MW00586793

Tuolumne
Free Climbs

Second Edition

Tuolumne
Free Climbs
Second Edition

Greg Barnes
Chris McNamara
Steve Roper

Contents

Published by
SuperTopo
2 Bradford Way
Mill Valley, CA 94941
www.supertopo.com

Topos and text by Greg Barnes, Chris McNamara
History by Steve Roper
Managing Editor: Chris McNamara
Contributing Designer: David Safanda
Editors: Steve McNamara, Chris McNamara, and Greg Barnes

Front cover: Kuan Chang at East Cottage Dome. *Photo by Corey Rich.*
Frontispiece: Brad Goya on Eichorn's Pinnacle, but feeling on top of the world. *Photo by John Brooks.*
Back cover: Greg Haverstock riding the wave of one of Tuolumne's most incredible climbs, The Matthes Crest. *Shawn Reeder.*
 ISBN: 978-0-9765235-7-4

Maki Grossnick on the first ascent of Push It. Greg Barnes photo.

Warning!

Climbing is an inherently dangerous sport in which severe injuries or death may occur. Relying on the information in this book may increase the danger.

When climbing you can only rely on your skill, training, experience, and conditioning. **If you have any doubts as to your ability to safely climb any route in this guide, do not try it.**

This book is neither a professional climbing instructor nor a substitute for one. **It is not an instructional book. Do not use it as one.** It contains information that is nothing more than a compilation of opinions about climbing in Tuolumne Meadows. **These opinions are neither facts nor promises.** Treat the information as opinions and nothing more. Do not substitute these opinions for your own common sense and experience.

Assumption of Risk

There may be errors in this book resulting from the mistakes of the authors and/or the people with whom they consulted. The information was gathered from a variety of sources, which may not have been independently verified. Those who provided the information may have made mistakes in their descriptions. The authors may have made mistakes in their conveyance of the information in this book. **The authors cannot, therefore, guarantee the correctness of any of the information contained in this book.** The topographical maps, photo-diagrams, difficulty ratings, protection ratings, approach and/or descent information, suggestions about equipment, and other matters may be incorrect or misleading. Fixed protection may be absent, unreliable, or misplaced. **You must keep in mind that the information in this book may be erroneous, so use your own judgement when choosing, approaching, climbing, or descending from a route described in this book.**

DO NOT USE THIS BOOK UNLESS YOU [AND YOUR ESTATE] PROMISE NEVER TO TRY TO SUE US IF YOU GET HURT OR KILLED.

Disclaimer of Warranties

THE AUTHORS AND PUBLISHER WARN THAT THIS BOOK CONTAINS ONLY THE AUTHORS' OPINIONS ON THE SUBJECTS DISCUSSED. THEY MAKE NO OTHER WARRANTIES, EXPRESSED OR IMPLIED, OF MERCHANTABILITY, FITNESS FOR PURPOSE, OR OTHERWISE, AND IN ANY EVENT, THEIR LIABILITY FOR BREACH OF ANY WARRANTY OR CONTRACT WITH RESPECT TO THE CONTENT OF THIS BOOK IS LIMITED TO THE PURCHASE PRICE OF THE BOOK. THEY FURTHER LIMIT TO SUCH PURCHASE PRICE THEIR LIABILITY ON ACCOUNT OF ANY KIND OF NEGLIGENT BEHAVIOR WHATSOEVER ON THEIR PART WITH RESPECT TO THE CONTENTS OF THIS BOOK.

Acknowledgements

SuperTopo is a team of climbers who are equally motivated to avoid real jobs, climb a lot and, as a result, be poor. Greg Barnes is our top author who has endless Tuolumne climbing beta permanently wired into his head. Randy Spurrier is the force behind the SuperTopo web site. Steve Roper is the SuperTopo historian. David Safanda is a pro designer who helps keep SuperTopo looking slick. Chris McNamara is the publisher who spends way more time thinking about guidebooks and human flight than anyone should.

Many thanks go to the following people who helped out with feedback and beta: Austin Archer, Karl Baba, Andrew Betts, Norman Boles, Tony Calderone, Per Calleberg, Tom Carter, Peter Croft, Joe Denicola, John Dill, Jan Eickoff, Bowe Ellis, Lincoln Else, Alan Eustace, Chris Falkenstein, Michael Finger, Bill Folk, Tom Frost, Doug Fulford, Mike Fyten, Steve Gerberding, Mark Gray, Ted Hansen, TM Herbert, John Hutchinson, Chris Johns, Mark Johnsson, Adam Klauber, Neal Konami, Sean Leary, Charles Leggett, Rainer Malaka, Gene Malone, Kristin Tara McNamara, Kay and Steve McNamara, Bill Maney, Matt Markell, Dennis Mullane, Bill Patrick, Markus Raschke, Don Reid, George Ridgley, Karen Roseme, Paul Rosenberg, Florence Scholl, Tim Seaman, Erik Sloan, Todd Snyder, Elmar Stefke, Marty Steiger, Carrie Sundra, Bill Twinting, Chris Van Leuven, Monica Viziano, Randy Vogel, Mike Waugh, Karin Wuhrmann, and Dan Zimmerlin. Special thanks go to Bryan Law for his meticulous comments, edits, and photos, and to Mikey Schaefer for his detailed topo of Rise and Fall of the Albatross.

A big thanks from Greg to my partners Karin Wuhrmann, Austin Archer, Barry Hutten, Florence Scholl, Bryan Law, George Ridgley, Linda Jarit, Jonathan duSaint, Maki Grossnick, Paul Rasmussen, Joe Denicola, Josh Janes, Rachel Nelson, Drew Rollins, Julie Haas, and I'm sure many others who I forgot to include.

Thanks to the rebolters for putting so much elbow grease into replacing bolts! Thanks to Roger Brown, Karin Wuhrmann, Bruce Hildenbrand, Clint Cummins, Drew Rollins, Bob Jensen, Patrick Warren, Sean Kriletich, Benjamin Kumli, Greg deMatteo, Jerry Anderson, Bryan Law, Rachel Nelson, Joe Denicola, and many others.

Many thanks to all the previous guidebook authors and their guides which were referenced when writing this book: *The Climber's Guide to the High Sierra:* by Steve Roper, four editions of *Rock Climbing Tuolumne Meadows* by Don Reid and Chris Falkenstein, *Tuolumne Rock: An Underground Climber's Guide* by Alan Nelson, and *The Good, The Great, and the Awesome* by Peter Croft.

All Tuolumne climbers should thank the first ascensionists who established these wonderful routes, mostly hand drilling ¼" bolts from sketchy stances! Thanks to Chris Falkenstein for his great Tuolumne web forum at www.tuolumnemeadows. org. In addition, we acknowledge the hard work the following organizations do to improve and preserve the Tuolumne climbing experience: the Access Fund; www.accessfund.org, and the American Safe Climbing Association; www.safeclimbing.org. Please support them!

- *Greg Barnes*

Your choice...

New stainless steel bolt rated to 8000 lbs or more...

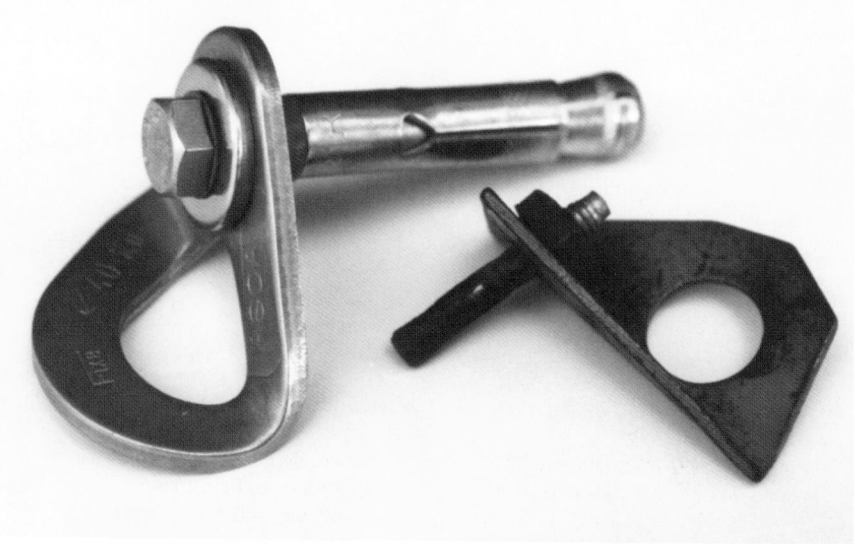

...or old 1/4" bolt with recalled Leeper hanger.

Help us replace old bolts with top-quality stainless steel bolts. The American Safe Climbing Association has helped replace over 6,000 bolts throughout the country. Donate today to help us replace old bolts!

www.safeclimbing.org

asca
American Safe Climbing Association

The ASCA is a 501(c)3 organization and donations are tax deductible.

Introduction

by Greg Barnes

Just a short drive and almost a vertical mile higher in elevation than Yosemite Valley, Tuolumne Meadows is an alpine rock climbing paradise. With its giant golden domes, pine trees, and lakes, Tuolumne offers some of the finest scenery of any climbing area on the planet.

While Half Dome is visible from Tuolumne's higher peaks, the climbing is completely different than Yosemite Valley. Instead of smooth, polished cracks and blank faces, Tuolumne has sharp, angular cracks, endless fields of knobs, and golden glacier polish with incut edges. Popular in the middle of summer when Yosemite Valley can be uncomfortably hot, Tuolumne has little traffic in early and late season, and generally little traffic anytime aside from at the popular routes. And compared to the near-urban atmosphere of Yosemite Valley in the summer, Tuolumne is practically tranquil.

With spectacular granite peaks, dramatic views, and approaches that meander through isolated backcountry meadows, Tuolumne has one of the finest collections of moderate alpine routes anywhere. Cathedral Peak, Matthes Crest, the North and West Ridges of Mt. Conness, and the Northwest Buttress of Tenaya Peak all provide outstanding long routes at the 5.5-5.7 level. Tuolumne also offers a good deal of shorter climbing routes with quick approaches, including some face routes that are both moderate and well-bolted.

However, one particular facet of Tuolumne rock climbing deserves explanation: runouts. Most routes were developed in the 1970s and 1980s. On lead and bolting from a stance, the safest way for the leader to stop and place a bolt was to stand on good holds. So the leader would keep going until getting to some good holds, then stop to place a bolt. On easier climbs there are often no bolts or pro placements on entire pitches, and many hard climbs are very dangerous. The Bachar-Yerian, a vertical knob climb established in 1981, remains one of the most serious and runout face climbs anywhere. On this climb and other testpieces, many of the world's strongest climbers test their psychological strength.

The tradition of runout face routes in Tuolumne, in combination with the poorly defined "R" ratings in the U.S., led to many visiting climbers running into much longer runouts compared to "R" rated routes in many other areas. In this edition we have introduced an intermediate rating of "R-" in order to help define runout routes. With detailed beta and gear information, plus variations to avoid some runouts, leaders can pick routes where they feel comfortable. Still, be aware that many Tuolumne classics are very runout compared to "R" rated routes elsewhere. We've also included many climbs you can toprope so you can develop your skills in relative safety.

Equipment

Most face routes in Tuolumne need some trad gear - even some "sport" routes. The crack routes require a good selection of gear, and it's nice to have many extendable draws.

While most routes in Tuolumne were developed with shorter ropes, a 60m or longer rope has become the Tuolumne standard, and a number of new routes detailed in this guide require 70m ropes (or two ropes). Dozier Dome in particular requires two 60m ropes for most routes.

On long routes, avoid the hassle of climbing with a pack by using a Camel back and clipping your lightweight hiking shoes to your harness. The Camelback holds enough water for most long climbs as well as space for a few essentials such as food, a small LED headlamp, compact rain shell, and sunscreen.

Peter Croft on a project in Glen Aulin. (Chris Falkenstein)

Anchor Conditions

Between 1998 and 2008 the American Safe Climbing Association replaced 1,055 bolts on 208 routes in Tuolumne. While most popular climbs now have safe bolts, some bad bolts remain. View which routes the ASCA has replaced at the ASCA web site, www.safeclimbing.org, and please make a tax-deductible donation. Even a mere $5 will replace at least one bolt. And that bad bolt could be the one that blows on somebody.

Essential Tuolumne Beta

Below is some fundamental information for planning a trip to Tuolumne. However, for more updated and extensive information you should visit the Tuolumne Beta Page on the SuperTopo web site: www.supertopo.com/climbingareas/tuolumne.html

Getting There

Tuolumne Meadows is located 1.5 hours northeast of Yosemite Valley. Since most climbers start their trip to Tuolumne by first driving through or near Yosemite Valley, you should visit the SuperTopo Yosemite Beta Page at www.supertopo.com/climbingareas/yosemite.html. There you will find more information and links for airports, buses, trains, and car travel.

Air Travel

Reno/Tahoe Airport is the closest airport to Tuolumne. From there, you will need to rent a car (3-hour drive) or take a bus or shuttle to Mammoth. The bus service is The Crest/Inyo-Mono Transit (800-922-1930), and the shuttles are the Mammoth Shuttle (760-934-6588) or Sierra Express (760-937-8294). From Mammoth take YARTS to Tuolumne (see Bus Travel). Oakland or San Francisco airports are farther from Tuolumne but are preferred over Reno/Tahoe because there are more flights to choose from. You can also fly into Sacramento or Fresno. Each of these places is a 3.5- to 5-hour drive from Tuolumne Meadows.

Bus Travel

YARTS (877-989-2787; www.yarts.com) provides bus transportation from Yosemite Valley to Tuolumne and from the Eastern Sierra to Tuolumne. During July through Labor Day, YARTS leaves from the Tuolumne Meadows Store every morning and from Yosemite Lodge each evening. It provides access between Yosemite and Mammoth, with the schedule and prices varying according to demand, even depending on day. Once in Tuolumne, a free shuttle bus provides convenient access throughout the Tuolumne Meadows area between the Tuolumne Lodge and Olmsted Point (including Tenaya Lake) during the middle part of the summer, and even sometimes to Tioga Pass a few times a day.

Car Travel

From Yosemite Valley, it's a 1.5-hour drive east on Highway 120 to Tuolumne Meadows. It's a 4.5-hour drive to Tuolumne from the Bay Area, a 3-hour drive from the Tahoe area, and about a 1.5-hour drive from Bishop.

Gas is available next to the Tuolumne Meadows Store, 15 miles east in Lee Vining, and on Highway 120 at Crane Flat.

If you don't have a car, you can rent one at any airport or major city. International climbers who stay in the United States for more than a month often buy a cheap used car in San Francisco or Los Angeles and sell it (or scrap it) at the end of their trip.

Driving times and distances to Tuolumne

From	Time (hours)	Distance (miles)
Boulder, CO	18:00	1,150
Fresno, CA	3:30	150
Truckee, CA	3:00	150
Los Angeles, CA	6:00	340
Mammoth, CA	1:00	50
Oakland, CA	4:30	220
Sacramento, CA	4:00	210
Salt Lake City, UT	10:00	620
San Francisco, CA	4:30	230
Yosemite Valley	1:30	60

When to Climb

Tuolumne Meadows has some of the best weather of any alpine rock climbing area on Earth. That said, Tuolumne is in a massive mountain range that receives severe thunderstorms, lightning, and rare major Pacific weather systems throughout the summer.

All climbing in Tuolumne is accessible from Highway 120. Because of its high elevation, Highway 120 east of Crane Flat and west of Lee Vining is closed in the winter. The road closes on the first snow of the year (usually November) and opens sometime in late May to June, depending on the snow year. During the winter, it is possible to climb in Tuolumne, but few people make the arduous ski in.

During early season (late May–June depending on snow year), Tuolumne conditions are often the best: no crowds, no mosquitoes, and long days. However, some approaches and climbs may be wet or snowy. Around June 15 the crowds arrive in Tuolumne – along with the mosquitoes. The crowds are not bad relative to Yosemite, but you will probably have to wait in line for the most classic routes. The mosquitoes, on the other hand, can be terrible. Be sure to bring long pants, long sleeve shirts, and bug repellent. In September, the crowds and mosquitoes leave Tuolumne and while the climbing conditions are still great, the days become short and the nights frigid.

Thunderstorm cycles are common in the summer. Typically, the storms hit in mid-afternoon and slowly increase in strength over several days, clearing up each night. However, heavy thunderstorms and rain can set in for days at a time. And in a few recent summers, an almost total lack of thunderstorms over the entire summer have perplexed locals.

Current Road and Weather

There is no specific weather phone report for Tuolumne so your best bet is to check the general High Sierra weather at www.supertopo.com. For current road conditions, call 209-372-0200, or the CalTrans voice-activated system for major highway conditions at 800-gas-road or 916-445-7623 (from outside California).

First Climbs

For those new to Tuolumne or with limited time, here's a list of good starter climbs:

Crags and Topropes:
Bunny Slopes, 5.6-5.9
Daff Dome, South Flank, 5.5-5.11c
Ellery Lake, 5.9-5.10d
Low Profile Dome, 5.7-5.11b
Pothole Dome, 5.0-5.11
Puppy Dome, 5.6-5.12c
Western Front, 5.9-5.10b

Multi-pitch Climbs:
Tenaya Peak, 5.5
Cathedral Peak, 5.6
Northwest Books, 5.6
Holdless Horror 5.6
West Country, 5.7
Zee Tree, 5.7
Erret Out, 5.7
Bull Dozier, 5.7
Hermaphrodite Flake to The Boltway, 5.8
South Crack, 5.8 R

Staying in Tuolumne

Unlike the Yosemite Valley experience, Tuolumne Meadows is relatively uncrowded and serene and provides just enough basic services to comfortably camp. If you are craving some better food, more services, or just a day excursion, Lee Vining, Mono Lake, and Mammoth Lakes are all less than an hour away.

Camping

The only campground in Tuolumne is the Tuolumne Meadows Campground, which is centrally located and very large (over 300 sites). Half of the sites can be reserved in advance at www.recreation.gov (reserve them at least 2-3 months in advance for peak times) and half of the sites are on a first come, first served basis (stand in line in early morning to ensure you get a site.) Sites cost $20 per night with a six-person, two-car limit. Be aware that mosquitoes can be particularly fierce and bears patrol the campground so proper food storage is mandatory.

Camping (cont)

Located 7 to 12 miles east from Tuolumne Meadows are ten Forest Service campgrounds, many of which are first come, first served. Several of these campgrounds are at elevations higher than Tuolumne Meadows and can help with acclimation. Twelve miles east of Tuolumne Meadows, the campgrounds in lower Lee Vining Canyon are lower altitude, more sheltered from the wind, and near to services in Lee Vining. You will pay between $12 and $17 per night on a first come, first served basis. The prices at these campgrounds have climbed steeply in recent years, in some cases more than doubling in less than a decade.

Along Highway 120 toward Yosemite Valley are several additional campgrounds with moderate to long drives (30 minutes to one hour). The campground reservation office in Tuolumne has information on current campground conditions.

Lodges and Cabins

In addition to campsites, there are more plush accommodations available in Tuolumne and the High Sierra, including the Tuolumne Meadows Lodge, White Wolf, and the High Sierra Camps (www. yosemitepark.com/html/accommodation. html). Just outside of the park boundary is the Tioga Pass Resort (www. tiogapassresort.com), which offers cabins, a small restaurant, and an espresso bar. Drive 15 miles east from Tuolumne Meadows and you will reach Lee Vining, a small town with a few motels, restaurants, and other basic services.

Food

A limited selection of high-priced groceries are available at the Tuolumne Meadows store. In addition, you can purchase groceries in Lee Vining at the Lee Vining Market. Mammoth has a large Vons supermarket.

The Tuolumne Meadows Grill serves hamburgers, fries, etc, but has very limited hours, closing hours before dark in mid-summer. The Tuolumne Lodge has a restaurant that serves breakfast and dinner in the midde part of summer. Eight miles

east of Tuolumne Meadows, the Tioga Pass Resort houses a cozy dining room with good food. Surprisingly, the Mobil Gas Station, located 14 miles from Tuolumne Meadows in Lee Vining, has the best food in the area. This isn't just any gas station – Tioga Toomey's Whoa Nellie Deli has a great selection of sandwiches, pizzas, fish tacos, and a variety of other savory treats for breakfast, lunch, and dinner. Frequent local bands and even a trapeze out front are other features of this unusual gas station.

Climbing Gear and Climbing Guides

The Tuolumne Mountain Shop (209-372-8436) located at the Tuolumne gas station offers a small selection of climbing equipment. For a more extensive selection of gear, you will need to drive 50 miles to Mammoth for Mammoth Mountaineering Supply (888-395-3951) www. mammothgear.com, 90 miles to Bishop for Wilson's Eastside Sports (760-873-7520) www.eastsidesports.com), or 60 miles back to Yosemite Valley for the Yosemite Mountain Shop (209-372-8396)www. yosemitegifts.com/wetoyomosh.html). You can get climbing instruction and

Third Pillar of Dana from the base – perfect alpine granite.

arrange for a guide through the Yosemite Mountaineering School (209-372-8344), which is based in Tuolumne at the Mountain Shop/gas station.

Altitude

At elevation it takes a few days for most people to adjust to the rarefied air, so drink plenty of water and take it easy. On your first day in Tuolumne, climb a route with a short approach to let yourself acclimate. In addition, eat a low-fat diet for the first day or two. Wear extra sunscreen and a hat – the UV levels are greater at altitude and severe sunburns can happen quickly.

Thunderstorms and Lightning

Tuolumne has mostly beautiful, sunny weather in the summer, yet severe thunderstorms occur. Small, puffy clouds seen before 10am are a frequent predictor of afternoon rain, hail and, worst of all, lightning. Thunderstorms often appear in cycles and generally during periods of hot, calm weather in the Central Valley.

Lightning tends to hit high points, trees, and water, but will also hit low points next to high rocks, flat areas near trees, and dry land around lakes. A climber was struck by lightning on Cathedral Peak in 2000, and many other close calls have occurred.

Know how to perform CPR. Unlike nearly any other type of injury that stops the heart, electrical shock victims can suddenly awaken even after extended CPR. But remember, the best strategy is to avoid thunderstorms in the first place. If you're on a climb and get nervous about developing clouds, it's time to turn around.

Bears, Marmots, and Mosquitoes

Bears have damaged cars for as little as a stick of gum or an empty soda can. If you want what's yours to remain yours, remember three things: bears are hungry, smart, and strong.

When bears smell food, even if it's locked in your trunk or glove compartment, they shift into high gear. They get turned on by odors of containers that used to contain food. They even go for toothpaste and sunscreen. Bears don't need to smell food;

they see something like a grocery bag or an ice chest and associate it with food. In fact, they don't even need to see that much. If a bear sees clutter inside a car, he'll think, "I wonder what's under all that stuff?" and go to work.

Breaking into a car is a trivial exercise for a bear. He inserts his claws at the top of the door frame and pulls down. Then he climbs in and trashes the car. You can't outsmart or outmuscle a bear. Always stash your food in one of the bear-proof storage lockers provided by the Park Service in the campground, at various trailheads including Cathedral Lakes, or at the Wilderness Permit Center.

If camping in the backcountry, use bear canisters, which are available at the Wilderness Permit Center. Tuolumne bears are experienced at cutting the lines to hung food, and the tattered remnants of the lines can be observed on nearly any tree near a backcountry campsite.

In addition to bears, be on the lookout for marmots. Cute from a distance, these plump critters love nothing more than scrounging for food in climbing packs while you watch helplessly from two pitches up. Be sure to hang your backpack high on a tree branch – even if it does not have food in it. Marmots are tough, smart, and strong-toothed and can quickly gnaw through nearly anything – leave zippers open.

Nasty mosquitoes are very common for most of the summer in Tuolumne, so come prepared. Consider long sleeve pants and shirts, which not only help with mosquitoes but help prevent sunburn.

Backpacking

Wilderness permits are required for camping in the backcountry (e.g. for Conness or Matthes Crest). They are available for free at the Tuolumne Wilderness Center (7:30 a.m.-5 p.m.), starting at 7:30 a.m. the day before you go in. There is often a long line to get permits, and popular trailheads frequently fill up, so plan ahead and get in line an hour early if you really need the permit. They can also be reserved up to 6 weeks (168 days) in advance, but not less than two days

Previously unpublished climbs

Cheesecake 5.5
DAFFy Duck 5.5
String Cheese 5.6
Frogger 5.7
Eddie Muenster 5.7
Chop the Hogs 5.7
Roof Rat 5.7
Black Nepalese 5.7
Bull Dozier 5.7
Obviously Not 5.7
Ripple 5.7
Pac-Man 5.8
R2-D2 5.8
West of the Witch 5.8
Udder Chaos 5.8
Pasture-ized 5.8
Cry Baby 5.8
Dastardly Rascal 5.8
Dope Show 5.8
Crystal Meth 5.8
Cheeseburgers & Beer 5.8
Bit by Bit (pitch 3) 5.8
Isostacy 5.8
Avocados & Tequila 5.8
X-Wing 5.9
Slasher 5.9
Wrest Day 5.9
Felsic 5.9

Aileron 5.9+
Trendy Bendy 5.10a
Mmmm…Crackahol 5.9 or 10a
Bust It Out 5.10a
Turbine 5.10a
Life in the Cretaceous 5.10a
Flash of the Blade 5.10a
Stemulant 5.10a
Chili Air 5.10a
Dumpster Evangelist 5.10a
Loud and Obnoxious 5.10a
Cheetos & Everclear 5.10a
You, Me, & the Dike 5.10a
Cyclone 5.10b
Flintstone (pitch 2) 5.10b
Anduril 5.10b
Tectonomagmatic 5.10b
Tourette's 5.10b
Plutonics 5.10b
Metalhead 5.10c
Five Ten, You Wuss 5.10c
Mordor 5.10c
City Girl 5.10c
Narsil 5.10d
Loco Yokel 5.10d
Push It 5.11a
Tooled 5.11b
Stinky T-shirt 5.11d
Rise and Fall of the Albatross 5.13a/b

Backpacking (cont)

in advance, and a non-refundable fee is required ($5 plus $5 per person as of 2009). Full information, including how to reserve through the internet, phone, or mail, is available at http://www.nps.gov/yose/ planyourvisit/wildpermits.htm

Miscellaneous Beta

Showers cost $2 and are available at the Tuolumne Meadows lodge between noon and 3 p.m.. There is a post office located next to the Tuolumne Store, which is open most of the season.

A message board is located outside the Tuolumne Meadows Store, and another larger one is along the entrance road to the campground. Most climbers use the Store board, but make sure if arranging messages with friends to specify which board.

The Tuolumne Meadows Stables (209-372-8348) is the pack station in Tuolumne.

The nearest ATM is at the Lee Vining Market. The nearest bank is Mammoth. You can get cash back with a credit card purchase from the Tuolumne Store.

Nearby Climbing Options

To take a break from Tuolumne, or if the weather deteriorates, there are many fine options. Yosemite Valley is the most obvious, but a plethora of bouldering and climbing areas are only an hour or so to the east near Mammoth and Bishop. These include (in approximate order of accessibility) the Bachar Boulders and Deadman Summit (bouldering), Sagehen Summit (trad/multipitch), Clark Canyon (sport), Dike Wall (sport) and Crystal Crag (sport/trad), Mammoth Crest (trad), Bear Crag (sport), Rock Creek (trad/sport), Benton Crags (trad), Owens River Gorge (sport), Pine Creek (trad/sport), Cardinal Pinnacle (trad), Buttermilks/Druids/Happys (endless awesome bouldering), and many others. Guides to these areas are available from Maximus Press (www.maximuspress.com).

Also, the huge endless granite alpine climbs of the Sierra are covered in SuperTopo's own *High Sierra Climbing*, which includes climbs on Mt. Whitney, Mt. Russel, Bear Creek Spire, and more.

Tuolumne Topropes

Tuolumne is known for its runouts on low-angle face. Compared to the Valley, the faces tend to be steeper, more featured, harder to spot bolts on, and more runout. In general, anyone comfortable slab climbing can get used to Tuolumne fairly quickly, but those without much slab experience should definitely introduce themselves to slick low-angle granite on toprope. Tuolumne has several easily accessible toprope crags for doing exactly that, and it's generally easy to walk or scramble to the top. Some topropes require a belay to safely set the anchor, and some require climbing adjacent routes of a lower grade.

In the table below, we've listed the more easily toproped climbs contained in this guidebook, along with key beta. There are dozens more toproping options not listed here available after leading various routes at many crags.

Area	Route	Rating	Anchor Access	Technique
Pothole Dome	many topropes	5.0-5.11	scramble 2nd-3rd class	slab, crack
Murphy Creek	several topropes	5.7-11c	walk, belay to anchor	cracks
Puppy Dome	several	5.7-12c	walk; scramble 3rd	cracks
Bunny Slopes	several	5.8-5.9	climb 5.6-5.7	slab, face
Ellery Lake	many topropes	5.9-10d	walk, belay to anchor	cracks, face
Western Front	many topropes	5.9-10b	scramble 3rd class	slab, face
Canopy World	several topropes	5.9-13a	scramble easy 5th	face, cracks
Medlicott Dome	Beer, Donuts	5.9-10	climb 5.7	face, cracks
Lamb Dome	Little Sheba, Lampoon	5.10a, 9+	scramble 3rd class	crack, face
Low Profile Dome	three 5.10 faces	5.10a-10c	climb 5.7 R	face
DAFF south flank	Fingertips	5.10a-b	climb 5.8	slab
Mountaineers Dome	three slab routes	5.10b-11a	climb 5.9	slab, crack
East Cottage Dome	many routes	5.10b-11a	scramble 4th, rap	face
Stately Pleasure Dome	Footnote	5.10c	climb 5.0	slab
Galen's Crack	two routes	5.10c-10d	walk	crack, face
Harlequin Dome	Chinese Handcuffs	5.10d	walk, bushwack	crack
Low Profile Dome	Memo From Lloyd	5.11b	long scramble 4th class	crack

Karin Wuhrmann follows pitch 3 of You Asked For It. photo by Greg Barnes

Leave No Trace

by Greg Barnes

Chris McNamara on top of The Third Pillar of Dana.

Fairview Dome, one of the most impressive domes in Tuolumne. Photo by Greg Barnes

Greg Barnes

The high country of Tuolumne Meadows is one of the most beautiful places on the planet. It has recovered well from the hordes of domestic sheep that ravaged the Sierra in John Muir's day, but the ecosystem is delicate, and we need to respect and preserve it.

The concept of Leave No Trace is fundamental, yet we can all do a better job of living up to it. Obvious things to do include carrying out all trash you find, using bear boxes in the campground, bringing bear canisters on overnight trips, and staying on trails. However, there are a lot of other things to do that are less obvious and often not done that well by climbers.

- Travel on rock when possible, otherwise stick to existing paths and trails. What looks like an empty dirt patch in June will be a flower garden in August – if you don't trample it first!

- Bring only minimal food and carry it on your person at all times when climbing. Rodents can and will chew through packs and into any food you leave at the base. Hanging food is a joke – we've all seen squirrels run up vertical rock – and a tree is home ground for these furry little acrobats.

- Pee on open rock or dirt and avoid plants. The salts in your urine can kill plants, which absorb water from the soil and breathe through pores in the leaves.

- Plan your day such that you use restrooms before heading out. This is easy to do, yet a surprising number of people munch a big breakfast at the car, hike to a climb, and then run to the nearest spot to take a dump. Parking areas for most climbs don't have bathrooms – plan ahead of time.

- When you have to go, follow the Leave No Trace guidelines: "Deposit solid human waste in catholes dug 6 to 8 inches deep and at least 200 feet from water, camp, and trails. Cover and disguise the cathole when finished. Pack out toilet paper and hygiene products." Packing out TP is distasteful to most people, but it's easy to do with a few large ziplock bags.

- In the campground or at picnic areas, immediately store food in the bear box or secure containers. Don't walk to your car and expect the birds, rodents, and bears to sit around and miss their chance to run in and grab food. Dinnertime is the favorite raiding opportunity; don't leave food unattended.

- Carry only gray, tan, or black webbing. If replacing fixed slings, cut off the old slings and take them with you.

- In places far from road noise, use rope commands instead of yelling "ON BELAY!" Loud belay commands are the number one impact climbers have on the solitude of others. Besides, it's good to practice rope commands for windy days and long pitches. Both partners tie in and double-check each other's knots. The leader uses a four-sharp-tug command for "off belay;" then waits a bit and pulls up the slack. Four sharp tugs from the leader then confirms that the follower is "on belay."

- When driving in Tuolumne at night, use your high beams and drive slowly. Many deer are killed every year by traffic, and several bears have been injured or killed (and YOU can be injured or killed in these accidents!). The entire stretch from Tioga Pass to Tenaya Lake, especially from the pass through the Meadows themselves, sees heavy deer traffic. Drive slowly at dawn and dusk. Animal eyes reflect light and are easily seen in high beams, so be on the lookout.

- Take the free Tuolumne shuttle to climbs. Check the hours at the store bus stop. The shuttle driver will stop at any pullout large enough to be safe, which includes most popular climbing areas. The shuttle runs the entire length of the climbing areas, except for the climbs approached from outside the Park (i.e. Mt. Conness, Third Pillar, and Ellery Lake).

Visit the Leave No Trace website at www.lnt.org to learn more about minimizing your impact on the wilderness.

Ratings

Tuolumne Meadows has a tradition of severely runout routes on slabby terrain, and also a tradition of stiff and sandbagged ratings on some climbs. In this book we include relatively few of the severely runout routes unless the routes are classic. With the increase in very tightly protected climbs over the last few decades, the definition of "well protected" has changed radically. For those who expect protection wherever they want it, and especially for those with little experience on granite slabs, there are very few routes in Tuolumne that meet the modern definition of tightly protected.

We also try to even out the difficulty ratings to current norms. After all, if ratings don't accurately compare climbs, and if some 5.10s are harder than other 5.11s, what is the point of a rating system? Rating climbs well is becoming increasingly difficult as very strong gym and sport climbing-trained climbers intersect with traditional climbs which require little physical strength but lots of technique and mental strength. In addition, the high elevation of Tuolumne often adds acclimation as a factor in perceived rating.

Ratings are decided by discussion and consensus, so we would like to hear your criticism and feedback. Please send a note to chris@supertopo.com or post a message on our route beta pages at www.supertopo.com/routebeta/tuolumne.html. Before your trip you may also wish to check these route beta pages for feedback from other climbers on particular routes that you anticipate climbing.

Runout Ratings

If a rating is followed by an "R-", the route is somewhat runout. This is obviously subjective, but it generally means there is a moderate runout on easy terrain (for that route rating), or a short runout on harder terrain.

If a rating is followed by an "R" it means the climb is substantially runout (has little protection) and a fall from the wrong spot is fairly likely to result in injury (ANY climbing fall can be serious or even fatal, so this is obviously a subjective rating). To climb an R rated climb you should be very solid at the grade. For example, most climbers want to feel solid on a well-protected 5.9 climb before trying a 5.7 runout climb.

An "R/X" rating is severely runout or runout in a really bad spot. This could be just a short runout with cruxy climbing and a big ledge to hit, or it could be a huge runout on a slab.

A climb with an "X" rating means that a fall will likely result in severe injury or death.

However, by the standards of many climbing areas, R rated climbs in Tuolumne are more runout. A good number of climbs that are rated R- in this guidebook would have a solid R rating in other areas. Likewise, routes listed here as R might be rated R/X or even X in other areas because of long fall potentials on steep, knobby terrain. Examples include Great Pumpkin and Hobbit Book. Many easier climbs also have very long fall potential on smooth low-angle granite, and these are not given R/X ratings because serious injury beyond road rash is relatively unlikely. Examples include South Crack, Great White Book, and the Dike Route.

International Ratings Comparison

USA (Yosemite Decimal System)	UIAA	France	UK	Australia
5.1	I	1	M	4
5.2	II	2	D	6
5.3	III / III+	2+	3A/3B VD	8
5.4	IV	3-	3B/3C HVD	
5.5	IV+	3		10
5.6	V-	3+	3C/4A S, 4A/4B HS	12
5.7	V	4	4A/4C VS	14
5.8	V+	4+		
5.9	VI-	5	4C/5B HVS	16
5.10a	VI	5+		18
5.10b	VI+	6A	5A/5C E1	19
5.10c	VII-	6A+	5B/6A E2	20
5.10d	VII	6B	5C/6A E3	21
5.11a	VII+	6B+		
5.11b	VIII-	6C		22
5.11c		6C+	6A/6B E4	23
5.11d	VIII	7A		24
5.12a	VIII+	7A+	6A/6C E5	
5.12b	IX-	7B		25
5.12c	IX	7B+		26
5.12d		7C	6B/6C E6	27
5.13a	IX+	7C+		28
5.13b	X-	8A	6C/7A E7	29
5.13c	X	8A+		30
5.13d		8B	6C/7A E8	31
5.14a	X+	8B+		32
5.14b	XI-	8C	7A/7B E9	33
5.14c	XI	8C+		34
5.14d	XI+	9A	7A/7B E10	35
5.15a		9A+		36

Crag Comparison - Single Pitch Crags

Crag	page	≤5.6	5.7	5.8	5.9	10a	10b	10c/d	11a/b	11c	Topropes	Face or Cracks?	Early Season?	Summary
Block Area	55					1	1			1	0	face and cracks	yes	*Sport routes and gritty crack/faces.*
Bunny Slopes	53	1	2	1	1	1					2	face	yes	*Slabby knobby face; great intro area.*
Canopy World	86	1	1		1		2	1	1		7	face and cracks	yes	*Secluded crag with long flat hike.*
Circle A Wall	52			1		1			1		1	face	no	*Short fun knobby face; wet early season.*
Daff Dome S. Flank	76	1	2	3	1	1	1	2	1		10	face and cracks	yes	*Golden slabs and easy cracks.*
Dike Dome	28	1	1	1		1					3	face and cracks	yes	*Slabby routes in a spectacular setting.*
Drug Dome Base	134		2	2	1	1		3		1	1	mostly face	yes	*Steep knobs, snow at base in very early season.*
East Cottage Dome	82					1	2	6	3		6	all face	yes	*Steep knobs and thin edging.*
Ellery Lake	192			1		1	1	2			5	face and cracks	no	*Very short top-ropes outside park; high altitude.*
Galens Crack	63		2	1	2	1	1	2	2		2	face and cracks	yes	*Short burly offwidth and face topropes.*
Low Profile Dome	60		2	1	1	1	1	1	2		4	mostly face	yes	*Excellent face climbs; short approach.*
Mariuolumne N. Wall	142		1	1	1	1					1	cracks	no	*Steep shady cracks, snow in early season.*
Medlicott Dome Right	152				2	1	2	1	3		0	face and cracks	no	*Tons of classics, often wet early season.*
Mountaineers Dome	50				1	1	1	1	1	1	3	face and cracks	yes	*Golden slabs, one crack (first pitch of multipitch).*
Murphy Creek	32		1	1	2	1	1	1	4	1	10	cracks	no	*Concentrated cracks with long but easy hike.*
Olmsted Canyon	30			1	1	1	1	4	1		9	cracks	yes	*Short cracks on scattered crags with a short hike.*
Pothole Dome	89	11						1			12	face	yes	*Beginner slab topropes and a 5.11 roof crack.*
Puppy Dome	98		1	1	1					3	5	cracks	yes	*Great easy and very hard cracks.*
Razor Back	116		1	1	1		1				0	face	no	*Thin edging slabs with snowbank in early season.*
Western Front	66		3	3	3	2	1				6	face	yes	*Great 5.9-10b slabby face topropes.*
Wind Tunnel	78	3	2	1	1						2	face	yes	*Low-angle slab and face in spectacular setting.*

Crag Comparison - Multipitch Crags

Crag	page	≤5.6	5.7	5.8	5.9	10a	10b	10c/d	11a/b	11c	Pitches	Face or Cracks?	Early Season?	Summary
Cathedral Peak	100	1	1	1							6	face and cracks	yes	The classic, spectacular, and very crowded spire.
Daff Dome	67				2	1	1			2	4-5	face and cracks	yes	Cracks and face, with some single-pitch at base.
Dozier Dome	160	1	5	4	3	4	2	1			1-4	face and cracks	no	Short multipitch, long single pitch; need two 60m
Drug Dome	130			1				3			3-5	face and cracks	yes	Classic 5.10d's, dirty 5.8, funky 5.10c/5.8 A0.
Eichorn's Pinnacle	107	1		1			1				2-5	cracks	yes	Spire with easy notch route, longer direct.
Ellery Bowl	193								1		2	crack	no	Awesome 2-pitch 5.11, cold high and snowy.
Fairview Dome	118			1	1		1	1			4-12	face and cracks	yes	Crowded classic 5.9 and 5.10c; runout shorter 5.8.
Harlequin Dome	43				1	2			2		3-5	face and cracks	yes	Roofs and dihedrals with few knobs.
Lamb Dome	126				3	1		1		1	2-4	face and cracks	yes	Cracks and golden faces; can link routes.
Lembert Dome	91	2		2	1	4	2				2-5	face and cracks	yes	Cracks, slabs, water chutes, and knobs.
Mariuolumne Dome	138		1	1	1	1	1	1			4-5	face and cracks	no	Hobbit Book and three 5.10s, high and cold.
Matthes Crest	110		1		1		1				4-15	ridge	yes	The long knife-edge, and a new 5.10 start.
Medlicott Dome	144	1		3	4	1	1	3	1		2-6	face and cracks	no	Long gold knobby dome; wet streaks early.
Mountaineer's Dome	47			1	1		1				3-5	face and cracks	yes	A 5.10 crack and runout varied slab routes.
Mt. Conness	176	2						1			5-10	face and cracks	no	High altitude moderates with lots of 3rd/4th class.
Phobos Deimos Cliff	57				2				1		3	cracks	yes	Steep golden cracks; steep approach hike.
Pywiack Dome	167	2	1		2						2-4	face and cracks	yes	Moderate slabs and steep face & cracks.
Stately Pleasure Dome	34	2	2	2	2		1				2-6	face and cracks	yes	Sunny white granite above Tenaya Lake.
Tenaya Peak	172	1									5-10	face and cracks	no	Long easy climb with early season snow.
Third Pillar of Dana	188						1				5-10	crack	no	High-altitude classic, snow early season.

Number of routes at each grade

Cam Sizes by Brand

Ref Size*	BD Camalots C3	BD Camalots C4	CCH Aliens	Metolius Cams	Trango Ballnutz and Big Bros	Wild Country Friends
0.2"					#1 Ballnutz	
0.3"	000 grey				#2 Ballnutz	
0.4"	00 purple		.33 black	00 gray	#3 Ballnutz	00 gold
0.5"	0 green		.375 blue	0 purple	#4 Ballnutz	0 blue
0.6"	1 red	.3 blue	.5 green	1 blue	#5 Ballnutz	.5 red
0.75"	2 yellow	.4 grey	.75 yellow	2 yellow		1 gold
1"		.5 purple	1 red	3 orange		1.25 purple
1.25"		.75 green	1.25 gold	4 red		1.5 silver
1.5"		1 red	1.5 orange	5 black		1.75 green
1.75"		1 red	2 purple	6 green		2 red
2"		2 yellow	2.5 clear	7 blue		2.5 gold
2.5"		2 yellow		8 purple		3 purple
3"		3 blue		9 burgundy	Big Bro 0.5	3.5 blue
3.5"		4 gray		10 dark blue	Big Bro 1	4 silver
4-4 5."		5 purple			Big Bro 2	5 red
5-6.5"		6 green			Big Bro 3	6 green
7-8"					Big Bro 3	
8-12"					Big Bro 4	
12-18"					Big Bro 5	

*"Ref size" is the optimal crack width for a given camming unit. It is not the range given by the manufacturer.

24

SUPERTOPO

TUOLUMNE FREE CLIMBS: SUPERTOPOS

Understanding the maps

Topo Symbols

Right-facing corner		Roof	⊥⊥⊥⊥	Bolt	x
Left-facing corner		Ledge	⊤⊤⊤⊤	Rappel anchor	
Straight-in crack		Slab	///	Face climbing	
Groove		Belay station	❶	Pine tree	
Arête		Pitch length	130' ●	Oak-like tree	
Flake		Optional belay	○	Bush	
Chimney		False belay	⊘	Knob	O
				Hole	●

Notes on Rack

• "nuts" refers to any nut, stopper, or chock. "micro"= #1, 2; "sml"= #3-5; "med"= #6-8; "lrg"= #9-13 (BD Stopper number)
• for cams, "2 ea .75-1.5" means bring two sets of all sizes between .75" and 1.5". Check the cam size chart to see which cam corresponds to which crack size.

Notes on Topo

• "belay takes .6-1" means while leading the pitch save enough .6-1" cams and nuts to build a natural anchor.
• a number next to a tree is its height.

Topo abbreviations

ow = offwidth
lb = lieback
p = fixed piton
R- = somewhat runout
R = runout (dangerous fall)

Metric system conversions

1 inch = 2.54 centimeters
1 foot = 0.305 meters
100 feet = 30.5 meters

Overview graphics

Low-clearance dirt road	·················
High-clearance dirt road	
Road or State Route	⑩
Federal Highway	⑩
Hikers' trail	
Climbers' trail	- - - - - - - -
Cross-country travel	·············

Star Ratings

★★★★★ - undisputed classic
★★★★ - excellent climb
★★★ - good climb
★★ - okay climb
★ - barely included in this book

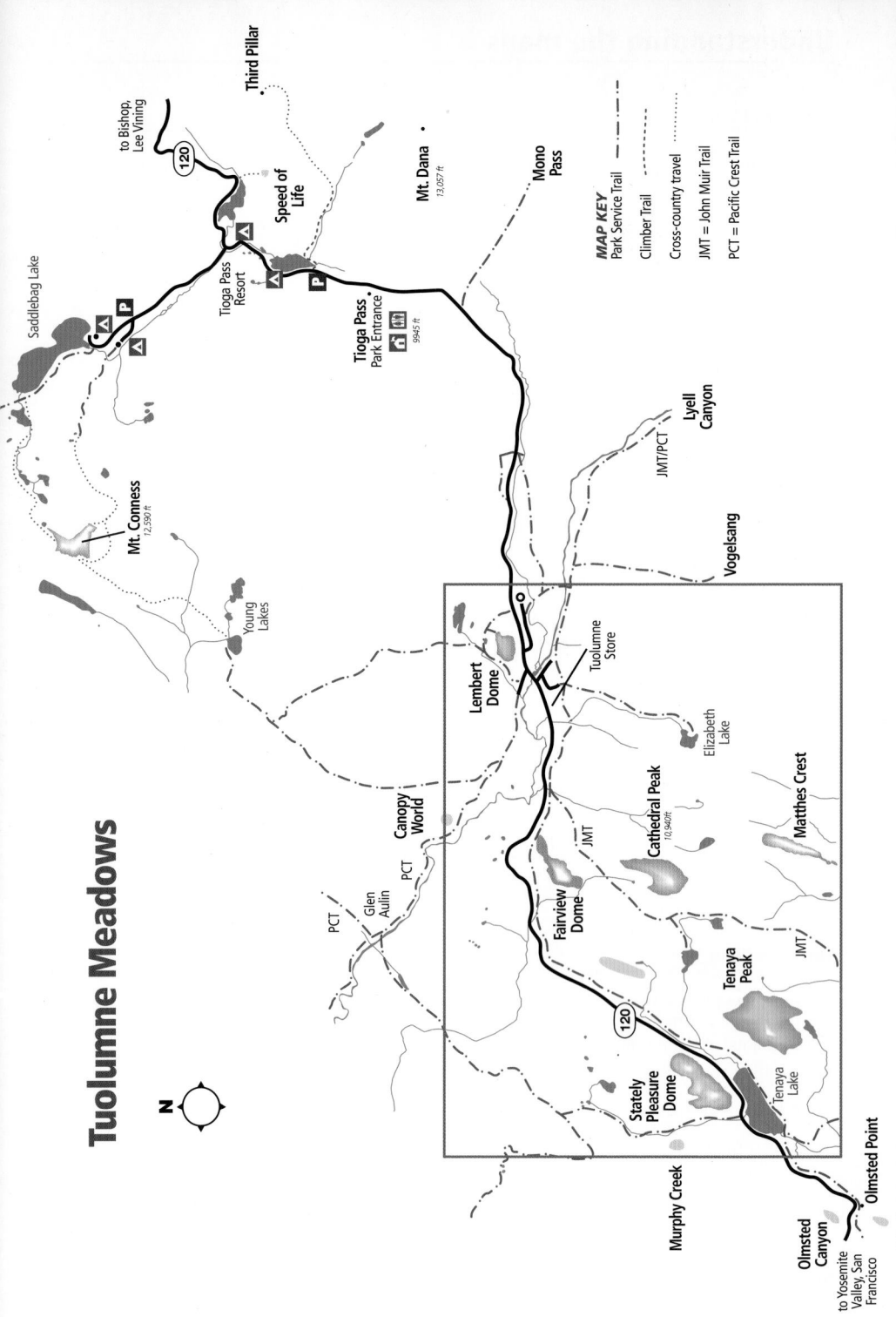

Tuolumne Meadows

N

MAP KEY
Park Service Trail ·—·—·
Climber Trail ·—·—·
Cross-country travel ·······
JMT = John Muir Trail
PCT = Pacific Crest Trail

Third Pillar

to Bishop, Lee Vining

120

Speed of Life

Mt. Dana
13,057 ft

Mono Pass

Saddlebag Lake

Tioga Pass Resort

Tioga Pass Park Entrance
9945 ft

Mt. Conness
12,590 ft

Young Lakes

Lyell Canyon

JMT/PCT

Vogelsang

Lembert Dome

Tuolumne Store

Elizabeth Lake

Matthes Crest

Canopy World

Cathedral Peak
10,940 ft

PCT

Glen Aulin

PCT

JMT

Fairview Dome

Tenaya Peak

JMT

120

Stately Pleasure Dome

Tenaya Lake

Murphy Creek

Olmsted Canyon

Olmsted Point

Dike Dome

to Yosemite Valley, San Francisco

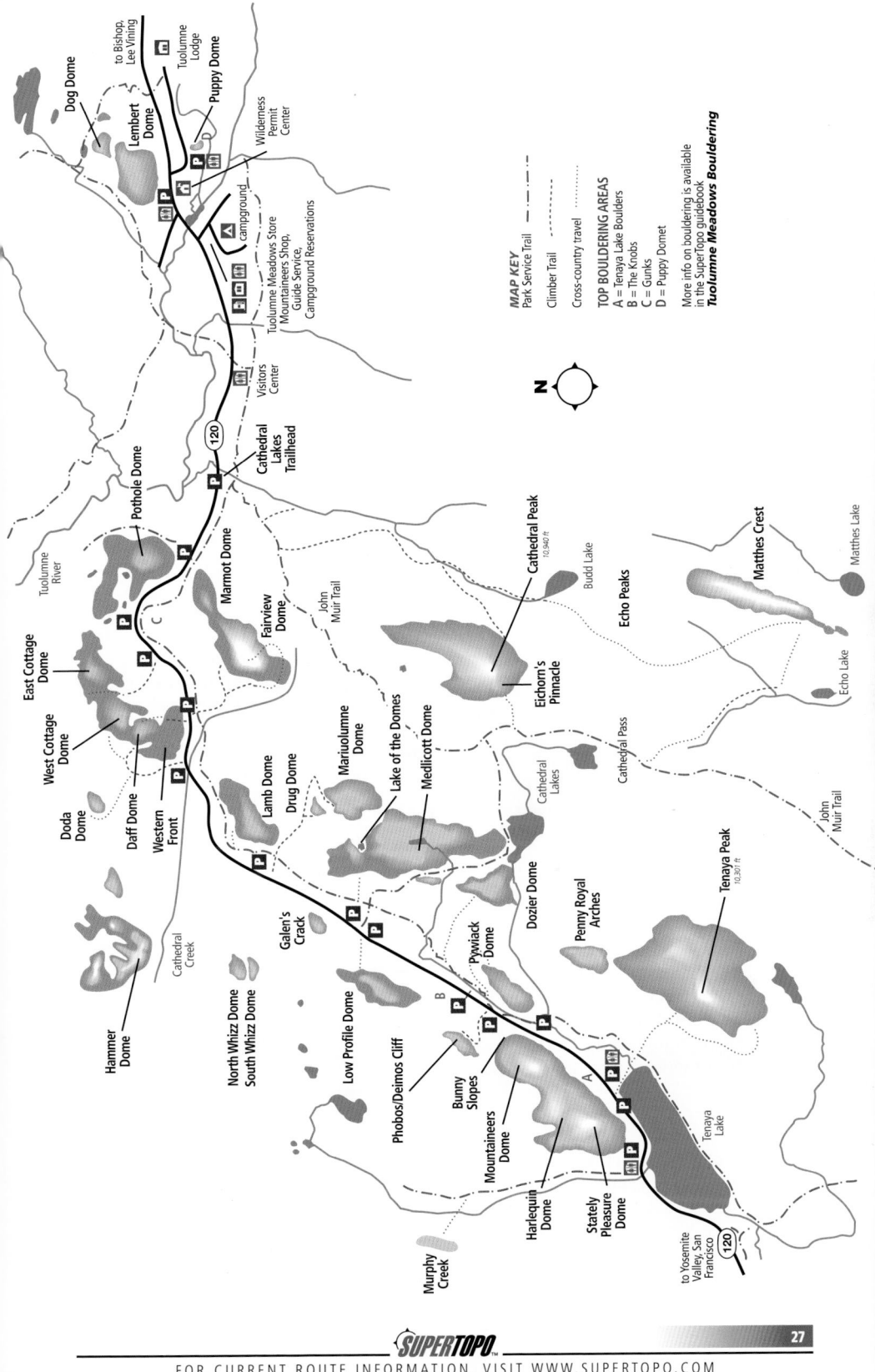

MAP KEY
Park Service Trail — ·· — ·· —
Climber Trail ------
Cross-country travel ···········

TOP BOULDERING AREAS
A = Tenaya Lake Boulders
B = The Knobs
C = Gunks
D = Puppy Domet

More info on bouldering is available
in the SuperTopo guidebook
Tuolumne Meadows Bouldering

N

to Bishop,
Lee Vining
Tuolumne Lodge
Dog Dome
Lembert Dome
Puppy Dome
Wilderness Permit Center
campground
Tuolumne Meadows Store
Mountaineers Shop,
Guide Service,
Campground Reservations
Visitors Center
120
Cathedral Lakes Trailhead
Pothole Dome
Tuolumne River
Marmot Dome
Fairview Dome
John Muir Trail
East Cottage Dome
West Cottage Dome
Doda Dome
Daff Dome
Western Front
Lamb Dome
Drug Dome
Mariuolumne Dome
Lake of the Domes
Medlicott Dome
Cathedral Peak
10,940 ft
Eichorn's Pinnacle
Budd Lake
Echo Peaks
Matthes Crest
Matthes Lake
Echo Lake
Cathedral Pass
Cathedral Lakes
John Muir Trail
Cathedral Creek
Hammer Dome
North Whizz Dome
South Whizz Dome
Galen's Crack
Low Profile Dome
Phobos/Deimos Cliff
Bunny Slopes
Mountaineers Dome
Harlequin Dome
Stately Pleasure Dome
Murphy Creek
Pywiack Dome
Dozier Dome
Penny Royal Arches
Tenaya Peak
10,301 ft
Tenaya Lake
to Yosemite Valley, San Francisco
120

Dike Dome

Dike Dome is less of a dome than a slabby shoulder of the extensive slabs below Olmsted Point. Overlooking Tenaya Canyon, Clouds Rest, and Half Dome, Dike Dome is in one of the most spectacular locations in Yosemite, but it is often too hot to climb in mid-summer. The climbing is similar to Yosemite Valley, but the slabs are better friction than most of the Valley. This is an excellent option for very cold days.

Approach

From the Olmsted parking lot, take the main trail to Olmsted Point. Fifty yards from the pavement, at the bottom of the first downhill, go right and down, following an old well-constructed trail to the right under a small cliff. Continue on the trail as it then turns left and down a drainage, where the trail fades and you hike down the drainage with slabs and brush (you're heading towards Half Dome). The brush gives way to a forest which is bordered on the left by an open slab. Hike along the left edge of the forest along the slab, then up a gentle hill to a collection of small boulders. You are now above the north (upstream) end of Dike Dome. Continue downstream along the top of the dome for about 50 yards, then down left where you can curve back left (upstream) in a gentle "scoop." The bolted anchor for the three routes detailed below is at the left end of the scoop.

Locating the dome, and especially locating the anchor on top of the routes, can be tricky. Approaching the anchors for toproping is very exposed 3rd and 4th class slabs and may require a belay for some. Sticky rubber footwear is recommended.

These three routes are at the south (downstream) end of the dome and require two ropes to rappel. If approaching from above, either fix a line, rap the single fixed rope, and lead with the second rope, or set up a two-rope toprope and just toprope all routes. All routes use the same two-bolt anchor, although a directional is needed for Twisted Sister.

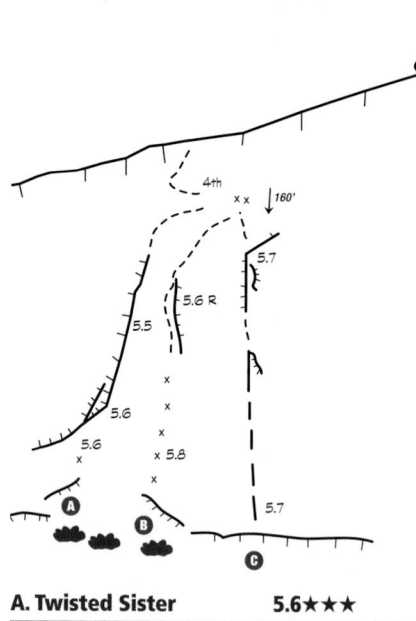

A. Twisted Sister 5.6★★★

FA: Steve Gerberding, August 1987.

A short cruxy face past a bolt leads to a wide lieback, then a long, beautiful crack/lieback. Slightly dirty in the crack, but excellent overall.
Rack: nuts: 1 set, cams: 1 ea. 0.6-.75", 3", 2 ea. 1-2", optional extra 1.25-1.5"

B. Black Leather 5.8 R★★★

FA: Grant Hiskes, August 1988.

Classic good-friction slab climbing with cool features, this is tightly bolted for an old-school 5.8 slab. The easiest finish is to the left. On toprope there are many possible variations.
Rack: cams: 1 ea. 0.5-1", 5 quickdraws

C. Bull Dike 5.7 R-★★★★

FA: Dave Bengston, July 1987.

A fun, varied adventure, this "crack" has everything from juggy face to slab to corner to pockets, with a little bit of actual crack climbing thrown in for good measure. Narrow, single-stem cams are needed for good protection in the final section.
Rack: nuts: 1 set cams: 2 ea. 0.5-2", narrow single stem cams 0.6-0.75", 1 ea. 3" optional extra 0.6-1.25"

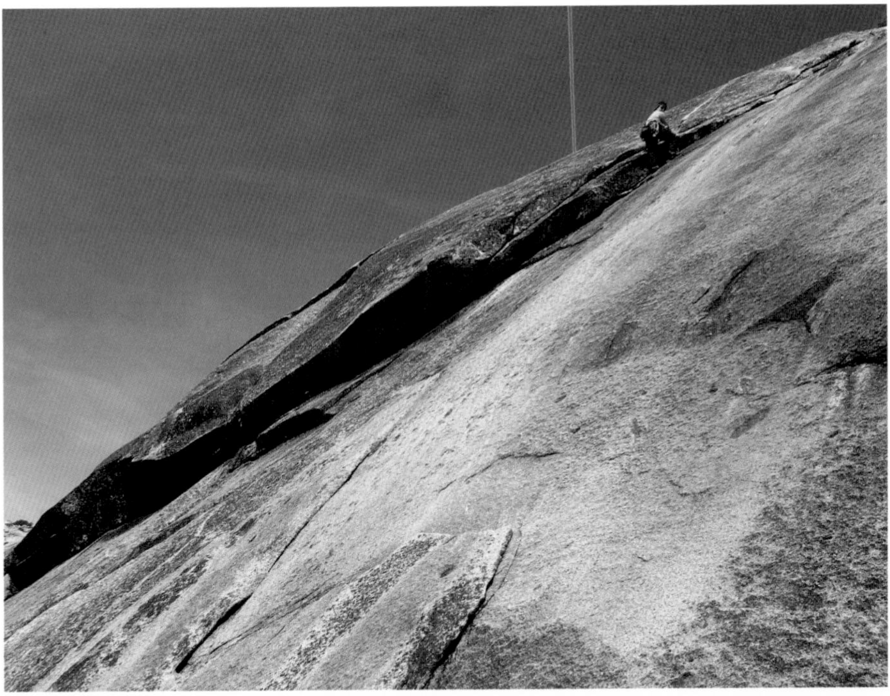

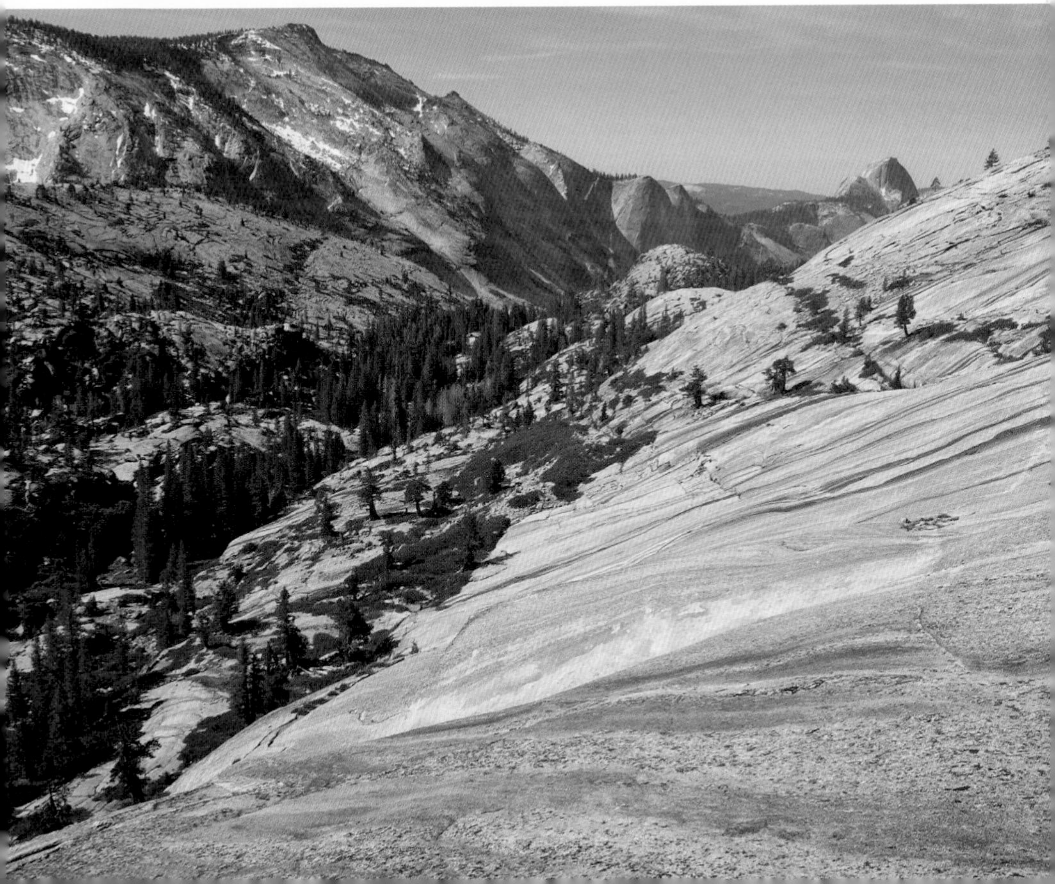

Olmsted Canyon

Olmsted Canyon is the main crack climbing crag of Tuolumne. More of a broad small valley than a canyon, Olmsted has lots of short crack routes close to the road. With rock more like Yosemite Valley (Half Dome granodiorite, as opposed to the knobby Cathedral Peak granodiorite), the cracks are parallel and much smoother than most Tuolumne cracks, although they can be a bit flakey and grainy. Olmsted Canyon also tends to be the last place that afternoon thunderstorms strike, making it a popular last-ditch destination on stormy days. Despite its popularity, the climbs at Olmsted are short even by cragging standards. Olmsted Canyon can get really hot on warm days, with the base resembling a solar oven. If you want to climb here on warm days, wait until late afternoon when the routes go into the shade.

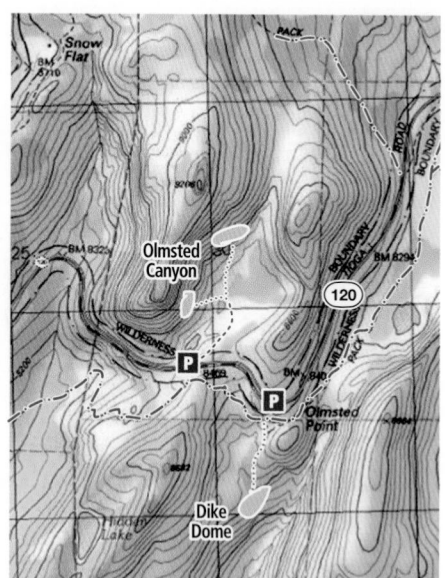

Approach

Park at a small paved turnout on the right (north) side of the road 0.3 miles west of the huge Olmsted Point paved pullout. If it's full, continue on until it's safe to turn around and park opposite in a tiny dirt spot, or at the main Olmsted Point parking and just hike back. From the paved pullout, follow an obvious hiking trail to the north. The trail winds among some boulders, then crosses a swamp on a granite ramp. Hike through a few yards of trees to a broad white slab, and hike up and left to A-D or up and right to E-K.

A. Grease Monkey   5.9 R-★★★

FA: Dave Yerian, July 1985

Good hand and low-angle fist crack to a slabby topout. The anchor is either a cam-wrenching crack at the back of the small ledge, or a directional anchor with the main anchor the tree to the left. Rack: nuts: 1 set, cams: 2 ea 0.6-3", long slings for tree

B. Age of Darkness   5.11a★★

FA: Dave Yerian, Merry McGrath, July 1985

Tough flared hands roof – tape gloves are highly recommended. The jams are very flared. Same anchor as Grease Monkey – use a directional anchor with the cams pulled sideways to the main tree anchor instead of over a right-angle break. Rack: cams: 2 ea. 0.6-3"

C. Lock of Ages   5.10c★★

FA: Scott Cole, Bruce Morris, Grant Hiskes, September 1988.

Fun climbing with a thin, well-protected crux, but usually pretty dirty. Rack: nuts: 1set, cams: 2 ea. 0.6-1.5", 1 ea. 2-3"

D. Double Feature   5.11d★★★

FA: Jeff Schoen.

An easy lieback to undercling leads to this hard, crimpy face on perfect rock. Rack: cams: 1 ea. 1-2", 6 quickdraws

E. Lord Caffeine   5.10d★★★★★

FA: Urmas and Becky Franosch, Bruce Morris, August 1986.

An outstanding, burly, leaning finger-and-offwidth crack, Lord Caffeine feels much longer than it looks. Nearly everyone thinks it's a sandbag – unless you climb 5.10 wide cracks in Yosemite Valley, in which case it seems about right. Finger locks, awkward smears, and good wide crack technique are the keys. It's possible to solo to the anchor to set a TR, but it's extremely exposed low 5th. Directionals are needed for toproping to prevent a swing into the slab. Rack: nuts: 1 set, cams: 2-3 ea 0.6-1.25", 1 ea 1.5-4"

F. Ivory Tower Left   5.8★★★

FA: Bruce Morris, Mike Hernandez, June 1987.

A great introduction to offwidth climbing. Not too hard for the grade, and straightforward. Often toproped after leading the Center route. Use a 3" cam as a directional between the bolted anchor and the top of the crack. Rack: cams: 1 ea 1-3", optional extra 1.25-2".

G. Ivory Tower Center   5.10a★★★

FA: Bruce Morris, Mike Hernandez, Stu Richie June 1987.

A classic narrowing hand crack, but only 30 feet tall. Wide hands off the deck to a thin hands crux at the top. The bolts are in a poor location for toproping, making it nearly impossible to keep the rope out of the crack. Rack: cams: 1 ea 1-3", optional extra 1.25-2"

H. Enemy Within   5.10b★★★

FA Bruce Morris, Mike Hernandez, July 1986.

Burly, steep offwidth, this route is on the narrow side of offwidths, so guys with big hands can get some fist jams too. Rack: cams: 2 ea. 2-6", extra 4-5"

I. The Thrill is Gone   5.10d★★★

FA Elliot Robinson, Bruce Morris, August 1987.

Wide lieback to offwidth to hard slab, a scary lead but a fun toprope. There's a great knee bar rest turning the lip of the lieback. Rack: cams: 0.6-7", extra 5-7"

J. The Stanley Edge   5.10c★★

FA Chris Falkenstein, Don Reid, Peter Mayfield, August 1985.

Kind of grainy leaning crack to the same slabby top-out as The Thrill is Gone. Rack: nuts: 1 set, cams: 2 ea. 0.6-2", 1 ea 3"

K. Tideline   5.11a★★★★★

FA Dave Yerian, Tom Herbert, Merry McGrath, August 1985.

Awesome steep thin hands to finger crack, one of the best cracks in Tuolumne. It starts near a huge, solitary Western Juniper tree. Rack: nuts: 1 set, cams: 2 ea. 0.6-2", 1 ea 3"

Broken Arrow   5.13d

FA Ron Kauk 1995.

To check out the hardest crack in Tuolumne, hike about 200 yards down and right from Tideline, then up the canyon a bit past a huge white flake to this 60-foot tall ultra-thin crack on a black and orange wall on the left. Broken holds have raised the difficulty of this extreme line, which used to be "only" 5.13b/c!

Olmsted Left

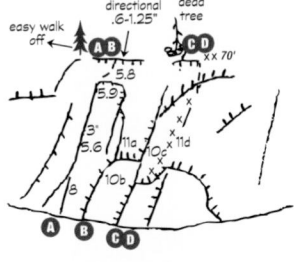

Olmsted Right

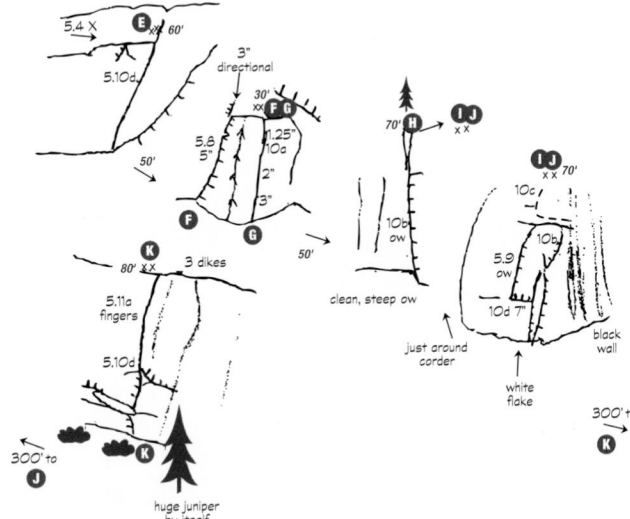

Murphy Creek

A fun crag similar to Olmsted Canyon, Murphy Creek has cracks galore, most of which are easily toproped. It's much further from the road and thus much less popular, but the hike is fairly flat and easy, and the climbs are more concentrated than Olmsted. Murphy Creek has an eastern exposure, with morning sun and late afternoon shade. Hiking to the crag can be very boggy in early season.

Most routes are shown here, but there are many additional topropes at this cliff. All of the harder routes were done by Scott Fry and Bird Lew in 1985. First ascents of most of the easier routes are unknown, but were probably free solos in the 80s. There is a mix of bolted and trad anchors, and a few of the TRs require directionals.

Approach

Coming from the main Meadows, park immediately after you pass Stately Pleasure Dome at the Murphy Creek Trailhead, which is just across the road from a picnic area with restrooms. A mellow 1.5-mile hike up the Murphy Creek trail leads to open slabs, and the crag is obvious as the only cliff taller than 30 feet. A short cross-country hike leads through the woods up to the crag, but this section can be very boggy in early season, and potentially wet enough to cause difficulty in crossing the creek.

A. Fluoridation   5.11a★★

Steep and sharply left-leaning thin to hand crack. Watch the penji for toprope – use directionals. The anchor has one bolt and cams.

B. Auto Bond   5.11b★★★

Excellent, steep liebacking and jamming with lots of finger locks, and a flared crux. Shares a two-bolt anchor with Mandric.

C. Mandric   5.10c R★★

Start up the ramp, and climb right with very delicate climbing to the dihedral, which gets wide above. Shares a two-bolt anchor with Auto Bond.

D. Mandric direct   5.11b★★★

Quality finger crack dihedral that gets wide above. Watch the severe penji for toprope – use directionals! Same anchor as Mandric.

E. Getting In the Groove 5.11d★★

Desperate moves off the deck leads to easier climbing above. The munge in the crack starting about 15 feet up attests to how few people manage to pull the first moves! Shares the two-bolt anchor with Penguin Café, but using that anchor it's not safe to TR all the way to the top.

F. Penguin Café 5.11a★★★

Awesome finger/hand crack (5.10c) to powerful lieback-to-hands crux to wide crack. The crux is very powerful and strange, and the great hand jams right before the lieback/cave crux are hard to leave! TR from bolts, but it's dicey to get to the bolts without a belay.

G. Gortlough RA 5.9★★

FA: Dennis Gleason, Anne Freund, 1990.

Hands, stemming, and a bit of offwidth. Quality but dirty. The arête on the right is a fun TR problem. The 2-bolt anchor is to the climber's right of the dying tree, with one bolt on the left face (newly added to substitute for the tree), and a bolt on the right.

H. Pac Man 5.8★★★

Left of X-Wing is a double crack through a short steep slot, which has a wide mossy left-leaning flake/crack to its left. Pac Man climbs the double crack with mostly hand jams and quality climbing. Make the trad anchor a little below the top to avoid rope drag.

I. X-Wing 5.9★★★

Good, varied climbing up cracks and dike, with a balancy crux. You can start up the main dike crack or to the left – if you start up the dike, double up on 1.5-2". Save a 2" cam for the anchor, which is one bolt plus a 2" cam-sized pod.

J. Frogger 5.7★★★

Save 2-4" pro for the anchor. Fun double hand cracks through a bulge. Climb left at the top to find a good 2-4" crack. You can stay in one crack or the other for variations, and you can also toprope the dike-to-thin crack-to-face.

Stately Pleasure Dome

Rising above the deep blue Tenaya Lake, Stately Pleasure Dome is the first dome encountered driving into Tuolumne from the west. Several high-quality routes start only a few hundred feet above the road. The climbs on the 500-foot dome are four to six pitches long and popular introductions to multi-pitch Tuolumne climbing.

The climbs are south facing and generally climbable any time the highway is open. However, on rare hot, windless days the face can be an oven. It's often windy up high, and balmy temperatures at the lake can trick the unwary into leaving windjackets in the car. As with all climbs in Tuolumne, do not start if thunderstorms are approaching.

Approach

Stately Pleasure Dome is located next to the east end of Tenaya Lake. From the car, scramble up slick 3rd class slab to the base.

Descent

Traverse up and left toward the headwall and a big tree about 200 yards away. Rappel from the tree or downclimb (4th class). Hike down intimidating 3rd and 4th class slabs, generally staying near the headwall. Climb down a short 4th class friction section (beware of water on the slab!) below a big roof. Then head left through a small notch to get down a four-foot drop-off, followed by more 3rd class friction traversing below the four-foot wall. Then, head straight down long 3rd class slabs toward the road and lake.

You can also hike up the dome above the tree, head west, and hike down behind the huge headwall. This requires a bit of routefinding, but is an option for those fearful of the 4th class friction, and is the wiser option if the slabs are wet.

It's also possible to hike up and north, then down the gully between Stately Pleasure and Harlequin Domes, but the bushwacking will get ugly.

A. White Flake   5.7 R★★★

FA: Jeff Foott, Jim Baldwin, Hope Morehouse, August 1962.

A good easy crack leading to big runouts on clean white slab, and finishing with a fun low-angle flake, White Flake used to be a standard beginner route back in the day when big runouts were all there was on easy slab. These days it sees little traffic, but it's still a great moderate climb for those confident on slab.

B. The Shadow Nose   5.9 R★★★

FA: Jack Miller and friends, July 1971.

A fun crack leads to a short section of slab to the first anchor. The second pitch has a huge runout on nontrivial terrain (above an old ¼" bolt), following a faint seam through pure gold polish. It's easy, and fun, to head left at the roof and finish on the cruiser flake of White Flake. This route was originally rated 5.7, but on the second pitch it likely climbed over to the right near (or on) the third pitch of West Country. The last pitch has one old bolt lost in a sea of featured slab.

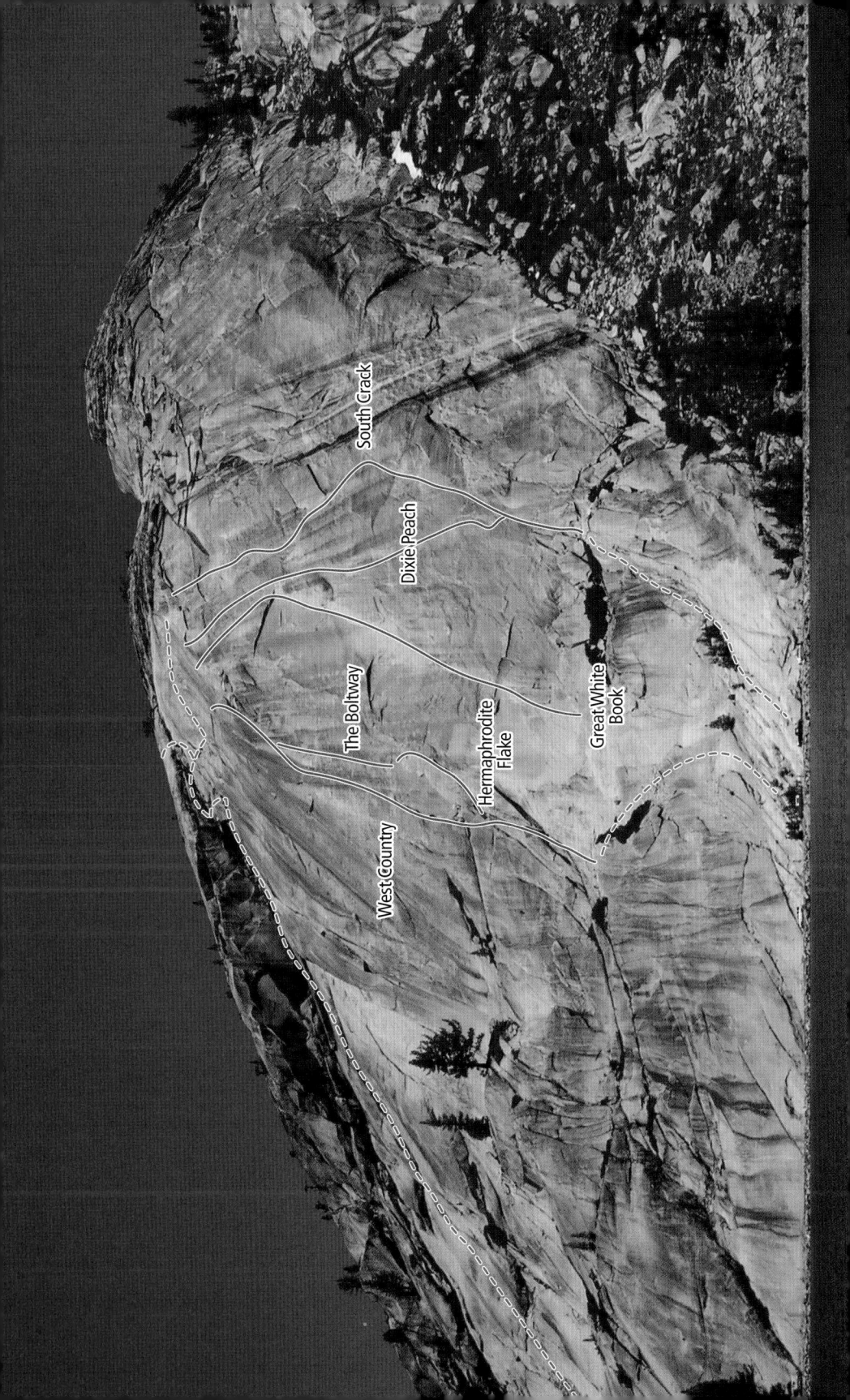

South Crack

Dixie Peach

The Boltway

Hermaphrodite
Flake

Great White
Book

West Country

West Country 5.7★★★★

Time to climb route: **1.5–2.5 hours**

Approach time: **5 minutes**

Descent time: **20–30 minutes**

Sun exposure: **morning to afternoon**

Height of route: **400'**

West Country is one of the more stout, classic, and accessible 5.7 multi-pitch climbs in Tuolumne. The second pitch, a slippery and tenuous 5.7 lieback, comes as a rude surprise for many leaders. The third pitch is well bolted by Tuolumne standards, but still has crux 5.7 friction 15-20 feet above the last protection. As with any climb at any grade in Tuolumne, those new to the area and especially those new to low-angle, slippery granite should take the ratings with a grain of salt.

FA: Bob Summers and John Fischer, 1970.

Strategy

West Country is popular and usually has a line. Hermaphrodite Flake starts from the same point, which adds to the wait. Luckily, the ledge is spacious and has great views. Many climbers avoid the original and much better first pitch in favor of an odd traverse start, which puts both leader and follower in danger of pendulum falls – this is recommended only for confident 5.7 climbers.

With two ropes, you can rappel from Pitch 3 to various rappel stations and toprope a variety of climbs. You will likely need to leave slings and rap rings to rappel from some stations.

Retreat

From Pitch 4, you would have to leave gear to rappel. From the two bolts at the Pitch 3 anchor, rappel with two ropes to the top of Hermaphrodite Flake. From Pitch 4 an intermediate station straight above the flake is used to gain the flake. Rappel straight down over the flake to a hidden station only 50 feet below the top of the flake. From here, two ropes reach the 3rd class ledge.

From the bolts on Pitch 2, either rappel to the Pitch 1 belay and leave gear (thread slings and/or large nuts), or rappel and aggressively pendulum left to gain a walk-off ledge.

If you top out just as it starts raining, either leave gear to rappel or consider a long walk-off around the back, as the normal 4th class slabs can be treacherous if wet. If thunderstorms (puffy clouds) are coming, rappel before you get any rain – remember that lightning can strike before the first raindrops do!

Hermaphrodite Flake to The Boltway 5.4 or 5.8 or 5.10b★★★

Time to climb route: **1–2.5 hours**

Approach time: **5 minutes**

Descent time: **20–30 minutes**

Sun exposure: **morning to afternoon**

Height of route: **400'**

Hermaphrodite Flake is one of the few climbs of the grade in Tuolumne. The flake itself resembles a mirror image of California and rivals El Capitan's Boot Flake in its mysterious ability to cling to the wall with no visible means of attachment. Climb the huge flake using a chimney tunnel-through or an exposed undercling. Once on top, many climbers continue up The Boltway, one of the first well-bolted 5.8 face routes in Tuolumne.

FA: Tom Naylor, Mary Olsen, and Earl Olsen, 1965 (Hermaphrodite Flake). Marty Steiger, 1992 (The Boltway).

Strategy

As with West Country or South Crack, be prepared to take a number and wait in line. The climbing is not well-protected in several wide cracks and in the tunnel-through. Yet no wide gear is needed since the cracks are either too wide for pro or it's possible to place small cams in other spots.

While this route climbed in its entirety is 5.8 or 5.10b, many parties rappel before the top. If you rappel after three pitches, the route is 5.7. If you rappel after two pitches, the route is 5.4.

You can toprope the excellent and sustained thin slabs Footnote (5.10c) and Cross Reference (5.11a) if rappelling from Hermaphrodite Flake.

Retreat

See West Country Retreat on facing page.

F. Footnote   5.10c R★★★

FA: Phil Bard, Jo Bentley, 1984.

Excellent, sustained thin edging slab, Footnote is outstanding training for hard slab, and easily top-roped. To set a toprope, you can climb the first 100 feet of West Country/Hermaphrodite Flake and traverse right on a ledge to the anchor. The route is just a shade longer than half a 60m rope, so by using slings at the anchor and great care on the ramp at the start, you can just toprope it with a 60, although a 70m is much better.

G. Table of Contents   5.10d R-★★★★

FA: p1: Dan Dingle, Steve Lesse, July 1979; p2: Vern Clevenger, Claude Fiddler, July 1981.

Table of Contents is probably the best thin edging 5.10 slab route in Tuolumne. With good but spaced edges, a natural weakness to follow (at least on the first pitch), and relatively good bolting, it's also quite popular (for a slab.). The first pitch is 5.10b and popular by itself. The second pitch is more tightly bolted, but harder.

H. Cross Reference   5.11a R★★★

FA: Alan Nelson, Vaino Kodas, July 1986.

Super sustained slab, Cross Reference is a good example of why many slab routes are so runout. It would be nearly impossible to try to stop and drill a bolt in the middle of the long crux section (it would be hard to clip a bolt even if was already there.), and thus a very bold and dangerous route resulted. Luckily, it's easy to toprope the first pitch from the anchor under the flake on Hermaphrodite Flake.

Great White Book 5.6 R★★★★

Time to climb route:	**2–3 hours**
Approach time:	**5 minutes**
Descent time:	**20–30 minutes**
Sun exposure:	**morning to afternoon**
Height of route:	**450′**

This is perhaps Tuolumne's most classic wide climb. It is intimidating, polished, and is many climbers' introduction to chimney and offwidth. Although it's low-angle, the climbing grabs your attention with frequent runouts or awkward chimney moves.

FA: Hope Morehouse Meek, Jim Baldwin, and Jeff Foott, 1962.

History

Why this classic, clean line on Stately Pleasure Dome wasn't done until 1962 beats me; it's easily the most obvious route in the Tuolumne area. Perhaps the answer is that the Great White Book simply fades into nothingness some 500 feet above the ground. It thus has no "summit," and in the old days the blank face above the book looked rather intimidating. Also, as seen from below, the thing looks steep! It isn't.

The route is great, it's certainly a gleaming white and it's a perfect example of an open book (a.k.a. dihedral). Thus the route would almost seem to be self-naming. But this is not the case. A woman named Hope was on the first ascent, and she was good. Good enough that we jokingly called her the Great White Hope, using that woeful boxing phrase from the early 20th century. We meant no racism by the expression; we just liked how it sounded. So it was an easy step by someone to call the route its present name, knowing that Great White Hope didn't sound like much of a route name.

Hope Morehouse Meek remembers the climb well. "Steve Roper mischievously put me together with Jim Baldwin. Jim had the reputation of being able to fall in love with a glass of water. Well, I lived with Jim in Camp 4, commuting from the Bay Area every weekend, for two years, climbing any route Jim would lead. Jim finally decided it was time for me to graduate to a first ascent, so we packed up our gear and drove to Tuolumne with Jeff Foott. The boys' selection of route delighted me. I love climbing but am a lazy walker, and I remember being able to drive almost to the bottom of the route. The book is very wide open with few cracks in its spine. A foot and hand on each leaf (to continue the metaphor of "book") with cross pressure and a few good hand holds did the trick most of the way. There was very little feel of exposure until the last pitch where one has to fiddle around a small ledge to get up to the friction at the end of the climb. The boys promised I could name it, and I wanted to name it Hope's Crack – but these wild and woolly and full-of-fleas boys demurred. I remember that we did the route without bolts, which pleased us greatly."

Baldwin died two years later in one of Yosemite's earliest climbing accidents; he was a wonderful fellow. Foott (and, yes, his name has two "t"s.) went on to become a world-renowned photographer, with more than a dozen wildlife films to his credit. Still climbing 5.10, he lives in the shadow of Castleton Tower, near Moab, Utah. Hope Morehouse Meek lives in La Jolla, California, where she regularly gets out into the desert and climbs when possible.

– *Steve Roper*

Strategy

Great White Book is popular, yet usually has smaller lines than the surrounding climbs. Wide gear is needed to protect the crux first pitch and large cams can be used to protect the upper half of the third pitch's wide chimney. Be aware that much of the climbing cannot be protected.

For all of the crux wide sections on Great White Book, the key to climbing comfortably is to wedge your right shoulder into the right wall and walk your feet up the left wall. While it sounds odd, the angle is so low that soloists have been seen walking down the whole corner, stemming one foot on each side.

On hot days the dihedral is shaded in the morning; on cold days wait until afternoon to avoid the icebox effect.

Retreat

Retreat from Great White Book is fairly easy, but gear must be left in several places. The first two pitches have blocks and horns that can be slung for retreat. In addition, immediately before the crux section on the first pitch is an excellent flake to sling and rappel off (careful!) and often leaders who don't like the looks of the wide slick dihedral bail from here. Two ropes are required to rappel unless you have lots of huge cams to discard. The book angles to the right, and becomes a waterfall in thunderstorms.

See topo page 40

J. Mosquito   5.7 R★★

FA: Vern Clevenger, Bruce Chimilesk, July 1971.

Mosquito is the "passing lane" for Great White Book. An easy crack to runout slab leads either back to the anchor on pitch 3 of Great White Book, or to the anchor for pitch 3 of Dixie Peach. From there, Mosquito joins Dixie Peach, allowing access to the upper pitches of Dixie Peach at a more moderate grade, but bypassing the best climbing.

K. Dixie Peach   5.9 R★★★★

FA: Vern Clevenger, Eric Schoen, Rob Frick, November 1973.

With clean, exposed climbing up the center of Stately Pleasure Dome, Dixie Peach is a step up from South Crack in both difficulty and head games. Fun, featured slab climbing makes up the bulk of the route, but with three slab pitches in a row with no protection at all, a solid lead head is required.

The first pitch is the crux, starting up the easy flake start of South Crack and then up a corner to flake to 5.9 slab past a bolt. The next pitch is the psychological crux, with sustained 5.8 friction climbing (with one rest knob) for 40 feet to larger holds and easier climbing. The next two pitches have generally easy climbing up wandering featured slab, and then you can use the finishes of either Great White Book or South Crack. It's easy to link the 2nd and 3rd pitches with a 60m rope, and you get to clip the intermediate anchor as a piece of pro.

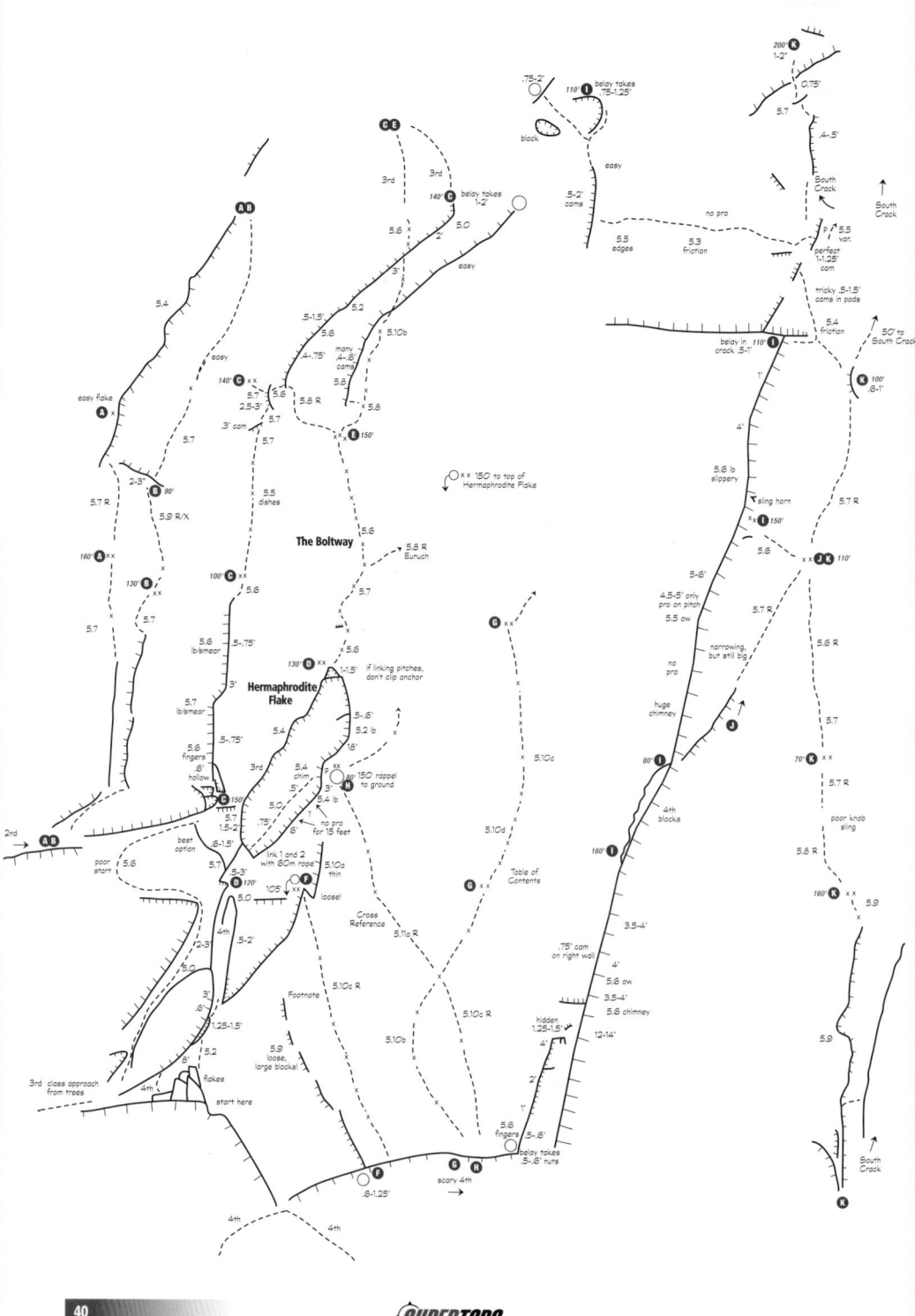

A. White Flake 5.7 R★★★
nuts: 1 set
cams: 2 ea. 0.6-2"
  1 ea. 3"

B. The Shadow Nose 5.9 R★★★
nuts: 1 set
cams: 1 ea. 0.6-3.5", 1 ea. extra 2-3" if belay
at roof

C. West Country 5.7★★★★
nuts: 1 set
cams: 1 ea .5-1.5", 2 ea 2-3"
optional: extra 2-4" cams for traversing crack on
4th pitch; recommended with novice followers.

D. Hermaphrodite Flake 5.4★★★
nuts: 1 set
cams: 1 ea .5-3"
many draws/slings

E. The Boltway 5.8 or 5.10b★★★
nuts: 1 set
cams: 2 ea .4-.6", 1 ea .75-3"
many draws/slings

South Crack Rack
nuts: 2 ea sml
  1 ea med-lrg
cams: 3 ea .6-.75"
  2 ea .5", 1-2"
  1 ea .3-.4", 2.5-3.5"

F. Footnote 5.10c R★★★
5 quickdraws
cams 0.6-1.25" for anchor at base

G. Table of Contents 5.10d R-★★★★
8 quickdraws

H. Cross Reference 5.11a R★★★
4 quickdraws

I. Great White Book 5.6 R★★★★
nuts: 1 set
cams: 1 ea .6-3"
  2 ea 4-5.5"
  1 ea 6-7"

J. Mosquito 5.7 R★★
nuts: 1 set
cams: 1 ea. 0.5-4"

K. Dixie Peach 5.9 R★★★★
nuts: 1 set
cams: 2 ea. 0.4-1.25"
1 ea. 1.5-3"

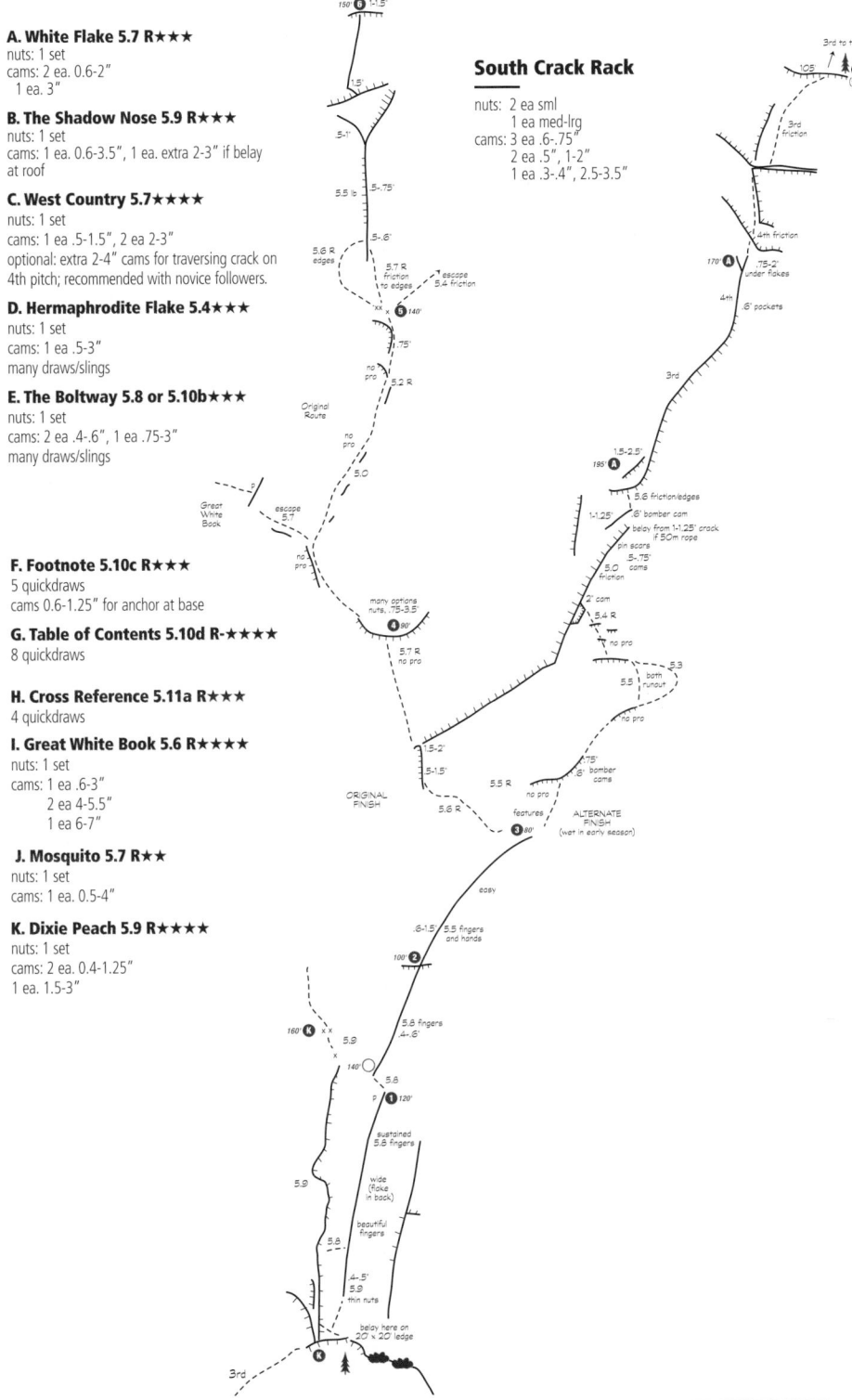

South Crack 5.8 R★★★★★

Time to climb route: **2–4 hours**

Approach time: **5 minutes**

Descent time: **20–30 minutes**

Sun exposure: **morning to afternoon**

Height of route: **500'**

South Crack is the ultimate 5.8 finger and hand crack. The route ascends a beautiful, long, splitter crack in a fantastic position. Beware of the runout slabs above – for those experienced on slabs they are a trivial walk-up; for those with less experience they can be terrifying and potentially dangerous.

FA: Gordon Webster and Frank de Saussure, 1965.

Strategy

South Crack often generates big lines. Once on the route, there is no way to pass other climbers until the slabs at the top. Faster parties often wait until late in the day to avoid the crowds. Amazingly, the route often goes unclimbed in perfect weather very early or late in the season. Watch for Highway 120 to open and quickly head up for a more serene and beautiful experience. You may even be lucky enough to see a big slab avalanche on Tenaya Peak.

The right start, with some thin face climbing protected by small nuts, gains the bottom of the crack. It's the more clean and sustained option, but a bit harder than the standard start. When the crack runs out at the end of the third pitch, the original route heads up and left across slabs. An easier escape heads up right.

If you finish early, consider climbing West Country, Hermaphrodite Flake, or Great White Book.

Retreat

You must leave gear, and two ropes are mandatory for retreat. If retreating from the end of the crack on the third pitch, your rappel anchor must be good for a direct outward pull, so cams are often the only safe bet. Below the right-traversing crack are several climbs, and aggressive searching on rappel will likely find a bolted anchor. You need two ropes to reach the ground from any of these bolted anchors. Once on the upper slab sections, retreat is even less appealing.

From the three-bolt belay below the top pitch, you can also rap down Great White Book, but you'll have to tension/pendulum far to the left on the first rap. You'll be leaving slings and gear down Great White Book, although there are many spots for nuts and/or slung blocks/horns.

Harlequin Dome

Approach time: 15 minutes

Sun exposure: all day

Height of routes: 450'

The golden and polished Harlequin Dome is located above Tenaya Lake, but doesn't have the crowds of Stately Pleasure Dome. It is home to wandering routes that are possible to link with various pitches of different climbs. Several wild routes climb through roofs on the steep right side of the dome.

Approach

Park at Tenaya Lake or at the huge parking lot with bathrooms a bit to the east of the lake. Hike up slabs below the dome, either skirting a short headwall or climbing through it at its shortest point (slick 4th class). Some bushwacking is necessary. The approach is somewhat steep but takes only 10-15 minutes.

Descent

Hike off left, then contour back down to the base through heavy brush. It's also possible to simply hike all the way down along Stately Pleasure Dome, but the bushwacking is just as bad if not worse, and you won't be able to get back to anything you left at the base.

A. Hoodwink   5.10a R★★★★

FA: Jim Bridwell and Roger Breedlove, July 1972.

hoodwink: 1) to deceive or trick. 2) to blindfold. 3) to cover or hide.

Yosemite master Jim Bridwell established this classic of the early 1970s. Hoodwink lives up to its name, which, if translated into modern climbing lingo, might be called "Sandbag." Most of the route is well protected. However, if the fixed piton on the crux roof pulled you would take a bad fall. Because of this, only confident 5.10 leaders

A Hoodwink		**D** By Hook or By Crook	
B The Sting		**G** Cyclone	
C No Rock Nazis			

should do this pitch.

The bottom section of the first pitch (also the first pitch of The Sting) is a fun 5.8 dihedral to roof. This can be done as a stand-alone climb by traversing left to a bolted anchor. You can single-rope rappel, but will need a 60m rope to lower off due to the traverse.

Slick, slabby, and awkward corners lead to the base of the roof – belay here. The crux of Hoodwink is the 10-foot horizontal roof on the second-to-last pitch. The roof is challenging, tricky, and wild – and protected by a single fixed pin at the lip. Be prepared for stout 5.10a. Immediately after pulling the roof there's a bolted belay.

The last pitch is a short 5.10a slab to an easy runout dike and the last bolt. Finally, climb a long runout to the anchor. It's easiest to stay to the right, but an apparent crack under a roof suckers many into 5.9 territory 40 feet from the last bolt.

B. The Sting   5.10b R★★★★

FA: Vern Clevenger, D. Ferries, Bob Locke, and Tom Carter, September 1975.

The second pitch of The Sting is one of those old-school 5.9+ pitches that will get your attention with tricky, hard climbing and a scary traverse left to a mantel. A long undercling traverse pitch above and a thin, technical crack, leads to a huge runout on relatively easy slab (or an escape right). Stingwink, a great linkup, starts by climbing The Sting. Then instead of heading up the final runout slab, traverse the roof and finish on the final two pitches of Hoodwink.

C. No Rock Nazis   5.11c★★★★

FA: Chris Falkenstein, Joe Rousek, and Dave Bengston, 9/85.

The crux first pitch of No Rock Nazis is technical, well-protected, and often overlooked. The second pitch starts with steep and hard-to-protect liebacking followed by a tightly bolted face climbing crux. This route joins the Sting at the end of the second pitch. A linkup of No Rock Nazis to The Sting to Hoodwink (or the 5.10d crux mantel pitch of Rock Lobster) adds even more fun climbing.

D. By Hook or By Crook   5.11b★★★★★

FA: Chris Falkenstein and Dave Hitchcock, 7/79.

Considered by many to be the best climb of its grade in Tuolumne, By Hook or By Crook winds its way up wild dihedrals and roofs. It has knobs, edges, thin cracks, and almost enough fixed protection to be called a sport climb. The start is slabby and cruxy, especially since a large block broke off 20 feet up, but a short stick-clip can be used to clip the first bolt from a good stance..

E. Heat Sensitive   5.12b★★

FA: Chris Falkenstein, Ed Barry

This short and very difficult face is easy to toprope from By Hook or By Crook. Consider stick-clipping the first bolt if leading..

F. Chinese Handcuffs   5.10d★★★

FA: Bruce Morris and Nick Badyrka, 1975.

This route climbs an excellent roof dihedral to a sharp finger crack that eats your fingers and gives the route its name. An off-balance crux at the lip of the roof leads to a pumpy finger, off-finger, and tight hand crack. You can easily toprope the climb with long slings from the tree and 2" pro (for a directional) at the top of the crack.

G. Cyclone   5.10b★★

FA: Greg Barnes, Jonathan duSaint, Karin Wuhrmann, Florence Scholl, October 2006.

The right side of Harlequin Dome has always been the realm of intimidating roofs and 5.11 and harder climbing. The roofs are still intimidating, but now there's a fun 5.10 route in the midst of the harder routes. Like its neighbors, Cyclone winds its way up through roofs, with one pitch only gaining 30 feet of vertical despite twice that length of climbing. The route is new and needs traffic to "buff" out the small flakes, grainy sections, and knobs – whether it proves popular or not will determine if it gets clean. The first two belays are semi-hanging and not very comfy. Rap twice with a single 60m rope, but be very careful watching rope ends (tie knots!).

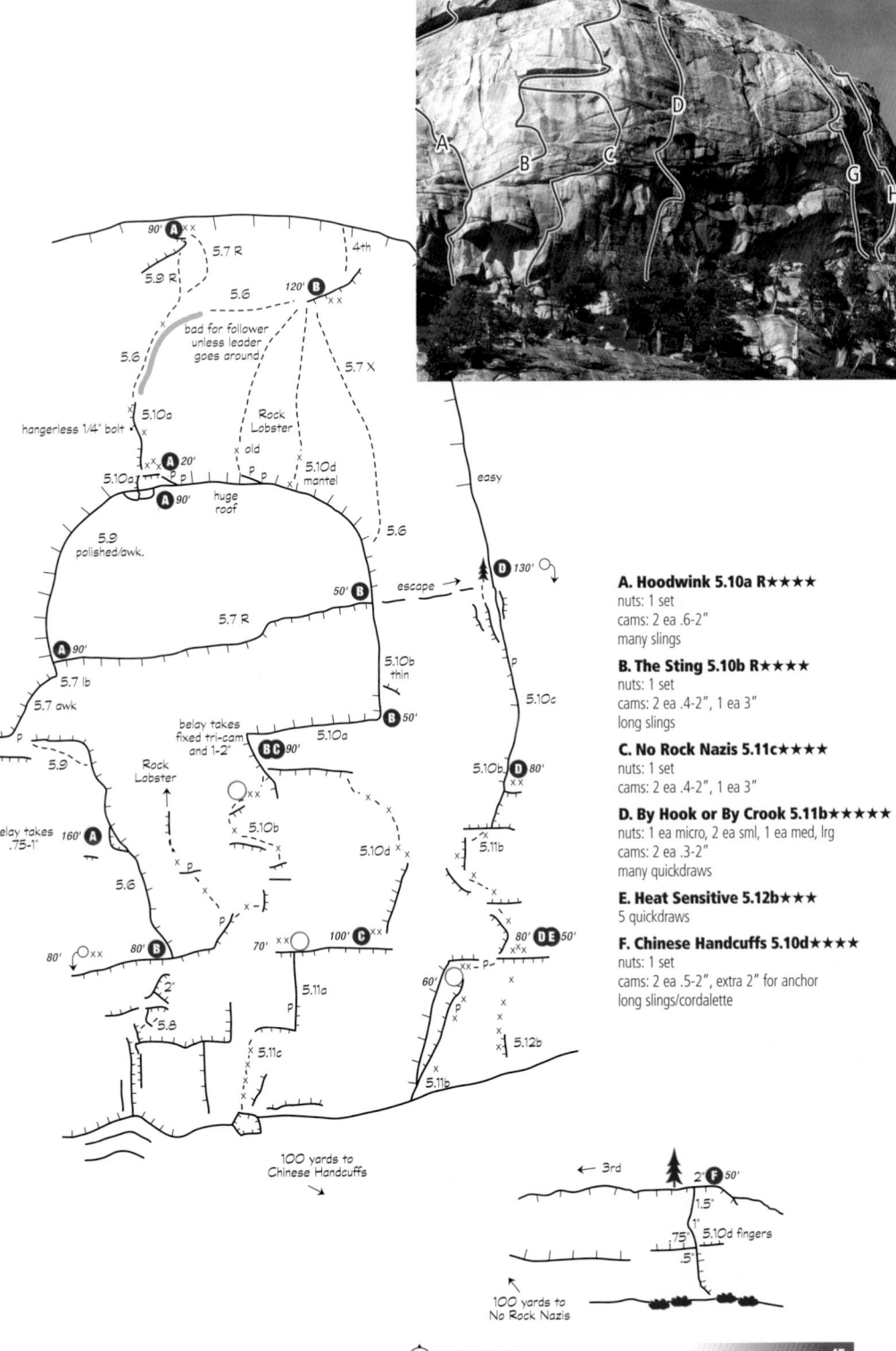

A. Hoodwink 5.10a R★★★★
nuts: 1 set
cams: 2 ea .6-2"
many slings

B. The Sting 5.10b R★★★★
nuts: 1 set
cams: 2 ea .4-2", 1 ea 3"
long slings

C. No Rock Nazis 5.11c★★★★
nuts: 1 set
cams: 2 ea .4-2", 1 ea 3"

D. By Hook or By Crook 5.11b★★★★★
nuts: 1 ea micro, 2 ea sml, 1 ea med, lrg
cams: 2 ea .3-2"
many quickdraws

E. Heat Sensitive 5.12b★★★
5 quickdraws

F. Chinese Handcuffs 5.10d★★★★
nuts: 1 set
cams: 2 ea .5-2", extra 2" for anchor
long slings/cordalette

H. Third World   5.11b★★★

FA: Ed Barry, Dave Hitchcock, July 1980.

With great climbing up steep cracks and face, Third World is a quality but rarely climbed route. With steep, well-protected crux cracks, and with the replacement of the old ¼" bolts in October 2006, the route is bound for renewed popularity. The first pitch is an excellent, varied, and challenging 5.10a, and is definitely worth climbing as a stand-alone pitch if the 5.11 crux is too difficult. The protection for the last hard moves on the first pitch is a recently reset old piton which should be backed up as best possible in the slightly hollow finger crack below. Beware of large loose blocks on top of the Pitch 2. Walk left on the ledge and rap Cyclone with one 60-m rope (watch rope ends!), or continue to the top and hike off left.

G. Cyclone 5.10b★★★
nuts: 1 set including thin
cams: 1 ea. 0.3-3.5"
long slings

H. Third World 5.11b★★★
nuts: 1 set
cams: 1 ea. 0.33-.5", 3"
2 ea. 0.6-2", opt. extra 0.75-1.25"

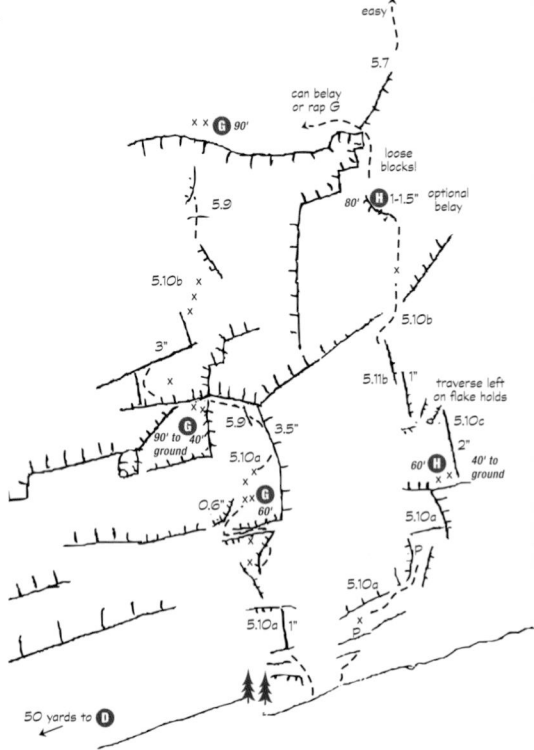

Mountaineers Dome

Mountaineers Dome is the last in the line of domes starting where Stately Pleasure Dome comes out of Tenaya Lake (collectively known as Polly Dome). Mountaineers Dome has neither obvious crack systems, nor sheer consistent angle faces. Despite the accessibility, it's one of the least climbed formations in Tuolumne.

Approach

Park at the parking lot 0.5 miles east of Tenaya Lake. Walk east up the road about 300 yards to Mountaineers Dome, and hike up to large white slabs at the base of the right central side of the wall. Faux Pas starts from the large ledge on the left side of the Dome, which is reached via 3rd class ramps, brush, and slabs. Pippin starts from the left side of the base of the dome. American Wet Dream starts on the right side of the dome at a groove leading to a hand crack on the right side of a gold slab.

Descent

After the 4th class up right, walk off left. No matter how you do it there's a lot of bushwacking, so long pants are nice. The sooner you cut back toward the start of the route, the more likely you'll cliff out, but it's not hard to backtrack a bit to get around.

An alternate descent follows 4th and easy 5th class left down the ramp system at the top of Pitch 5, however, it's not recommended unless you are comfortable on exposed and slick terrain. This descent winds its way down through the route Pippin.

A. Undisputed Truth   5.10a R★★

FA: Vern Clevenger, Dennis Oakeshott, July 1972

A fun edging and small-knob face climb with a short well-protected crux a few feet off the deck, and lots of easier but runout climbing. Currently, the crux bolt and one anchor bolt have been replaced, but the other bolts are old ¼" bolts. Two 60m ropes are required to rappel. A tiny cam offers at least psychological pro between the 3rd and 4th bolts.

B. Faux Pas   5.9 R★★★

FA: Vern Clevenger, Tom Higgins, Bob Kamps, July 1972.

A quality, sustained slab with edges and tiny knobs. The first pitch starts up a somewhat grungy corner, then traverses on easy terrain to a horizontal crack and a few thin edging slab moves to a bolted anchor. The second pitch climbs up then right, then up past three bolts and a significant runout with sustained climbing past the 3rd bolt to gain the two-bolt anchor. Rappel back left to the start ledge with two 60m ropes, or continue up for another pitch of easy climbing and walk off.

C. Pippin   5.8 R★★ or 5.9 R★★

FA: Vern Clevenger, Mike Munger, August 1971.

A varied climb with lots of easy climbing and some neat crux sections, Pippin wanders up disconnected features on the left side of Mountaineers Dome. A cool crux pitch up featured rock is the highlight of the route. Sections of dirty cracks and corners detract from the quality.

The first few moves off the ground are a slippery 5.9 lieback, but you can spot the leader, and then a shallow 1" cam protects 5.8 knobby slab past a tree. Except for the first 20 feet, this pitch is really easy, and it

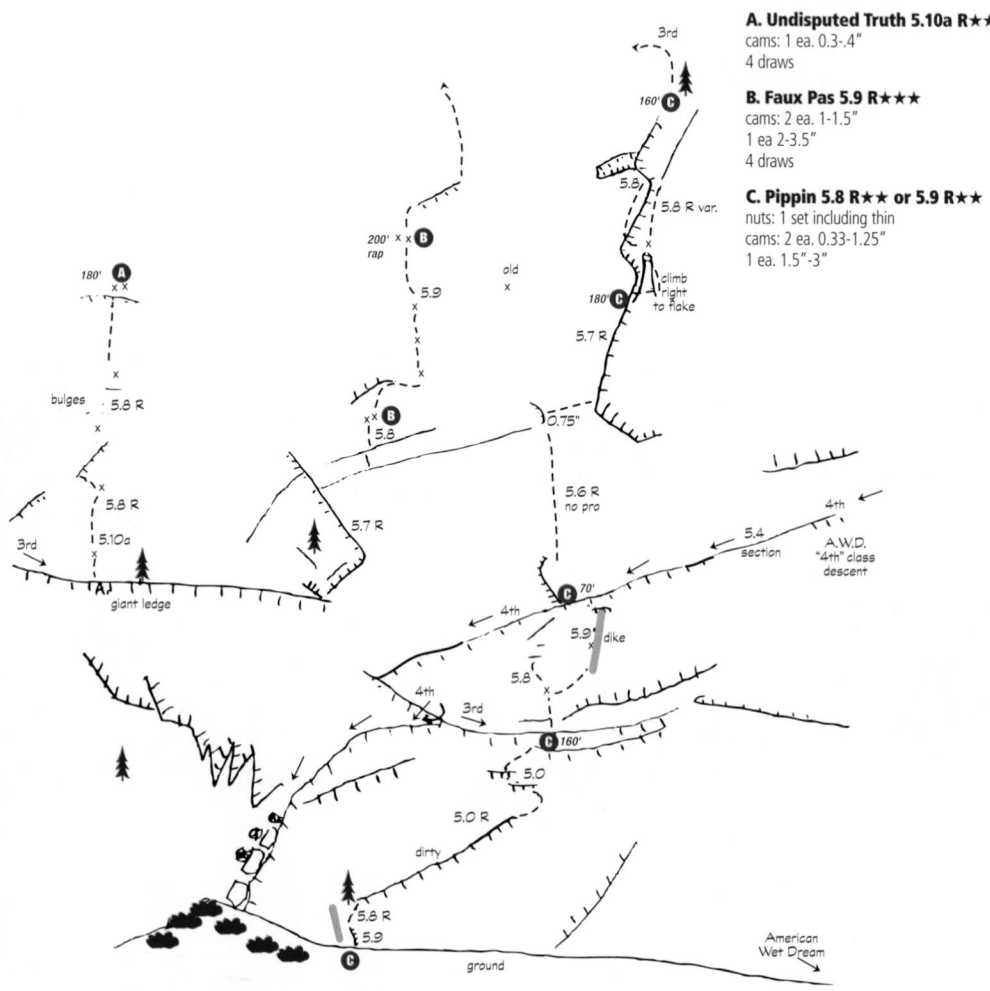

A. Undisputed Truth 5.10a R★★
cams: 1 ea. 0.3-.4"
4 draws

B. Faux Pas 5.9 R★★★
cams: 2 ea. 1-1.5"
1 ea 2-3.5"
4 draws

C. Pippin 5.8 R★★ or 5.9 R★★
nuts: 1 set including thin
cams: 2 ea. 0.33-1.25"
1 ea. 1.5"-3"

doesn't detract much from the route to do a simple 3rd class scramble around this pitch.

The second pitch is the crux. The two variations for this pitch – the original which follows a dike, and an easier variation to the left – are both fun-featured face and thin cracks.

The 5.6 runout pitch can be climbed various ways, but the cleanest is to head straight up the faint water streak to a 0.75" cam placement left of the base of the corner, then to traverse straight right into the corner.

The anchor after the 5.6 runout is poor (thin nuts and a shallow 1" cam), and it's best to continue up to the base of the flake where bomber 1-1.25" pro is found. The corner is very slick 5.7 with poor pro, and some dirt and moss.

The last pitch climbs the flake to stacked blocks perched on top (relatively solid), and a bolt placed from the blocks. Climb left from the bolt into the corner, which has a steep bouldery 5.8 crack section up top. Alternatively, you can climb the face above the bolt to the arête of the corner, then up right to a right-leaning groove/crack. This face variation has some 5.8 moves about 20 feet above the bolt. Walk off left.

This route is a waterfall in early season.

American Wet Dream

American Wet Dream

5.10b ★★★★

Time to climb route:	**3–4 hours**
Approach time:	**5 minutes**
Descent time:	**30 minutes**
Sun exposure:	**morning to afternoon**
Height of route:	**500′**

American Wet Dream is one of Tuolumne's most overlooked 5.10 routes. From the road, Mountaineers Dome looks somewhat monolithic, with no obvious features that would connect in a moderate route. However, American Wet Dream follows a staircase series of thin cracks that traverse diagonally across the entire dome. Some belay ledges are so spacious that many will be comfortable going off belay.

FA: Vern Clevenger, Rick Accomazzo, Tom McCabe, and Daryl Teske, 8/74.

Strategy

American Wet Dream is right next to the road yet sees little traffic. It is south facing and a good choice for cooler weather or early or late season, but a poor choice for the hottest days of mid-summer. A good selection of thin nuts and a 60m rope are recommended.

The crux climbing on the second and third pitches require placement of thin nuts while liebacking. Also, awkward hands/liebacks/mantels are found on several pitches. The fourth pitch features a big easy traverse to a stemming corner with thin pro above a good bolt. Modern tiny cams or a #3 Lowe Ball (aka Trango Ballnutz) offer adequate pro at the crux, but use caution since there is a slab to hit and it's easy to have the rope too slack because of the traverse.

Retreat

It's possible to retreat from slung blocks, horns, or bolts at the end of the first three pitches. After that, additional gear would be required. Use care while retreating – do not rappel over roofs onto blank faces. To reach the slung flake on the top of the first pitch requires downclimbing a ramp from the large ledge. Two ropes allow more rappel options. There aren't that many bolted belays below the upper section of the route (and some are still old bolts), so it's better to retreat the route.

Just left of the first pitch of American Wet Dream are 3 fun slab routes that can be led or toproped after leading the first pitch of American Wet Dream. You can finish American Wet Dream, or rappel off slings on the small arch.

B. Happy Hour   5.10b R★★★

An off-balance corner to wandering, edgy face to slab. Set anchor at the base of the corner below the base of the second pitch of AWD. Tricky moves at the very top up slightly crumbly face to a mantle.

FA: Alan Bartlett, Bruce Brossman, July 1984.

C. Vice Gripped   5.10c R★★★

Cool climbing up large dishes. Shares the start with How Does It Feel?, but heads left to dishes after the crack.

FA: Alan Roberts, Dave McMillan, 1980.

D. How Does It Feel?   5.11a R★★★

Start on easier terrain, then after the crack head up sustained slab through gold polish. Right off the deck you can do a direct start or you can start on Vice Gripped. Don't miss the traverse right to a small ledge with bolt (almost all the way to the first anchor of American Wet Dream). Set the anchor at the small natural arch plus 1.25-1.5" pro.

FA: Brian Harrington, John Pruett, August 1987.

A. American Wet Dream 5.10b★★★★
micro nuts: 1 set
nuts: 2 ea sml-med, 1 ea lrg
cams: 2 ea .33-1"
1 ea 0.3", 1.25-3"

B. Happy Hour 5.10b R★★★
5 draws
nuts: 1 set
cams: 1 ea. 0.5-2", 1-2" for anchor

C. Vice Gripped 5.10c R★★★
5 draws
cams: 1 ea 1-1.5", 1-2" for anchor

D. How Does It Feel? 5.11a R★★★
5-6 draws
cams: 1 ea 1-1.5", 1.25-1.5" and long sling for anchor

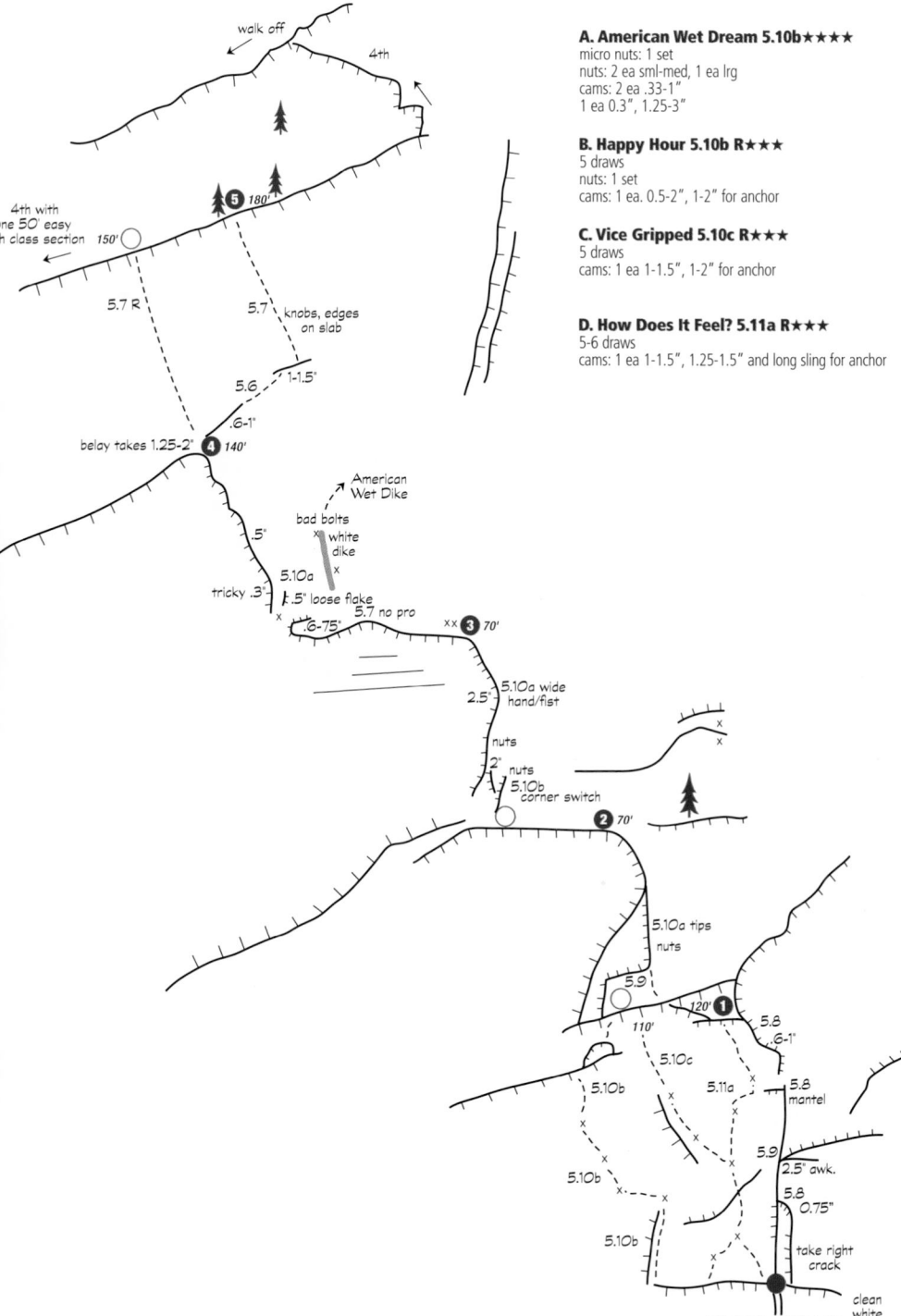

walk off
4th
4th with
one 50' easy
5th class section 150'
5.7 R
5.7   knobs, edges
on slab
5 180'
5.6   1-1.5"
.6-1"
belay takes 1.25-2' 4 140'
American
Wet Dike
bad bolts
white
dike
.5"
5.10a
tricky .3"   .5" loose flake
5.7 no pro
.6-75'   3 70'
5.10a wide
hand/fist
2.5"
nuts
2"   nuts
5.10b
corner switch
2 70'
5.10a tips
nuts
5.9
120' 1
110'
5.8
.6-1"
5.10c
5.11a
5.8
mantel
5.10b
5.9
2.5' awk.
5.8
0.75"
5.10b
take right
crack
5.10b
clean
white
ledges

Circle A Wall

Approach time: **10 minutes**

Sun exposure: **all day**

Height of routes: **60'**

Circle A Wall is a small dark cliff situated between the wide slab left of Bunny Slopes and Mountaineers Dome. A short scramble from the road (be careful not to drop anything!) leads to the base of this short black block of a cliff that becomes a waterfall in early season.

Approach

Park at Mountaineers Dome, walk up the road past some big boulders on the left. Hike up the bushy ramp on the left to Circle A Wall. You can also approach from the parking area for the Bunny Slopes by hiking down the road for 100 yards, then up loose blocky 3rd class (careful not to drop anything!).

Descent

Rappel Apex Predator with one rope.

A. Joe Mamba   5.10a R-★★★

Joe Mamba ascends slick, steep knobs on flawless polished rock.
FA: George Watson, Norman Boles, July 1988

B. Apex Predator   5.11b★★★

The climbing gets increasingly difficult and thin, but it also gets more tightly bolted.
FA: Michael Forkash, Jo Bentley, George Watson, Norman Boles, July 1988.

Joe Mamba

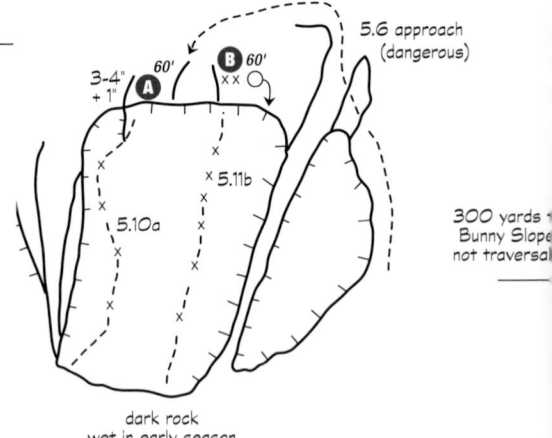

5.6 approach (dangerous)

3-4" + 1"   Ⓐ   60'   Ⓑ 60'
xx ○

x 5.11b
x

300 yards Bunny Slope not traversal

5.10a

dark rock
wet in early season

1st class approach
200 yards from American Wet Dream

3rd class approach (loose)

Bunny Slopes

Approach time: 5 minutes

Sun exposure: sunrise to evening

Height of routes: 165'

Just east of Mountaineers Dome and opposite Pywiack Dome is a large slab of low-angle rock. The Bunny Slopes is a small section of this slab starting from a wide ledge near the right side. While uninspiring from afar, up close the proliferation of awesome knobs, occasional thin cracks, and a striking dike add flavor. But the Bunny Slopes' main attraction is a combination not often seen in Tuolumne: easy face routes with adequate protection. Early season sees large streams running down the slabs, yet the Bunny Slopes sneak between two such streams and are usually dry as soon as the road is open.

The climbs are sunny and are good anytime except on the hottest days. Sometimes groups or classes occupy the routes, but you can easily see from the road whether anyone is at the climbs. While all the routes covered here have 3/8" protection bolts, many of these bolts were hand drilled on lead, and a long section of bolt protrudes. One of these bolts pulled,

and the hole was only 3/4" deep. For any of the bolts where an unusually long section of somewhat rusty bolt protrudes, do not clip in and lean back on the bolt – if you weight the bolt, pull downward only. Several of the climbs require pro, but a small rack of a few 0.5-1.25" cams is sufficient for all climbs.

Approach

The approach is short and easy. Park at the large dirt turnout for Pywiack Dome, or at a smaller one 100 yards down the road. Hike up 2nd class dirt and slabs to a short headwall to the right of the Bunny Slopes. Be very careful not to dislodge rocks onto the road (or on your partner!). Cross the headwall and hike left at the only spot possible (3rd class). The ledge at the base is huge and comfy, yet by the left edge the terrain below the ledge is distinctly 5th class, and some old runout routes to the left actually start well below the ledge.

Descent

Rap the routes, and reverse the approach, again being careful not to knock rocks onto the road.

A Wild in the Streaks   **D** Biscuit and Gravy
B Black Diamond   **E** Mere Image
C Hot Crossed Buns

A. Wild in the Streaks   5.7★★

With a consistent angle, good bolting, and many small knobs, this route is quite popular. The thin edging of the first 30 feet is harder than the upper part of the climb. In turn, the bolts on the upper part are more widely spaced and harder to spot since they blend into the knobs.
FA: Grant Hiskes, 1980s.

B. Black Diamond   5.9 R★

Severe runouts in the wrong places mean that Black Diamond is for advanced leaders only. The first bolt was recently replaced, and the third bolt is still 1/4", but the headwall with no pro at the top is the real danger. This is an excellent toprope that begins with thin edging on slab and gold polish and finishes on steeper knobs.
FA: unknown

C. Hot Crossed Buns   5.6★★★

Fun knobs at the start soon give way to low-angle knobs. An excellent first lead for Tuolumne novices, it nevertheless has long runouts. Those unfamiliar with low angle climbing and those inexperienced with slabs should toprope it first.
FA: Grant Hiskes, 1980s.

D. Biscuit and Gravy   5.8★★

Steep and varied, the only concern most have with Biscuit and Gravy is the slick crux before getting to the first bolt. While only a few feet off the ground, the slightly slanted rock landing warrants care and a spotter. Toprope from the shared anchor of Hot Crossed Buns.
FA: Grant Hiskes, 1980s.

E. Mere Image   5.7 R-★★★

FA: Kim Townsend, 1975.

With excellent, varied climbing up a slick white dike, Mere Image is the best, and oldest, climb at the crag. The widely spaced 1/4" bolts scared many off for years, but they were replaced by the ASCA in June 2002. While the dike is very slippery, the climbing meanders around on knobs and edges and only rarely gets near or on the dike.

A. Wild in the Streaks 5.7★★ 5 quickdraws

B. Black Diamond 5.9 R★ TR recommended; for lead, 3 quickdraws, 1 ea 2"

C. Hot Crossed Buns 5.6★★★ cams: 1 ea .6-1.25", 4 quickdraws

D. Biscuit and Gravy 5.8★★ cams: 1 ea .5-1.25", 5 quickdraws

E. Mere Image 5.7 R-★★★ cams: 1 ea .5-1", 4 quickdraws

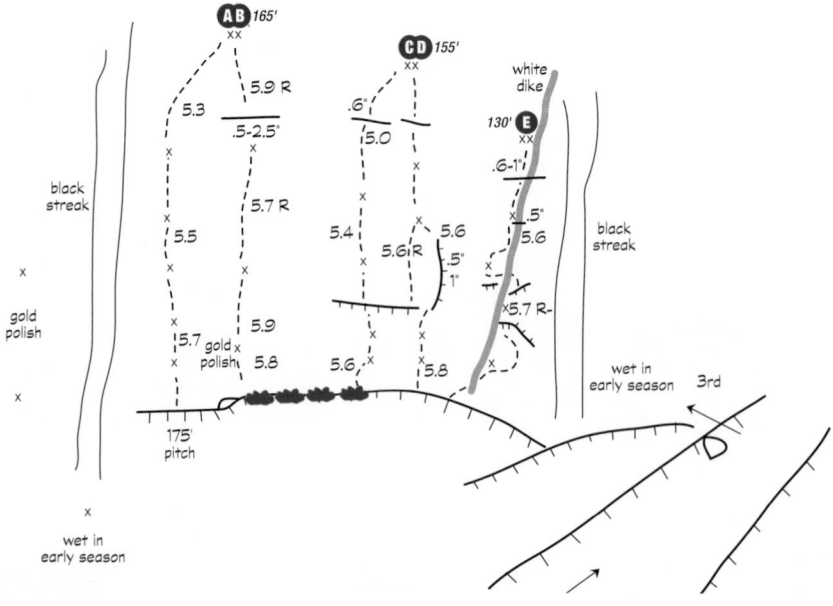

The Block Area

Approach time: **5-10 minutes**

Sun exposure: **morning to afternoon**

Height of routes: **70-100'**

Named after a huge block leaning against the face (with two old squeeze chimneys and a death-route thin seam), The Block Area is just uphill of the Bunny Slopes. Relatively untraveled, this area is best for those comfortable with some less-than-perfect rock. Close to the road, with short pitches, this area is a good option for some quick routes.

Approach:

Approach as for the Bunny Slopes, but then continue up the ramp until you reach the climbs. It is possible to approach from below, but brush and small overhangs can block the way. Also, loose blocks are perched on a sand slope, and anything knocked down will hit the road.

Descent:

Reverse the approach.

A. Aileron   5.9+★★

FA: Greg Barnes, Karin Wuhrmann, July 2005.

A wild but dirty line up a steep flake, Aileron is an alpine adventure that starts with climbing past plants, loose flakes, and a bit of moss. The flake above is fun, with hand jams and good jugs. There's a large detached plate above the top of the flake - don't pull out! Slings around a large tree for the anchor.
Rack: nuts: sml-med, cams: 1 ea. 0.6-1", 2 ea. 1.25"-3.5", optional extra 2-3", double shoulder-length sling for hole.

B. Obviously Not   5.7 R★

FA: Florence Scholl, Karin Wuhrmann, July 2005.

A shallow leaning corner, with munge and intermittent cracks. Originally finished by traversing off the ledge to the right, it's more convenient to continue up to the bolted anchor for Trendy Bendy.
Rack: nuts: 1 set, cams: 2 ea .6-1.5", 1 ea. 2-3"

C. Trendy Bendy   5.10a★★★

FA: Greg Barnes, Julie Haas, Florence Scholl, July 2007.

A fun sport route with some flexible flakes and grit, Trendy Bendy climbs straight up the face right of Obviously Not. There are some spots for optional pro, particularly before the first bolt and after the last bolt. Bolted anchor.
Rack: 6 draws, optional cams: 1 ea. .6-.75", 3"

D. Fuel Rod   5.10d★★★★

FA: Chris Falkenstein, Matt Trent, August 1990.

A great sport route up the golden and knobby face off the upper ledge, Fuel Rod starts out with a hard crux right after the first bolt. After the initial crux, the climbing is sustained easy 5.10, with some optional small cam placements under overlaps. The bolted anchor can be a bit hard to spot.
Rack: 5 draws, optional cams: 1 ea. 0.6-1"

Phobos/Deimos Cliff

Approach time: 30–45 minutes

Sun exposure: all day

Height of routes: 300'

Steep, golden, and imposing, Phobos/ Deimos Cliff sits at the top of a ridge opposite Pywiack Dome. It's one of the tallest vertical cliffs in Tuolumne and has the best collection of steep crack routes. Phobos, the Greek god of battlefield panic, and Deimos, the god of fear, are appropriate names for the two testpiece 5.9 cracks that give this cliff its name. With a steep approach hike, sunny exposure, and awesome views, it's a unique place known for hard cracks and perfect weather (as long as the thunderstorms are holding back).

Approach

A 30- to 45-minute approach up a steep trail guards the cliff, and unacclimatized climbers have quite a trudge ahead of them – it's best to climb at this cliff later in a trip when you're used to the altitude. From the parking lot follow the climbers' trail up and left, then either through or around a short cliff band. Head left below a steep slab area, then up the obvious switchbacking trail that ends in boulders a few yards left of the start of Phobos. Take note of the approach as many miss the trail on the descent.

Descent

From the top of the cliff hike west and follow cairns into a steep 3rd class ramp system that deposits you in the midst of annoying brush. Various pathways through the brush lead back down, but remember where the trail up was, and connect to it by going left. If you left anything at the base you will have to go back up the trail a bit.

A	Phobos	**C**	Deimos
B	Blues Riff	**D**	John Lee Hooker

A. Phobos 5.9★★★★★

FA: Tom Higgins and Jack Miller, 1970.

Phobos is the easier, better-protected, and better-known of the two 5.9s – if there is a car at the parking area there's surely a party ahead of you. In fact, it's common to have three or four parties lined up for Phobos, and another party looking at, then deciding not to try, Deimos. A good strategy for Phobos, especially considering the danger from thunderstorms, is to climb something else in the morning, then hike up around noon (assuming no clouds are forming) and climb it in the afternoon.

The intimidating start of Phobos has turned many climbers away before they even rope up. The second pitch's perfect double hand cracks on a near-vertical wall are the best steep cracks at the grade in Tuolumne. Sharp hand jams, wild stemming, steep jugs, and endurance climbing make Phobos both feared and sought-after.

Retreat requires leaving gear – with two ropes less gear will be needed. There is a loose, but well-wedged, large block at the top of the first pitch which usually has rappel slings on it. This is a very bad place to get caught in a thunderstorm due to the height of the cliff, lack of cover, and the large trees on the descent trail.

B. Blues Riff 5.11b★★★★★

FA: Dale Bard, Bob Locke, Claude Fiddler, Alan Bard, 1976.

Blues Riff is one of the best crack climbs in Tuolumne. In the winter of 1998–1999 a gigantic block forming one wall of the first pitch 5.10a offwidth fell off, but an alternate face climbing variation was established soon thereafter. The 140-foot-long crux pitch was undamaged by the rockfall. The endless, slightly overhung endurance liebacking and hand jamming of this pitch is an awesome pumpfest.

The first pitch is still loose and a bit chossy, but the climbing is easier than it appears. Near the top of the second pitch, a 15-foot section of the flake is too delicate to place pro behind. Most of the climb requires 1.5" pieces. A cool head is needed to fire this lead, especially since the short, desperate crux comes before the long endurance climbing. Luckily, there's a huge but sapping jug to "rest" on before the long hand and lieback crack. The third pitch, a 5.9 lieback off a wide and sharp flake, is often avoided by rapping.

Two 60m ropes are best for rappel from Pitch 2. If you only have two 50m ropes, it is difficult to swing back into the first pitch ledge – the first to rappel should place a directional at the crux, then the second should remove it while the first uses the ends of the rope to swing the second back to the ledge.

C. Deimos 5.9★★★★

FA: Tom Higgins and Tom Gerughty, August 1970.

Deimos is the steeper and stouter cousin of Phobos. It turns most people away who are just trying to reach the bottom of the climb, which is located on a blocky terrace after a 5.8 chimney boulder problem. The intimidating inverted V-slot roof on the first pitch is followed by wide hand, fist, and offwidth climbing on a leaning ramp. Deimos is one of the few climbs in Tuolumne where a prior introduction to burly Valley climbs is a good idea.

With afternoon shade, Deimos is the only climb at Phobos/Deimos Cliff that is appropriate for the hottest days of mid-summer. Usually the weather is just perfect – one less excuse for not getting on this testpiece. Hollow flakes on the first pitch and offwidth sections require some commitment. Extra large protection is a good idea for most climbers. Strong parties can run it out a bit and use long slings to link the first two pitches into one spectacular lead using a 60m rope.

Retreat requires leaving gear – two ropes will require less gear to retreat.

D. John Lee Hooker 5.11b or 5.10bA0★★★

FA: Greg Barnes, Hung-Chen Chang, Rachel Nelson, August 2003 FFA: Chris Falkenstein, Sean Gindt, September 2005

A fun alternate start to Blues Riff, John Lee Hooker climbs a thin crack to crux gold polish face to a long traverse right, with some wild moves past a bolt on the roof. The route was started in June 2001 near the date of Hooker's death.

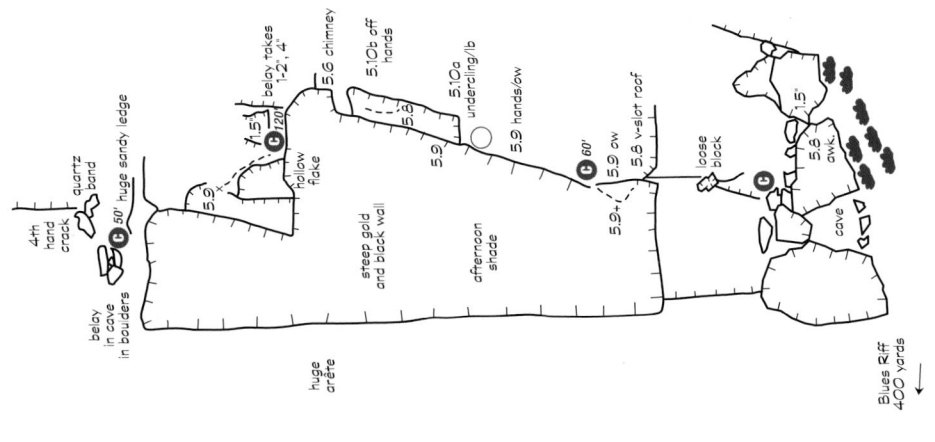

A. Phobos 5.9 ★★★★★
nuts: 1 ea med, lrg
cams: 1 ea .6-1.25"
 2 ea 1.5"
 3 ea 2-3"
 1 ea 3.5-4"
 1 ea 6" (optional)
 extra 2-3" (optional)
slings

B. Blues Riff 5.11b ★★★★★
nuts: 1 set
cams: 2 ea .6-1"
 3 ea 1.25"
 4 ea 1.5"
 2 ea 2-3"
 3.5-6" (optional for last pitch)
slings

C. Deimos 5.9 ★★★★
nuts: 1 set
cams: 2 ea .6-1.25"
 3 ea 1.5-3"
 1 ea 3.5-4.5"
slings

D. John Lee Hooker 5.11b or 5.10A0 ★★★
nuts: 1 set
cams: 1 ea .6-2"
 2 ea 3-4"
 1 ea 5"

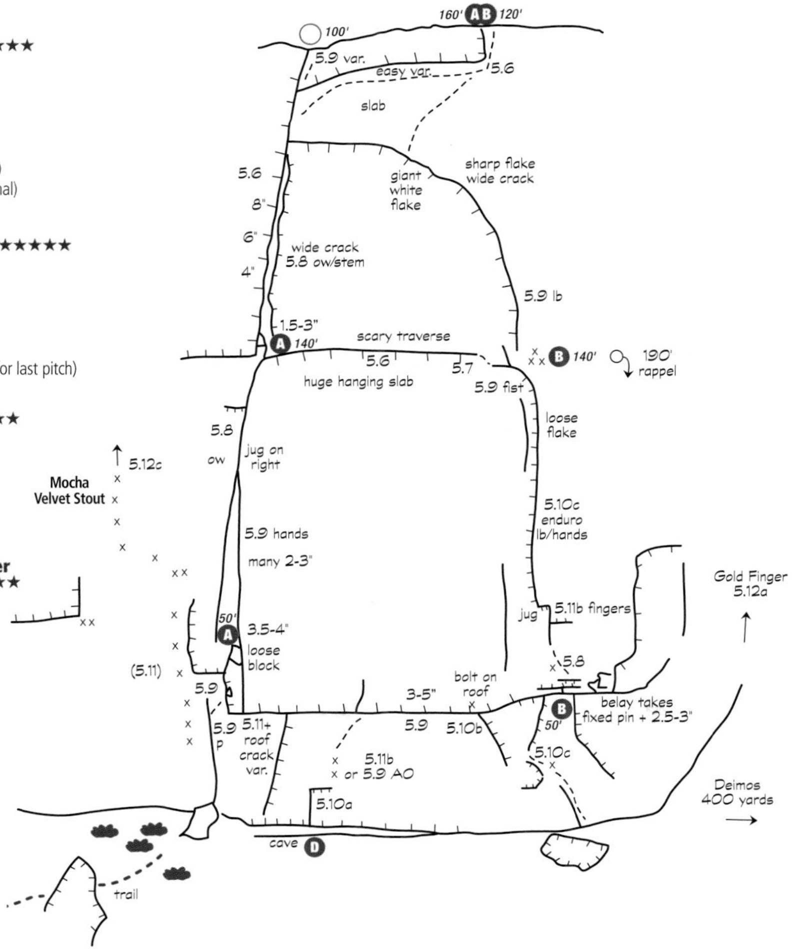

SUPERTOPO

Low Profile Dome

Approach time: 5 minutes

Sun exposure: morning to afternoon

Height of routes: 180'

Low Profile Dome is a small, dark cliff in a region of soaring golden granite domes. It has steep and excellent quality moderate routes with an unusual abundance of bolts, and the climbs are only a few hundred feet from the road.

In early season the routes are often wet. However, due to south-facing exposure, Low Profile Dome is often a warm place to climb on colder days. The routes are short and have excellent rappel anchors, making them a great choice for climbing before thunderstorms (lightning hits everywhere, so don't push it!).

B Golfer's Route **D** Darth Vader's Revenge
C Orange Man **E** Shit Hooks

Approach

Park at a wide paved pullout on the east side of the road, 2.1 miles east of Tenaya Lake and 5.5 miles west of the Tuolumne Store. Low Profile Dome is the cliff a few hundred yards to the west. Follow the trail which leads straight from the road toward the cliff. Golfer's Route is on the toe of the wall right where the trail ends. A huge granite ledge is about 30 feet to the right and a short scramble gets you to the base of the 5.10 routes.

A. R2-D2   5.8 R-★★★

FA: Greg Barnes, John Hovell, 10/06.

About 100 yards left of Golfer's Route, up on a higher terrace, is a section of steep knobby rock that leads to a broad slabby ledge about 50 feet up, with a black bulge/ roof above (and another slab above that). R2-D2 takes a steep knobby, pocketed face up a white streak between two black streaks, with one bolt visible about 20 feet up. There's a flat area with small boulders near the base. The steep face with hidden pockets getting to the first bolt is a bit runout. The route goes up and slightly right to a steep corner and a nearly invisible two-bolt anchor in the roof.

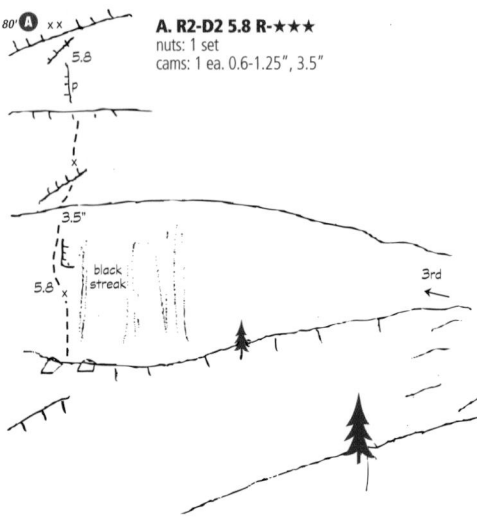

A. R2-D2 5.8 R-★★★
nuts: 1 set
cams: 1 ea. 0.6-1.25", 3.5"

B. Black Widow   5.7★★★ or 5.9 R★★★★

FA: Alan Bartlett and Bruce Bossman, 1980.

Black Widow is rarely climbed even when there are lines a few feet to the right on Golfer's Route. The first pitch is a fun knobby crack, with a newly replaced anchor, and allows you to toprope a 5.11a face. The second pitch is a very bold lead up awesome knobs and pockets. Very narrow camming units and/or Tricams are required to adequately protect this pitch (e.g. red Aliens, 0.5 Tricams). Two raps with a single 60m rope, but tie knots in the ends on the raps since there's not much rope to spare.

C. Family Affair   5.9 R-★★★

FA: TM, Tom, and Don Herbert, 7/85.

The face to corner left of Golfer's Route, Family Affair is rarely done since the (original) bolts were not indicated in previous topos. While not too runout, the face is comparable to a 5.9 version of Golfer's Route, and so should only be led by those comfortable at the grade. Fun flake and knob climbing on the first pitch leads to a belay ledge, and the somewhat runout 5.9 crux face starts the second pitch, with an interesting (although often dirty) corner crack finish.

D. Golfer's Route   5.7 R★★★★

FA: Don Reid and Mike Corbett, 8/79.

Golfer's Route is the perfect introduction to runout knob climbing. It's a varied and sustained route with two short pitches that can be linked with a 60m rope. The climb is runout and often that means 20 feet between protection. The rock is slick, requiring confident footwork. Once at the top you can climb over to the right and toprope the three 5.10 climbs with two ropes (or with a single 60m rope, you can rappel to the mid-anchor on Darth Vader's Revenge and toprope the first pitch of that climb). The traverse is 5th class; both leader and follower must be careful as any slip would result in a nasty pendulum fall. Make sure not to drop ropes on leaders below.

E. Orange Man   5.10c★★★

FA: unknown.

A beautiful line with plenty of great knob climbing, Orange Man will challenge you with its two sections of 5.10c micro-edge slabs. By starting to the left of the normal start and traversing in, the first crux can be skipped. Also, the second crux can be climbed around at runout 5.10a.

F. Darth Vader's Revenge   5.10a★★★★

FA: Chris Falkenstein and Herb Davis, 7/78.

This is an outstanding route with a variety of 5.10a cruxes. The intimidating, overhung black roof is only one of your problems – there's also a reachy traverse near the start, a section of climbing protected by a single improbable small nut placement, and a section of hard friction climbing above the roof. Most people either skip the shorter second pitch or link it with the first pitch as a single lead.

G. Shit Hooks   5.10b★★★

FA: Dave Hitchcock and Bruce Brossman, 1980.

Formerly runout with an ugly, dirty crack finish off right, Shit Hooks now sports more bolts on a long single pitch. The route is excellent and varied with a middle section of sustained climbing on small holds.

H. Memo From Lloyd   5.11b★★★

FA: Don Reid and Grant Hiskes; 1980.

Steep, burly, and pumpy, Memo From Lloyd is a great workout and often toproped. It takes good protection on lead, but use care as it's very strenuous to place pro in the crux first 20 feet. To set a toprope, scramble around to the right and down an easy ramp to the bolts.

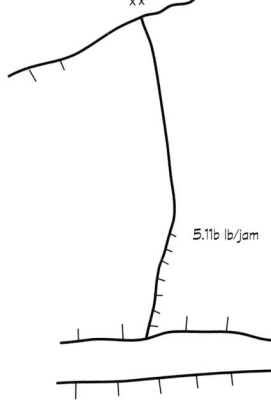

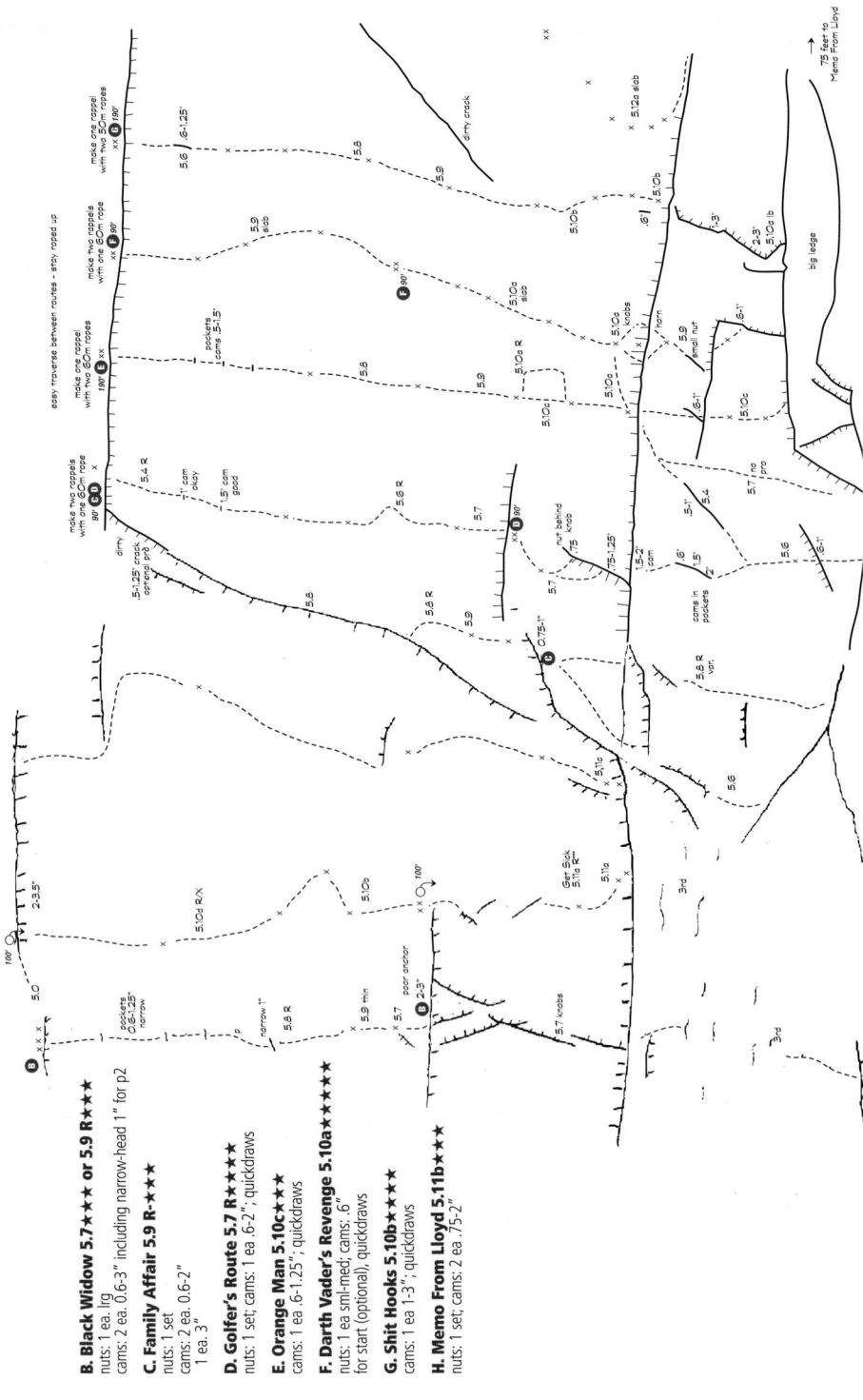

B. Black Widow 5.7★★★ or 5.9 R★★★
nuts: 1 ea. lrg
cams: 2 ea. 0.6-3" including narrow-head 1" for p2

C. Family Affair 5.9 R★★★
nuts: 1 set
cams: 2 ea. 0.6-2"
1 ea. 3"

D. Golfer's Route 5.7 R★★★★
nuts: 1 set; cams: 1 ea .6-2", quickdraws

E. Orange Man 5.10c★★★
cams: 1 ea .6-1.25", quickdraws

F. Darth Vader's Revenge 5.10a★★★★★
nuts: 1 ea sml-med; cams: .6"
for start (optional), quickdraws

G. Shit Hooks 5.10b★★★★
cams: 1 ea 1-3", quickdraws

H. Memo From Lloyd 5.11b★★★
nuts: 1 set; cams: 2 ea .75-2"

Galen's Crack

Approach time: 30 seconds

Sun exposure: mid-morning to afternoon

Height of routes: 30'

Galen's Crack is the Generator Crack of Tuolumne – a short, powerful, overhung fist to offwidth crack. Even though it's narrower than Yosemite's Generator Crack, it is still very challenging, especially for those with small hands.

Approach

Driving toward the lake from the store, look for a small rock outcropping with an obvious offwidth crack on the right side of the road about 0.5 mile past Lamb Dome. There's a small dirt pullout on the right, or a larger dirt pullout on the left.

If coming from the west, look for a dirt pullout about 0.5 mile past Low Profile Dome, below the left end of Medlicott. The small crag to the left of the road is Galen's Crack.

A. Galen's Crack   5.10c★★

FA: Galen Rowell.

The overhung start is 5.10c for those with large hands. It requires a fist jam to pull out of the most overhung section into the lower-angle offwidth. The grade is substantially more difficult for those with small hands.

You will need 3-4" pro, plus long slings, to set a toprope. Bolts have been added and chopped on top.

B. Falkenstein Face   5.10d TR ★★★

FA: Chris Falkenstein.

The fun face right next to Galen's Crack.

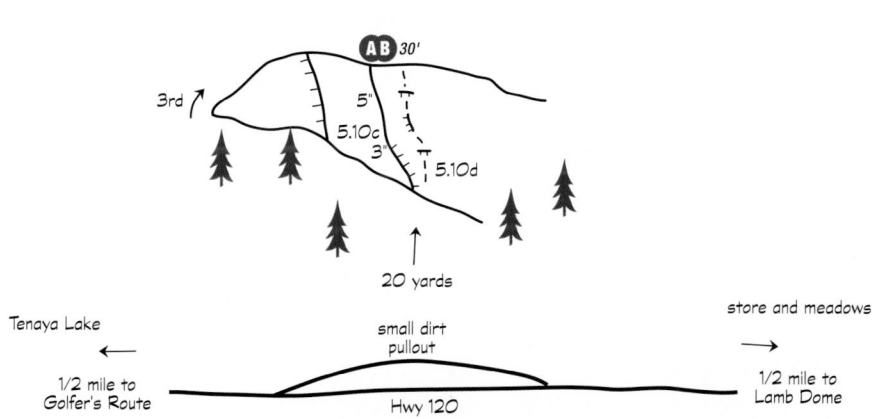

Doda Dome

Approach time: **35-40 minutes**

Sun exposure: **afternoon**

Height of routes: **400'**

Doda Dome is the next dome northwest of Daff Dome, and while it's pretty close to the road, it is rarely visited. Only the west face has technical climbing, and this face is not visible until reached. The west face is surprisingly large, but much of it is fairly low-angle, with varied climbing including slab, horizontal and vertical cracks, and knobs. The routes have seen little traffic (whether the route is 25 years old or newly climbed), so some lichen, dirt, and suspect knobs can be found.

The obvious line on the west face is the huge dihedral of Silicone Corner. Reaching the corner requires some wandering up easy 5th class to reach an improbable section to gain the ledge at the base of Silicone Corner.

If you view Doda Dome from the road near Lamb Dome, you'll see why it was named by Grant Hiskes after Carol Doda, the famous stripper who was the first woman to get silicone breast enhancements.

Approach:

The approach to Doda Dome is not particularly long, but as most of it is cross-country with no path or trail to follow, careful attention should be paid to route finding. Please note that the forest between Daff and Doda has a lot of evidence of bear activity.

Hike the main approach trail for the West face of Daff Dome past the Western Front and more slabs to the steep cliff (Cowabunga Cliff – the spectacular overhung flake is Cowabunga, 5.12c). At the upper end of the Cowabunga Cliff, just as the Daff Dome trail turns right towards West Crack, turn left into the woods and

Mt. Conness

Photo by Bryan Law

head towards Doda Dome (visible through the trees). After 100 yards across open terrain, drop down a short slab and then down into a short, steep ravine. Hike up the other side and angle slightly left through the trees, aiming for the left side of Doda Dome. Short sections of dense forest and longer sections of open terrain lead to the gentle notch on the left side of Doda Dome. Hike down slabs to the west face of Doda.

Descent

Enjoy the spectacular view, then hike off the back side of the dome and around either direction to the base.

When returning to the car, if you get off-track, just head downhill to the main creek (Cathedral Creek), then up the creek to the road.

A. Silicone Corner 5.7 R-★★★★

FA: Grant Hiskes, Pat Ranstrom, Greg Rustler, August 1982

An outstanding, burly, old-school route, Silicone Corner will test your hand jamming, stemming, liebacking, and low-angle chimney/flare technique. Tape gloves are strongly recommended, as there is a lot of wide hands jamming with very sharp, rough rock.

The initial section of the main corner is cruxy and poorly protected until a thin hands crack is reached about 30 feet up. A thin flared crack about 15 feet up can be protected only with an offset finger-sized cam (eg. green/yellow offset Alien). Use slings to reduce rope drag, which can be significant on this long pitch.

The approach pitches are wandering, with a distinct steep 5.7 crux just before reaching the huge ledge at the base of the corner. An intermediate belay just above this section is recommended, and then the belay can be moved to below the corner. The base of the corner has no good pro, but a belay can be set below the corner near the lower end of the down-sloping ledge.

B. Bust It Out 5.10a★★

FA: Greg Barnes, Mark Miller, George Ridgley, Linda Jarit, Bryan Law, June 2007

A fun route with a short but wild crux pitch out a roof. Horizontal cracks offer great pro for the approach to the headwall. The severely overhung hand crack is bypassed just to the left with a short, bouldery crux up a thin crack to an undercling left. A cool traverse back right leads to a hand crack splitting the top of the steep section. Belay just above the roof to reduce rope drag. A short bulge leads to a final fun hand crack. Tape gloves are recommended for the somewhat knobby and dirty hand crack. Lichen and moss on the upper half of the route detracts from the quality.

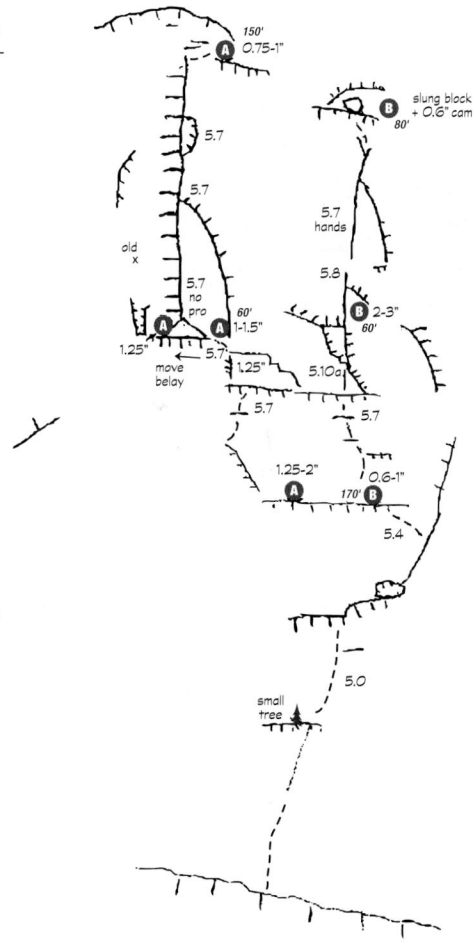

Western Front

Approach time: **5 minutes**

Sun exposure: **midday to afternoon**

Height of routes: **70'**

Western Front is a small cliff below Daff Dome with easily accessed moderate topropes. Slabby, thin, and all in the 5.9–5.10b range, these routes are outstanding training for Tuolumne face climbing. The few lead bolts will give you an idea of the typical runouts of most Tuolumne routes. As you toprope, think about what it would be like to lead these climbs – look for rest stances and practice your routefinding.

The bolted anchors are near the edge and somewhat dangerous to get to – many will want a belay. Even with occasional crowds, there are generally enough climbs to go around.

All you need is gear for setting topropes off bolts and one rope.

Approach

Park at any of the Daff Dome parking areas (see page 62). Be very careful on the road, which has a 45 m.p.h. speed limit and poor visibility around the blind curve. While only a hundred yards from the road, it's actually surprisingly easy to miss Western Front among all the white granite ridges. Locate a trail which starts where the creek comes out under the highway and head up a tree-filled gully between ribs of low-angle granite toward the huge west face of Daff Dome. After only about 100 feet, head left up the short slabs and look for a big tree-filled ledge down to the left. The five bolted anchors are another 50 to 150 feet up the ridge, and fairly hard to spot. It's best to find the wall itself – the only 40- to 80-foot-tall steep wall around – then to locate the anchors.

Descent

Reverse the approach.

A. Green Eggs and Ham   5.9 R★★

FA: Tom Malzbender, 1985.

This left-most route starts up an easy flake then traverses right at the crux. There is some pendulum potential even if you clip the bolt.

B. March of Dimes   5.10a R-★★★

Good and varied climbing, and the only route here that is fairly well protected for the leader. Still, it is rarely led because it's so easy to toprope.

C. New Tricks for Old Dogs   5.10b R★★

Fun climbing up small edges and polished slab. The tricky crux is moving left to the second bolt.

D. Touch of Grey   5.9 R★★

Sustained and good climbing.

E. Ace in the Hole   5.10a R/X★★

Fun, meandering climb on knobs.

F. Deadheads Delight   5.9 R★★

Tricky start off the deck – keep a tight toprope or give the climber a spot.

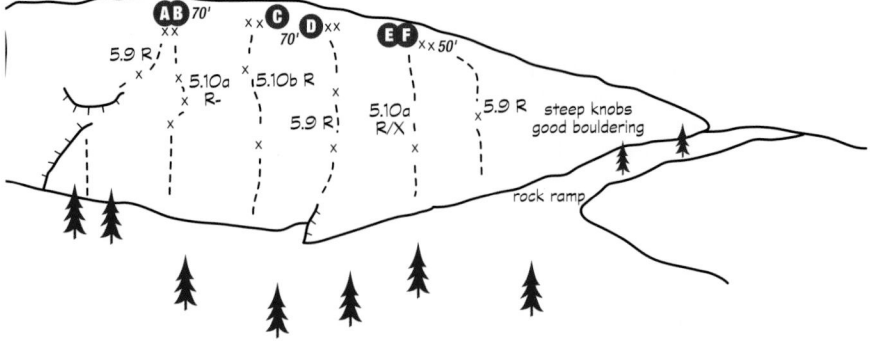

Daff Dome

Daff Dome springs suddenly into view when driving up Highway 120 from the west. Steep and monolithic, it offers some of the finest climbing in Tuolumne. The golden west face, which appears completely sheer and has a roof near the bottom, looks to be the realm of the 5.13 climber. Yet West Crack splits the middle of the huge face and the huge books on either side are each superb moderate free climbs (Cooke Book is out of sight to the left, and Crescent Arch is the obvious curving giant dihedral).

Approach

Drive 3.6 miles west of the Tuolumne Meadows Store or three miles east of Tenaya Lake. Park either at a tiny dirt pullout in trees just north of the creek or at a dirt pullout just south of the creek. If both of these are full, park on the other side of the road next to trees immediately opposite the small dirt pullout. All of these parking spots are relatively small and located at a sweeping turn of Highway 120 with a 45 m.p.h. speed limit – so take great care in parking and moving around the vehicles.

Locate the trail which starts where the creek comes out under the highway. It heads up a tree-filled gully between ribs of low-angle granite toward the huge west face of Daff Dome. Follow the trail up for about 300 yards, then down a gentle slope and slowly up again below a 100-foot-tall overhung cliff (home of Cowabunga, a 5.12c roof flake). The trail then curves up and right around the cliff and brings you to the wall below West Crack. Hike up and right to the ledge that traverses left to West Crack and Cooke Book, and hike 50 feet right to get to Crescent Arch.

Descent

Rappel Route (best option) - photo page 74
Use one rope. From the top, walk to the east end of the dome and locate bolts with chains on top of a big block next to the only large tree. Rappel to an anchor in the middle of the face. Another rappel gets you to the ground. Meander down along the dome until you see a few good looking cracks (5.6-5.8 with bolts at the top) on the wall to your right. Next, follow the trail down the gully to the road then walk a few yards back to the car.

Walk-off
Wear climbing shoes. From the top, go south down exposed and polished 4th class slab. Use intelligent routefinding to avoid steep sections. Most climbers sit down and use hand, foot, and butt friction to descend one short, steep section of golden polish. Work back right (west) to easier slabs and the base of the climbs. Do not attempt the walk-off if the rock is wet.

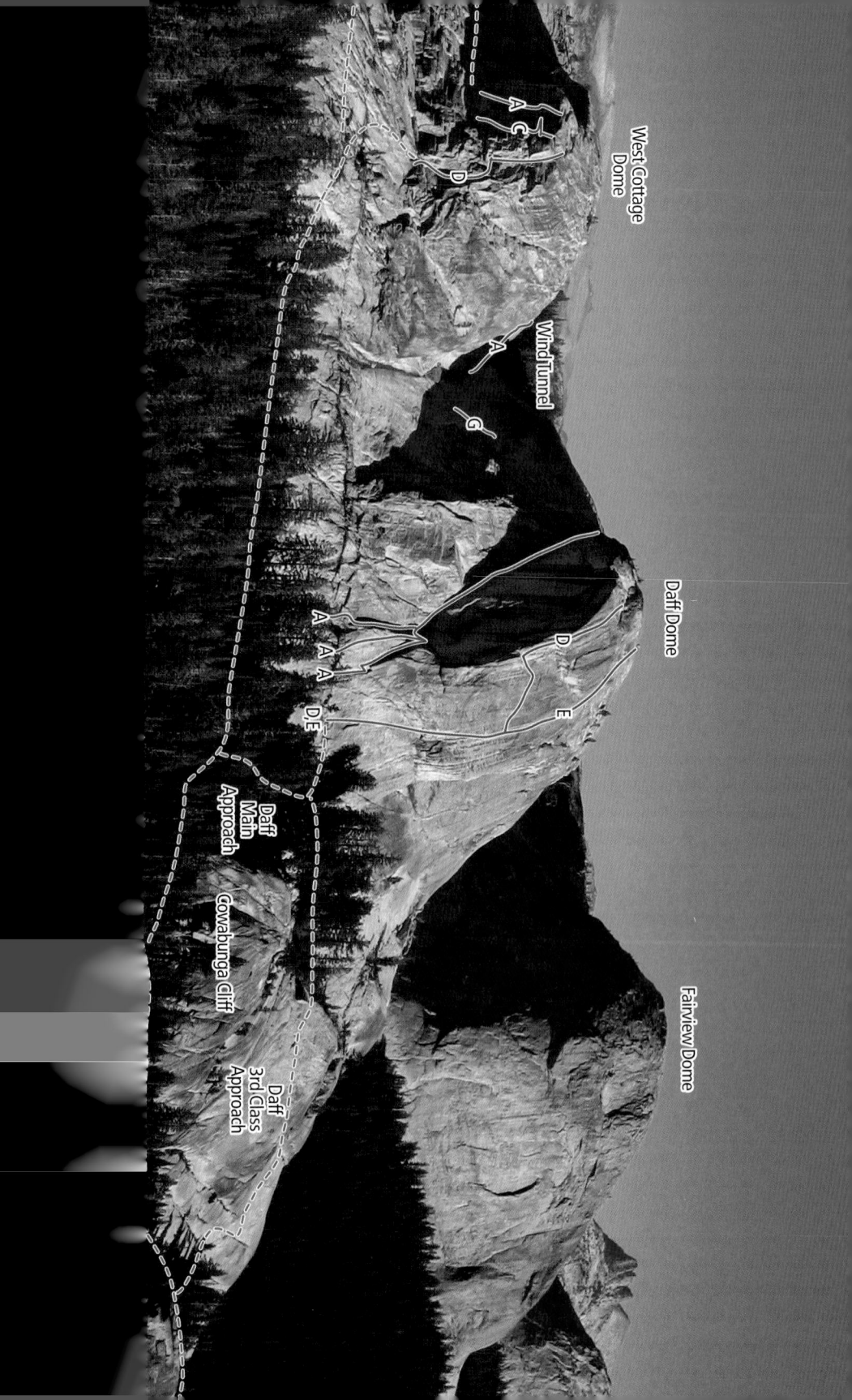

West Cottage Dome

Wind Tunnel

Daff Dome

Fairview Dome

Daff Main Approach

Gowabunga Cliff

Daff 3rd Class Approach

Cooke Book 5.10a★★★

Time to climb route:	**3–4 hours**
Approach time:	**20 minutes**
Descent time:	**30 minutes**
Sun exposure:	**never**
Height of route:	**700′**

Cooke Book is one of the most overlooked climbs in Tuolumne, partially because even from the base the route is hidden. The route's huge dihedrals wind around the north side of Daff Dome. Many see the intimidating steep dihedral higher on the north face and, assuming Cooke Book ascends this, decide on another route. This steep dihedral is the newly climbed testpiece Rise and Fall of the Albatross. Lower pitches include optional offwidth, and mandatory stemming/liebacking with intermittent protection and somewhat grainy feet. The crux features outstanding technical liebacking.

FA: Bob Kamps and Tom Higgins, 6/67.

Strategy

Cooke Book is located on the north face of Daff Dome in an often windy location. It is one of the coldest climbs in Tuolumne – even when those on West Crack are in shorts and T-shirts, climbers will often be shivering under fleece and windjacket on Cooke Book. The route is an excellent choice during the hottest days of summer.

Most start Cooke Book in the main dihedral, which is long, sustained, and physical. A short 5.8 offwidth/lieback section gives many trouble on this pitch. After a belay at slung blocks at the top of the initial corner, most traverse along

obvious knobs and flakes in the main dihedral. However, if you do this, a tricky 5.10c downclimb into a corner is especially treacherous for the follower. Instead, downclimbing or rappelling 40 feet from the belay to gain easy flakes allows this section to be bypassed at 5.7. An alternate start comes straight up to these flakes after a steep, exciting headwall.

The fourth pitch of Cooke Book has a short, well-protected 5.10a crux right after an excellent no-hands rest, and 5.9 climbing on lower pitches is all well protected. The 5.7 to 5.8 climbing on lower pitches, with liebacking and slightly grainy slabby feet, is of more concern to most, especially since protection is sometimes a bit sparse. Pitches 2, 3, and 4 can be linked into two pitches with an alternate belay.

Since Cooke Book is tucked into dihedrals on the north face, it's often hard to see approaching thunderclouds. As with all longer routes in Tuolumne that gain high summits, be careful of electrical storms.

The first pitch of Bombs Over Tokyo (5.10c), which shares the start of Cooke Book, is probably the best moderate 5.10 crack in Tuolumne, and is an excellent way to round out the day. Fast parties may wish to run up West Crack, Blown Away, or tackle the technical Crescent Arch.

Retreat

Retreat requires leaving gear. Irregular cracks and flakes offer excellent nut and sling placements.

B. Rise and Fall of the Albatross 5.13a/b★★★★

FA: Mikey Schaefer, Sept. 2007.

This new testpiece extends an old project into spectacular terrain on the steep north face of Daff. The short first pitch (actually the 3rd pitch after a couple approach pitches) was completed in the '90s by Dave Bengston and Chris Falkenstein, and was a sandbagged 5.12c called Flight of the Albatross.

See topo page 74

Photo by Bryan Law

Bombs Over Tokyo

5.10c or 5.12c R★★★★

Time to climb route: **3–4 hours**

Approach time: **20 minutes**

Descent time: **30 minutes**

Sun exposure: **noon to sunset**

Height of route: **700'**

Bombs Over Tokyo climbs the spectacular steep arête of Daff Dome. It used to be that the high grade and bad bolts scared most away from all but the first pitch of this route. The 5.11d R second pitch of this climb was one of the most serious of its era. Fortunately, the ASCA replaced all bolts (except the 5.12c crux bolt ladder) in 2002. A new route, Blown Away, meets Bombs Over Tokyo at the 4th pitch belay, so it's now possible to toprope the amazing 4th pitch 5.10d arête. For those interested in an adventure, it's also possible to bypass the 5.11d R pitch and aid the original 3rd pitch, then lead the spectacular 4th pitch.

FA: Vern Clevenger, Claude Fiddler, 1981.
FFA: John Bachar.

Strategy

The first pitch is very popular on its own, being probably the best 5.10c single-pitch crack in Tuolumne (the corner high on OZ is the undisputed best 5.10 crack).

The second pitch is a very serious 5.11d slab with only a few small RPs and a fixed #1 knifeblade. You can reach the top of this pitch with little difficulty by climbing any of the variations on the first pitch of Cooke Book and making an easy 5.7 traverse right.

The crux pitch is a 5.12c face past old bolts to a horizontal crack. The bolts are currently old ¼" with Leepers. There is a lower traverse dead right along the lip of the roof on somewhat loose holds – this is the Bombs Under Tokyo variation. Bolted years ago but never freed, the bolts were replaced recently and a few attempts have been made, but apparently it has not yet been freed and may be 5.13. Of course, the original variation is a John Bachar 5.12+, so it may be 5.13 as well!

The fourth pitch is a radically exposed gem, and easily toproped from Blown Away.

Retreat

Retreat is possible with two 60m ropes. At the fourth pitch belay, a nut is needed to back up the single bolt.

See topo pages 74-75

F. Witch of the West   5.9 R-★★★

FA: unknown, 1980s

A good climb up knobby and slabby face to the right of West Crack. The anchor for this route is directly below the first anchor on West Crack, and it is often used by parties retreating off of West Crack.

H. West of the Witch   5.8 R-★★★

FA: Greg Barnes, Karin Wuhrmann, Florence Scholl, 7/05

The face starting directly from the left large tree, West of the Witch goes through a small roof (optional tiny pro above roof) to a varied face. The bolts can be hard to spot.

Karine Croft on Pitch 1 of Bombs of Over Tokyo. Chris Falkenstein Photo

Blown Away 5.9★★★★★

Time to climb route: **3–4 hours**

Approach time: **20 minutes**

Descent time: **30 minutes**

Sun exposure: **noon to sunset**

Height of route: **700'**

Blown Away combines the first two pitches of the classic West Crack with spectacular face climbing and mind-numbing exposure. A huge traverse pitch that is never too runout (but not exactly tightly bolted either) challenges the leader and follower. The first ascent team couldn't believe that such a cool route could still be done on one of Tuolumne's most popular domes in 2002. This, and a "little bit of wind" one day, inspired the name.

FA: Greg Barnes, Karin Wuhrmann, Rachel Nelson, June 2002.

History

I had been fascinated with the golden knob face to the left of West Crack for many years, but never felt strong enough to dare either of the testpieces which ventured onto it (Clevenger's Bombs Over Tokyo and Gerberding's Wienie Roast). Finally in 2002, after several years of experience establishing new face routes from stance with a hand drill, my girlfriend Karin Wuhrmann and I gave it a go. After two attempts to find the easiest route, we established the traverse pitch. When we returned the next day, we were nearly ripped off the wall by gusty winds. Finally we came back with our friend Rachel Nelson and did the fourth pitch, which originally went around into space over left, avoiding the dirty and ugly-looking dihedral. That variation turned out to be harder than it looked, especially after a large block broke off. When we cleaned

out the dihedral a bit we realized that it was much better, and far easier, than it first appeared – definitely the logical line. A few weeks later, I ran into Vern Clevenger in the grill parking lot and told him about the route. He swore at himself for not thinking of doing the line back in the 1970s. "Do you realize how hard we worked to get up there? Why didn't I think of traversing in?"

– *Greg Barnes*

Strategy

West Crack is super popular and therefore climbing Blown Away requires patience and luck with crowds. In cold weather, climbing the route in the afternoon is your best bet, but you must move quickly. Two 60m ropes are required to retreat, but carrying a second rope on the big traverse is a pain. On windy days, head elsewhere.

On the crux third pitch, the leader should be careful getting to the first and second bolts. The second bolt is the two-bolt belay for the second pitch of Wienie Roast (5.11c R). If leading on a 50m rope, use this as an intermediate belay. At the last bolt, you can see an anchor 30 feet higher, but the climb goes left and down to a big ledge (unless you need to retreat, then go to the upper belay). Because the pitch traverses, both leader and follower should be confident 5.9 climbers.

The fourth pitch goes through a steep dihedral at the top – while intimidating, it's surprisingly easy, with good protection, wild stemming, and hand jams right when you need them. Once at the low-angle knobby slab look for the bolted anchor 20 feet up and left next to the arête (hard to spot). Use care if retreating from the fourth pitch anchor as it is difficult to avoid swinging left.

Retreat

Retreat from the end of Pitch 3 by climbing up to the optional anchor, then make two rappels with two 60m ropes.

Retreat from Pitch 4 by carefully angling back to the ledge (may need to clip bolt as directional), then climb up to the optional anchor and make two rappels with two 60m ropes (the last rap is 190 feet).

West Crack 5.9★★★★★

Time to climb route: **2–4 hours**

Approach time: **20 minutes**

Descent time: **30 minutes**

Sun exposure: **noon to sunset**

Height of route: **700'**

Except for a few face moves off the ground which are protected by a bomber bolt, the entire route is 5.8 or easier. While the roof at the start of the second pitch is intimidating, hidden holds make it reasonable. Even the offwidth on Pitch 4 is climbed via great face holds to the right.

FA: Frank Sacherer and Wally Reed, 7/63.

History

It's hard to believe that this handsome chunk of granite had no name as late as 1963. Frank Sacherer and Wally Reed, in July of that year, climbed the classic West Crack, one of the earliest Tuolumne climbs. When Valley climbers asked where this gem was, Sacherer hesitated only a moment before replying: "Dome across from Fairview." Within weeks this had been shortened to Daff.

The admirable Tuolumne ethic of never using aid perhaps originates from the climb of West Crack (Pratt and Reed, on Fairview in 1958, had used lots of aid, but this was in the Dark Ages and the cracks brimmed with dirt, meaning that jamming was out of the question). By 1963 Sacherer and Reed were superb free climbers and as they stood beneath the west face of Daff they spotted crystals and dikes and knobs and cracks everywhere. This was high-country granite, weathered far more than the smooth walls of the Valley. It seems safe to say that as they roped up they were thinking of a free ascent. Trouble was, about 20 feet above the ground the rock was, for a short distance, smooth and featureless, almost Valley-like. But it posed little problem, going at 5.9. Higher, the climbing proved thrilling and amazingly easy, and pitons could be driven anywhere for protection. Because Sacherer had a huge free-climbing agenda down in the Valley, he never again put up a first ascent in Tuolumne. One wonders what he would have done had he lived in the Meadows for a few months!

– Steve Roper

Strategy

Come prepared to wait in line or climb nearby routes. Large cams are needed to protect the fourth pitch or you can run it out. Beware of the possibility that the rope may drag cams into the crack on this pitch. If you have a #11 Hexcentric, bring it and use it at the bottom of the offwidth – not only is it great pro, it also keeps the rope running smoothly. With a 60m rope you can climb the route in four pitches with no difficulty.

The crux of the route is the first 30 feet. Clip the bolt with a single locker and stand on thin polished edges, working up to a good crimp. A few easier moves gain the crack, which stays easy for the next 60 feet. For the roof on the second pitch, jam with the right hand and use bomber jugs up and left to work your way through the overhang. This section is easier if you are tall.

West Crack is high up and often windy. Since it gets afternoon sun, strong parties often finish the day by running up it, while most people begin their climb as soon as the sun hits the wall. In the hot days of mid-summer it is an excellent morning route.

Retreat

Retreat with two ropes by leaving gear and/or using anchors on Blown Away, West Crack, and Witch of the West. Be careful on the rappel from the top of the first pitch – it just makes the anchors of Witch of the West.

See topo pages 74-75

Crescent Arch 5.10b★★★★

Time to climb route: **3–4 hours**

Approach time: **25 minutes**

Descent time: **30 minutes**

Sun exposure: **noon to sunset**

Height of route: **700′**

Crescent Arch is not only the most natural line on Daff Dome, it is one of the best routes in Tuolumne. From Highway 120, it's hard not to gawk at the elegant arc of large dihedrals and roofs that dominate the face.

FA: Layton Kor and Fred Beckey, 6/65.
FFA: Bob Kamps and Tom Herbert.

History

The "no aid climbing" ethic established early on in Tuolumne wasn't respected by everyone, and perhaps non-California climbers weren't aware of this unspoken "rule." In 1965 along came two historic figures, the famous Northwest master Fred Beckey and the pride of Colorado, Layton Kor. To the right of West Crack curved a gigantic dihedral, soon to be known as Crescent Arch. To many climbers, including me, this appeared to be an obvious aid route and was therefore to be avoided. But to Beckey, a first-ascent maniac, this was a route that begged to be done, and he must have been surprised to find it virgin as late as 1965. On June 2 he persuaded Kor to accompany him. Beckey described the climb later: "The first two leads were primarily difficult 5th class, and the next two leads involved nailing under the curve of the arch, with a hanging belay en route. The final exit, led beautifully by Layton, was both wet and difficult – about 45 pitons were used."

Within months TM Herbert and Bob Kamps had done the route without aid, as if to show the world that the vast majority of Tuolumne routes could be done free – and should be done free on the first ascent. I would guess this team eliminated 25 aid points, a startling achievement considering the stature of the first ascensionists.

Even after many years, Crescent Arch is a slick testpiece for the grade. Alternately awkward and delicate, the line requires surprisingly careful routefinding for such an obvious line. The climbing is often a tricky balance between protecting the crack and easier climbing on the face to the right. I once saw a leader take a 50-foot whipper near the top. This fellow had been lured onto the face and had forgotten about protection. Be warned!

– Steve Roper

Strategy

While not as popular as the neighboring West Crack, Crescent Arch draws crowds. Start early to avoid them and the danger of being near the summit during afternoon thunderstorms. This route is often wet in early season, especially on the crux pitch. Be prepared to climb either West Crack or Cooke Book if the climb looks wet.

The crux pitches require delicate footwork with small holds. Although the rock is often low-angle, the footholds are small and require subtle technique.

Pitches 2 through 4 traverse out slanting dihedrals and the occasional roof, making rope drag a big issue. Use many slings, especially on pieces that are around a roof or bulge. The crux pitch is 5.10b and requires skill with placing thin pro, and a steady head for the steep and dramatic knob moves.

After Crescent Arch, many people climb either Cooke Book or West Crack.

Retreat

Retreat requires two ropes. Because the route traverses, it becomes more difficult to retreat the higher you climb.

See topo pages 74-75

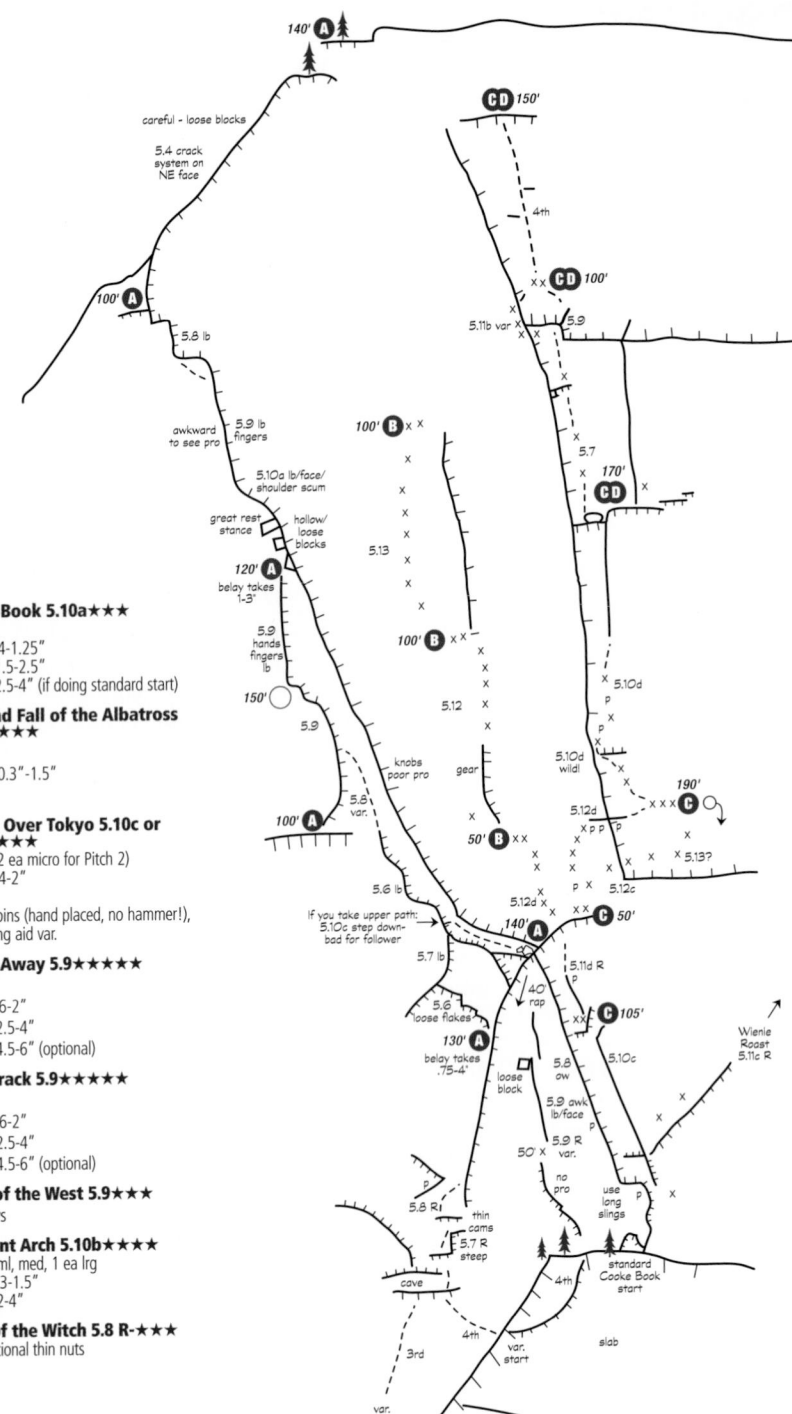

A. Cooke Book 5.10a★★★
nuts: 2 sets
cams: 2 ea .4-1.25"
1 ea 1.5-2.5"
1 ea 2.5-4" (if doing standard start)

**B. Rise and Fall of the Albatross
5.13a/b★★★★**
nuts: 1 set
cams: 1 ea. 0.3"-1.5"
draws

**C. Bombs Over Tokyo 5.10c or
5.12c R★★★★**
nuts: 1 set (2 ea micro for Pitch 2)
cams: 2 ea .4-2"
long slings
hooks, thin pins (hand placed, no hammer!),
aiders if doing aid var.

D. Blown Away 5.9★★★★★
nuts: 1 set
cams: 2 ea .6-2"
1 ea 2.5-4"
1 ea 4.5-6" (optional)

E. West Crack 5.9★★★★★
nuts: 1 set
cams: 2 ea .6-2"
1 ea 2.5-4"
1 ea 4.5-6" (optional)

F. Witch of the West 5.9★★★
4 quickdraws

G. Crescent Arch 5.10b★★★★
nuts: 2 ea sml, med, 1 ea lrg
cams: 2 ea .3-1.5"
1 ea 2-4"

H. West of the Witch 5.8 R-★★★
4 draws, optional thin nuts

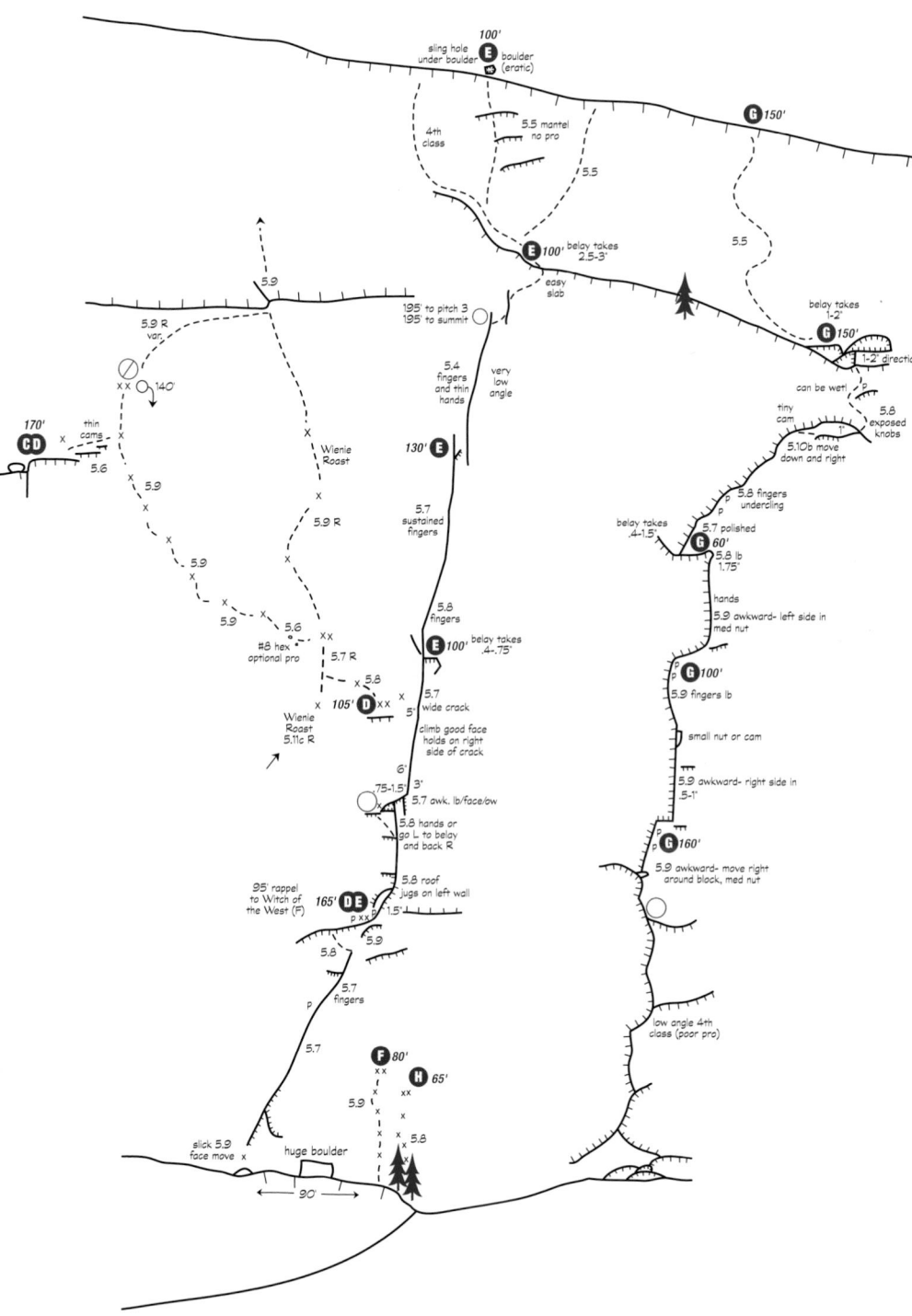

sling hole
under boulder
E 100'
boulder
(eratic)

4th
class

5.5 mantel
no pro

5.5

G 150'

5.9

5.5

5.9 R
var.

E 100'
belay takes
2.5-3'

easy
slab

195' to pitch 3
195' to summit

belay takes
1-2'

G 150'

1-2' directional

xx

140'

5.4
fingers
and thin
hands

very
low
angle

can be wet

p

170'
CD

thin
cams

5.6

5.9

Wienie
Roast

E 130'

5.7
sustained
fingers

tiny
cam

1'

5.8
exposed
knobs

5.10b move
down and right

5.8 fingers
undercling

5.9 R

5.9

5.9

5.6

#8 hex
optional pro

5.7 R

Wienie
Roast
5.11c R

xx

x

5.8
105' **D** xx

E 100'

5.8
fingers

belay takes
.4-.75'

5.7
wide crack

climb good face
holds on right
side of crack

belay takes
.4-1.5'

G 60'

p

5.7 polished

5.8 lb
1.75'

hands
5.9 awkward- left side in
med nut

G 100'

5.9 fingers lb

small nut or cam

5.9 awkward- right side in
.5-1'

6'

.75-1.5'
3'

5.7 awk. lb/face/ow

5.8 hands or
go L to belay
and back R

95' rappel
to Witch of
the West (F)

165' **DE**

5.8 roof
jugs on left wall

p xx
1.5'

G 160'

5.9 awkward- move right
around block, med nut

5.8

5.9

5.8

5.7
fingers

p

low angle 4th
class (poor pro)

5.7

F 80'
xx

H 65'
xx

5.9

5.8

slick 5.9
face move

huge boulder

90'

Daff Dome, South Flank

Approach time: **10 minutes**

Sun exposure: **all day**

Height of routes: **80-160'**

The South Flank has an easy approach, short climbs, and a sunny exposure – a completely different experience from the West Crack area. This popular area has the best concentration of easy cracks in Tuolumne.

Approach

See "Daff Dome Approach" for directions to the creek. Fifty yards east of the creek, head up low-angle slabs and a tree-filled area along the southeast side of the dome. If parking in the few spots tucked in the trees, you'll need to head up and left to get to the trail. Follow the trail up to the first steep area, marked by beautiful shiny gold polish and then a bunch of good-looking cracks.

Descent

Rappel the routes and reverse the approach.

A. Fingertips   5.10a R★★★★

FA: Bruce Morris, Bill Taylor and Tom Judson, 8/73.

Excellent slab climbing on slick golden granite with perfect incut "fingertip" edges. The right variation is more difficult (5.10b). It's easy to set up the first pitch on toprope by climbing Alimony Cracks and rappelling twice with a single 60m rope.

B. Alimony Cracks   5.8★★★

One of the few easier crack climbs in Tuolumne, with a short crux and a long easy top section. With a single 60m rope you can rappel twice, and have a 100-foot toprope on the first pitch of Fingertips.

C. Perspiration   5.11c★★

Short, hard crux to slabby knobs.

D. Liberation   5.10c R★★★

Fun, but runout for leader and follower.

E. Guide Cracks   5.5-5.8★★★

FA: Chris Falkenstein, 8/75.

Guide Cracks (aka Honeymoon's Over) are four short, fun, well-protected cracks to two shared bolted anchors 80 feet off the deck. Very popular with the Yosemite Mountain School and climbers introducing friends to cracks, they are often gang-toproped and too crowded to get on. If climbing here, please be considerate and don't hog the climbs.

F. Great Circle   5.10a R-★★★★

FA: Bruce Morris and Bill Taylor, 1974.

A great crack to slab route, the first pitch is 5.9; the second is more heady.

G. It is Finished   5.11a R-★★★

Usually toproped from Great Circle, this is a brutally slick, polished slab testpiece. It's also a good lead but a bit runout.

H. Hogwash   5.10c R-★★★

FA: Dennis Oakeshott and Bruce Morris, 1975.

Usually toproped, but also a reasonable lead.

I. Tips Ahoy   5.11a R★★

FA: Rob Settlemeyer and Dave Caunt, 1981.

A runout lead, Tips Ahoy is a fine toprope from the tree on top of Unnamed. To toprope from the anchor on Great Circle, traverse right (5.5) to set an anchor.

J. Unnamed   5.7 R★★

The poorly protected ramp to the right of Tips Ahoy; anchor off the tree and use directionals to toprope.

A. Fingertips 5.10a R★★★★ 4 quickdraws

B. Alimony Cracks 5.8★★★ nuts: 1 ea med, lrg; cams: 1 ea .6-1.25", 2 ea 1.5-3"

C. Perspiration 5.11c★★ 4 quickdraws; rivet hanger and nut for hangerless 1/4" bolt

D. Liberation 5.10c R★★★ 4 quickdraws

E. Guide Cracks 5.5-5.8★★★★ nuts: 1 set; cams: 2 ea .6-1.25", 1 ea 1.5-3"

F. Great Circle 5.10a R★★★★ nuts: 1 set; cams: 1 ea .5-2"; 2 quickdraws

G. It is Finished 5.11a R★★★ 7 quickdraws

H. Hogwash 5.10c R★★★ 7 quickdraws

I. Tips Ahoy 5.11a R★★ 4 quickdraws plus 1-2" cams for directional at top

J. Unnamed 5.7 R★★ cams: 1 ea .6-2"

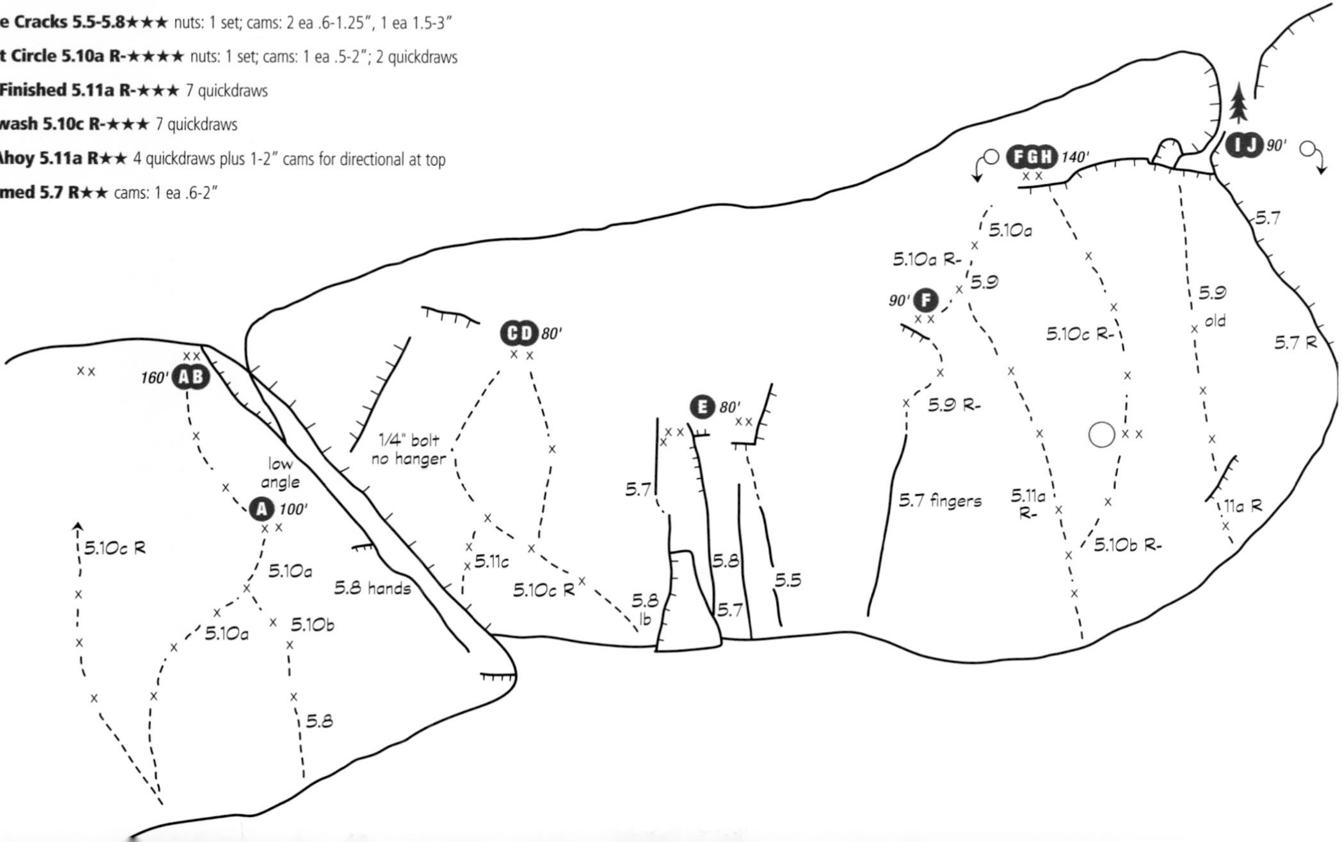

The Wind Tunnel

Approach time: **25-30 minutes**

Sun exposure: **mid-morning to late afternoon**

Height of routes: **100'-160'**

The notch between Daff Dome and West Cottage Dome is home to some fun new easy routes in a spectacular setting. Previously home to some obscure Walt Shipley routes (with basically zero pro), there are now several new routes. As the name implies, this area is typically windy and can be cold.

While the routes are moderate, the protection on several of the routes is a bit tricky, mostly thin cams in horizontal cracks.

The south-facing routes get sun from mid-morning on and the two routes on the north side of Daff get partial afternoon sun, except in late season (October) when they are in the shade (cold!). Because it is always windy, The Wind Tunnel is a good place to go on hot days, even though the area gets a lot of sun.

Approach

Routes A-E are about 200 yards right of Cottage Cheese, on West Cottage Dome in the notch between West Cottage and Daff Domes. Routes F and G are opposite of route A, on Daff Dome, on the lower (right) side of the low-angle slabs but before the steep section and the drop-off. All of these routes are hard to spot, so use the photos and descriptions to help locate them. They are best approached from the south flank of Daff. They can also be approached at 3rd/4th class up the big gully between Daff and West Cottage Dome (or after rapping off of Daff).

A. Udder Chaos   5.8 R-★★

FA: Bryan Law, George Ridgley, 9/08

The left-most route starts with climbing past a tan-camo bolt 15 feet up. The crux is just after the bolt, and the climbing gets easier above, with horizontal cracks for pro and a bolted anchor. Two ropes required for the 160' rap.
Rack: 1 draw (tan camo hanger), pro to 2"

B. String Cheese   5.6★★★

FA: Bryan Law, George Ridgley, 10/07.

A fun, varied route starting with big orange edges on a white face, with slab, knobs and cracks (both vertical and horizontal). The route is 130' long, so to descend climb right to the anchor for Eddie Muenster and rap with a single 60m rope.
Rack: cams: 1 ea. 0.75-2", 5 draws

C. Pasture-ized   5.8 R-★★

FA: Bryan Law, George Ridgley, 7/08.

A slabby start to a hard-to-spot bolt leads to some horizontal cracks, and a second bolt which protects a short, steep knob crux. Climb to the anchor for String Cheese, and traverse to Eddie Muenster if you want to rap with a single 60m rope. The direct start is a bit runout to the first bolt.
Rack: cams: 1 ea. 0.33-1", 2", 2 draws

D. Eddie Muenster   5.7★★★

FA: Bryan Law, George Ridgley, 10/07.

Another good route with lots of horizontal thin cracks and an exciting bulge crux. Use long slings if the best pro is too far one side or another. It is a 100' rap back to the ground.
Rack: cams: 2 ea. 0.33-1", 3 draws

E. Cheesecake   5.5 R-★★★

FA: Bryan Law, George Ridgley, 7/08.

An easy climb up the right side of the slab, Cheesecake takes golden slab past a tan camo bolt to a series of thin horizontal cracks. Just after the bolt is the crux, and just past that is a good horizontal crack over to the right that is easy to miss.
Rack: cams: 2 ea. 0.33-1.5", 1 draw

F. DAFFy Duck   5.5 R★★

FA: George Ridgley, Bryan Law, 8/08

Opposite the other routes, on the side of Daff, there is a steep green slab on the left, a low angle section in the middle, and a steeper section down and right. On this lowest section, to the right of the very low angle slab, climb a bumpy light-grey water streak past a couple of cam placements in horizontals and a single bolt to easier runout terrain (5.0) above. 2-bolt anchor. 90'
Rack: cams: 1 ea. 0.5-2", 1 draw

G. Turbine   5.10a★★★

FA: Bryan Law, George Ridgley, Denis Morel 8/08

To the right of DAFFy Duck, Turbine is a bolted face with the first three bolts tan camouflaged. The first four bolts are closely spaced, with the crux after the 4th bolt. The 5th bolt is up and left, and the last bolt is up and a bit right. There is a 5.6 runout above the last bolt. Also, beware of a semi-detached flake after the last bolt. 2-bolt anchor. 100'
Rack: 6 draws

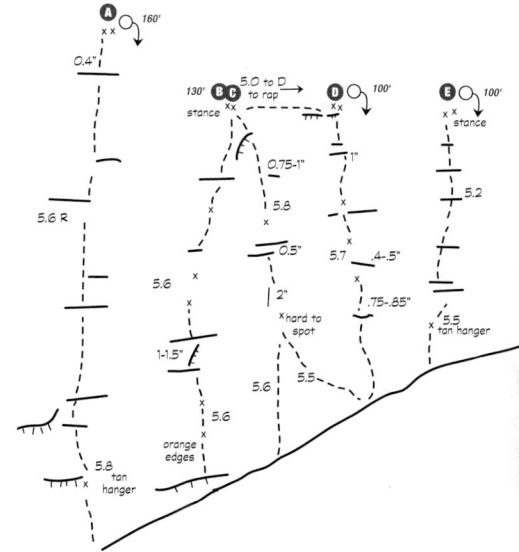

Photo by Bryan Law

West Cottage Dome

Approach time: 20-30 minutes

Sun exposure: none

Height of routes: 80-160'

Steep and north facing, West Cottage Dome has several excellent crack routes which see very little traffic considering their quality. In fact, the main detraction to the north face routes is some grainy rock and lichen due to the lack of traffic. All the bolts were replaced on this dome in 2001. However, several key pitons are required and should be backed up where possible.

Approach

Approach as for Daff Dome via the trail to the West Face. When you reach the base of Daff below Cooke Book and West Crack, hike left along the base of the slab to the next dome – this is West Cottage Dome. A couple hundred feet of 3rd class slab leads to the lower right side of the north face, where Cottage Cheese begins. The easy approach zigzags left then right to below the starting dihedral. To reach the other routes, continue all the way to below the left edge of the north face, then go up and back right at 3rd class (all other approaches are blocked by short headwalls).

Descent

Hike off the back side (3rd class), then down right, past the Wind Tunnel routes, down the 4th class slab gully back to the base. This gully can be nasty when it's wet, and can have ice and snow in early season. In early season or heavy snow years, it might be best to gear up at the car and not leave packs at the base – then after scrambling down the back side of the dome, head towards the east shoulder of Daff and down past the south flank routes to the road.

A. Pencilitis   5.11a R★★★

FA: Ed Barry, Dave Hitchcock, Mike White, July 1979.

A serious route up the left side of the north face of West Cottage Dome, Pencilitis

is a liebacking test piece with old pitons protecting the crux. The first pitch is relatively easy, but has a substantial runout on low 5.10 liebacking. This is a good warmup, since the crux lieback faces the same direction and is much harder and protected primarily by two old fixed pins. Backup pro is hard to get, and consists of small cams in flared finger cracks. The single bolt near the top is pretty far up, particularly in light of the huge ledge at the start of the pitch. It's very easy to escape the crux second pitch by simply walking right on the huge ledge and either rappelling or finishing Pencil-Necked Geek. Somewhat grainy and flaky. Narrow and/or offset small cams may be helpful, but it may be best not to be fiddling with them instead of just gunning the lieback!

B. Geekin' Hard   5.10d★★★

FA: Scott Cole, Urmas Franosch, July 1986.

A bouldery start leads to some easy climbing, then a flared hand crack to a powerful undercling/lieback crack that leads to a thin hand crack and the first belay of Pencil-Necked Geek. Originally protected by a piton (that pulled out with a single finger in 2008!), the bouldery start takes some good thin nuts and thin cams. A bit grainy.

C. Pencil-Necked Geek 5.11a R-★★★

FA: Alan Roberts, Alan Bartlett, Dan McMillan, Tom Prentice, July 1980.

A tricky boulder problem start, protected only by a questionable old thin piton, leads to an excellent finger and hand crack in a steep groove. You can easily avoid the crux boulder problem by climbing the start of Geekin' Hard (bouldery 5.10d, but with good pro), then stepping right. The second pitch steps left up wild, steep liebacking with poor pro (RPs, tricky 3-3.5"cam), leading to a burly hand traverse/mantel and a bolt. Make a tenuous step left onto a ramp, and another bolt (which protects the follower very well). You can climb up then straight left to a bolted belay, but it's best to skip this and climb right past another bolt to a knobby thin crack which leads to the summit. If you use the intermediate belay, the traverse from the belay to the bolt is very intimidating, especially for the follower. Like the neighboring routes, expect a bit of lichen and grainy rock.

D. Cottage Cheese 5.10b★★★★

FA: Tom Higgins, Ben Borrison, August 1968.

An overlooked gem, and another tribute to the free climbing standards of the 60s, Cottage Cheese is the best, and cleanest, route on the north face. Starting with an excellent technical and sustained first pitch with great pro, the big belay ledge reveals an intimidating start to the second pitch. A burly overhung boulder problem that was 5.10a in 1968 leads into 5.9 hands, chimney, and a stretch of old-school 5.7 offwidth. Make sure to set an anchor at the top of the first pitch, then move the belay for the second.

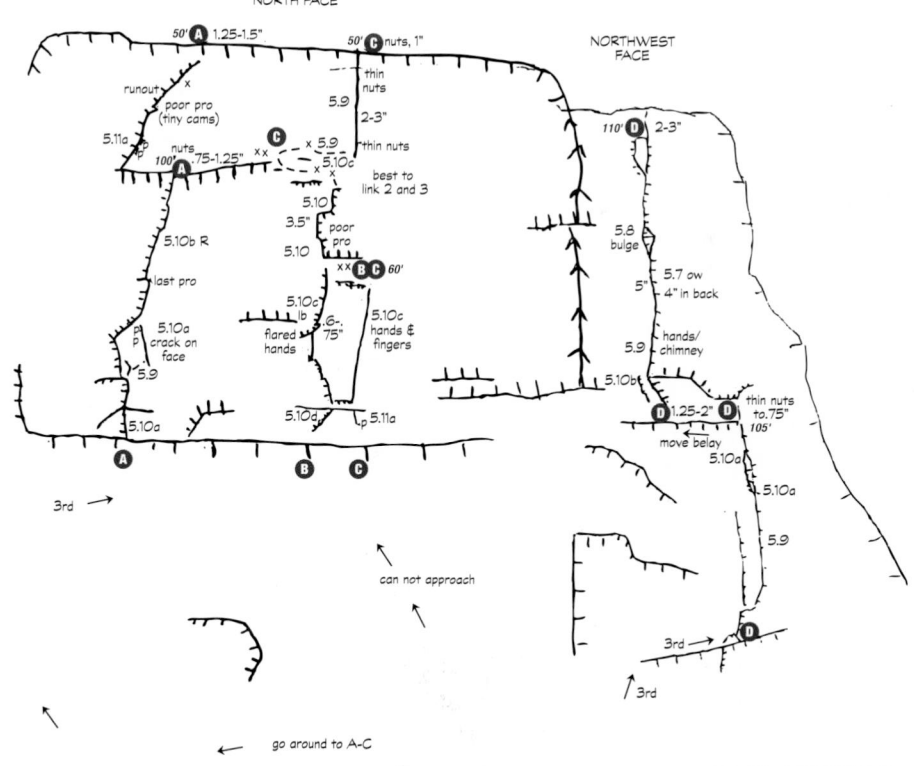

East Cottage Dome

Approach time: **20 minutes**

Sun exposure: **afternoon**

Height of routes: **80'**

Home of one of the most popular sport climbing areas in Tuolumne, East Cottage Dome has long been a favorite for steep, thin knob climbing. With many routes in the 5.10 to 11a range, a relatively short hike, and plentiful afternoon sun, this is a great cragging destination. Good edging shoes are mandatory, and good footwork and crimping strength are the name of the game.

While these are mostly sport routes, many were established in the first wave of sport development, and what were tightly protected routes for the late 80s now sometimes seem well spaced or even runout. Some of these route require a few thin cams for supplemental pro. The base of the wall is unfriendly to falls before the first bolt, so a stick clip is a good idea for some of the routes. Many of these routes require care getting to the first bolt, and an attentive belay near the 2nd (or even 3rd) bolt.

The base of the middle of the wall is a sloped 3rd class ramp that leads to a 10 to 15-foot dropoff to a broad low-angle slab. There is one 4th class step which can be sketchy to downclimb. The split at the base of the wall often has pools of water, and it's common to dunk the rope in water even on a warm and sunny day. It's also common for people to drop water bottles, shoes, or even entire packs and watch them roll and bounce downhill for a long way.

It's possible to toprope some of these routes by doing a short rappel off of anchors on the top. However, even getting to the top anchors requires 3rd or 4th class knobby slab right before a dropoff, and some of the anchors have been partially chopped, leaving only a single bolt (or one bolt plus a stopper slung on the other bolt when one is missing a hanger).

The main issues as far as weather are the lack of afternoon shade (it can get really hot), and the exposure to winds – the routes are high up and exposed.

Approach

The parking area is a small dirt pullout with a steep sandy parking area. It's easy to miss the parking, so carefully note the mileage as you pass the paved parking lot for the tourist trap Pothole Dome. Only 0.6 miles west, along a downhill stretch of the road, the small pullout is hidden on the right. Use great care parking, and especially when leaving this pullout. Follow the obvious trail up to slabs, and then pay careful attention to the trail, which climbs to a saddle. From the saddle, contour north up huge exfoliating flakes, then around to the west face of the dome.

A. Life in the Cretaceous   5.10a★★★

FA Bryan Law, Linda Jarit, George Ridgley, November 2007.

A fun new route with thin moves off the deck. While this route is more tightly bolted than most of the other routes, the section from the last bolt to the anchor reminds you that this is still Tuolumne. The first bolt is camouflaged tan.

A. Life in the Cretaceous 5.10a★★★
6 quickdraws

B. Linda's Sandbag 5.8★★ toprope
Climb the thin seam straight below the anchors
of Life in the Cretaceous.

C. Flintstone 5.10b R-★★★★
70m rope or 2 ropes for 2nd pitch!
Pitch 1: 5 quickdraws, optional 0.6" cam; pitch 2:
7 quickdraws, 110'.

D. Disintegration 5.10d★★★★
6 quickdraws, one 0.6" cam

E. Liposuction 5.11a★★★
5 quickdraws, cams 0.3-0.75"

F. Orange Plasma 5.11a★★★★
7 quickdraws

G. Ballroom Dancing 5.10b R★★★
4 quickdraws, pro tiny-.5"

H. Comfortably Numb 5.10c★★★★
4 quickdraws, optional cams 0.5-0.75"

I. Old Folks Boogie 5.10d R★★★
6 quickdraws

J. Knobvious 5.11a R★★★★
7 quickdraws, optional knob tie-off

K. Rover Take Over 5.10d R-★★★★
6 quickdraws

L. Knobnoxious 5.10d★★★★
7 quickdraws

M. Unknown 5.10d★★★★
6 quickdraws

N. Knobulator 5.10c★★★
4 quickdraws

B. Linda's Sandbag   5.8★★★ toprope

FA Linda Jarit, November 2007.

Climb the thin seam straight below the anchors of Life in the Cretaceous.

C. Flintstone   5.10b R-★★★★

FA Scott Burk, Chris Cantwell, 1981.

A great two-pitch adventure, this route was ignored for decades, and for good reason. The bolts were almost all hangerless ¼" stud bolts, nearly impossible to spot among the knobs and lichen. Not only did you have to bring keyhole hangers (or use the wire of a nut to sling the bolts), the bolt type was weaker than standard ¼" bolts. Now, with all the bolts newly replaced, Flintstone is posed for popularity, especially with the wildly exposed second pitch. This and the chopped route Skeletal Remains (the dike at the far right end) were named in the theme of dinosaurs, since for some climbers at the time, East Cottage Dome was called Dinosaur Dome. Despite being the oldest sport route at the dome, this

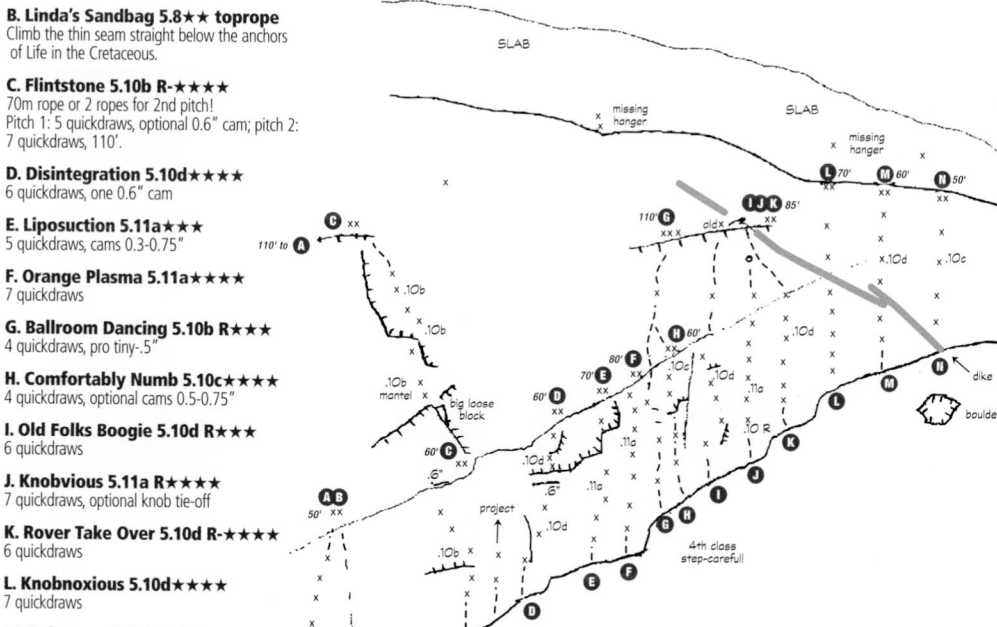

route has seen nearly zero traffic, and it has large knobs, many of which (especially at the top of the second pitch) are likely to break if cranked or stepped on (use suspect knobs lightly). A 70m rope is required to lower off the second pitch.

Unknown old project – two bolts

D. Disintegration   5.10d★★★

FA Paul Granthem, Jim Schwarz, August 1988.

Outstanding climbing up a thin seam to a wild roof/bulge (some call this route The Bulge). While the thin face first half is technically harder, the bulge crux may be tricky for shorter folks, but luckily two very closely spaced bolts protect it tightly.

E. Liposuction   5.11a★★

FA Jim Schwarz, Paul Granthem, August 1988.

Sequential, thin climbing leading to a fun crack/corner and a great finish bulge.

F. Orange Plasma   5.11a★★★★

FA Jim Schwarz, Paul Granthem, August 1988.

Sustained, excellent small knob climbing up the bright orange streak.

G. Ballroom Dancing   5.10b R★★★

FA Jim Matthew, Mike Waugh, 1986.

Fun route with positive but suspect knobs, runout up high but easy. Like Flintstone, the lack of traffic coupled with large incut knobs means that extra care is needed to avoid snapping knobs.

H. Comfortably Numb   5.10c★★★★

FA Phil Bard and friends, August 1981.

An intermediate anchor on this excellent route lets you lower off with a 50m rope, but you can also continue to the upper anchor and lower off if you have a 70m rope. While you can place pro in the flakes after the second bolt, the climbing is very positive and fairly easy, and falling on the pro might well break the flakes.

I. Old Folks Boogie   5.10d R★★★

FA: Phil Bard, Paul Tradani, August 1983.

Reachy on medium sized knobs at the crux, and runout on easy terrain at the top. You can either climb left from the last bolt, or head straight up easier knobs on a big runout to the top ledge. A single ¼" bolt

marks the original finish of the route, and you can go about 25 feet either way on the 5th class ramp/ledge to a good anchor.

J. Knobvious   5.11a R★★★★

FA Dan and Sue McDevitt, Dave Gardner, July 1990.

Sustained, thin climbing, runout off the deck but well protected after the first bolt. A good candidate for stick-clipping, if you have a long enough stick-clip. An optional knob tie-off near the anchor protects easy climbing to the top.

K. Rover Take Over   5.10d R-★★★★

FA Grant Hiskes, Errett Allen, Ken Yager, 1988.

Fun route with a mix of hard-to-spot stainless SMC hangers and big light-grey camouflage Fixe hangers. Finish either left or right on easy but runout climbing.

L. Knobnoxious   5.10d★★★★

FA Dan and Sue McDevitt, Dave Gardner, July 1990.

Somewhere near this route (perhaps to the right where one old bolt is about 15 feet up) was a very bold John Bachar free solo first ascent called Edging Skills or Hospital Bills. While it seems that these routes are pretty straightforward if you have strong fingers and good footwork, consider that many holds broke off during the first ascents – making a free solo first ascent even more intimidating.

M. Unknown   5.10d★★★★

FA unknown

Good route up through the split in the dike.

N. Knobulator   5.10c★★★

FA Dan and Sue McDevitt, July 1990.

Start at the beginning of the dike, but go straight up. Fun knobs with bigger feet than most of the other routes.

The spectacular position of East Cottage Dome (the wall to the right) with the Southwest Face of Mt. Conness in the background.

Canopy World

Approach time: 1-1.5 hours

Sun exposure: morning to afternoon

Height of routes: 80-100'

Canopy World is a fun crag along the trail to Glen Aulin. The approach is a little over two miles, but it is almost entirely flat on a heavily used trail (the Pacific Crest Trail), and it goes quickly. In late season when the river is very low, you can take almost a mile off the approach by parking near Pothole Dome and crossing the river near the crag.

In the full sun all day, Canopy World can be pretty hot in midseason, but it's a great crag for cooler weather or cloudy/stormy days when multipitch is questionable. Shade is available below trees, but the climbs are in the sun. There are more routes on the shady northwest and northeast faces, mostly sport and mostly 5.12 (one 5.11 and one 5.13).

By scrambling to the top, you can set top-ropes on some of these climbs.

However, the scramble is Sierra 4th class, so sticky rubber and a cool head are recommended. The best way to the top is to lead a route.

Currently, the two bolted anchors at the top of the south face of the crag have one good bolt and one old ¼" bolt. Make sure to use a non-extending method when setting anchor slings/cordalettes.

Approach

Park at the Soda Springs trailhead (take the dirt road past the Lembert Dome parking area until it turns right, and park there; the trail heads straight), then follow the signs towards Glen Aulin. Canopy World is the crag about 100 yards right after the trail drops down a large slab, around two miles from the trailhead. If the river is very low, you can cross below Pothole Dome and take a mile off the approach.

A. One-Eyed Jack   5.10d X★★★

FA: Ed Barry, Tom Herbert, 1985

A great toprope, this extremely runout

route defines the difference between old-school and new-school ratings. If it were bolted today, there would be tons more bolts and the rating would be closer to 5.11d than 5.10d. Ed Barry is one of the many little known strong California climbers, who 12 years after doing this route did the second ascent of Übermensch (5.14a) at Pinnacles. From the anchor of Kill Pickle, a directional can be set with tricky tiny micro-nuts at the ledge. Use great care setting this directional – if it fails the climber will be dropped a bit and will pendulum to the right.

B. Kill Pickle   5.10c R★★★★

FA: Vaino Kodas, Mike Beck, June 1983

Quality, technical route with just enough bolts to keep a well-belayed leader from hitting the ground (assuming you make it to the first bolt…). Easy to toprope from bolted anchor. The third protection bolt was originally doubled – two ¼" bolts next to each other. This is sometimes seen on old routes before dangerous runouts – even when new, ¼" bolts didn't inspire too much confidence!

C. Sudden Impact   5.13a★★

FA: Tom Herbert, Doug McDonald.

Easily toproped by rappelling 25 feet from the Kill Pickle anchor to a two-bolt anchor at the lip. If you can get up this, then there are tons of hard crimpy testpieces all over Tuolumne and California with your name on them (many, like this one, put up by Tuolumne pioneer TM Herbert's son Tom).

D. Trick Shot   5.9★★★★

FA: Ed Barry, Tom Herbert, 1985

Excellent hand and finger cracks in a corner, one of the better Tuolumne 5.9 crack routes to push your lead grade. The climb gets steeper and harder as you head up towards the transfer into the lower-angle left crack at the top. You can set an anchor in the crack at the top, but it's best to just scramble over right to the bolted anchor of Polski Wyrob, since that anchor is more directly above the corner.

E. Polski Wyrob   5.11b R-★★★

FA: Vaino and Toivo Kodas, June 1987

A fun face climb with a cruxy start. Crimp and crank, or do what many do and just pull on the draw. While it looks like a sport climb, the section above the very low first bolt is runout and should be treated as if you have no pro (since the first bolt won't do any good for most of it). Currently all bolts on this route (except one at the anchor) are ¼" and should be treated with caution.

F. Billiard Room   5.10a X★★★

FA: Ed Barry, Tom Herbert, 1985

Cool juggy face to groove climb with no pro until halfway up the route. A good toprope – see Sweet'n Low description for toprope info.

G. Kick Back Crack   5.10a R★

FA: Tom Herbert, Brian Wheat, 1986

Cruxy start to dirty lieback crack to easy hand crack. Dangerous as a lead, but a fun toprope – see Sweet'n Low description for toprope info.

H. Sweet'n Low   5.7★★

FA: Don Reid, free solo

A wandering climb with some heads-up moves including power lieback and short face climbing above not-super-bomber pro in flakes. Fun double hand cracks at the top lead to a ledge with 1.25-1.5" crack for the anchor. A few 5th class moves must be done to top out, but there is no pro for an anchor. Thus, to toprope the previous two routes, lead Sweet & Low, set the anchor, toprope, then have the second-to-last climber belay at the anchor, with the final climber leading past the anchor up and over the top to a large tree, then belaying the partner as they clean the anchor and top out.

A. One-Eyed Jack 5.10d X★★★
nuts: 1 ea sml, set micro
cams: 1 ea 0.5-0.75

B. Kill Pickle 5.10c R★★★★
3 draws

C. Sudden Impact 5.13a★★★
6 draws

D. Trick Shot 5.9★★★★
nuts: 1 set
cams: 2 ea. 0.6-3"

E. Polski Wyrob 5.11b R-★★★
5 draws

F. Billiard Room 5.10a X★★★
cams: 1 ea. 1.25-3"

G. Kick Back Crack 5.10a R★
cams: 1 ea. 0.6-3"

H. Sweet'n Low 5.7★★
nuts: 1 set
cams: 1 ea. 0.5-.75", 2-3"
2 ea. 1-1.5"

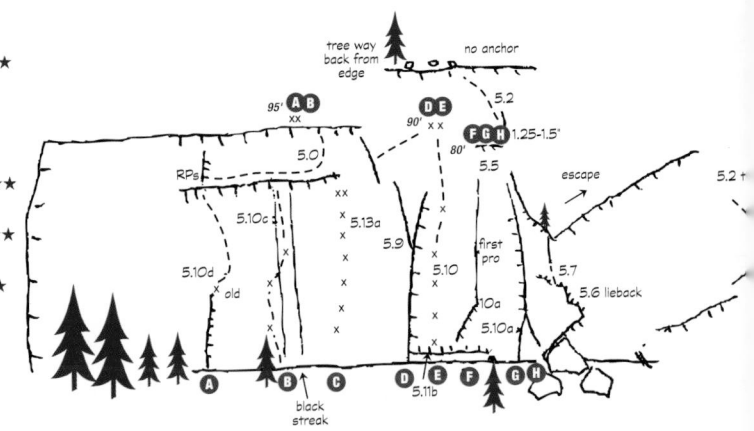

The view from Canopy World downstream toward Glen Aulin.

Pothole Dome

Approach time: **5 minutes**

Sun exposure: **midday**

Height of routes: **25–110'**

Pothole Dome is the low-angle "tourist-walk-up" dome at the west end of Tuolumne Meadows just before the road heads up into the trees toward Fairview Dome. The steeper left side is home to two sets of three bolted toprope anchors dating from the 1970s, with a variety of slabby topropes from 5.0 to 5.10a. It's also home to a steep short handcrack roof, Potluck (5.11). With the very short approach, absence of drop-offs or boulder fields, plus the easy climbs, this is by far the best location in Tuolumne to introduce beginners (or children) to Tuolumne climbing.

The bolted toprope anchors are far back from the edge. Very long slings are needed to toprope with the rope over the edge, but since the edges are rounded, it's possible to toprope with shorter slings if you don't mind some wear on your rope. Also, nearly every climb is around 100-110 feet tall, but starts with 3rd class climbing – use either long slings plus a single long rope, or some scrambling is required (or two ropes).

All anchors have two good bolts, thanks to ASCA volunteers. Bring gear for setting topropes off of bolts, very long slings and/or cordalettes, and one 60m or longer rope.

Approach

One of the easiest approaches anywhere in Yosemite, just follow the nature trail (keeping off the meadow!) as it loops around. To get to the first set of anchors, hike up 3rd class slab and look for anchors above the steep section to the left. The anchors are WAY back from the edge – if you don't see them, look behind you. The second set of anchors is about 300 yards to the north along the west side of the dome. Halfway along the gentle hike, you'll see a very short overhung wall above with a cave-like crack; this is Potluck, which requires some scrambling to get to the top. After the short hill, the next climbs are at the only steep section of the dome, and it's easy to scramble up on either side to get to the top.

Descent

Reverse the approach. You can also hike down the dome in pretty much any direction – enjoy the views of the meadow. If you hike along the meadow, please stay on the trail instead of trampling the grass and flowers. Also, the end of the meadow away from the road is a favorite place for deer to congregate away from the constant cars and buses – don't disturb them.

Left side

This wall is steeper than the right side topropes, with incut ledges and more knobs and holds.

A. Toprope #1

Good 5.1 friction climbing on the left is the easiest way up. Straight under the anchor is 5.6, and to either side is a little easier.

B. Toprope #2

Again, 5.1 is the easiest way up, but this time the other options are harder: The water streak on the left is 5.10a, the bulge on the right is 5.9, or to the right of the bulge is 5.5.

C. Toprope #3

The easiest toprope on the right is 5.0, with harder possibilities on the left up to 5.6. This is the shortest of the six easy topropes and the only one suitable for a single 50m rope.

D. Potluck   5.11★★

Short, very pumpy hand crack roof to face holds at the lip. Bad pendulum potential if you fall at the start – you could swing into the ground and it's easy to smack your belayer.

Right side

This wall next to the meadow is polished and slick and lower angled than the left side topropes. Excellent training for slabby polished routes such as West Country.

E. Toprope #4

Staying to the left is a good 5.1 friction and knob climb. Sticking to the edges in the middle is a good 5.8, with two 5.3-5.4 friction and knob climbs on the right.

F. Toprope #5

The hardest of the six easy topropes. The easiest way up is 5.6 on the left side of the gold polish. Straight up the middle is 5.10a micro-edges and polish, and the right is 5.9 thin edges and knobs.

G. Toprope #6

Straight up under the anchor is a great 5.1, or 5.4 just to the left; further to the left is the same 5.9 as for Toprope #5, and to the right is a 5.6–5.10a through squeaky clean polish (difficulty depending on where you go).

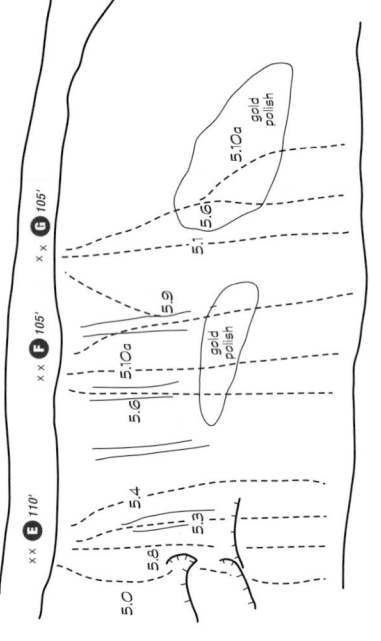

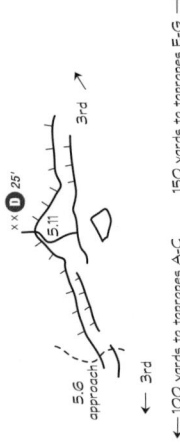

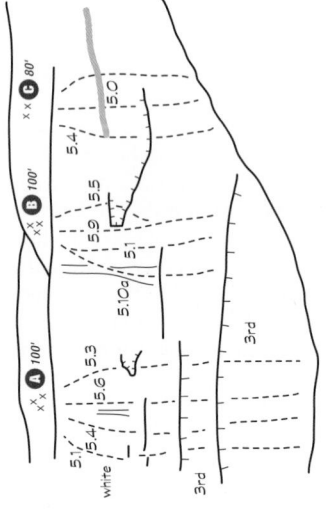

Lembert Dome

Lembert Dome is the only major dome near the inhabited sections of Tuolumne making it a tourist trap and a bustling picnic area. Directly above the parking area are two obvious grooves; these are the Water Cracks, which are runout polished grooves. Next to the Water Cracks are a variety of slab climbs on slick golden rock. However, most climbers come for the great crack and knob routes on the steep northwest face, which is shady and cool in the morning and warm late in the day.

A Crying Time Again **G** Mega Beam
C Direct Northwest Face **A** Truck' N Drive
E Northwest Books **B** Left Water Crack
F Beginner's Route **C** Werner's Wiggle

Approach

Park at the well-signed Lembert Dome parking lot. Approach to the Water Cracks is obvious. For the northwest face, hike up to the open granite then contour left along the base of the dome.

Descent

Various descents are possible. From the top of Crying Time Again and Direct Northwest Face, you can hike to the top of the Dome then off the back side. You can also hike down the front side to the top of Northwest Books. From there you can contour east, or hike down towards the Water Cracks. From about 200 feet above the Water Cracks, there is a 4th class descent which goes east, then down, then east more, then finally cuts back to the parking lot. The hike off routes are poorly defined, and depend on your comfort on 3rd and 4th class open slabs. Many descents are possible but many of the slabs cliff-out, so be careful.

Lembert Dome and Tuolumne Meadows. Greg Barnes Photo.

Crying Time Again
5.10a R★★★★★

Time to climb route: **3–4 hours**	
Approach time: **10 minutes**	
Descent time: **20–30 minutes**	
Sun exposure: **noon to sunset**	
Height of route: **450'**	

Crying Time Again ascends an amazing golden and knobby wall and is sustained and improbably steep for the grade. The route winds its way through steep bulges, following the natural line of weakness. It is unusually well-protected for a face climb at its level in Tuolumne, but is still heady.

FA: Bruce Morris et al.

Strategy

While this is a popular route, many people have problems finding the start of Crying Time Again, leaving it often free.

The first pitch is the only slab pitch and the 5.8 slab traverse gives both leader and follower something to think about. The third pitch has a poorly protected mantel. The top of the fourth pitch has a short hard traverse that is scary for the follower. The crux last pitch is tightly bolted.

In early and late season the wall can be too cold, but generally the climbing is perfect in the morning on hot days or in the afternoon on cooler days.

Retreat

Rappel with two ropes off of stations at the top of Pitch 2, 4, or 5. Rappelling is also possible off of the very top bolts (Pitch 6). If rappelling from the top, rappel 6 to 4, 4 to 2, and 2 to the starting blocks, then downclimb the 3rd class to the ground.

B. Cry Baby   5.8 R-★★★

FA: Brian Bennett, George Ridgley, Sept. 2008.

A new alternate start to Crying Time Again, Cry Baby starts a bit right of the normal start and takes a more direct route to the second pitch anchor. The crux is after the first bolt.

Direct Northwest Face
5.10b★★★★

Time to climb route: **2–3 hours**	
Approach time: **10 minutes**	
Descent time: **20–30 minutes**	
Sun exposure: **noon to sunset**	
Height of route: **400'**	

This follows an impressive, splitter crack. With sustained 5.9 climbing and short, well-protected cruxes, it's an excellent climb for those breaking into the grade.

FA: Russ Wayne, late 1950s. FFA: Bob Kamps, Mark Powell, and Beverly Powell 7/62.

Strategy

While popular, the grade keeps the crowds down. With a 60m rope you can do the route in two pitches, although rope weight makes the top 5.9 slab moves harder.

The 5.10a crux on the third pitch is powerful and challenging and is best done as a long reach while liebacking to the right. The 5.10b crux is thin finger locks in pin scars – get small cams ready, and go for it.

In early and late season the wall can be too cold, but generally the climbing is perfect in the morning on hot days or in the afternoon on cooler days.

Retreat

Retreat is possible with the sacrifice of a few nuts and slings, and is easier with two ropes. If you're hit by a big thundershower be aware of lightning and the huge quantities of rain and hail that can flow down everywhere.

D. John Henry   5.10a R-★★★

FA: Chris Cantwell, Barry Chambers, 1997.

A fun addition to the area. Sustained and slabby with steps to slabby bulges, the crux second pitch is both well-protected by Tuolumne standards and somewhat heads-up at many of the harder moves. A bit of lichen detracts from the quality. Runout but easy on the first pitch, with a 3rd class approach from the left. Two ropes are required.

Northwest Books 5.6★★★

Time to climb route: **1–2 hours**

Approach time: **10 minutes**

Descent time: **10–30 minutes**

Sun exposure: **noon to sunset**

Height of route: **300'**

The Northwest Books on Lembert Dome was one of the first technical climbs in Tuolumne and remains one of the most popular. Two pitches of varied climbing and some polished rock make this a challenging route. Due to the grade and the quick, easy access, it's extremely popular. Many parties miss the traverse out of the corner of the second pitch, giving 5.6 leaders their first encounter with a 5.9 crack.

FA: Warren Harding and Frank de Saussure, 1954.

History

Warren Harding, soon to become a Yosemite legend, was just beginning his exalted career in 1954. Following his bold foray up the Arrow Chimney (the second ascent) and his new route on the east buttress of Middle Cathedral that summer, he relaxed and headed for the Meadows, establishing the first real route on that glaciated masterpiece called Lembert Dome. A bit of a come-down? Yes, but this route proved to be a non-serious outing beloved by thousands since. Harding couldn't remember why he chose this line. Many years ago he told me that his memory about routes was deficient – and that this was a decided advantage. "Every time I do a route that someone claims I've already done," he declared, "it's a brand-new experience – and so I get to do it for the first time again!" I would guess that Harding was simply trying to repeat a short scrambling route done nearby in 1951 (now called the Beginner's Route). I'll bet he looked up, spotted these nice dihedrals above him, and went for it. If so, it was a typical Harding adventure, featuring a man always willing to do something different.

– Steve Roper

Strategy

There is almost always a line on this route. Since it's quick to access, it is worth hiking up for a look. If there is too much traffic on the route you only have a ten-minute walk back to the car.

Because the corner never gets sun, this climb tends to be wet in early season. In fall it tends to be cold. But, of course, it is normally perfect in high season.

Retreat

Retreat the route by rappelling and leaving gear. Since the corner traverses, you need two ropes to reach the 3rd class ledge from most spots on the first pitch. The corner will channel water during a cloudburst, but lightning is the greater danger.

F. Beginner's Route   5.4 R-★

FA: Dorothy Dern, Richard Leonard, H. Stewart Kimball, Philip Dern, Alfred Dole, 1951.

The earliest known technical route on Lembert Dome, the Beginner's Route takes staircase ledges to a short face with a bolt protecting the crux. While not runout in general, the very traversing nature of the route and the angled ledge beneath the crux would make it difficult to catch a lead fall without slack in the system leading to a ledge fall. Dick Leonard was one of the first technical rockclimbers in the U.S., with ground-breaking ascents of the Cathedral Spires and Shiprock in the 1930s, and he was, like his frequent partner David Brower, a prominent environmental activist.

G. Mega Bleam   5.10a★★★★

FA: Mark Spencer, 1985.

A technical and unique pitch, this is an excellent route with cool liebacking and stemming between folds of rock. The best approach is to climb Beginner's Route. You can also scramble onto the base ledge from the top on your way down from another route, or after topping out on routes like Water Cracks. A runout 5.8 start leads to tightly bolted face. Finish with some slab climbing to the anchor. Pitch 2 is 5.8 and is severely wandering, flakey, and has no pro. A single rap with one rope returns you to the ledge.

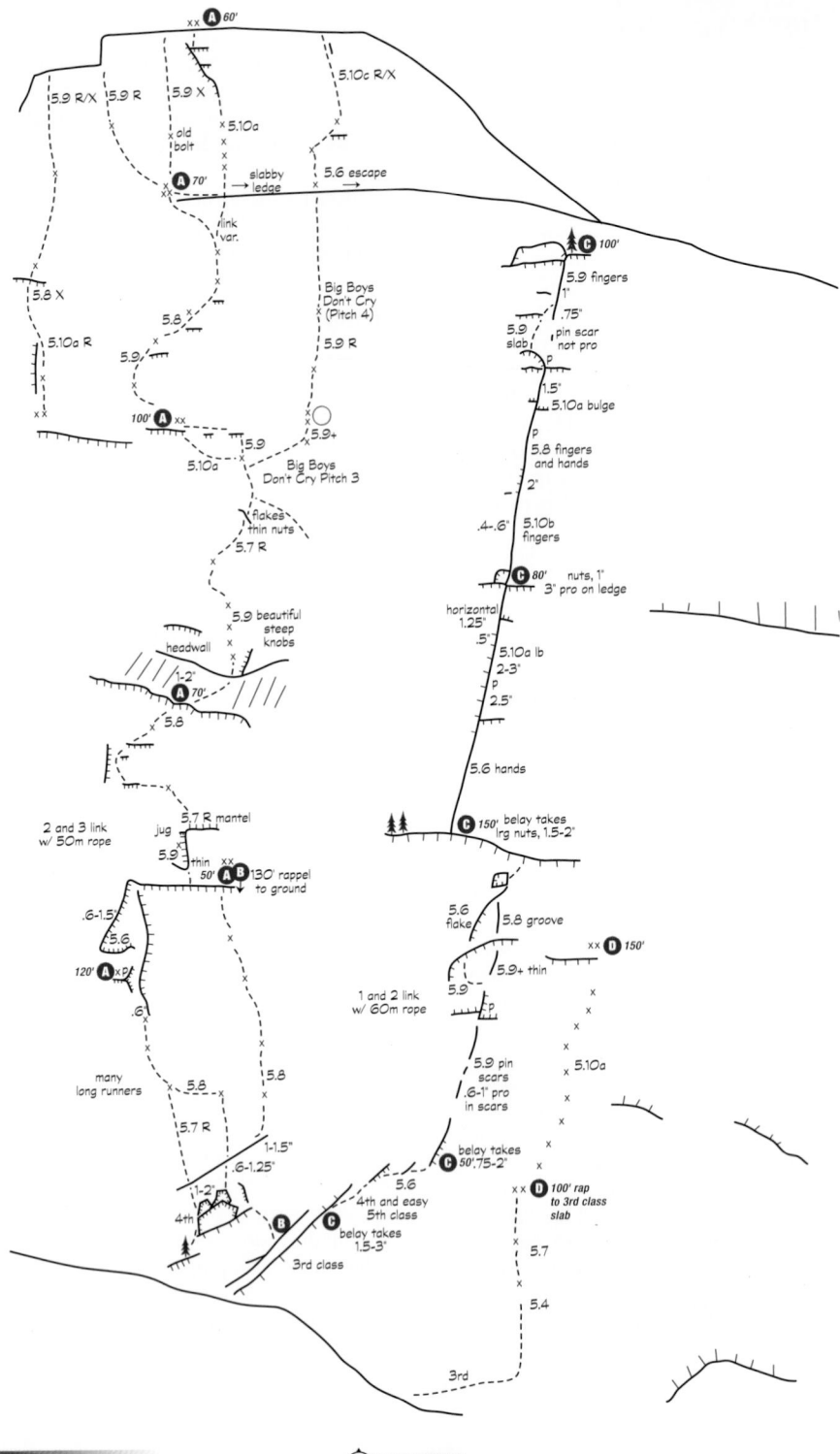

XX Ⓐ 60'

5.9 R/X   5.9 R   5.9 X   5.10c R/X

X old bolt   X 5.10a

Ⓐ 70'   slabby ledge   5.6 escape

link var.

Ⓒ 100'   5.9 fingers

1"
.75"

5.8 X   5.9 slab   pin scar not pro

Big Boys Don't Cry (Pitch 4)   1.5"
5.10a R   5.9   5.9 R   5.10a bulge
p

5.8 fingers and hands

2'

5.10b fingers   .4-.6'

100' Ⓐ XX   5.9   5.9+   Ⓒ 80'   nuts, 1" 3" pro on ledge
5.10a   Big Boys Don't Cry Pitch 3

flakes thin nuts
5.7 R   horizontal 1.25'   .5"   5.10a lb
2-3'
p
2.5'

5.9 beautiful steep knobs

headwall   5.6 hands

1-2'   Ⓐ 70'
5.8   Ⓒ 150' belay takes lrg nuts, 1.5-2'

5.7 R mantel

2 and 3 link w/ 50m rope   jug   5.6 flake   5.8 groove
5.9   thin   XX
50'   Ⓐ Ⓑ 130' rappel to ground   5.9+ thin   XX Ⓓ 150'

.6-1.5'   5.9
5.6   1 and 2 link w/ 60m rope   P
120' Ⓐ XP   5.9 pin scars   5.10a
.6   .6-1" pro in scars

many long runners   5.8   5.8

5.7 R   belay takes 50'.75-2'   Ⓒ
1-1.5"   100' rap to 3rd class slab   XX Ⓓ
.6-1.25"   5.6
1-2"   4th and easy 5th class
4th   Ⓑ Ⓒ belay takes 1.5-3'   5.7
3rd class
5.4

3rd

A. Crying Time Again 5.10a R★★★★★
nuts: 1 set; cams: 1 ea .6-2"; quickdraws, long runners

B. Cry Baby 5.8 R-★★★
cams: 1 ea. 0.75-1.5"
4 draws

C. Direct Northwest Face 5.10b★★★★
nuts: 2 ea sml, 1 ea med-lrg; cams: 2 ea .6-2", 1 ea .5, 2.5-3"

D. John Henry 5.10a R-★★★
10 draws, 2 ropes

E. Northwest Books 5.6★★★
nuts: 1 set; cams: 2 ea .6-2", 1 ea 3-4"

F. Beginner's Route 5.4 R-★
cams: 2 ea. 0.6-2"

G. Mega Bleam 5.10a★★★★
cams: 2 ea. 0.6-.75"
7 draws

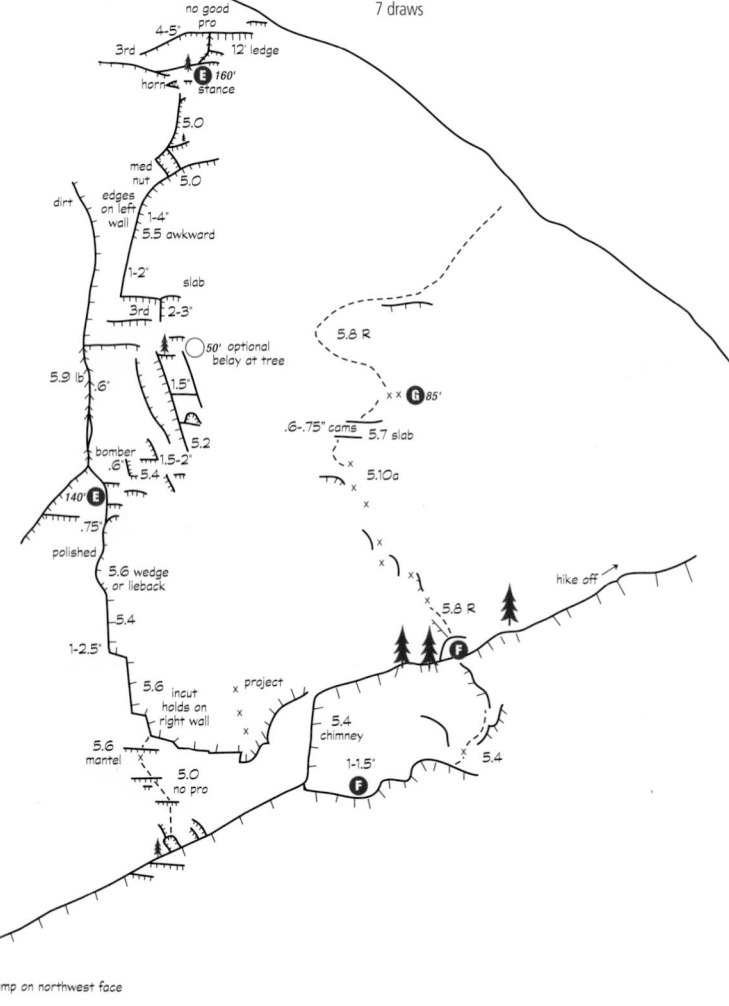

Lembert Dome, Right

A. Truck'N Drive   5.9 R★★★★

FA: Dick Dorworth, Chris Vandiver August 1971.

A beautiful route up a crack to golden face, Truck'n Drive is the most varied and perhaps the best route on the front side of Lembert Dome. Slab and flakes lead to a neat step-over into a leaning hand crack which narrows and leads to a bolted belay on the slab above the arch. The second pitch is not that runout, but every hard move comes a ways out from the last bolt, and thus it's definitely good to be solid on friction climbing.

B. Cucamonga Honey   5.10b R★★★★

FA: Dan Dingle, Mike Lucero, June 1979.

Right off the bat on Cucamonga Honey, pure gold polish slab climbing provides the crux of the route. Fun, runout, and typically toproped from the rap bolts on top of the Water Cracks.

C. Left Water Crack   5.7 R★★★★

FA: Warren Harding, 1950s.

The Left Water Crack was the single most popular route in Tuolumne for decades. The most obvious moderate route in the Meadows, the Left Water Crack is a wide groove with staircase-like steps formed by thousands of years of water coursing down the dome. Awkward, strange, weird, and runout, it's one of the few routes where many people deliberately use their knees. It's possible to start up the right crack then make a big step left to the left crack, or you can start low in the left crack. A couple bolts can be clipped either from the left or right cracks.

D. Right Water Crack   5.8 R★★★

FA: Warren Harding, 1950s.

More shallow and slabby than its neighbor, the Right Water Crack is somewhat harder and more of a slab climb. A couple of bolts can be clipped from either crack.

A Truck' N Drive	**E** Head Rush
C Left Water Crack	**F** Werner's Wiggle

E. Head Rush   5.10a R★★★

FA: unknown, late '70s

Head Rush is a classic slab which is very sustained and thin. All five bolts have been replaced, but two of the bolts had broken years ago, so this was in previous guides with only three bolts.

F. Werner's Wiggle   5.8 R★★★

FA: Werner Braun, August 1969.

A polished groove leads to wandering slabby climbing to join the upper section of the groove. A good, varied route.

A. Truck'N Drive 5.9 R★★★★
nuts: 1 set
cams: 1 ea. 0.6-0.75"
  2 ea. 1-2"

B. Cucamonga Honey 5.10b R★★★★
3 quickdraws

C. Left Water Crack 5.7 R★★★★
4 quickdraws
optional thin nuts

D. Right Water Crack 5.8 R★★★
3 quickdraws
optional thin nuts

E. Head Rush 5.10a R★★★
5 quickdraws

F. Werner's Wiggle 5.8 R★★★
3 draws
nuts: 1 ea. sml
cams: 1 ea. 0.4-0.75"

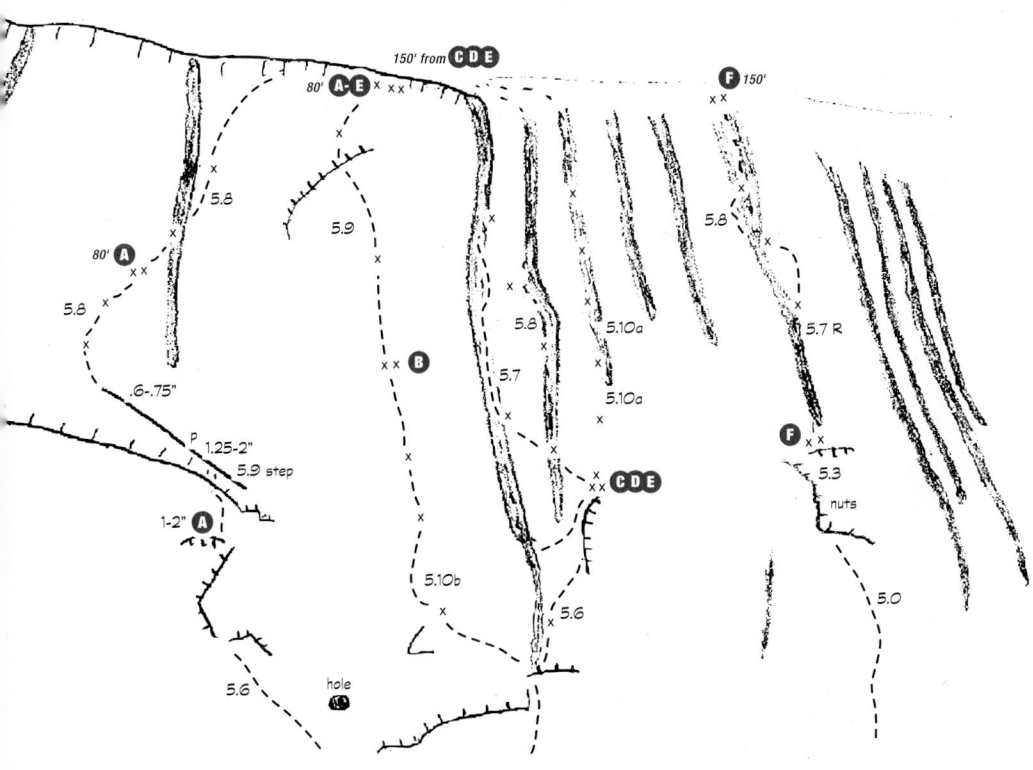

Puppy Dome

Approach time: 2 minutes

Sun exposure: morning to afternoon

Height of routes: 40–100'

Puppy Dome is close to the road and the river yet tucked away in the trees. It has an easy upper section that has long been home to basic climbing classes. A nice short hand crack on the lower section is a great first lead. The side facing the river has a drastically different nature with its overhanging cracks above a cool boulder field. Do or Fly (5.11c) is typically toproped, but the beautiful crack on the right, Horseshoes and Handgrenades (5.12a), traverses too severely to be toproped easily. Grenade Launcher (5.12c) is also easy to set up on toprope, but is simply too hard for most folks.

Approach

Park at the Wilderness Permit Center. In the southwest corner of the parking lot, cross a heavy horse trail, then follow a small trail straight toward the dome 100 yards ahead. Contour around the west side of the dome. Puppy Crack is on the left and obvious at the first clearing. The other climbs are all the way around the dome on the overhung wall above the obvious boulder field.

Descent

Descend Puppy Crack by walking off left. Rappel or walk off the other routes (4th class from Do or Fly, 3rd class from Grenade Launcher and Horseshoes and Handgrenades).

A. Puppy Crack   5.7★★★

FA: unknown.

Great but short finger and hand crack. Be very careful not to damage the small tree at the top with the rope.

B. Battle of the Bulge   5.8 R★★★★

FA: unknown

One of the best single-pitch cracks of its grade in Tuolumne, Battle of the Bulge is the first corner left of the overhung river face of Puppy Dome. Starting with cruxy runout climbing past funky pockets up the dihedral, the climb has a good hand crack middle section, and as the name implies, a challenging hand crack bulge at the top. It is possible to protect the start using tricky Tri-cam placements.

C. Do or Fly   5.11c★★★

FA: Chris Falkenstein and Bob Finn, 1974.

This awesome testpiece climbs hand jams up a steep, right-slanting crack. There are two starts: The left is 5.10d and runout (the original bolt is currently missing) and is dangerous to attempt on toprope due to severe pendulum potential. The right start is 5.11c and excellent once you get past the tricky boulder problem start with a very bad landing. A crash pad is recommended to cover the large sharp flake.

The climb traverses, and therefore it's unsafe to toprope without setting directionals from the few fixed pins. Getting to the bolted anchor requires a very exposed 4th class ledge traverse. The best plan is to get a belay to the anchor, then once the first person is secured to the anchor, the second runs around to the bottom while the first sets up the toprope anchor off the bolts. Then the belayer (now on the ground below) puts the first person on belay and lowers them, leaving them free to swing around wildly trying to clip the directionals. It's a good idea to bring a few 1-2" cams. Even when set up properly, there's a pendulum potential right off the deck, so this climb is not recommended for climbers uncertain of their abilities.

D. Grenade Launcher   5.12c★★★

FA: John Bachar, 1980s.

Start up wherever you can get off the ground (two optional starts) and climb through the roofs above. The protection bolt is a good directional but is hard to clip. It's difficult to set directionals that allow you to get back on – if you fall, start again from the ground.

E. Horseshoes and Handgrenades 5.12a★★★★

FFA: Dale Bard, 1978.

The obvious, beautiful, right-leaning off-finger crack on the right. If overhung ringlocks are your thing, go for it! It may be possible to set a toprope if you really work at it, but you might as well lead it. On-sight free soloed by Peter Croft.

A. Puppy Crack 5.7★★★ nuts: 1 set; cams: 1 ea .75-3"

B. Battle of the Bulge 5.8 R★★★★
cams: 1 ea. 0.6-.75", 2 ea 1-3" nuts: 1 set tri-cams useful for pockets at start

C. Do or Fly 5.11c★★★★ nuts: 1 set; cams: 2 ea .6-2"; many draws

D. Grenade Launcher 5.12c★★★ 1 set, cams 2 ea 0.4-1.25", 1 ea 1.5-3"

E. Horseshoes and Handgrenades 5.12a★★★★ nuts: 1 set; cams: 2 ea .4-3", 1 ea 3.5-4"

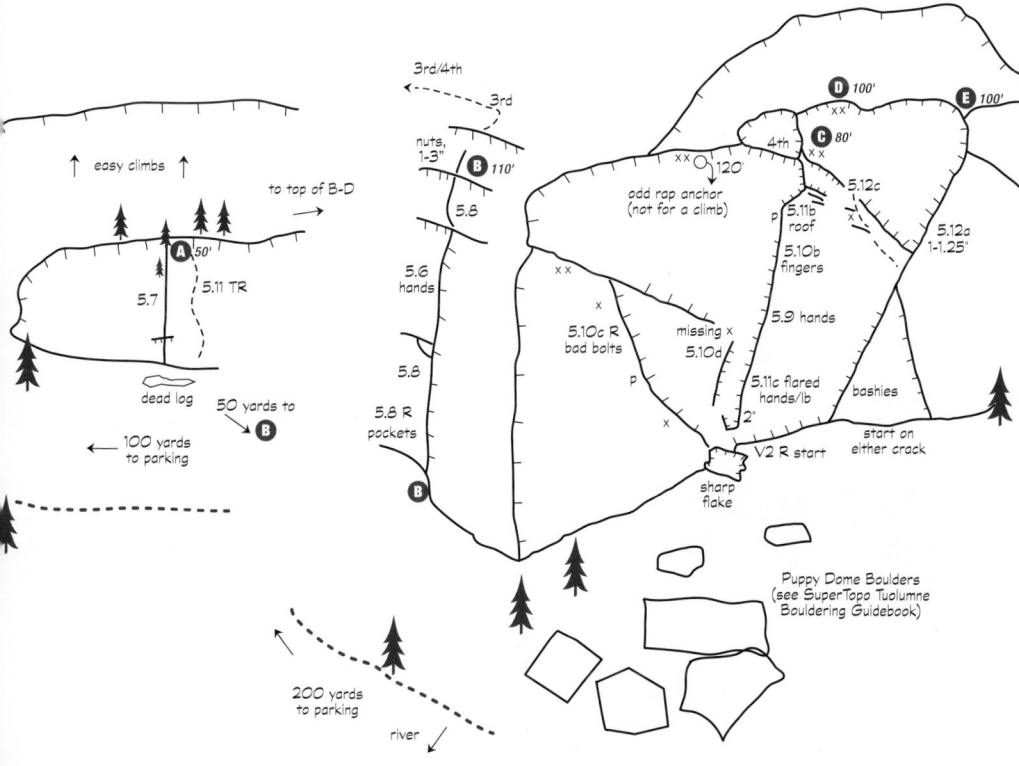

Cathedral Peak

Cathedral Peak is not only the most striking peak visible from Tuolumne Meadows, it is one of the best 5.6 alpine rock climbs anywhere. Everything about the experience is incredible: the approach, the rock quality, the climbing, and, most of all, the summit. Not surprisingly this is also one of Tuolumne's most popular climbs, so be prepared to share the experience with others.

Approach

Park on the side of Highway 120 at the Cathedral Lakes trailhead. Follow the John Muir Trail for about eight minutes, passing a trail to the left (this is the wrong trail). The trail will bend right, ascend 30 granite steps and then cut left. After 200 feet, find a well-traveled, three-foot-wide, sandy climbers' trail that heads off left (about 15 feet before a stone runoff diverter and often blocked by logs so that tourists stay on the John Muir Trail). Follow this trail, most of which parallels Budd Creek, for about 45 minutes (1.5 miles) until the trail cuts right up a slope. The trail continues and eventually splits several times. All branches lead to the route, but if you stay to the right,

make sure not to go too steeply upward as you approach the rock – you may stray onto the steep, sandy descent trails.

Descent

From the summit, downclimb without a rope or downlead the final 30 feet. While this section is only 4th class, most will want a belay. The first climber should place pieces of pro intended to catch downward falls and clip them to the rope. Then the second will downclimb on lead, belayed by the first. You will be downclimbing the original line of ascent done by John Muir (without a rope and in heavy boots) in 1869.

From below the summit, move away from the climbing route on 3rd class. Once on a big ledge, traverse 15 feet down right, then down left for 150 feet on 3rd class ledges, then work back right on 4th class ledges and slabs. From the base of the ledges and slabs, walk north to a ridge. Walk the ridge for 100 feet and then drop down (3rd class) to heavily used sandy trails and hike back down to the base. Walk out the way you came in. Snow and ice in very early or late season can be treacherous near the top.

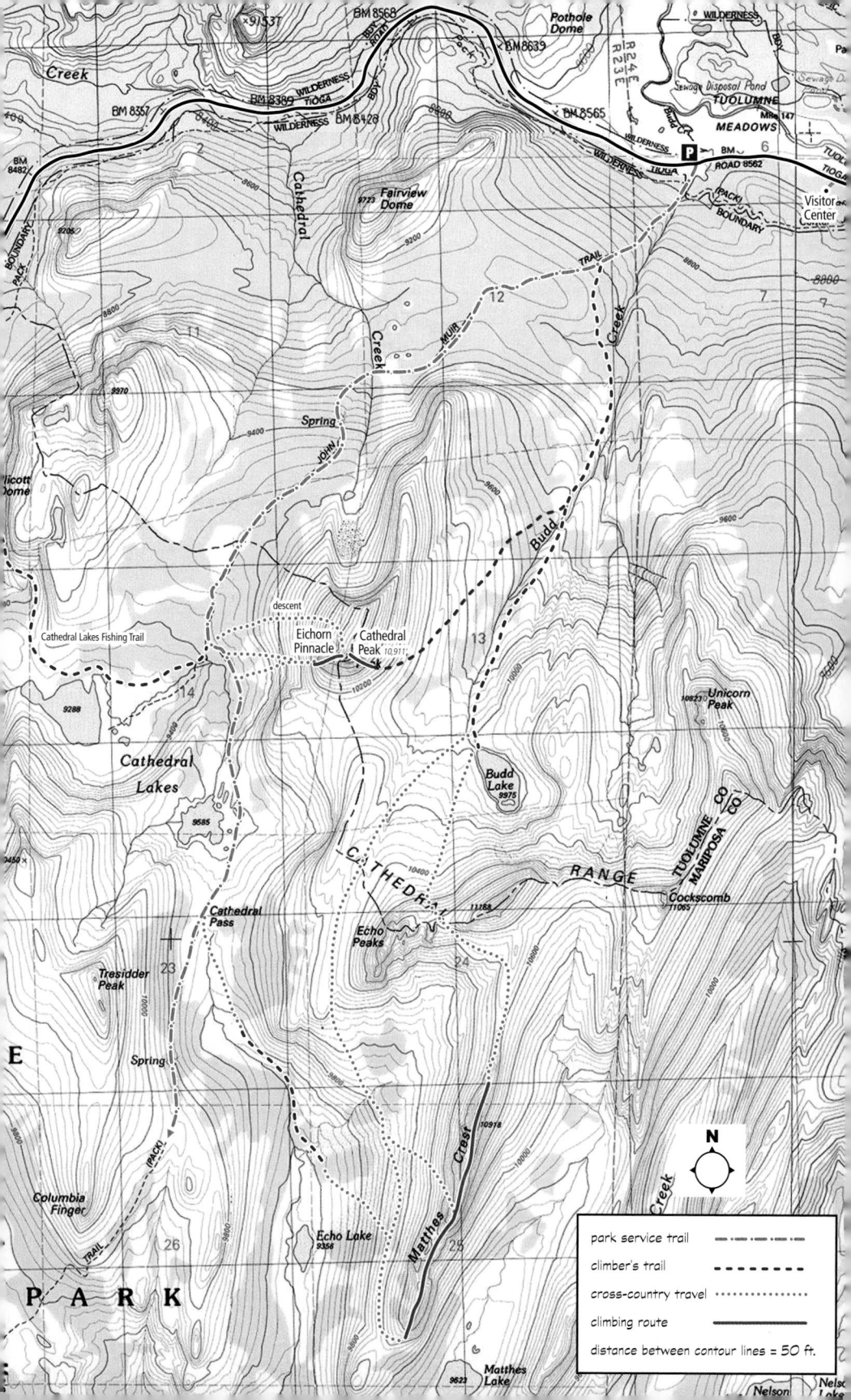

Southeast Buttress

5.6★★★★★

Time to climb route:	**2–4 hours**
Approach time:	**1.5 hours**
Descent time:	**1.5–2 hours**
Sun exposure:	**sunrise to afternoon**
Height of route:	**700'**

Cathedral Peak is one of the most aesthetic routes in Tuolumne. The climb consists of five pitches of easy and moderate crack and face climbing in a perfect setting. The first few pitches are on low-angle terrain that gradually steepens and becomes more difficult. Because of its quality and moderate grade, this is one of the most crowded routes in Tuolumne. Luckily there are a number of variations if you need to pass a party.

FA: Chuck Wilts and Spencer Austin, mid-1940s.

History

John Muir didn't take long to seek out the most beautiful peak of the Tuolumne region. On his first trip to the Meadows, in 1869, he strolled up through virgin forests (no John Muir Trail then!) and scrambled to the top of what he named Cathedral Peak. The last bit was bona fide class 4, making it the hardest climb yet done in the country. Muir said afterwards, "This I may say is the first time I have been at church in California."

Muir, naturally, chose the easiest way, and his was the only route on the peak for the next 76 years. Along came Chuck Wilts, one of the Valley giants of the 1940s. An electrical engineer, Wilts was fortunate to spend the war years on Army/Navy rocket projects in Southern California. This meant that he was able to get away often to climb in the Sierra. His wife, Ellen, herself a brilliant climber, remembers his gear, ancient indeed by modern standards: "tennis shoes, hiking boots and even, on occasion, nailed boots. His clothing consisted of army-surplus full-cut climbing pants, a pullover parka, and a brimmed shade hat."

Wilts and Spencer Austin often climbed in the Valley on weekends in the early 1940s, and they were almost the only people in the Valley, with climbers and tourists alike involved in the war effort. Super climbers, they were the first to free the Regular Route on the Higher Cathedral Spire (1944). Later (1946 and 1947) they made valiant attempts on the Arrow Chimney, only to lose the route to John Salathé and Ax Nelson.

Virtually nothing is known about the history of the Wilts/Austin route on the Southeast Buttress of Cathedral Peak, even the year of the ascent. They never mentioned the climb in any major publication and, being modest men, never bragged about their soon-to-be classic route. The only clue – seven trivial words – appears in a mimeographed Sierra Club newsletter dated September 9, 1943, which states that in late July the pair "climbed the south side of Cathedral Peak." This could well have been the route we are talking about.

Whatever the year, it seems safe to say that they got the idea for their route by looking at that amazing profile of the buttress seen from many places along the Tioga Road east of the Meadows. It would be hard for a climber to scope that view and not want to be up there. Why no one had done the buttress in the 1930s is unclear, except that the pioneers back then usually sought out unclimbed summits rather than put up new routes.

By the mid-1950s the route was a standard one, middling 5th class, and done by a few people on virtually every Sierra Club trip to Tuolumne. I did it when I was 16, in the company of an even-less experienced 17-year-old. We joyfully pounded our soft pitons into the decomposed cracks, taking hours (it

SUPERTOPO

TUOLUMNE FREE CLIMBS: SUPERTOPOS

seemed) to get them out, all twisted and scarred. Our excitement mounted as we got close to the top, manteling those big blocks of ultra-clean high-country granite. On top of our first "big" climb, we realized we had become rockclimbers as well as mountaineers.

– *Steve Roper*

Strategy

There are no real routes up the Southeast Face, just an incredible sea of features that can be pieced together in an infinite number of variations. Because the face often has 10-15 people on it at a time, it's important to utilize these variations to avoid bottlenecks and slower parties. We highlight three main ways to climb the face, but you may create your own climb that combines pitches from all three. Route A gets most of the traffic, and although slightly easier it is no more classic than routes B and C. In fact, many pitches on routes B and C are considered the best on the face.

To avoid crowds start early or, if you can climb fast, get a late start. Often if you start climbing before 8 a.m. or after 3 p.m. you will have most of the face to yourself. Because of the numerous climbers on the route, definitely wear a helmet and be careful of loose knobs and loose rock, especially 100 feet above The Chimney.

The summit is a 10,940-foot lightning rod and it's a miracle that no climbers have been killed by lightning. A climber was struck in summer 2000 and only luck, his partners, and the Tuolumne SAR team were between him and the afterlife (see *Accidents in North American Mountaineering 2001* for details). Puffy clouds at the trailhead mean one thing: go climb something else.

For those who finish early, an amazing, improbable, and short 5.4 route will take you to the top of Eichorn's Pinnacle. Hopefully, you'll have a friend to take pics because the spectacular picture of you on top of Eichorn's Pinnacle, taken from the notch, is one to show off to family and friends. (See the SuperTopo for Eichorn's Pinnacle for more info.)

Before you start climbing, hang your backpack and any other gear in a tree as marmots will eat anything you leave at the base, including packs with no food.

Retreat

High Sierra thunderstorms and lightning sneak up on many Cathedral Peak climbers; be prepared in case you have to retreat. It is possible to retreat with just one 50m or 60m rope. However, two ropes will make retreat much faster and require leaving less gear. Many perfect nut placements and natural threads/horns mean that even a multi-pitch retreat will be reasonable. Of course, if a thunderstorm is on you just leave the dang cams and live to zap some food in a microwave, instead of learning what it feels like to be zapped yourself.

To retreat from the base of The Chimney, walk right on the ledge, rappel off a slung flake (see topo) for two rappels with one 50m rope. If it's getting dark and you just need to get to the top quick, there are many spots on Pitches 4 and 5 where you can bail off left onto 4th and easy 5th class terrain.

The view of Cathedral Peak from the approach to the south side.

Rack

nuts: 1-2 sets
cams: 1-2 ea .6-2.5"
many slings

A. Standard Route 5.6

B., C. Variations 5.7

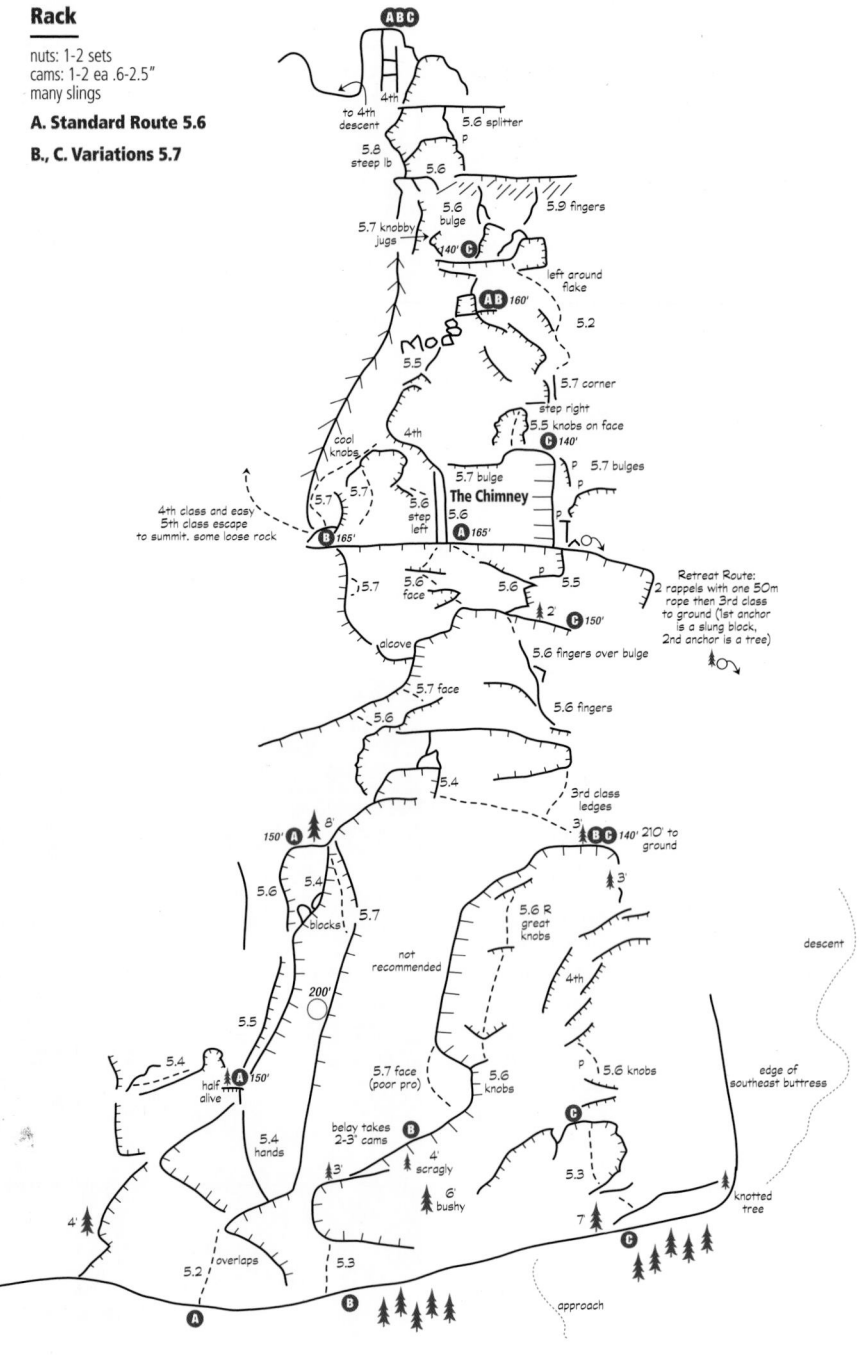

Eichorn's Pinnacle

Justin Bastien enjoys a winter ascent of Cathedral Peak. (Corey Rich)

One of the most spectacular spires of the Tuolumne region lies on the western flank of Cathedral Peak. Eichorn's Pinnacle, named after Jules Eichorn, one of the first ascensionists in 1931, must be the most photographed splinter of rock in Tuolumne. Seen from near the summit of the main peak, Eichorn's is beautifully outlined against Lower Cathedral Lake. It's worth doing just to get a picture.

— Steve Roper

Approach

West Pillar

Allow about 1.5 hours for the approach. Park on the side of Highway 120 at the Cathedral Lakes trailhead. Follow the John Muir Trail for about 2.5 miles and after a long gradual climb switchbacking up a hill, the trail will head down a hill toward Cathedral Lakes. At this point, leave the trail to the left and walk cross-country to the base of the west face of Eichorn's Pinnacle. The route starts up the obvious wide crack.

North Face

Most climbers approach the North Face route by first climbing Cathedral Peak, then downclimbing and traversing 150 yards to Eichorn's Pinnacle. If not climbing Cathedral Peak, follow the approach for the West Pillar, but instead of walking to the base of the West Pillar stay to the left (north) and walk up 3rd class slabs to the notch between Eichorn's Pinnacle and Cathedral Peak.

Descent

A 70-foot rappel from the summit leads to 3rd class ledges. From here there are two descent options:

1) Scramble down 3rd class slabs back toward Cathedral Lake and the John Muir Trail.

2) Walk up a few hundred yards and pick up the descent for Cathedral Peak (see Cathedral Peak SuperTopo page 82).

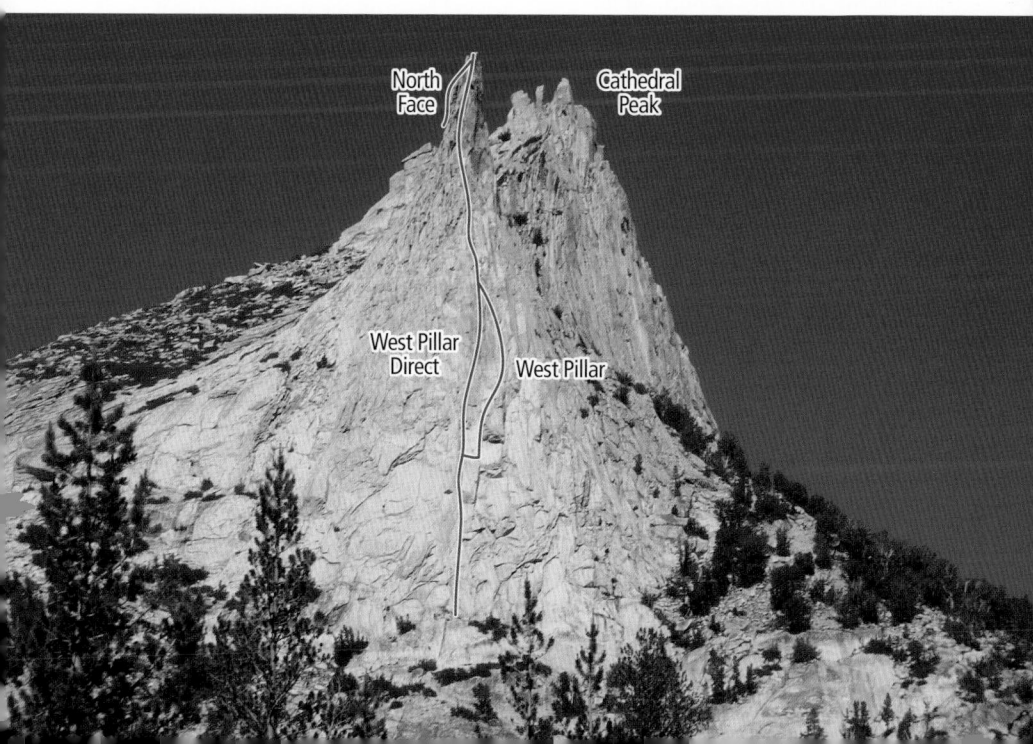

North Face

Cathedral Peak

West Pillar Direct

West Pillar

West Pillar Direct 5.10b★★★★
West Pillar 5.9★★★

Time to climb route: **2–4 hours**

Approach time: **1.5-2 hours**

Descent time: **1.5 hours**

Sun exposure: **noon to sunset**

Height of route: **700'**

A few hundred feet from the summit of Cathedral Peak stands Eichorn's Pinnacle – one of the most spectacular features in Tuolumne. While Cathedral Peak is an outstanding climb in its own right, combine it with Eichorn's Pinnacle and you will have ticked two of the most classic summits in Tuolumne.

The North Face, the most popular line, is one of the most exhilarating 5.4 climbs you will ever do. The West Pillar climbs five good pitches of sustained 5.8 and 5.9 (or a 5.10b variation) and joins up with the North Face before the summit.

FA: Gary Colliver and Mike Cohen, 7/72.
West Pillar Direct: : Alan Bartlett and Don Reid, 1979.

History

The North Face route was first climbed by Glen Dawson and Jules Eichorn on July 24, 1931. According to *Sierra Classics,* "As Eichorn and Dawson did not learn proper belay techniques until the next week at the Sierra Club's Underhill Camp, the ascent of Eichorn's Pinnacle was a daring adventure." In addition, the pair made the ascent without pitons and wearing tennis shoes. While this ascent was bold, a few years later Eichorn would make ascents of two far more dangerous and technical routes: Higher Cathedral Spire and Lower Cathedral Spire in Yosemite Valley.

The West Pillar of Eichorn's Pinnacle

was first climbed in 1972 by Gary Colliver and Mike Cohen. On an attempt to repeat the original route in 1979, Don Reid and Alan Bartlett got off route and accidentally established the popular 5.10b variation.

– Chris McNamara

Strategy

There are rarely crowds on this climb. During the normally cool Tuolumne temperatures, it is better to start the climb after noon when the route goes into the sun. This route is well-protected even in the wide sections.

Despite the ominous look of the wide first pitch, there are only a few short offwidth sections that can be stemmed around on knobs. After the first pitch there are two alternatives: the standard route traverses right while the 5.10b variation continues straight up. The direct variation has some loose rock, but has better climbing than the 5.9 route.

For a great linkup, start the morning with Cathedral Peak, then descend the 3rd class slabs to the West Pillar of Eichorn's Pinnacle.

Retreat

It is possible to retreat with just one rope, but you will have to leave gear. From the second belay on the standard route it's easy to bail off to the shoulder with one rappel and some downclimbing. From the top of the third pitch walk off on mellow 3rd and 4th class ledges.

A. North Face   5.4★★★★

FA: Glen Dawson and Jules Eichorn, 7/31.

This climb starts with a traverse off a large ledge onto tremendously exposed terrain. Though the moves are well-protected and rated 5.4, the exposure will get the blood pumping of even the most experienced climbers. The climb ends on a beautiful summit making a fantastic encore to climbing Cathedral Peak.

You may want to climb this route in two pitches to avoid rope drag. For a spectacular photo, have friends on the summit of Cathedral Peak take a shot of you while you stand on the summit of Eichorn's Pinnacle.

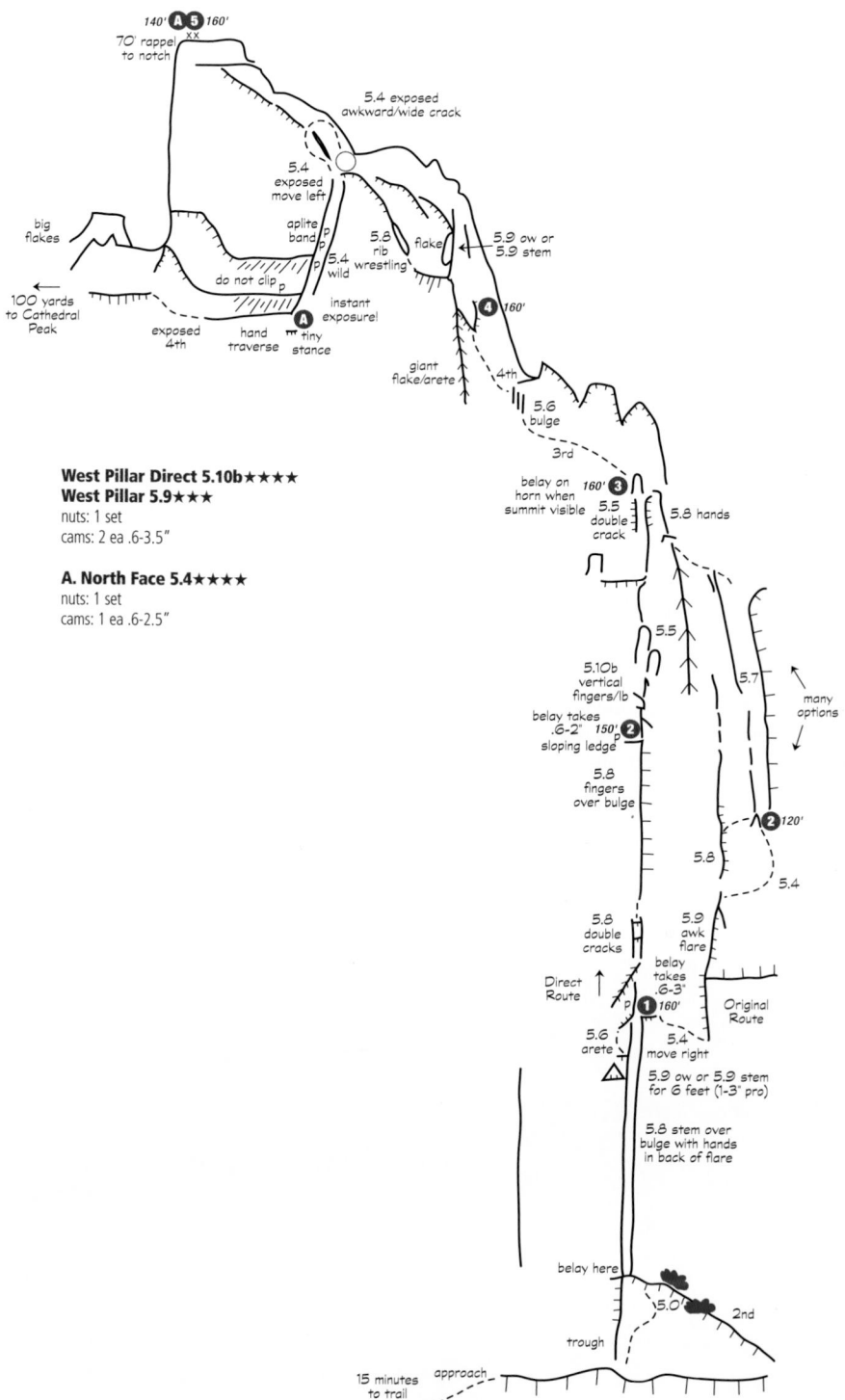

140' **A** **5** 160'
70' rappel
to notch

5.4 exposed
awkward/wide crack

5.4
exposed
move left

big
flakes

aplite
band

5.8
rib
wrestling

flake

5.9 ow or
5.9 stem

100 yards
to Cathedral
Peak

do not clip

5.4
wild

instant
exposure!

4 160'

exposed
4th

hand
traverse

tiny
stance

giant
flake/arete

4th

5.6
bulge

3rd

West Pillar Direct 5.10b★★★★
West Pillar 5.9★★★
nuts: 1 set
cams: 2 ea .6-3.5"

belay on
horn when
summit visible

160' **3**

5.5
double
crack

5.8 hands

A. North Face 5.4★★★★
nuts: 1 set
cams: 1 ea .6-2.5"

5.5

5.7

many
options

5.10b
vertical
fingers/lb
belay takes
.6-2" 150'
sloping ledge

2

5.8
fingers
over bulge

2 120'

5.8

5.4

5.8
double
cracks

5.9
awk
flare

Direct
Route

belay
takes
.6-3"

1 160'

Original
Route

5.6
arete

5.4
move right

5.9 ow or 5.9 stem
for 6 feet (1-3" pro)

5.8 stem over
bulge with hands
in back of flare

belay here

5.0

2nd

trough

15 minutes
to trail

approach

Matthes Crest

Matthes Crest is a true knife-edge ridge; a long fin of rock sculpted by glaciers. And unlike most such ridges, it is not a low point between peaks, but a completely independent formation. High and spectacular in a region of sweeping expanses of granite, Matthes Crest is unique. The entire climb is above 10,000', and tops out at 10,918'.

Approach

Park on the side of Highway 120 at the Cathedral Lakes trailhead. Follow the John Muir Trail (JMT) for about eight minutes, passing a trail to the left (this is the wrong trail). The JMT will bend right, ascend 30 granite steps and then cut left. After 200 feet, find a well traveled three-foot-wide sandy climbers' trail that heads off left (about 15 feet before a stone runoff diverter and often blocked by logs so that hikers stay on the John Muir Trail). Follow this trail – most of which parallels Budd Creek – for about 1.5 miles to a creek crossing where a small trail heads up on the right bank of the creek. This is the Cathedral Peak climbers' trail. Instead of taking it, cross the logs and head up the main trail on the west side toward Budd Lake. From the west end of the lake head south and a little west contouring around the steep slopes of Echo Peaks. When Matthes Crest is visible, descend a little and walk cross-country for about 30 minutes to the south end.

An alternate approach is to simply take the JMT to Cathedral Pass, then hike down the east side of the meadow to a use trail which leads to Echo Lake., and then hike straight up to the south end of the Crest.

A third approach, but only for those who are familiar with the area, is to park at Medlicott Dome, take the Cathedral Lakes fishing trail to Lower Cathedral Lake, then once past the lake, cut cross-country up and right to Upper Cathedral Lake, joining the JMT just before that lake.

Descent

If rappelling off the North Summit, either retrace your steps by the Echo Peaks or head west to the large meadow, join the John Muir Trail at Cathedral Pass, and hike north on the JMT. While this second option looks attractive to those wary of the hike back up through the Echo Peaks, it is substantially longer in both distance and time. For those finishing the entire Crest, it's easiest to hike back by the Echo Peaks and Budd Lake.

Traverse From South to North

descent

approach

Traverse from South to North 5.7★★★★★

Time to climb route: **3–6 hours**

Approach time: **3-4 hours**

Descent time: **2-3 hours**

Sun exposure: **morning shade for first 3 pitches**

Height of route: **500' (length is 1 mile)**

The Matthes Crest is one of the most classic knife-edge ridges anywhere. Stunning scenery, fun climbing, and stomach-churning exposure combine to make Matthes Crest a true gem. Not only that, Matthes Crest is LONG. Most parties take a long day to only do the southern two-thirds of the ridge and rappel off of the North Summit, but the harder climbing to the north is even more spectacular.

FA: Chuck and Ellen Wilts, 1947.

History

No tourist has ever set eyes on Matthes Crest. A generalization, yes, but it depends on the definition of a tourist. Mine: one who goes through a national park quickly, never getting more than a few miles from the road. Matthes Crest, hidden away south of Tuolumne Meadows, is visible from no road and from no close trail. Only those who look directly south or directly north from close up will find this stupendous blade of granite worthy of attention. The writer and climber Michael Cohen has enjoyed a long love affair with the peak and recently wrote, "When you get up high, it sometimes appears as a striking, dramatic form blazing white in the sun, but on cloudy days Matthes Crest seems to fade into the bare bones of the region, being only one small part of a vast collection of exposed granite ribs that punctuate the domes and peaks of the Tuolumne region." Cohen also called the formation "a knife edge, a serrated white cleaver, great and wondrous." How true!

Once called Echo Crest, the blade attracted 1930s climbers looking for virgin summits. On July 26, 1931 Jules Eichorn, Walter Brem, and Glen Dawson made the first ascent. In their concise words, "We climbed the highest point from the east. It also looked possible from the west. The rock is weathered so as to be rotten and insecure. We found no record of former ascent."

Around 1949 the peak was christened after the Sierra's most eminent geologist, Dr. François Matthes, who had recently died. Wrote Reid Moran at the time, "He was the rare man of science who, through the clarity and simplicity of his prose, made his great knowledge of the geological story available not merely to his professional colleagues but also to the mountain-loving layman." Matthes wrote extensively about the Sierra and invented the term "cockscomb" to describe the rooster-comb-like formations that so dominate the mountains immediately south of Tuolumne Meadows.

Chuck Wilts (first free ascent of the Higher Spire; first ascent of the Southeast Buttress of Cathedral Peak) made the first ascent of the now-classic south-to-north traverse in 1947 with his favorite climbing partner, his bride Ellen. Typical of the pair, they didn't bother to write anything about their route. For them, it was just another wonderful day in the mountains.

The route appeared in the first High Sierra guide, in 1954, but the description didn't much help. Here it is in full: "Ascend the south arête above a group of pines and traverse along the ridge." Even worse is the description from my 1972 guidebook: "The most pleasant route is a complete traverse of the ridge from south to north; this is 5.3 and a true classic." R. J. Secor's 1992 guidebook added more information – but it was still vague: "Four Class 4-5 pitches lead to the top of the crest. Many spectacular and enjoyable Class 3-4 pitches over slabs, pinnacles, and knife-edges lead to the base of the north peak." Secor rated the climb 5.6. My 5.3 rating came from the memory of a crazy cragrat who did the route unroped as a teenager. Me.

– *Steve Roper*

Strategy

The standard route done on Matthes is the traverse from the South end to the North Summit, then rappel. This section is predominantly 3rd class. The last section of the ridge is much more involved, with mostly 5th class climbing that many consider to be the best climbing along the Crest. This section is awesome, but much tougher, with the follower often in more danger than the leader. No details on the route finding of the last section will be presented here, since those strong enough to do the whole Crest in a day shouldn't need that beta.

Despite the long approach, Matthes often has a line. Luckily, it's usually easy to pass people. The climb is at least 18 pitches if you belay every pitch. Most parties, however, will only belay the handful of 5th class pitches and simul-climb or free solo the 3rd and 4th class sections. The climb can take as little as three hours if simul-climbed and over 12 hours if every pitch is belayed. Two ropes are needed for the descent from the north summit, making lightweight double ropes useful. Beware of loose rock, especially in the first few pitches.

Rappelling from the south summit is the most common mistake – it's unusual for the ropes not to get snagged. Instead, climb back down the ridgetop for 100 feet then traverse easy ledges on the east side of the ridge. Place pro to protect followers. Most parties rappel from the north summit (two double-length rappels to the west); continuing north presents increasing difficulties and great climbing but poor protection, especially for the follower.

The Matthes Crest is highly exposed and should not be attempted in any sort of inclement weather, especially during the common Sierra afternoon thunderstorms.

Slower parties should consider backpacking in and camping at Echo Lakes to the west of Matthes Crest. A small number of overnight permits are available at the Tuolumne Meadows Wilderness Permit Center (see introduction).

Retreat

It is possible to retreat off of the west side of Matthes Crest by leaving slings and pro at almost any point. Care should be taken to avoid rope snags – multiple short rappels are better than long rappels. Do not attempt to rappel the taller, steeper east side of the Crest. Many parties have retreated the west side over the years, and routes up the side have also been done, so it is common to find old nuts, slings, and pitons – do not trust these alone!

The start of the Traverse from South to North.

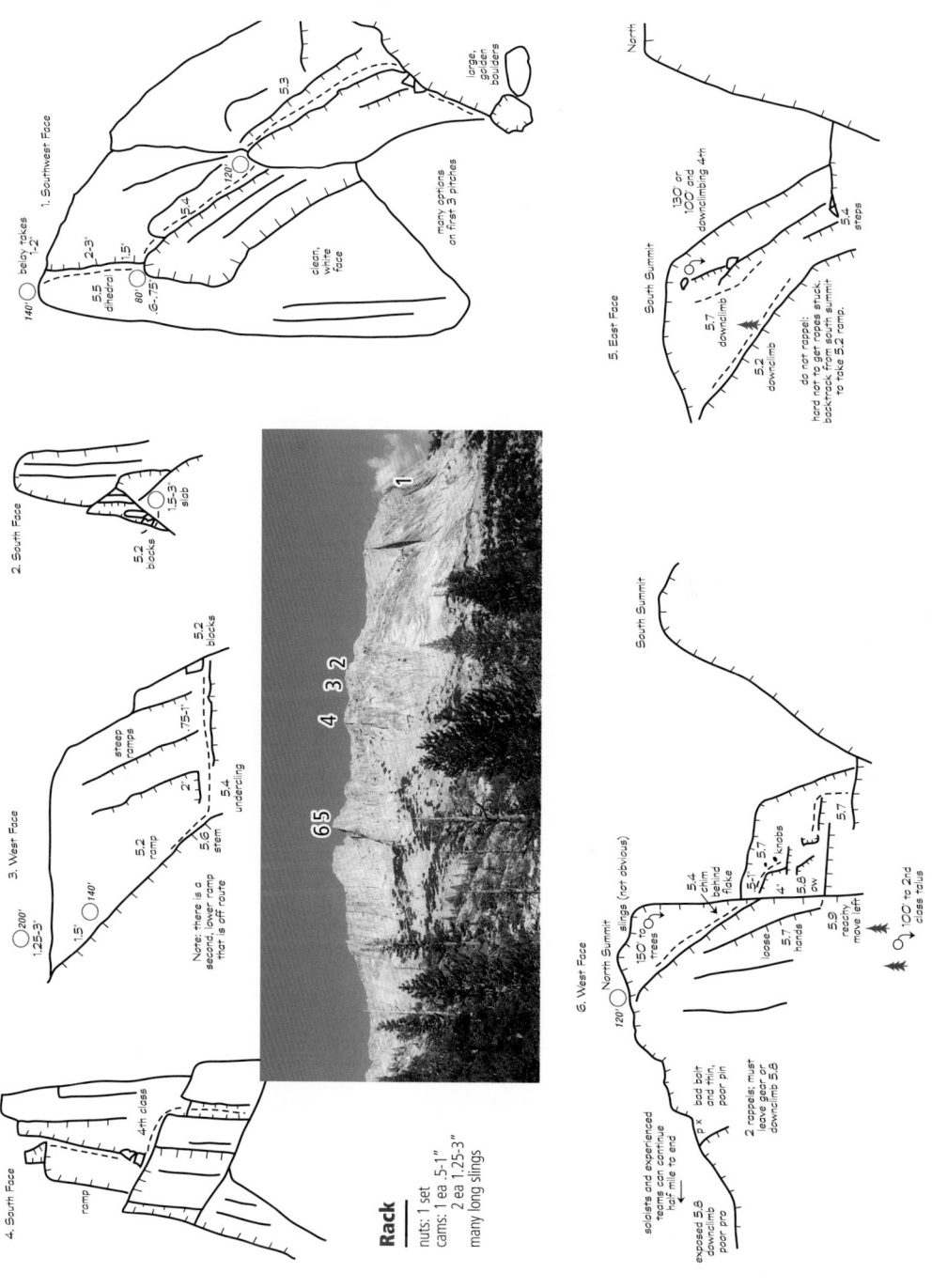

Anduril 5.10b R-★★★★

Time to climb route: **5–9 hours**

Approach time: **3-4 hours**

Descent time: **2-3 hours**

Sun exposure: **morning sun**

Height of route: **500'**

FA: Greg Barnes, Karin Wuhrmann, Florence Scholl, Maki Grossnick, September 2007.

A cool new route up the east face of the south end of Matthes Crest, Anduril offers a more challenging start to the majestic Matthes Crest south-to-north traverse. Anduril has lots of featured fins, stemming, and knobby face climbing with tremendous exposure in a wild setting.

The first 3 pitches have bolted anchors, and with the combination of face climbing and spaced pro in cracks, a light rack and a good supply of long draws are sufficient.

While not particularly runout, Anduril has several sections with runout 5.8 and a few harder sections with slightly poor pro. While there are short sections of offwidth, all but a couple short wide crack sections are avoided by climbing featured fins.

Strategy

The route starts from the lower ledge at the edge of the drop-off. If the ledge has a belay bolt, you are too high (the ledge with the belay bolt is the start of Narsil). The first pitch is the crux, with runout face climbing off the deck, flakes, and two small roofs. Two bolts protect the crux second roof.

The second pitch starts with a handcrack and fin, then transfers left to a slightly runout bit up double fins to a flared shallow hand crack and a bolted belay.

The third pitch climbs up and then steps down right, and reachy climbing (slung horn for pro) gains a flared chimney between fins. A bolt protects the stemming/arête climbing up to a handcrack and a bolted anchor on a ledge to the right.

The last pitch climbs up neat grey and gold rock, then walks right on a two-foot ledge, and climbs the featured arête/fin, stemming back left occasionally for pro.

At the very top of the pitch, just before reaching the crest, take care to avoid large loose blocks on the left.

Anduril sees morning to early afternoon sun.

Retreat

Don't try to rappel the route after Pitch 2, due to the traversing nature of the route and many rope-catching spikes and notches below the route. It is possible to retreat from the summit by climbing left and down a rope-length (south) from the notch, then by leaving slings, rappel to horns down the usual start of Matthes Crest. However, there are many horns and such a rappel has a high chance of getting the rope stuck.

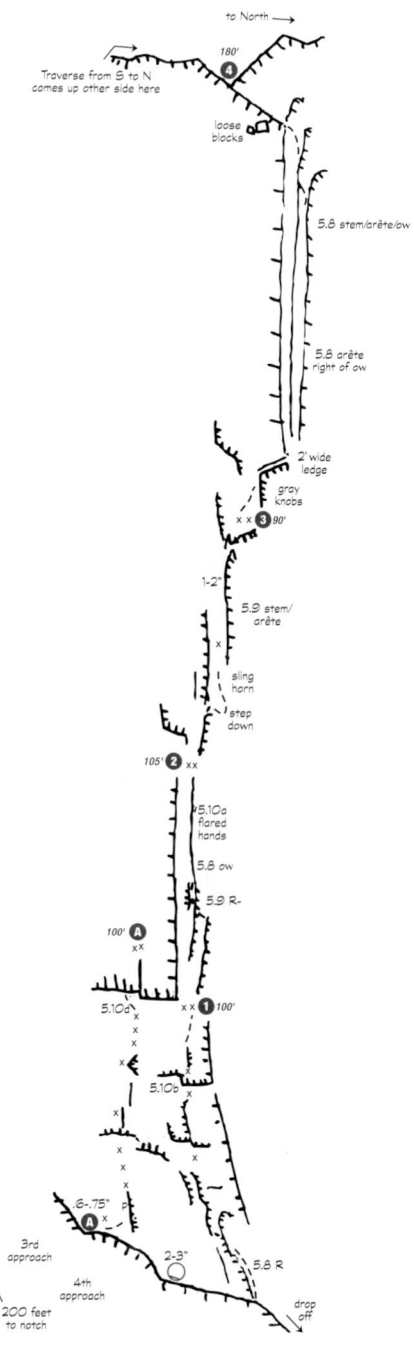

Anduril 5.10b R-★★★★
nuts: 1 set
cams: 1 ea. 0.3-4", optional 5", optional extra 2-3"
slings for horns

A. Narsil 5.10d★★
cams: 2 ea. 0.5-1"
draws

A. Narsil   5.10d★★

FA: Greg Barnes, Florence Scholl, 8/08.

Narsil starts from the upper ledge about 30 feet above the start ledge for Anduril. Thin cams plus a belay bolt provide the anchor. Climb right, then follow bolts and thin cracks up a sustained face to the crux moves past the last bolt to gain the roof with a fixed nut, and a final pumpy lieback past the roof to easy terrain and the anchor. The FA team intends to continue the route higher. Several pro bolts are currently ¼" with small custom hangers. Rap with a single 60m rope.

Razor Back

Razor Back is the upper and larger of the two walls left of Fairview Dome (the lower is Whale's Back, home to some severely runout, hard slab routes). It connects to the upper right side of Marmot Dome, the dome directly above the big parking area at Pothole Dome. Home to a few obscure old routes, Razor Back has seen some recent route activity on the clean steep slab at the end nearest Fairview Dome. A large snowbank at the base is common in early season.

Approach

There are various ways to approach Razor Back. One approach is to park at the Gunks bouldering, follow the trail towards the Gunks for 50 yards, then contour left and up to gain an open granite ridge (the top of Whale's Back). Hike up this, then through the forest when you're almost to Fairview Dome. The other easy approach is to park at Pothole Dome, then hike steeply uphill to Marmot Dome, then follow the right side of the wall to Razor Back.

A. Dastardly Rascal   5.8★★

FA: Bryan Law, Greg Barnes, September 2008.

Fun climb which wanders left up the line of least resistance.160-foot pitch, 130-foot rap.

B. Flash of the Blade   5.10a R-★★★★

FA: Bryan Law, Linda Jarit, September 2008.

An improbable new three-pitch route that climbs up the steep golden face in the middle of Razor Back, Flash of the Blade tackles the imposing wall left of the only old route on this part of the wall, First Verse, an Ed Barry 5.10d R from 1985. Flash of the Blade takes golden edges, knobs, and features up the face at a surprisingly moderate grade.

The first pitch starts with a short heady section on tan knobs and features to a bolt 25 feet up, then climbs to a small cam placement and undercling/slab right up a shallow dihedral past a bolt to two large holes on golden rock. From the holes, climb straight up on beautiful golden edges and slab to a ledge and bolted anchor just below the big flake undercling/crack (which is hollow). There is a 5.9 section with a 15-20 foot runout in the middle of the golden slab. The second pitch starts up runout easy knobs past a small roof, then continues straight up the face past a gear placement in the top of the flake and four bolts. The final pitch climbs up past seven bolts and some runouts. Rap with one 70m or two ropes. Two 60m ropes just reach the ground from the second belay. Make sure not to lower the rope into the flake from the second pitch belay – coil and toss it to the side.

C. Slasher   5.9★★★★

FA: Bryan Law, Linda Jarit, September 2008.

An excellent and well-protected face route up slick tan slab to thin golden edges. Crux near top.

D. Chop the Hogs   5.7★★

FA: Brian Bennett, Greg Barnes, August 2008.

This is a fun little climb that's a good warm-up for the area. Three bolts protect featured face and slab to an easy section past a flake (optional 2" cam) to a ledge and the bolted anchor. An old and seriously runout Ed Barry route, First Verse (5.10d R), starts up the handcrack flake to the left and continues up the face above. If you look closely you can spot an old bolt above a grey knob about 20 feet left of the anchor.

E. Metalhead   5.10c★★★★

FA: Bryan Law, Greg Barnes, August 2008.

A quality, very sustained steep edging slab up cool golden and black rock. Starting with easy knobs, then a short runout on some friction, Metalhead gets progressively more difficult for the first 60 feet. At the 4th bolt, take a rest, because except for one not-so-great rest spot, the next 70 feet are sustained low 5.10 thin slab. The route is very tightly bolted after the 4th bolt. Grab the tree at the top and climb around the right side to keep the rope from running over the tree; a two-bolt anchor is on the big ledge just right of the tree. Two ropes required to rappel.

SUPERTOPO

A. Dastardly Rascal 5.8★★
6 bolts 160' pitch, 130' rap

B. Flash of the Blade 5.10a R-★★★★
cams: 1 ea. 1.25", 1.5"
7 draws
one 70m rope or two ropes

C. Slasher 5.9★★★★
9 draws 90'

D. Chop the Hogs 5.7★★
cams: 1 ea. 2"
3 draws

E. Metalhead 5.10c★★★★
12 draws

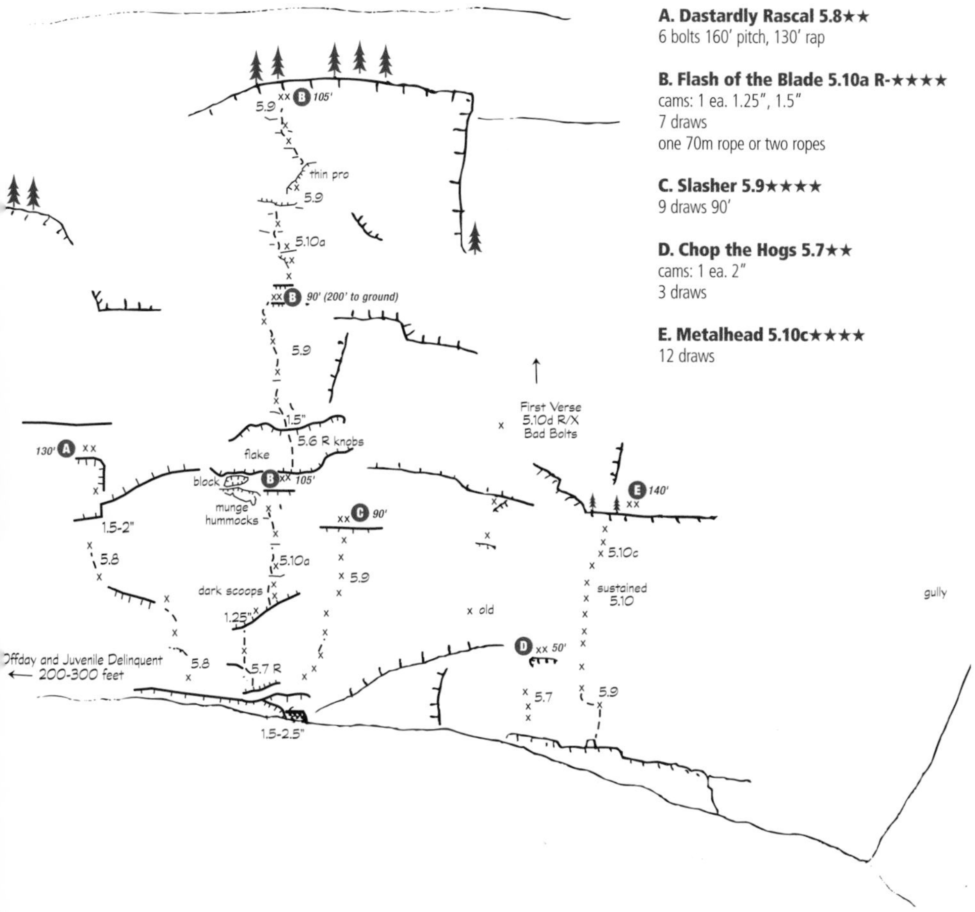

Labels on topo:
5.9 · B 105'
thin pro
5.9
5.10a
B 90' (200' to ground)
5.9
First Verse 5.10d R/X Bad Bolts
130' · A
flake
1.5"
5.6 R knobs
block
B 105'
munge hummocks
E 140'
C 90'
1.5-2"
5.8
5.10a
dark scoops
5.9
5.10c
sustained 5.10
gully
Offday and Juvenile Delinquent ← 200-300 feet
5.8
1.25"
5.7 R
old
D 50'
1.5-2.5"
5.7
5.9

Fairview Dome

Fairview is the preeminent dome in a region geologists claim has the highest proliferation of granitic domes on earth. The symmetrical 900-foot-high north face displays fascinating evidence of exfoliation. Enormous overhangs and arches clearly demonstrate that for millennia the outer shell of rock has been peeling off as the elements pry at natural flaws. Although there were obvious ways to bypass the curving overhangs, the face remained unclimbed as late as 1958.

Approach

Park in an obvious six-car pullout in trees – the only pullout on the south side of the road – 3.4 miles west of the Tuolumne Store and 4.2 miles east of Tenaya Lake. From the pullout, follow an obvious trail that heads directly from the left (southeast) corner of the parking lot toward the dome. Follow climbers' trail signs; please do not stray from the trail. When the trail splits near the base of the dome, stay on the left trail for the Regular Route or the right trail for Lucky Streaks. Great Pumpkin starts 50 yards right of Lucky Streaks.

Descent

There is only one descent route: walk south down the giant knobby slab of the dome. The descent is mostly 2nd class with one 3rd class section. Bring approach shoes unless you want to kill your toes. Climbing shoes are not needed for the descent.

After getting down to the bottom, contour back right along the face until you reach the base of Lucky Streaks, then follow climbers' signs back to your car.

From the top of Great Pumpkin, traverse 200 feet of 4th class straight back from the edge to a bowl on the 2nd/3rd class descent. It's wise to stay roped for this section. From there, join the normal descent route.

Regular Route 5.9★★★★★

Time to climb route: **6–8 hours**

Approach time: **20 minutes**

Descent time: **40 minutes**

Sun exposure: **afternoon to sunset**

Height of route: **900'**

The Regular Route of Fairview is listed in *Fifty Classic Climbs of North America* – "routes which ambitious climbers dream of doing" – and there is no doubt it's one of the climbs to dream about in Tuolumne Meadows. The route follows the longest steep line in Tuolumne and contains pitch after pitch of sustained and rewarding cracks. Views of Daff Dome and the Grand Canyon of the Tuolumne River are outstanding, surpassed only by the 360-degree panorama from the summit. The climbing features good pro and variable cracks. As you climb higher the climbing eases and speeds up.

FA: Chuck Pratt and Wally Reed, 8/58.
FFA: Steve Roper and Mark Powell, 1962.

History

Few mountaineers have the good fortune to stumble upon a climbing area as undeveloped as Tuolumne Meadows was in 1958. One such lucky person was Wally Reed, who felt like a child turned loose in a toy store as he puzzled over which should be the first big climb of the region. Reed had noticed half a dozen intriguing route possibilities, but his thoughts kept turning to the symmetrical 900-foot-high north face of Fairview Dome. On its steep north face were two long, conspicuous cracks; the right-hand one looked promising, for it shot up 300 feet and ended in broken rock.

At the 450-foot level was a huge crescent-shaped ledge, and if it could be reached, the remainder of the route looked easier.

Early in the summer of 1958 Reed met 19-year-old Chuck Pratt, who at that time had been climbing for less than a year, and asked him if he would be interested in making an attempt on the north face of Fairview. Pratt agreed immediately, flattered that a man who had labored on El Capitan with Warren Harding would ask him along on a new route. When Pratt arrived in Tuolumne and saw the marvelously direct route Reed had picked out, he knew at once it had the ingredients for a memorable climb.

The first pitch of the climb went free and fast. But higher, as the cliff steepened, the two men were forced into direct-aid techniques. Since he had never done such extensive aid work, Pratt regularly tangled his feet in his aid slings, much to the amusement of Reed, who was completely at home on a long piton ladder. Twice it was necessary to belay in slings, an awkward technique Pratt had done only on practice climbs. So attentive were the men to their world of stone that when the sun disappeared behind a nearby ridge, they were caught by surprise. From a small ledge 400 feet above the ground, the pair hurriedly abandoned the face, satisfied that the route was feasible at least as far as what they called Crescent Ledge.

It was not until August that the two climbers found time to return. They decided to carry bivouac gear on this attempt, which was a wise decision, for it was dusk when they reached Crescent Ledge, and the temperature quickly plunged to the freezing point. Insulated in their sleeping bags, the pair watched the moon rise over the Sierra crest and illuminate a world glowing with granite.

Early the next morning Reed and Pratt began noticing subtle changes in the character of the rock. In the vicinity of Crescent Ledge, flakes and knobs began to appear, and the excited climbers stowed their aid slings and rapidly gained elevation. A four-foot ceiling that cut across the face at the 600-foot level looked formidable, but hidden, juglike holds permitted the obstacle to be free climbed easily. By noon, the two men had reached the rounded summit, amazed by the fact that they had covered the final 500 feet so easily.

In the decades following Reed and Pratt's first ascent, many more climbs have been established on the weathered knobby granite of Tuolumne, but none as long, and few so pleasing from afar.

– Excerpt from Fifty Classic Climbs of North America, *Steve Roper and Allen Steck.*

Strategy

This is one of the best climbs in Tuolumne, so expect a big line and slow parties. It's common to have to return many times before getting a chance to get on the route, and coming mid-week does not help. Early season can be a good way to beat the crowds, but the compromise is that the whole crux section is flowing with water, which raises the grade a notch or two. Also, you must start the route from a receding snow field and it can be difficult trying to keep the rope(s) dry. Late season is another strategy, but often the temperatures have dropped and because the route gets nearly no sun the rock can be frigidly cold.

The best strategy for fast teams is to start the route in the early afternoon after confirming that there are no slow parties above. For most folks, coming early and waiting in line is often the only option. Depending on the speed of the teams in front of you, this can be frustrating. Remember that returning another day is a smarter idea than starting late with slow parties above.

The Regular Route eats up nuts, therefore a double set is recommended. In addition, there are no fixed rappel anchors so nuts

are needed if retreating. Extra nuts, slings, and rappel rings or extra biners are a good idea for any team uncertain of their ability. The crux on the first pitch requires good footwork on small polished edges and a great trick is to toprope some 5.10 faces the previous day, making the edges on the Regular Route seem huge. Almost every section of difficult climbing higher up can be mellowed by stemming and good footwork.

The main safety rule on Fairview, like on any long route in Tuolumne, is NEVER to climb when puffy clouds are in sight – even a tiny one. They usually indicate later thunderstorms, which can easily be deadly high on the exposed dome.

Windjackets and warm gear can be important on the cold north face. The best strategy is to harness and rack up at the car and carry everything with you, thereby avoiding the need to return to the start of the route and robbing marauding rodents of the chance to dine on your pack. Always bring headlamps and consider safety gear depending on your skill level and the season. Nights are freezing even in mid-summer.

For strong parties who get an early start, consider finishing up the day on West Crack, right across the road on Daff Dome (Dome Across From Fairview).

Retreat

Retreat with two ropes by leaving natural pro. At most places on the route, two or three nuts plus slings can be used to safely set a retreat anchor. With two 60m ropes you can reach the ground from the tree on the last rappel, otherwise you'll need to either leave gear or downclimb. From Crescent Ledge you can rappel other routes with two ropes. The anchor conditions on these rappels are unknown.

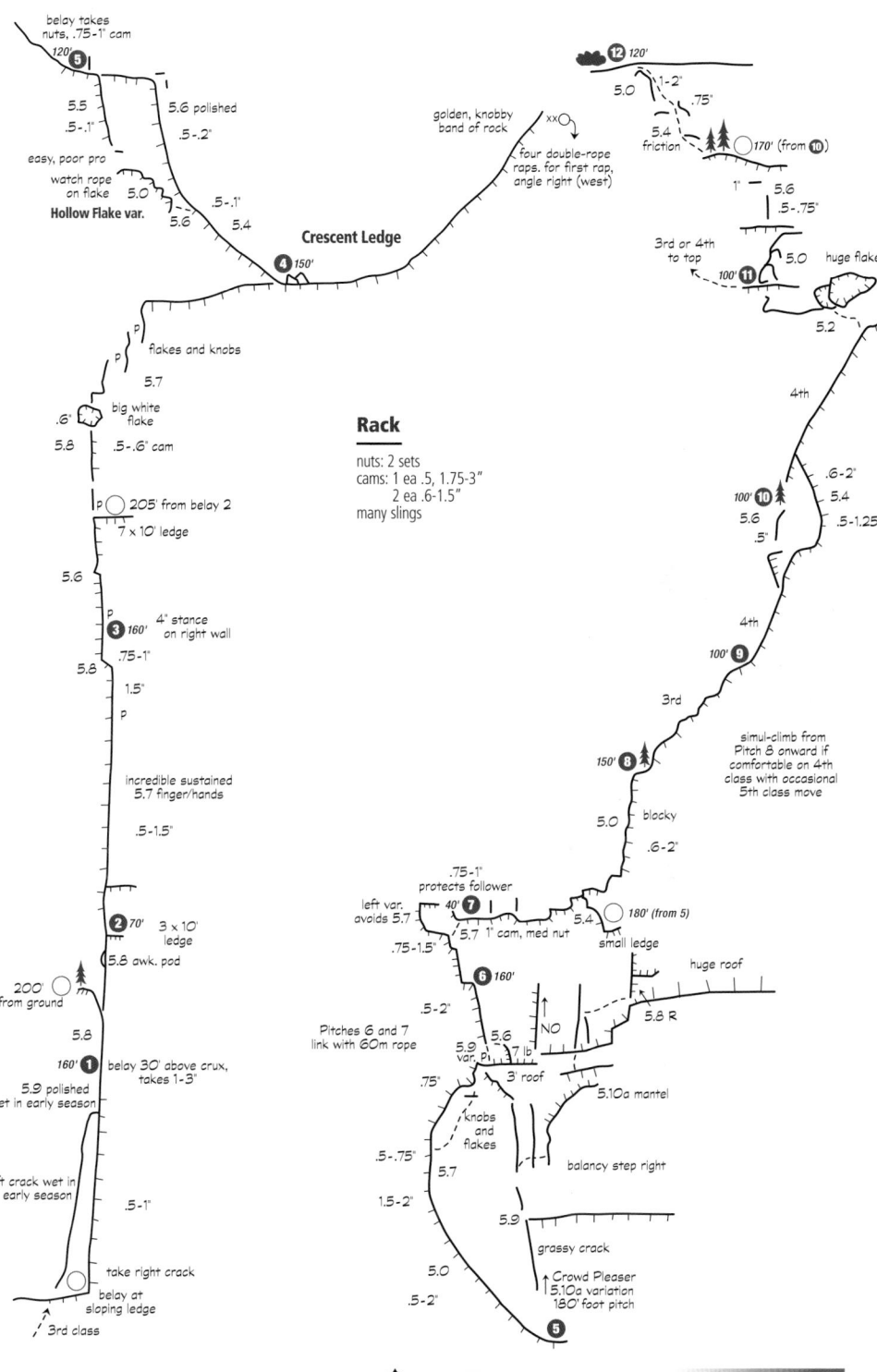

belay takes
nuts, .75-1" cam
5 120'
5.5
.5 - .1"

5.6 polished
.5 -.2"

easy, poor pro
watch rope
on flake
Hollow Flake var.
5.0
5.6
.5 -.1"
5.4

Crescent Ledge
4 150'

12 120'
5.0
.1 - 2"
.75"

golden, knobby
band of rock
xx
four double-rope
raps. for first rap,
angle right (west)

5.4
friction
170' (from **10**)

1" — 5.6
.5 -.75"

3rd or 4th
to top
11 100'
5.0
huge flakes

5.2

4th

P
P
flakes and knobs
5.7
P
.6"
big white
flake
5.8
.5 -.6" cam

P
205' from belay 2
7 x 10' ledge

.6 - 2"
10 100'
5.4
5.6
.5"
.5 -1.25"

5.6

P
3 160'
4" stance
on right wall
.75 -1"

5.8
1.5"
P

incredible sustained
5.7 finger/hands
.5 -1.5"

4th

9 100'

3rd

simul-climb from
Pitch 8 onward if
comfortable on 4th
class with occasional
5th class move

2 70'
3 x 10'
ledge
5.8 awk. pod

200'
from ground

5.8

160' **1**
belay 30' above crux,
takes 1-3"
5.9 polished
wet in early season

left crack wet in
early season
.5 -1"

take right crack

belay at
sloping ledge
3rd class

Rack

nuts: 2 sets
cams: 1 ea .5, 1.75-3"
　　　 2 ea .6-1.5"
many slings

8 150'

5.0
blocky
.6 - 2"

.75 -1"
protects follower
left var.
avoids 5.7
40' **7**
5.7 1" cam, med nut
.75 -1.5"

5.4
180' (from 5)
small ledge

huge roof

5.8 R

6 160'

.5 -2"

5.6
5.9
var. P
5.7 lb
NO

3' roof

5.10a mantel

.75"

knobs
and
flakes
.5 -.75"
5.7

balancy step right

1.5 -2"

5.9

grassy crack

5.0
.5 -2"

Crowd Pleaser
5.10a variation
180' foot pitch

5

Pitches 6 and 7
link with 60m rope

Lucky Streaks 5.10c★★★★★

Time to climb route: **4-5 hours**

Approach time: **25 minutes**

Descent time: **45 minutes**

Sun exposure: **noon to sunset**

Height of route: **600'**

Looking up from the base, Lucky Streaks may look intimidating. However, the rock is covered with knobs making the climbing easier than it appears. The quality of this route rivals that of the Regular Route on Fairview Dome and Crescent Arch on Daff Dome. The pitches tend to be long and the protection bomber (except for the first pitch).

FA: Bob Kamps and Tom Higgins, 7/67.

Strategy

This route is popular so start early. Because the pitches are long and the cracks often take just a few sizes of gear, it's important to strategically use nuts and cams. All belays are either at a ledge or a fairly good stance.

The third pitch 5.10c crux can be avoided by a 5.10a variation to the right. However, this variation is runout and the rest of the pitch is technical stemming protected by thin gear. Should you choose to climb up the thin crack variation on Pitch 5, be careful of the detached flake. In addition, the 5.7 face above is quite runout.

Retreat

Carry two ropes to retreat. The first and second belays have fixed rappel anchors. If you retreat from above, you will need to leave gear.

Rack

micros nuts: 1 set
nuts: 2 ea sml,med
     1 ea lrg
cams: 2 ea .4-2"
     1 ea 3-3.5"

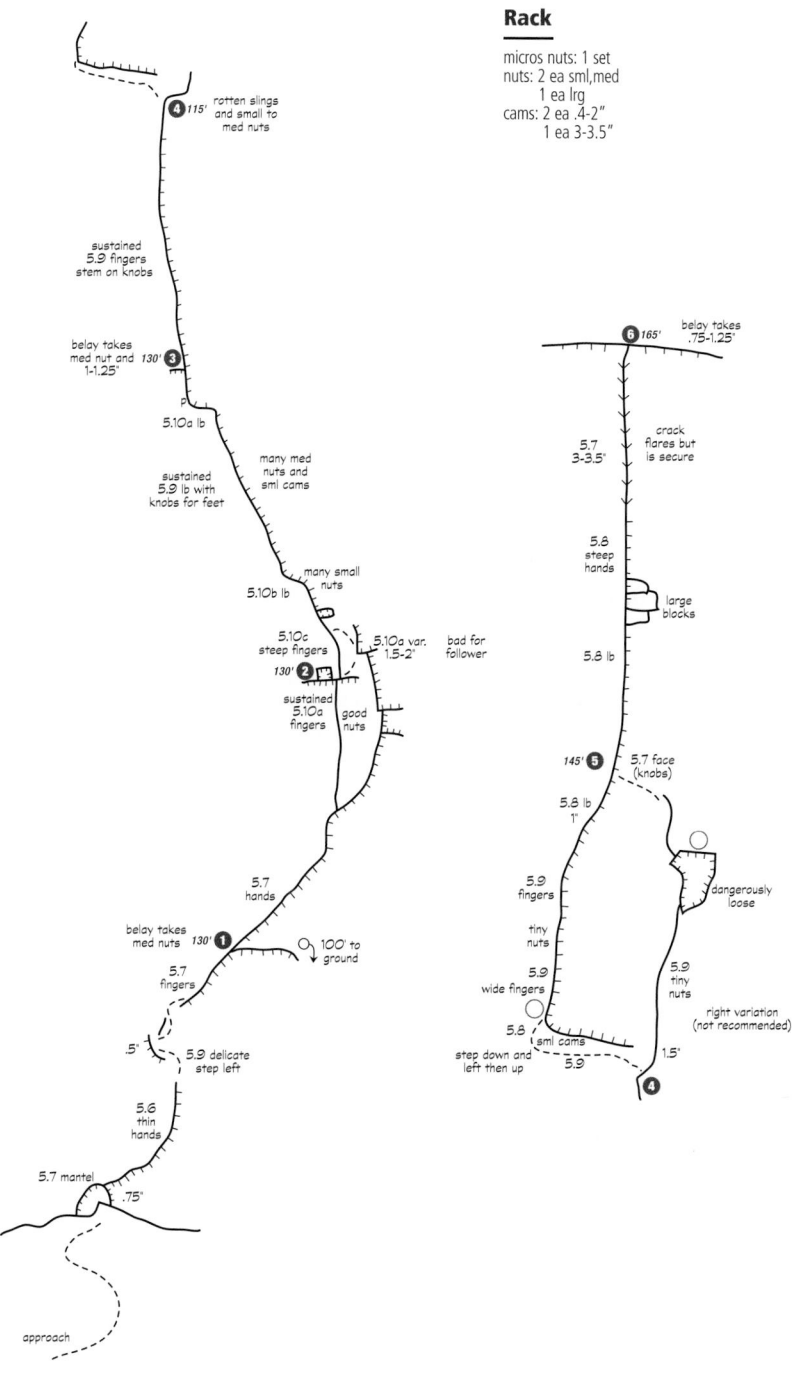

4 115' rotten slings and small to med nuts

sustained 5.9 fingers stem on knobs

belay takes med nut and 130' **3**
1-1.25"

5.10a lb

sustained 5.9 lb with knobs for feet

many med nuts and sml cams

many small nuts

5.10b lb

5.10c steep fingers   5.10a var. 1.5-2"   bad for follower

130' **2**

sustained 5.10a fingers   good nuts

5.7 hands

belay takes med nuts 130' **1**   100' to ground

5.7 fingers

.5'   5.9 delicate step left

5.6 thin hands

5.7 mantel

.75'

approach

belay takes .75-1.25"
6 165'

5.7 3-3.5'   crack flares but is secure

5.8 steep hands

large blocks

5.8 lb

145' **5**   5.7 face (knobs)

5.8 lb 1"

5.9 fingers

tiny nuts

5.9 wide fingers   5.9 tiny nuts

right variation (not recommended)

5.8 sml cams   1.5'

step down and left then up   5.9

dangerously loose

4

Great Pumpkin 5.8 R★★★★★

Time to climb route: **2–4 hours**

Approach time: **20 minutes**

Descent time: **30 minutes**

Sun exposure: **mid-morning to sunset**

Height of route: **500'**

Great Pumpkin is an improbable face and flake climb up the right side of Fairview Dome. Seriously runout for both the leader and follower, it is not to be taken lightly. However, for those comfortable on very runout 5.8 face in Tuolumne, it is an outstanding romp up perfect granite. The remaining 1/4" bolts were replaced by the ASCA in 2002.

FA: Bob Kamps and Ivan Couch, 7/69.

Strategy

The route is somewhat popular so it's a good idea to get an early start. Due to the sun exposure, Great Pumpkin is usually perfect regardless of when you climb it. In cold weather, start around noon when the route is in the sun; in hot weather, start early. Sections can be wet, especially after heavy thunderstorms. A snowbank is often present at the base in early season.

The first pitch is a rude awakening for those not used to the typical runouts on Tuolumne face climbs. After 60 feet of easy climbing comes a field of knobs and edges with no apparent protection. Meandering climbing for 30 feet requires patience and concentration until you gain a single protection bolt. From there, tricky routefinding up left, then back right for a long slick traverse, subjects both the leader and follower to long fall potential.

The second pitch has fun climbing up flakes with somewhat suspect pro that leads to a huge move right on friction. Placing extra backup pro before this crux is wise. More flakes and a great shallow corner system past a few more tricky sections gains the belay ledge. Be sure to sling the tree (or clip retreat webbing) for the follower.

The third pitch has tricky climbing with poor protection. A slung horn/knob is the only pro for a thin traverse 30 feet off the belay ledge. Easier but still runout climbing leads to a bolted anchor 70 feet off the ledge. It's best to belay here.

The last pitch climbs awesome knobs past two bolts and a belay station (best skipped) to a long runout. About 40 feet from your last pro is a 5.8 section, followed by the last bolt at about 60 feet from the optional belay. From here, easier climbing leads to the top.

Like all longer routes in Tuolumne, don't get caught on Great Pumpkin in a thunderstorm.

Strong parties often climb both Great Pumpkin and the Regular Route or Lucky Streaks in a day. Start with Great Pumpkin to let the crowds on the more popular crack systems disperse.

Retreat

Retreat by rappelling with two ropes; however, it may not be possible to regain the first belay due to the traversing nature of the route, so an alternate belay would need to be constructed somewhere below the midway ledge.

Rack

nuts: 1 set
cams: 2 ea .4-1.25"
     1 ea 1.5-3"
long slings

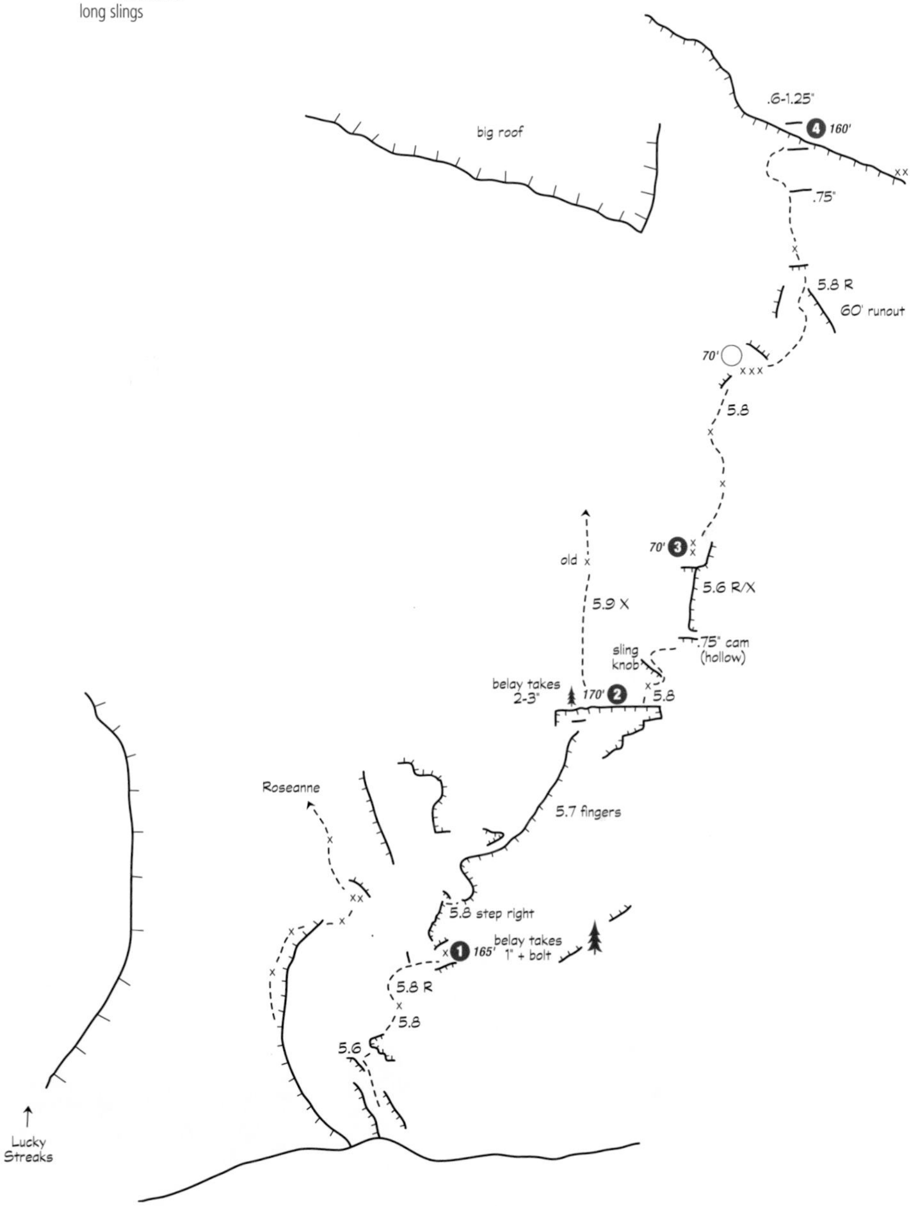

big roof

.6-1.25'

4 160'

xx

.75'

5.8 R
60' runout

70' ○ x x x

5.8
x

x

70' **3** x
x

5.6 R/X

x
.75" cam
(hollow)

sling
knob

old x

5.9 X

belay takes
2-3" ▲ 170' **2** x = 5.8

Roseanne

5.7 fingers

5.8 step right
belay takes
x **1** 165' 1" + bolt

5.8 R
x
5.8

5.6

↑
Lucky
Streaks

Lamb Dome

Located right next to the road midway through Tuolumne, the somewhat pyramidal 500-foot Lamb Dome (aka The Lamb) is surprisingly overlooked by climbers. With no tourist parking and little chance to stop, it's often just one of the cliffs whizzing by. Upon closer inspection, the northwest face is somewhat broken, with the only distinct feature being a long horizontal crack near the top. This is the unusual multi-pitch traverse called On the Lamb.

Approach

If driving from the east, park at the large dirt turnout on the left along the first straight section of the road, about one mile after passing Fairview and Daff Domes. Lamb Dome is next to the road, and is obvious from the parking area. You can either hike straight from the parking lot, or start up the trail to Drug Dome/ Mariuolumne Dome, then take a left after 100 yards on a major hiking trail. Take the obvious trail from the right side of the parking lot and approach the standard route by hiking north along the base, then up and around to the northeast side of the dome.

There are three approaches to climbing On The Lamb. The standard is to approach from below and left via 4th class cracks and flakes; the second is to hike around to the end of the climb and climb it in reverse. The third approach is to climb one of the routes below the start such as Five Ten, You Wuss. Most parties choose the standard approach, but many do not start far enough to the left, and end up trying to approach via runout 5th class friction.

The key to finding the correct start is to go completely around left to the northeast face, where you cannot see any part of the climb, then to climb a long, slabby hand crack groove.

To get to routes B-F, skirt the base of Lamb Dome until you reach the large right-slanting 3rd class ramp that starts near the left side of the face. Routes B and C start to the left, left of the big corner. Route D starts about 150 feet up the 4th class ramp along the orange headwall. Routes E and F start at the top of the huge 3rd class ramp on a giant ledge with trees. Sleeper starts in the right-facing corner next to the highest part of the 30-foot-wide sandy ledge.

Descent

An easy hike off the back on 2nd and 3rd class slab joins the trail from Drug and Mariuolumne Domes.

SUPERTOPO

TUOLUMNE FREE CLIMBS: SUPERTOPOS

A. On the Lamb 5.9★★★★

Time to climb route: **3–4 hours**

Approach time: **30 minutes**

Descent time: **10 minutes**

Sun exposure: **afternoon to sunset**

Height of route: **600'**

On the Lamb is one of the most spectacular, exposed, and unusual climbs in Tuolumne Meadows. It follows a 500-foot-long horizontal crack near the top of Lamb Dome. Few climbs have long traverses, and nearly no climbs have such a huge number of juggy holds – especially in Tuolumne. Many find On The Lamb so fun that they immediately turn around and reverse the climb. In fact, one of the best ways to climb this route is to start at the end, climb three pitches to the start of the traverse, then reverse.

Unlike most climbs, On The Lamb is as intimidating for the follower as for the leader – indeed, more so if the leader has placed a piece that is difficult to remove. While there is abundant protection, don't climb On The Lamb unless both partners are solid at the grade.

FA: Bruce Brossman and Drone Stephens, 7/74.

Strategy

On The Lamb is fairly popular. You can see if anyone is on the main part of the climb from the parking lot, but you can't see the start of the route, or anyone near the end of the route.

Bring a large selection of nuts, especially medium to large, and extra cams in the 0.5-1" range. It can be tricky to set belays without damaging the stems of cams, so bring tri-cams and small to medium hexes if you have them. Rigid-stemmed cams should be tied off short.

The crux is 40 feet of intimidating, steep traversing with poor feet. Climb quickly without hesitation and place gear fast to gain the rests on either side.

Retreat

Retreat from On The Lamb is difficult. A variety of bolted anchors on other routes are found below the climb, but reaching them may require more than half of a 60m rope, and taking a second rope will be a hassle unless double ropes are used. Lamb Dome is exposed to lightning danger.

B. Tectonomagmatic 5.10b★★

FA: Bryan Law, Greg Barnes, September 2008.

The left of the two black streaks left of Dukey Corner. Starting with a boulder problem surmounting the shortest section of a vertical wall, climb up cool knobs, flakes, edges, and slab up the black streak. The route takes its imaginative name from a funky grey streak/dike to the left of the start – a geological feature that is not (yet) described in scientific literature. The crux is short and well protected, and there's loads of very fun 5.9 range climbing on the pitch. There are some runouts on easier terrain near the top. This is a great approach to the upper pitch of route C, actually a more logical approach than that route.

C. Five Ten, You Wuss 5.10c★★★

FA: Greg Barnes, Bryan Law, George Ridgley September 2008.

A new three-pitch route on the left side of Lamb Dome, Five Ten, You Wuss climbs the right of the two black streaks left of the big corner on the left end of Lamb Dome. The first pitch climbs up a ramp to horns, then left past a bolt to the black streak, up past overlaps, and then up funky, reachy friction bulges. The second pitch is short, climbing up the face to a low-angle corner, then traversing left on a ledge to belay from gear in a scoop. Rope drag makes linking these pitches difficult. Tectonomagmatic can be used to approach this belay in a single long pitch. The third pitch is a long pitch with face to corner to face, ending at the right end of the lower ledge at the top of the 4th class approach for On The Lamb. To the right of the 3rd pitch is a mysterious, unrecorded old route with a couple of very old ¼" bolts and homemade hangers, which was presumably approached from Dukey Corner and the big ledge.

D. Tooled 5.11b★★★★

FA: Joe Denicola, Maki Grossnick, Karin Wuhrmann, Greg Barnes, July 2008.

Climb the big left-leaning dike on the left side of Lamb Dome. Steep golden climbing up a pumpy rail to a thin crux leads to a huge flake and great knob climbing. The bolted belay is shared with an old 5.10 R/X route, Lamb Chops, which climbs sharply left-to-right. The second pitch leads up and left on golden slab to the heavily featured dike, and ends at the bolted belay of another 5.10 R/X route, Hip Boots, which came in from the left and then continues up the upper part of the dike with a substantial 5.10 runout. Rappel the route with a single 60m rope, which requires swinging over on the second pitch, and be careful to stay to the right when rappelling the first pitch. When dropping the rope on the first pitch, coil the rope and toss it instead of just letting it fall down the slab, since it's easy for it to snag in the big detached flakes.

E. Sleeper 5.9 R★★★★

FA: Tom Higgins and Bob Kamps, 7/74

Sleeper is one of the overlooked gems of Tuolumne. The route is distinguished by outstanding, burly climbing up a flared corner, beautiful knobs, and a great thin crack. The first two pitches are 5.8 and fairly well-protected, but the third and fourth pitches are dangerously runout. Escape is simple via the last 80 feet of On The Lamb, and Jailbreak is a great option for climbing to the top of the dome.

F. Carpet Crawler 5.10a R/X★★★★

FA: Steve and Dave Gerberding, 10/85.

A very dangerous route due to the crux having 20-foot fall potential off the roof onto a slab. All bolts were replaced by the ASCA in 2002. The second pitch is crumbly.

G. Jailbreak 5.9 R-★★★★

FA: Greg Barnes, Karin Wuhrmann, July 2003.

A great finish to On The Lamb, Jailbreak heads up a golden knobby dike just before the end of On The Lamb (assuming you do On The Lamb in the "normal" left-to-right direction). Jailbreak follows the left-leaning dike all the way to the summit of Lamb Dome. A short section up a dihedral past a bulge with a bolt leads to an anchor only 30 feet above On The Lamb, allowing climbers on Jailbreak to get out of the way of On The Lamb. The next pitch shares a section and the belay with the runout 3rd pitch of Sleeper, and the start of the last pitch of Jailbreak is also runout.

H. Lampoon 5.9+ R/X★★

FA: Alan Bartlett, Kurt Smith, Shari Schubot, July 1984.

Old-school climbing. This is a fun toprope and a sketchy lead. The crux, moving left from the bolt, indicates the 5.9+ rating you expect to find on many more obscure routes.

I. Little Sheeba 5.10a★★★★

FA: Chris Falkenstein and Dennis Oakeshott, 1975.

Little Sheba, the thin crack about 100 yards left of the right toe of Lamb Dome, is one of the finest single-pitch cracks in Tuolumne. It is also an easy toprope to set up with a 60m rope for those confident on the 3rd class friction and routefinding necessary to reach the anchor. It's very popular, especially late in the afternoon. To toprope the face climbs (see topo), rappel from the tree to gain the bolted anchor.

George Ridgley on Five Ten, You Wuss, Lamb Dome Photo by Bryan Law

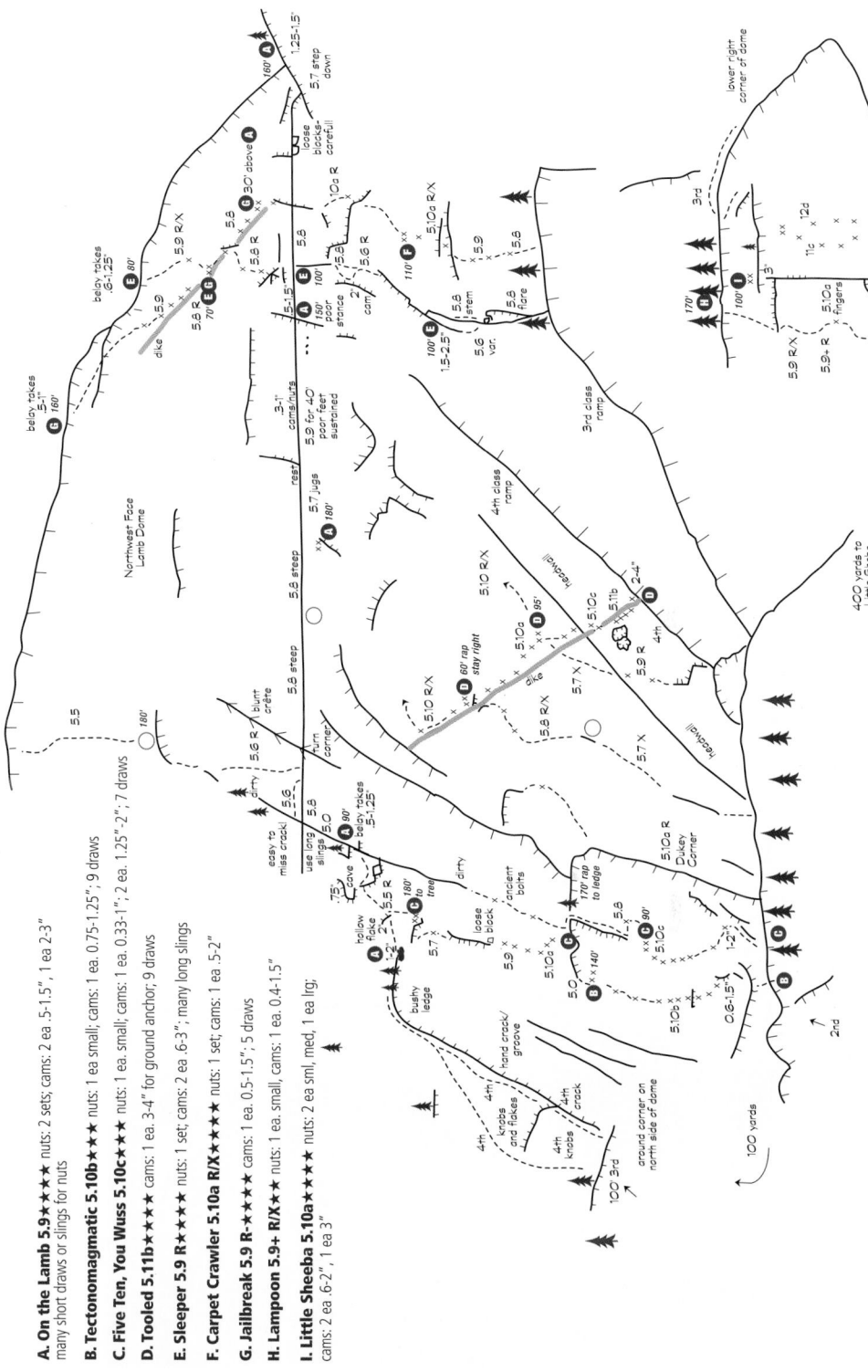

A. On the Lamb 5.9 ★★★★ nuts: 2 sets; cams: 2 ea .5-1.5", 1 ea 2-3" many short draws or slings for nuts

B. Tectonomagmatic 5.10b ★★★ nuts: 1 ea small; cams: 1 ea. 0.75-1.25", 9 draws

C. Five Ten, You Wuss 5.10c ★★★ nuts: 1 ea. small; cams: 1 ea. 0.33-1", 2 ea. 1.25"-2", 7 draws

D. Tooled 5.11b ★★★★ cams: 1 ea. 3-4" for ground anchor, 9 draws

E. Sleeper 5.9 R ★★★★ nuts: 1 set; cams: 2 ea .6-3"; many long slings

F. Carpet Crawler 5.10a R/X ★★★★ nuts: 1 set; cams: 1 ea .5-2"

G. Jailbreak 5.9 R-★★★★ cams: 1 ea. 0.5-1.5", 5 draws

H. Lampoon 5.9+ R/X ★★ nuts: 1 ea. small, cams: 1 ea. 0.4-1.5"

I. Little Sheeba 5.10a ★★★★ nuts: 2 ea sml, med, 1 ea lrg; cams: 2 ea .6-2", 1 ea 3"

Drug Dome

Drug Dome is somewhat obscured from the road by trees and overshadowed by Mariuolumne Dome, which towers above it. However, up close Drug Dome is one of the steepest and most distinctive domes in Tuolumne. Mostly too steep for free routes, the left-most route to the top of Drug Dome is the mega-classic route up steep face to the huge dihedral.

This is OZ [pronounced "ounce" or "oh zee"], easily the cleanest and steepest 5.10 in Tuolumne.

Approach

If driving from the east, park at the large dirt pullout on the left along the first straight section of the road, about one mile after passing Fairview and Daff Domes. Take the obvious trail out of the right side of the parking lot, skirting the right edge of Lamb Dome, and head straight toward Mariuolumne and Drug Domes. This trail turns toward Drug Dome after about 10-15 minutes of hiking. Scramble up through the boulders to the base of the wall about 50 yards right of the gigantic, apartment-sized boulder at the base of the dihedral.

Descent

This descent takes about 45 minutes from the summit to the base, but it can be tricky the first time. Bring hiking shoes as it is too long to do in climbing shoes. Remember that the first part of the descent is about 300 yards of horizontal traversing and loses only a little elevation.

From the summit of Drug Dome walk east cross-country for 200 feet until you run into a wall and are forced slightly north (toward Daff Dome). A 30-foot section of exposed 3rd class above a 20-foot-wide gully (don't take the gully!) leads to more traversing on trail and ledges. After 150 yards, you cross a small talus field and 200 yards after that you meet an open slab.

Angle down the slab and enter a big talus field just above a clump of bushes. Diagonal down the talus looking for cairns and angle left (back toward Drug Dome) as soon as safely possible. A few hundred yards of traversing (losing only a little elevation) leads back to the base. Note: on the final traverse west back to the base of Drug Dome many climbers make the mistake of staying too low.

OZ 5.10d★★★★★

Time to climb route: **3–4 hours**

Approach time: **10 minutes**

Descent time: **45 minutes**

Sun exposure: **afternoon to sunset**

Height of route: **500'**

OZ is a sought-after testpiece with tightly-bolted, hard 5.10 face climbing and the longest, most sustained 5.10 crack in Tuolumne. Unlike most Tuolumne routes, OZ is vertical instead of slabby and ascends a steep face into a giant clean dihedral, and continues up to a roof. OZ is neighbored by several projects, a 5.11 X, two new 5.12c routes, and Sunshine (5.10b X), which is one of the best (and least protected) face climbs in Tuolumne.

FA: Dale Bard and Bob Locke, 1975.

Strategy

OZ is popular and sometimes has lines. However, it has a short approach hike, and there are several great short routes to the right. The climb is north facing and cold – often too cold to comfortably climb in early or late season. Even on hot days, a windjacket is recommended. The long dihedral crack is consistently about one inch wide and requires many extra 1" cams.

Linking the crux face pitch to the base of the dihedral pitch is a great setup for the long perfect dihedral. The exit pitch is wandering and good use of slings helps reduce rope drag.

After OZ, many parties finish the day on Hobbit Book or Seconds to Darkness.

Retreat

It is possible to rappel with two ropes from most points on OZ.

A. Gram Traverse   5.10d★★★★★

FA: Dale Bard and Bob Locke, 6/76.

This adds two more hard 5.10 pitches under the huge roof and is one of the most stunning traverses you will ever encounter.

The second pitch is somewhat loose, but well-protected in the difficult sections, and not deserving of its reputation of being dangerous. Still, use care around several large and hollow blocks and flakes.

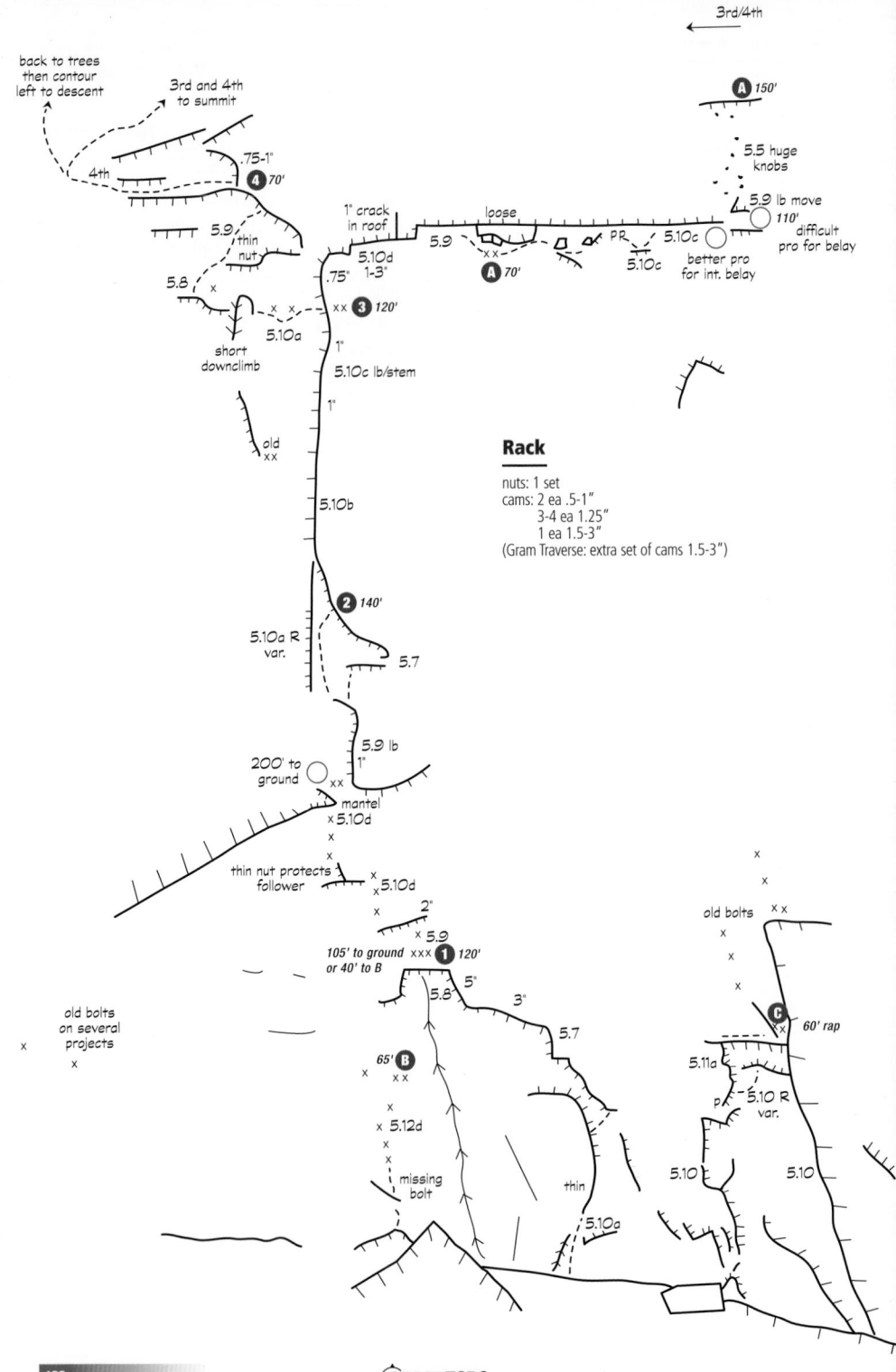

Rack

nuts: 1 set
cams: 2 ea .5-1"
　　　3-4 ea 1.25"
　　　1 ea 1.5-3"
(Gram Traverse: extra set of cams 1.5-3")

Drug Dome Base Routes

In addition to the classic OZ, Drug Dome has a number of new routes and old routes with recently replaced first pitch anchors, making it an excellent cragging destination.

The base routes have morning shade and afternoon sun, and the hike is relatively short. Most of these routes have seen very little traffic, so beware of suspect knobs, and some grit and lichen.

Several of these routes require a 70m rope to lower the leader to the ground, and even then can be just at the end of the rope. Do not assume that a rope will reach for lowering – tie knots.

B. Ice   5.12d★★

FA Tom Herbert, September 1989.

Brutal, slick face climb which is fairly easy to TR if rapping from first pitch of OZ. The first bolt is missing. Cold shut anchor. There is also one cold shut about 15 feet left of the anchor.

C. Just Say No (pitch 1)   5.11a R★★★★

FA Roland Arsons, Dimitri Barton 7/88

Steep, wild flakes and face climbing with thin and a bit sketchy pro, and some hollow rock. Powerful crux at top. Awesome climbing for experienced leaders. The leaning corner/chimney to the right is an alternate start which can be led or toproped with directionals.

D. Anatolio (pitch 1)   5.11b★★★

FA Chad Shepard, Dimitri Barton 7/04.

Good climbing with a short, well-bolted lieback crux, but there's definitely some lichen. Higher up the route sports a 5.12c undercling with big pendulum potential. This first pitch was originally done in the late 80s by Dimitri Barton with nearly zero pro at 5.10 X (took a slightly different line).

E. Acapulco Gold (pitch 1)   5.10c R★★

FA Sean Leary, Dimitri Barton, Ivo Ninov 2004.

Great knob climbing, but pretty contrived route finding, and runout. It's easy to skip the lower bulge crux by climbing up to the ramp then way left. It's also not clear exactly where you're "supposed" to climb on the first bulges. Up higher this route takes a much more natural line up an arête to a wild overhung 5.12c steep knob pitch.

F. Sunshine (pitch 1)   5.9 R/X★★★★

FA Dennis Oakeshott, Bob Harrington 1976

Beautiful golden knobs and cool features on perfect golden rock. While it sports long runouts, the first pitch of Sunshine is one of the better protected pitches on this old-school runout testpiece, and it's possible to sling a few knobs. Higher up, this route is 5.10 and even more runout. 70m rope to rap.

G. Push It   5.11a★★★★

FA Maki Grossnick, Greg Barnes, Karin Wuhrmann, Linda Jarit 9/07.

The prominent arête between the two starts of Sunshine. Tricky crux (can A0) with fun, varied climbing, most of which is no harder than 5.10b. You can just barely lower with a 70m rope if the leader swings to the right – tie knots in end of rope. 125' pitch.

H. Roof Rat   5.7★★

FA Greg Barnes, George Ridgley, 7/07.

Stellar golden rock and great crack start this long pitch. Lichen-covered foot holds at the end of the pitch detract greatly from the star rating. It's nearly a full rope length to the shared bolted anchor with Black Nepalese and Dope Show. Start climbing

the main dihedral right of Sunshine (the first 60 feet of which are the start of the right variation of Sunshine), and continue out the arch to the right of Stemulant to the shared anchor on the roof above the arch.

I. Stemulant   5.10a★★★★

FA Greg Barnes, George Ridgley, 7/07

Cool route up the steep gold dihedral right of the right start of Sunshine. Climb fun flakes and knobby face to the main dihedral, then past a roof with a bolt and up the steep dihedral to a bolted anchor out left at the big roof. The hanging belay anchor has mussy hooks for lowering, but a 70m rope just barely makes it down. It's possible to lower to the far left edge of the Black

B. Ice 5.12d★★
cams: 1 ea 0.4-0.75", draws
C. Just Say No (pitch 1) 5.11a R★★★★
nuts: 1 set including micro, cams: 2 ea. 0.4-2", optional extra 0.6-.75"
D. Anatolio (pitch 1) 5.11b★★★
11 draws
E. Acapulco Gold (pitch 1) 5.10c R★★
cams: 1 ea. 0.4-1", 7 draws
F. Sunshine (pitch 1) 5.9 R/X★★★★
nuts: 1 set, cams: 1 ea. 0.6-1.5"
G. Push It 5.11a★★★★
nuts: 1 set, cams: 1 ea. 0.6-1"
H. Roof Rat 5.7★★
nuts: 1 set, cams: 2 ea. 0.6-3"
I. Stemulant 5.10a★★★★
nuts: 1 set, cams: 2 ea. 0.6-2"
J. Black Nepalese 5.7★★★
cams: 1 ea. 2-3" for belay anchor, 5 draws
K. Dope Show 5.8★★
cams: 2 ea. 0.6-1", 1 ea. 2-3" for belay anchor, 4 draws
L. Lord of the Overhigh (pitch 1) 5.8★★
nuts: 1 set, cams: 2 ea. 0.6-3"

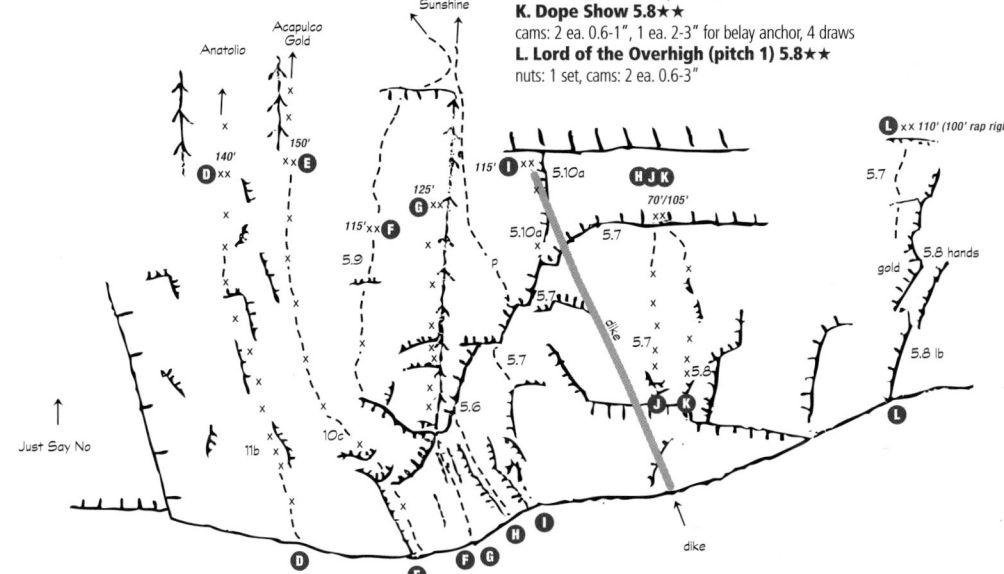

Nepalese ledge with a 60m rope and belay from there, then scramble off the ledge to the right. Tie in or use knots in rope ends. 70m rope needed to lower.

J. Black Nepalese   5.7★★★

FA George Ridgley, Greg Barnes, 7/07

A fun route starting off the middle of the ledge. Use 2-3" pro for a belay anchor. Climb the hollow white flake to the very knobby face. The shared anchor is on the roof.

K. Dope Show   5.8★★

FA Greg Barnes, George Ridgley, 7/07

Knobby route starting off the right edge of the ledge. Use 2-3" pro for a belay anchor. Start just right of the flake at a right-leaning undercling. Climb past a bolt 10 feet up (crux) to fun knobs and flakes – use care with the hollow flake at the third bolt. The shared anchor is on the roof.

L. Lord of the Overhigh (pitch 1) 5.8★★★

FA Gary Slate, Jeff White 1980.

A good climb, but pretty dirty. Climb the harder-than-it-looks right-leaning lieback to a handcrack under a golden bulge, then up face left of dirty flakes past an overlap with good thin pro. A bit runout up the face but not too hard. Pitch one anchor replaced 2007, but old rusty bolts higher (5.10c R). A 100-foot rap down to the right, but just over half a 60m rope straight down, so be very careful with rope ends. 70m rope to lower.

M. Crystal Meth   5.8 R-★★★

FA: Greg Barnes, Bryan Law, Joe Denicola, August 2008.

Crystal Meth takes fun flakes, face, and cracks up the face just right of the huge black streak on the right side of Drug Dome. The first pitch of Crystal Meth was established by accident when trying to climb Crystal Ball, a 5.10c route which is on the left edge of the huge black streak. Crystal Meth is on the steep wall of Drug Dome before the break to the very low-angle stepped slabs below Hobbit Book. Euro Trash is on the left side of these low-angle slabs, starting about 50 yards uphill of Crystal Meth.

Crystal Meth is wet in early season, especially in wet years, and even when it appears that the route is dry you have to pay attention to spray from the waterfall (especially if there's any breeze or wind from the north).

The first pitch starts just right of the right edge of the black streak, and actually uses one flake which is just in the black streak, and sometimes wet.

It's possible to approach Hobbit Book and other routes on the main Mariuolumne Dome by climbing Crystal Meth. From the third pitch anchor, climb a 4th class slab (many options) to the forest which is about 50 yards before the roping-up spot for the 4th class approach ledge for Hobbit Book. You can rappel the route with a single 70m rope.

N. Euro Trash   5.10c★ or 5.8 A0★★

To the right of Drug Dome is a wide, low-angle white slab with many ledges. This slab is directly below the approach ledge for Hobbit Book. On the left side of the slab is an unusual route which, like Crystal Meth, can be used to approach Hobbit Book and other routes on the main Mariuolumne Dome.

A fun romp up easy slabs, Euro Trash is easily the most contrived route in Tuolumne. It is an example of a style of climb somewhat common in Europe but rarely seen in the U.S. Consistently avoiding easier climbing by finding the hardest way up easy slabs, the contrived routefinding is highlighted by the crux – a 5.10c bulge through the steepest rock around, when climbing 40 feet to either side is 5.8 or so. Established on rappel by a French guide, the most surprising thing about Euro Trash is that it wasn't chopped in the aggressive bolt wars that were occurring around the same time.

Despite the contrived nature of the route, the first three pitches are very fun, well protected by many bolts, and only 5.8. The last pitch has very few bolts when compared to the first three pitches, but the crux has two right in a row, and with good pro supplementing the bolts, the pitch can be done at 5.8 A0.

The first four bolts off the ground can be hiked around – literally – at 2nd/3rd class. The bolts are there mainly as route markers, sort of like cairns on trails. The last pitch traverses sharply right above the last bolt along a ramp, then finishes back left at a bolted anchor. It's best to use long slings

after the fifth (last) bolt.

Careless parties on the approach to Hobbit Book can easily dislodge rocks in the section near the roping-up spot for the 4th class approach ledge, and any rocks dislodged in this area will rain down Euro Trash. Also, even careful parties on Stomper or Mordor may drop blocks that could fall here. Helmets are strongly recommended.

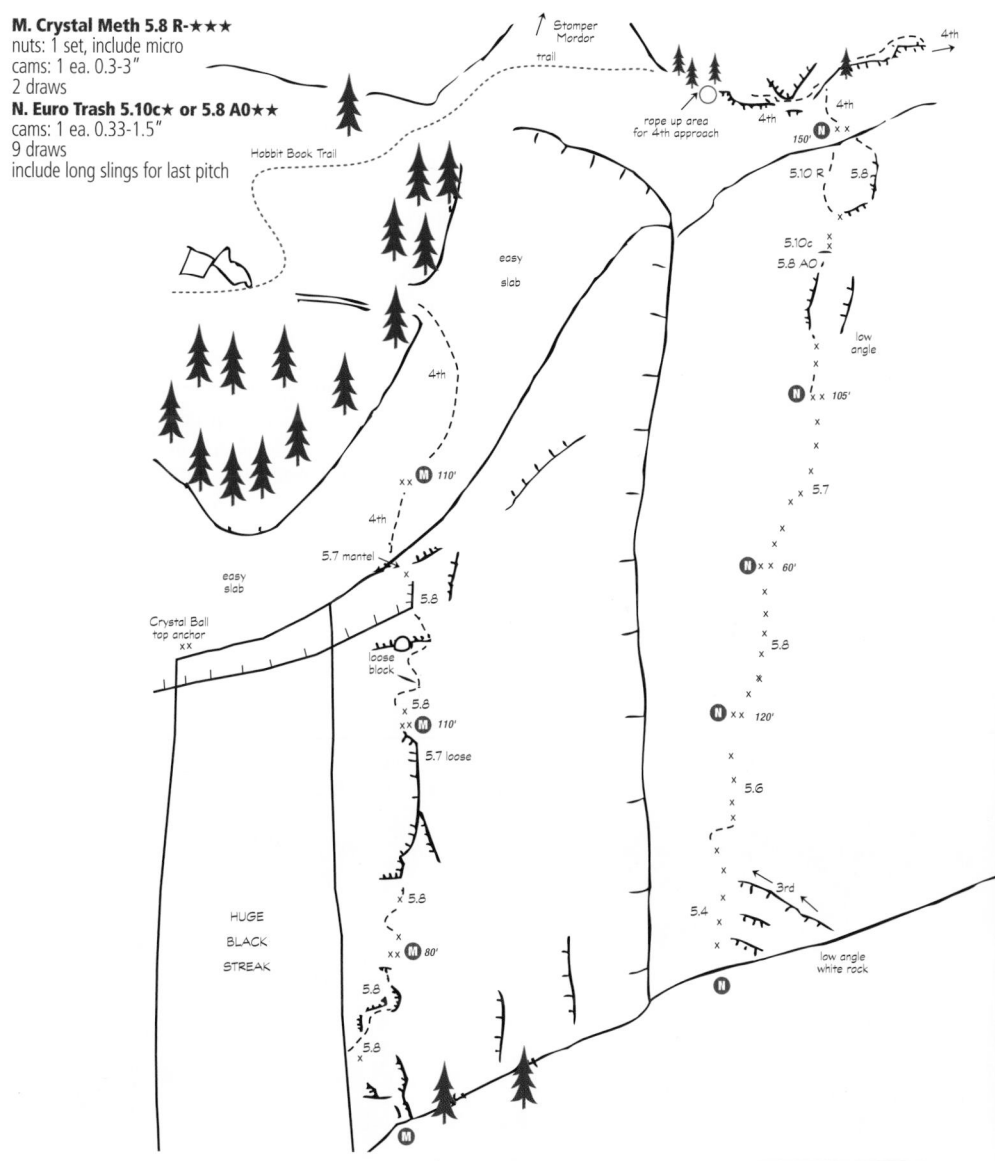

M. Crystal Meth 5.8 R-★★★
nuts: 1 set, include micro
cams: 1 ea. 0.3-3"
2 draws

N. Euro Trash 5.10c★ or 5.8 A0★★
cams: 1 ea. 0.33-1.5"
9 draws
include long slings for last pitch

Mariuolumne Dome

Tucked in between Lamb and Medlicott Domes, and with Drug Dome at its foot, Mariuolumne Dome is 900 feet tall and second only to Fairview Dome in size. The most obvious feature of the Dome is a giant corner on the right edge of a large golden wall – Hobbit Book. Steep, high, and exposed, the climbing feels far different from the usual lower-angle climbs on most Tuolumne domes. This dome is near the boundary of Mariposa and Tuolumne counties – hence the unusual name.

Approach

This approach is strenuous and involves tricky routefinding. If driving from the east, park at the large dirt pullout on the left along the first straight section of the road, about one mile after passing Fairview and Daff Domes.

Take the obvious trail out of the right side of the parking lot, heading up to the right of The Lamb and straight toward Mariuolumne and Drug Domes. After a couple minutes you will cross a park service trail which parallels the highway. The approach trail heads through the forest towards Drug Dome. When you reach the huge boulder field below Drug Dome, cut left on a trail along the base of the boulders. The trail will wander through boulders and trees below the base of the cliff left of Drug Dome. At the end of this cliff, hike up along the slab with a giant boulder field on your left. The trail ends and you scramble through boulders to pass a steep section, then back to a huge hanging slab below a steep cliff (the North Wall of Mariuolumne Dome).

Hike right along the base of the steep cliff above. You can either climb 4th class straight up the wall, or more common is to follow a use trail to the right. While easy, there is exposed 4th class near the end, and some may want a rope. After gaining the upper wooded ledges (about 400 feet wide), you pass the top of Drug Dome and climb up and right aiming for the upper right end of the trees. Rope up at the end of the trees. Stomper starts from the alcove above this point. Be very careful about knocking rocks off in this area, since they will fall down onto Euro Trash. From the last tree, rope up, and traverse 100 feet of extremely exposed 4th class ledges. The remaining 150 feet of ledges are wide and spacious, and do not require a rope. Hobbit Book starts at the end of the ledge in a low-angle, friendly corner.

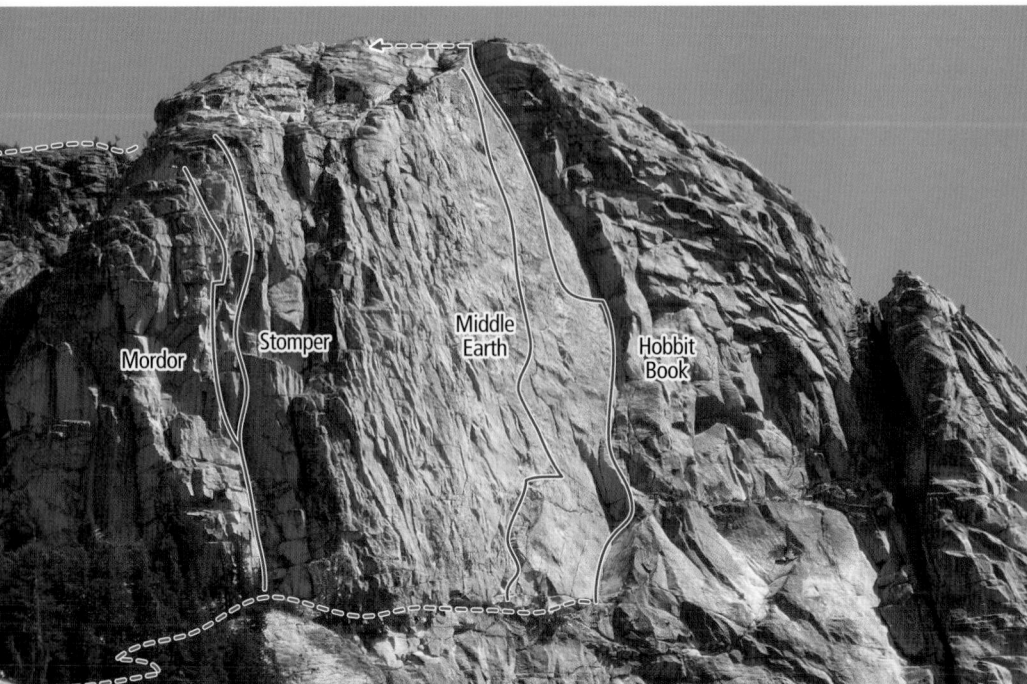

Mordor   Stomper   Middle Earth   Hobbit Book

Descent

From the top of the dome, head down dirty low-angle slabs and trees toward Fairview Dome. Do not take the first gully, which looks narrow and forbidding, unless you wish to downclimb the first 4th class section of the approach. After about 500 yards the slabs enter some large trees. Look for the apparent gully on the left, which is split in the middle by a granite tower. Go down easy dirt and boulders to the right of the tower. You come out above the boulder field and at the east end of the North Wall of Mariuolumne Dome. The boulder field is most easily skirted on the right, although it's also possible just to go straight down. The descent will take most people 1-1.5 hours.

An alternate descent is to simply hike across toward the left end of the Cathedral Peak ridge and join the John Muir Trail, which is then followed to the Cathedral Lakes trailhead. This will necessitate a car shuttle or hitching a ride, but is far easier on the knees and is a pleasant hike.

A. Mordor   5.10c ★ ★

FA: Greg Barnes, Joe Denicola, Linda Jarit, September 2008.

A new route that climbs through the huge roofs on the left side of Mariuolumne Dome, Mordor is a wild, steep crack climb with outrageous exposure. As with its neighbor Stomper, Mordor has an alpine feel in sections and climbers should watch out for a few loose blocks throughout the climb, particularly on the easy 5th top out pitches.

The first pitch is shared with Stomper and has multiple variations: a 5.6 offwidth on the left, a 5.8 dihedral with a small roof just to the right, or the main corner which starts with a bouldery 5.9 section up hollow blocks. Regardless of which start you use, beware of loose blocks. The second pitch heads up the classic hand crack dihedral left of the 5.9 fist/offwith corner of Stomper, and ends at the same set of large belay ledges as that route. You can easily mix and match the second pitches of the two routes.

The third pitch is the roof. Starting with a short, hard stemming dihedral, then traversing left on face past a bolt to an offwidth corner (a 6" cam is nice here), the crux is the first section of the roof, with powerful underclinging to gain good footholds. At the end of the roof, layback and jam past a small second roof/block to a hand rail (5" crack, but with hidden 2" pro), then traverse right under the next roof with awkward handjams, good footholds, and stomach-churning exposure. Set the belay at the end of the second roof, standing on a 6" wide ledge, about 10 feet above the lip of the main roof. It's very easy to dangle a loop of the lead rope down to the second belay to haul anything the follower doesn't want to carry.

The fourth pitch climbs the golden hand crack past some bulges to a steep offwidth which you climb around using knobs to the right. It's easiest to do a ridiculously exposed step sharply to the right to a lieback flake, then climb back left above the top of the offwidth. The climbing eases dramatically at this point, and various belays are possible. Low 5th class climbing for another pitch (watch for loose blocks) leads to 4th class to the top.

With some sharp edges and steep overhangs, a thick lead line or double ropes are recommended. It's possible for the follower to fall out of the roof, with the rope sawing on edges as they swing in space. To prevent this, it's important for the leader to protect the end of the first part of the roof.

B. Stomper   5.10a ★ ★ ★

FA: Alan Bartlett, Don Reid, Dimitri Barton, August 1980.

Steep, burly, old-school crack climbing up fractured rock, Stomper is a lesser traveled climb up the main wall of Mariuolumne Dome. On the second pitch, Stomper has a physical 5.9 fist/offwidth that will be the crux for many people, especially those with smaller hands. The crux pitch has really cool, thought-provoking moves up a leaning corner/chimney/lieback, but starts with a short (but powerful and awkward) crux moving from an overhung hand crack to a flare.

The fourth pitch is relatively easy,

but involves delicate climbing on slightly crumbly face and knobs around dangerously perched blocks. This pitch mandates extreme care for both leader and follower – especially since any block kicked loose would land in the roping up area for the 4th class traverse to Hobbit Book, and also likely continue down onto Euro Trash.

Despite the bomber pro and good climbing, Stomper has seen very little traffic since it was established, and this is reflected in the flakey rock and lichen in many spots. It's easy to bypass the fist/offwidth pitch by climbing the second pitch 5.8 handcrack of Mordor.

C. Middle Earth   5.10b R★★★

FA: Bruce Brossman, Mike Breidenbach, 1985.

An old-school route that manages to wind its way up the steep face left of Hobbit Book at a moderate grade, Middle Earth is a sustained, wandering climb with many heady face climbing sections.

It's easy to confuse the start of Middle Earth with an old abandoned project that starts just left of Hobbit Book in another right-leaning crack. Middle Earth starts in a fist crack near the big right-facing corner of Serrated Edge (old-school 5.10 wide), while the project starts just left of Hobbit Book and is thin hands.

Starting up an awkward leaning fist crack that ends 60 feet up, it's best to end the pitch at an awkward belay 15 feet before the end of the crack at a foothold next to the hand crack. If you set the belay at the end of the crack, you risk a Factor 2 fall on the belay (and straight onto the belayer if the leader takes the bulge on the right).

The second pitch starts with the crux of the route, a 5.10 bulge with a couple different options, both of which lack protection and have a bad landing on the sloping ledge. While the route has traditionally been rated 5.10a, this bulge is pretty hard and heady for that rating, and the 1982 Alan Nelson guide to Tuolumne called it 5.10+. After pulling the bulge, a thin piton gives at least psychological pro up a slopey ramp to a bolt. A long traverse right to the dike crack gets easier the further

right you move, so it isn't bad for the leader, but the follower risks a big penji.

The third pitch has two hard sections, one up a featured face right of the first bolt, and the second a downward traverse to the flake from the second bolt. The flake is fairly hollow, and the thicker stronger sections of the flake should be used for protection.

The fourth pitch follows a featured dike up and right with intermittent pro. Near the top, an excellent hand crack leads to a short knobby face to a small belay ledge with anchor pro in an arching undercling. Don't continue up to the bigger ledge with a cave up and left, since the only pro is behind a large detached block.

The last pitch has a couple options – follow the dike at 5.9 R/X with tiny cams and nuts as the only pro, or follow thin cracks up and right to the very top of the last pitch of Hobbit Book.

D. Hobbit Book 5.7 R★★★★★

Time to climb route:	**2–4 hours**
Approach time:	**1.5–2 hours**
Descent time:	**1.5–2 hours**
Sun exposure:	**late afternoon**
Height of route:	**500′**

The Hobbit Book has the feeling of a remote alpine climb, despite being only a mile from the road. An airy 4th class traverse above a sweeping 500-foot wall brings you to the start of the route. Add the major runouts on a steep reachy face pitch, the time-consuming approach hike, and roped 4th class traverse, and the Hobbit Book adds up to a day far more comparable to the Regular Route of Fairview Dome than to West Crack or other multi-pitch climbs with short approaches.

FA: Charlie Raymond and Gordon Webster, 1965.

History

On Mariuolumne Dome there exists a beautiful curving open book, quite visible from the road and just begging to be climbed. When Charlie Raymond and Gordie Webster did the first ascent in 1965, they knew they had a winner. The upper pitches were a fantasy come true: knobs covered a steep wall that had looked intimidating from below. The climbing was easy and "fantastic" – a favorite word of the day. This fantasy wall had to have a dramatic name, and thus was born the Hobbit Book.

During the 1960s an obscure series of books became mandatory reading for an enormous number of youthful Americans seeking a temporary escape from the terrible crises of that era (assassinations, Vietnam, race riots, loss of faith in institutions, and so on). *The Hobbit*, written in 1937, and the trilogy *Lord of the Rings,* published during World War II, stemmed from the vivid imagination of one J.R.R. Tolkien, a South African professor later known as the "father of fantasy literature." The books mentioned above have sold 85 million copies at last count and have

spawned a major motion picture trilogy.

Tolkien's hobbits were furry "little people" who loved to luxuriate outside their burrows, never exercising, simply preferring to be left alone. Hobbits were thus the opposite of the climbers who read these wondrous tales, but the more heroic characters appealed to us all.

Climber Joe Kelsey named (and still names) all his myriad golden retrievers after his favorite Tolkien characters. I remember one named Arwen Evenstar and another called Samwise. I briefly succumbed to this naming trend in 1968 when Dick Erb and I christened a meaningless new route not far left of the Hobbit Book. We called it Strider after an enigmatic character who had a role in the books.

– Steve Roper

Strategy

Start early as the route is popular, the approach is long, and there is no way to pass slower parties. Survey the parking lot. If there are cars and no one is on OZ (passed after ten minutes on the way up), there are almost certainly climbers ahead of you. The lack of an approach trail for a big section of boulder scrambling coupled with a long 4th class traverse from around the corner makes it easy to get off route and lose time.

Hobbit Book is generally perfect in the high season of mid-summer. However, it is high and shaded, and can be frigid in colder or windy weather. There is some loose rock, especially on Pitches 2 and 4. The best time to climb is mid- to late summer once the snowbank on the 4th class traverse has melted.

The third pitch is the business. A short run up the dihedral leads to a 30-foot traverse to a bolt. Above is a steep 60-foot face of plates with no easy protection, which demands a calm and cool head. It is possible to tie off plates with long (double-length) runners for those familiar with slip knots, especially with thin modern slings. The climbing is difficult for those under 5'10" due to repeated reachy moves. Use delicate footwork to get the best handholds and avoid pulling straight out on the thin plates.

Hobbit Book Retreat

Thunderstorms mandate immediate retreat due to the high location and long and difficult descent. Retreat by leaving pro at a variety of spots. Several fixed pins exist on the first two pitches that can be used in combination with your own gear. Stay roped up for the 4th class traverse and place lots of gear if descending this ledge system in the rain.

Climbs on the Descent

The Mariuolumne Dome descent gully, which bypasses all the 4th class approach terrain, comes down next to a steep 200-foot wall called the North Wall of Mariuolumne Dome. Immediately next to the descent gully are a couple of steep hand cracks including the classic Seconds to Darkness.

A. Mmmm…Crackahol   5.9 or 10a★★★★

FA: Greg Barnes, Jonathan duSaint, September 2006.

An excellent end-of-the-day route just left of Seconds to Darkness, with great crack climbing which winds around the arête. There are two possible starts – the overhung hand crack on the left, or the handcrack corner on the right. The 5.10a left start has a block behind it that mandates great care for the leader, as a backwards fall might see the leader hit the block. The right start has a challenging hand traverse/mantle crux.

B. George's Toprope   5.9+★★★

FA: George Ridgley, 2007.

Toprope knobs to flakes left of Seconds to Darkness, join Seconds for a short bit, then traverse right across face to a small roof and thin face. Good, challenging, and varied.

C. Seconds to Darkness   5.8★★★★

FA: Don Reid, Alan Roberts, July 1989.

Perfect for the end of the day (hence the name), Seconds to Darkness takes a zig-zagging hand crack through a roof. Burly, steep climbing, it'll feel a lot harder if you have no experience with steep hand cracks. With no holds over the roof except the 2-3" crack, this route is substantially harder for people with really small hands.

A. Mmmm…Crackahol 5.9/10a★★★★
nuts: 1 set
cams: 1 ea. 0.6-1", 3-4"
        2 ea. 1.25-2"

B. George's Toprope 5.9+★★★

C. Seconds to Darkness 5.8★★★★
nuts: 1 set
cams: 2 ea 1.5-3"
        extra 2"

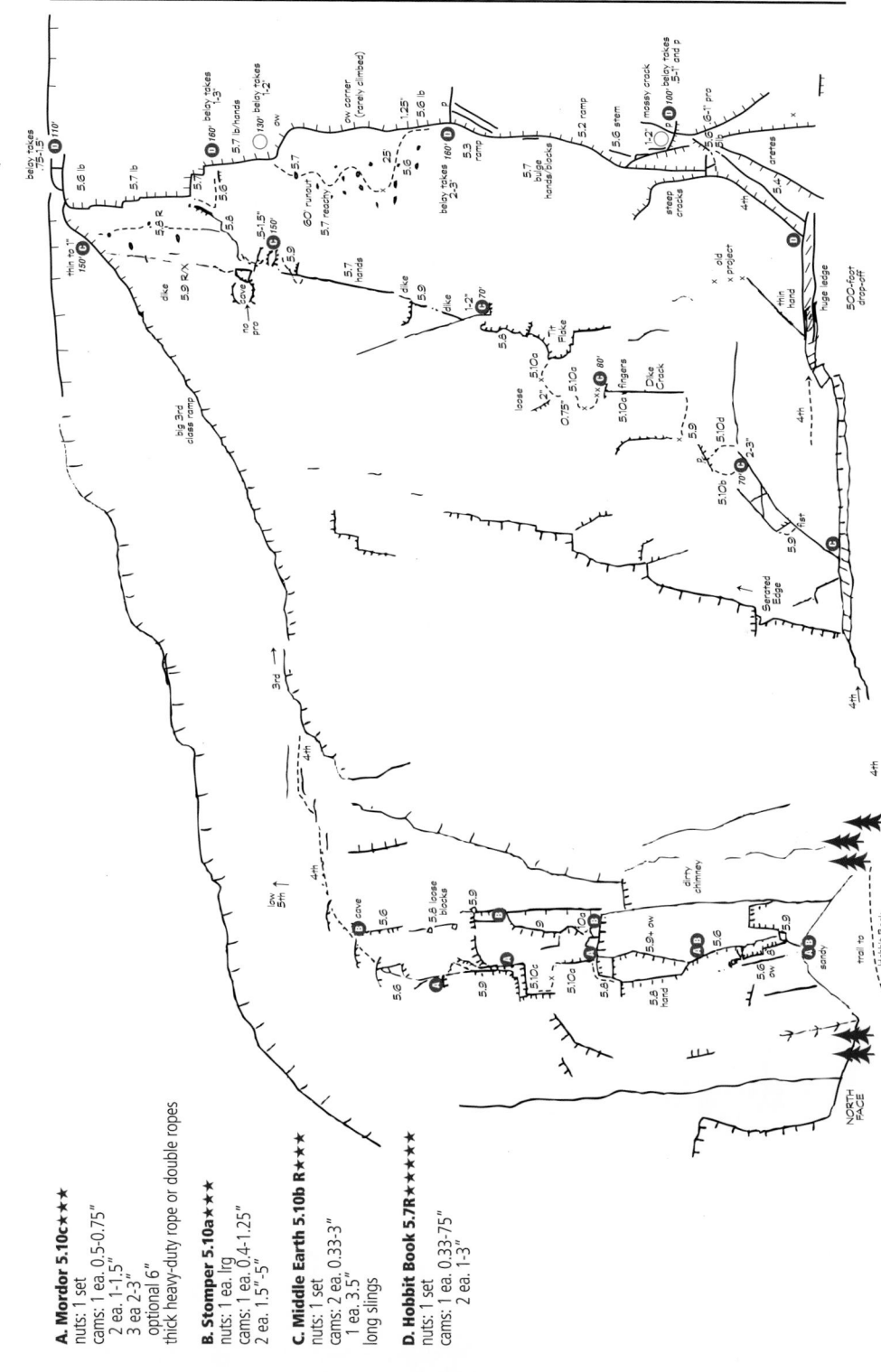

A. Mordor 5.10c ★★★
nuts: 1 set
cams: 1 ea. 0.5-0.75"
2 ea. 1-1.5"
3 ea. 2-3"
optional 6"
thick heavy-duty rope or double ropes

B. Stomper 5.10a ★★★
nuts: 1 ea. lrg
cams: 1 ea. 0.4-1.25"
2 ea. 1.5"-5"

C. Middle Earth 5.10b R ★★★
nuts: 1 set
cams: 2 ea. 0.33-3"
1 ea. 3.5"
long slings

D. Hobbit Book 5.7R ★★★★
nuts: 1 set
cams: 1 ea. 0.33-75"
2 ea. 1-3"

Medlicott Dome, Left

Approach time: **30–40 minutes**

Sun exposure: **mid-morning to sunset**

Height of routes: **500'**

The mile-long west face of Medlicott Dome is home to some of the best face and crack routes in Tuolumne. The left end has a nearly detached buttress of lighter-colored rock, which is home to excellent crack and face climbs, including the 1976 Dale Bard classic Scorpion (5.11b). All old bolts have been replaced on the routes listed here.

Approach:

Park at a small dirt pullout in the trees on the east side of the highway about 200 yards north of the Low Profile Dome pullout. Do NOT park in the large pullout that is directly across from where you're headed (the pullout for Galen's Crack). While this is the closest to the wall, it's a nasty bog and dense small tree forest with no trail. Please try to minimize climber impact by using the main Medlicott parking. This lot is often full since it is popular with hikers, climbers, and also used to access the Cathedral Lakes for fishing. If it's full park along the road, or at the large Low Profile Dome parking area and walk. The free shuttle will drop you at the latter lot.

From the parking lot, follow the obvious trail through a muddy bog – stay on trail, please don't damage the delicate meadow by trying to take a shortcut. Immediately after the meadow the trail contours right – go straight ahead into the forest past a boulder.

A major hiking trail is only about 100 feet ahead – take this to the left through a zone of densely packed small trees (major avalanche zone in winter). After about 200 yards, you will see larger trees and more open country, with a climbers trail which is often cairned. This leads to Medlicott Center. Keep going another quarter-mile, then head up shortly before a dense stand of smaller trees. An alternate approach is to hike up the Center trail, then hike down along the base of the wall. This is easier to follow, but steeper and gains extra elevation.

Descent

Rappel the routes (usually with two 60m ropes). For the routes that top out, hike south along the top of Medlicott Dome, then down 3rd class rocky gullies and slabs, and pick up the fishing/hiking trail which leads back to the Bachar-Yerian area. Make sure to find the trail as it heads down directly below the Bachar-Yerian, and follow this back to the road.

A	South Country	F	Scorpion	F'	Shagadellic
E	Super Chicken	E'	Excellent, Smithers	A'	The Coming

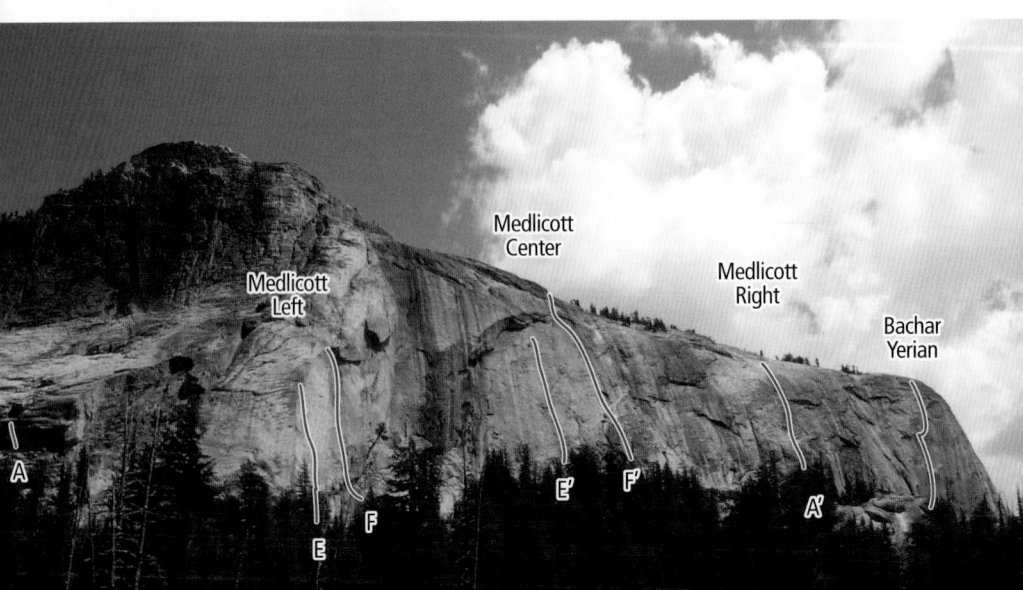

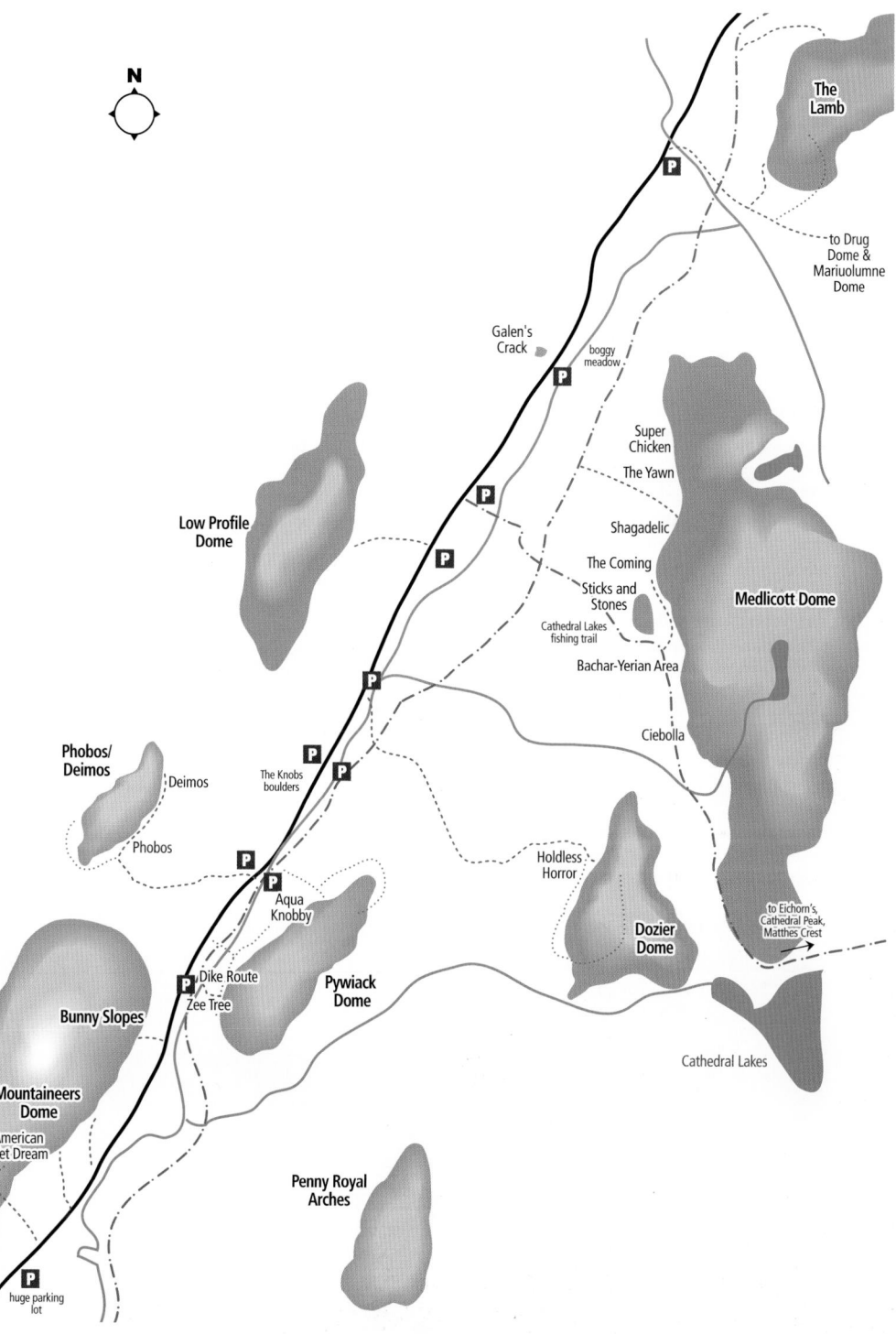

N

The Lamb

P

to Drug Dome & Mariuolumne Dome

Galen's Crack

boggy meadow

P

Super Chicken

The Yawn

Low Profile Dome

P

Shagadelic

The Coming

P

Sticks and Stones

Medlicott Dome

Cathedral Lakes fishing trail

Bachar-Yerian Area

P

Ciebolla

Phobos/ Deimos

Deimos

P

The Knobs boulders

P

Holdless Horror

Phobos

P

to Eichorn's, Cathedral Peak, Matthes Crest

P

Aqua Knobby

Dozier Dome

Dike Route

P

Pywiack Dome

Zee Tree

Bunny Slopes

Cathedral Lakes

Mountaineers Dome

American Wet Dream

Penny Royal Arches

P

huge parking lot

A. South Country 5.10c★★★

FA: Greg Barnes, Karin Wuhrmann, August 2003.

This steep short route climbs the right wall of the huge chimney splitting an overhung section of cliff about 100 yards left of Chicken Little.

A steep, varied sport climb in a wild setting, South Country climbs the right (south) wall of the beginning chimney of Another Country, a 1962 route up the north face of Medlicott Dome. South Country climbs a slightly overhung offset offwidth to face to arête. Originally done with big bros, sketchy thin pins and pro, and a single bolt. A ground anchor should be set for the belayer (two 3" cams work best).

B. Chicken Little 5.9 R★★

FA: Alan Bartlett, Dimitri Barton, 1984.

A fun old-school route, Chicken Little starts up a 4" crack, then slab climbs up a dike to a horizontal crack belay, then up slabby lieback cracks to the top of the dome. Lots of runouts on this old-school route – even the lieback cracks up high often have no pro. A selection of smaller cams (.4-1.25") is required for setting the horizontal crack anchor on top of pitch 1.

C. Pussy Paws 5.10c X★★★

FA: Dimitri Barton, Alan Bartlett, Jack Roberts, 1984.

Very runout slab climbing, and a bit crumbly. Only extremely confident leaders should even consider this route. The third pitch starts with a runout of over 100 feet off the belay!

D. Loco Yokel 5.10d★★★

FA: Greg Barnes, Karin Wuhrmann, Jonathan duSaint, September 2007.

Burly, technical dihedral to a long pumpy lieback. Steep, powerful, and tenuous climbing up the initial dihedral is tightly protected with bolts and gear, and then a lieback with thin gear leads to a flake lieback pumpfest with bolts once the gear runs out. If lowering from the first pitch, it's a couple feet longer than half a 60m rope. If continuing, the belay is basically a hanging belay and a butt-bag is nice. The second pitch starts with thin moves that ease quickly to a cool, knobby, airy arête that is the left arête of the entire mile-long face of Medlicott. You can just barely rap with a single 60m rope – tie knots in the ends.

E. Super Chicken 5.9 or 5.9 X★★★★

FA: Jim Wilson and Rick Accomazzo, June 1974.

Super Chicken is an excellent, steep climb up a knobby hand crack dihedral, with a cool face traverse to finish.

Avoid the unprotected third pitch by a rappel with two 60m ropes from the second belay.

Retreat from the first pitch can be problematic; slings around loose blocks on the right end of the ledge is probably the best option.

F. Scorpion   5.11b★★★★★

FA: Dale Bard, Bob Locke. July 1976.

A classic, wildly steep testpiece of the 1970s, Scorpion is easily one of the best routes of the grade in Tuolumne. Steep face, slab, and crack climbing on three superb pitches leads to a quick rappel to the base. The bolts are camouflaged tan and can be hard to spot.

G. Wailing Wall (p1)   5.11d★★★★

FA (5.7 A3): Dave Calfee, TM Herbert, 1967. FFA: Rick Accomazzo, Dale Bard, Jim Bridwell, 1975.

This burly testpiece was one of the first 5.12 routes in the U.S., although the introduction of sticky rubber dropped the rating a notch. Wild stemming leads to a powerful, tricky

crux to easier but very pumpy climbing. Watch out for the rope dragging cams into the crack at the lip. The route continues up with several excellent 5.10+ pitches including a burly 5.10d roof flare.

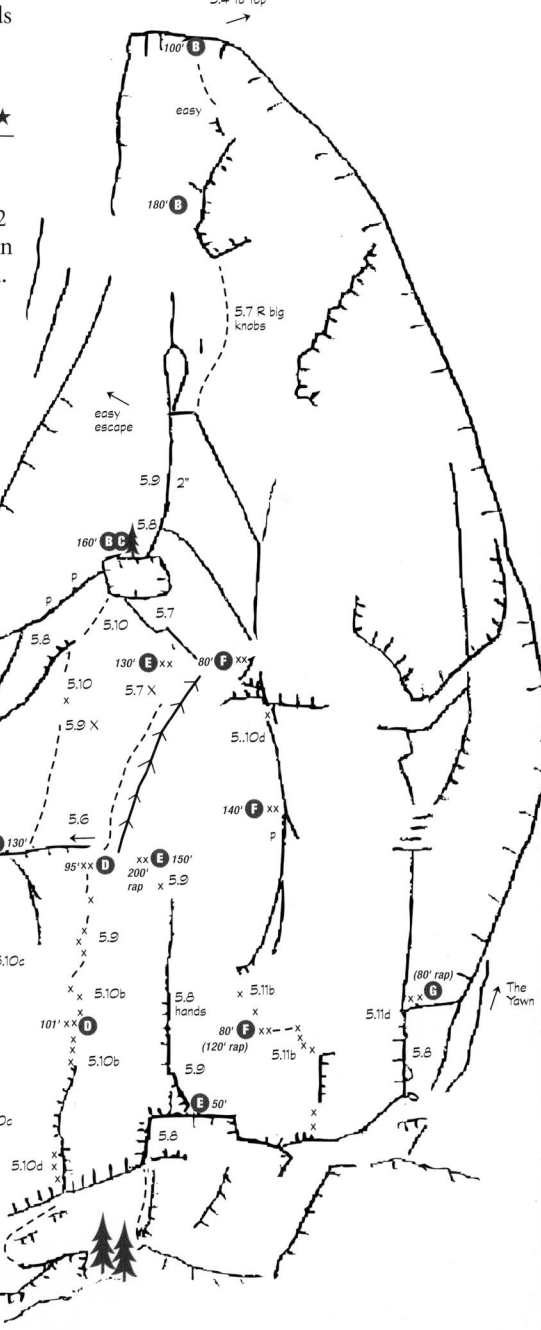

A. South Country 5.10c★★★
5 quickdraws,cams: 2-3 ea. 3" for anchor,
optional 0.75-1" for route

B. Chicken Little 5.9 R★★
·nuts: 1 set, cams: 2 ea. 0.4-1.25", 4"
1 ea. 1.5-3"

C. Pussy Paws 5.10c X★★
cams: 1 ea. 0.4-2"

D. Loco Yokel 5.10d★★★
nuts: 2 ea. small, medium, cams: 2 ea. 0.33-1"
1 ea. 1.25-3", 7 quickdraws

E. Super Chicken 5.9★★★★
nuts: 1 ea sml, med, 2 ea lrg; cams: 1 ea .5-1.25",
2 ea 1.5-3", opt. extra 1.5-3"; many slings

F. Scorpion 5.11b★★★★★
nuts: 1 set cams: 2 ea. 0.6-1.5" 1 ea. 0.5, 2"
optional extra 1" 6 quickdraws

G. Wailing Wall (p1) 5.11d★★★★
nuts: 1 set cams: 2 ea. 0.6-3",
optional extra 1-2"

Medlicott Dome, Center

Approach time: 30–40 minutes

Sun exposure: mid-morning to sunset

Height of routes: 500'

Featured, moderate multipich slab and crack routes with excellent rock are the draw of the center section of Medlicott Dome. It has wide-open expanses of granite, well-protected moderate routes, great knobs, flakes, and dikes, and a large friendly base area with good views. Crowds are common for Shagadelic, but there are several single and multipitch options along the base.

Approach

Park at a small dirt pullout in the trees on the east side of the highway about 200 yards north of the Low Profile Dome pullout. The lot is often full since it is popular with hikers, climbers, and also used to access the Cathedral Lakes for fishing. If it's full park along the road, or at the large Low Profile Dome parking area and walk. The free shuttle will drop you at the latter lot. From the parking lot, follow the obvious trail through a muddy bog – stay on trail, don't damage the delicate meadow by trying to take a shortcut. Immediately after the meadow the trail contours right – go straight ahead into the forest past a boulder. A major hiking trail is only about 100 feet ahead – take this to the left through a zone of densely packed small trees (major avalanche zone in winter). After about 200 yards, you will see larger trees and more open country. Look for an obvious trail, often with a cairn at the start. This trail leads directly to below Excellent, Smithers, then cuts right towards Shagadelic. An alternate approach is to do the Medlicott Right approach, then hike along the base of the wall. This is more scenic, but much longer (see map).

Descent

Rappel the routes (usually with two 60m ropes). For the routes which top out, hike south along the top of Medlicott Dome, then down 3rd class rocky gullies and slabs, and pick up the fishing/hiking trail which leads back to the Bachar-Yerian area. Make sure to find the trail as it heads down directly below the Bachar-Yerian, and follow this back to the road. If you left gear at the base, continue along the base of the dome to your packs.

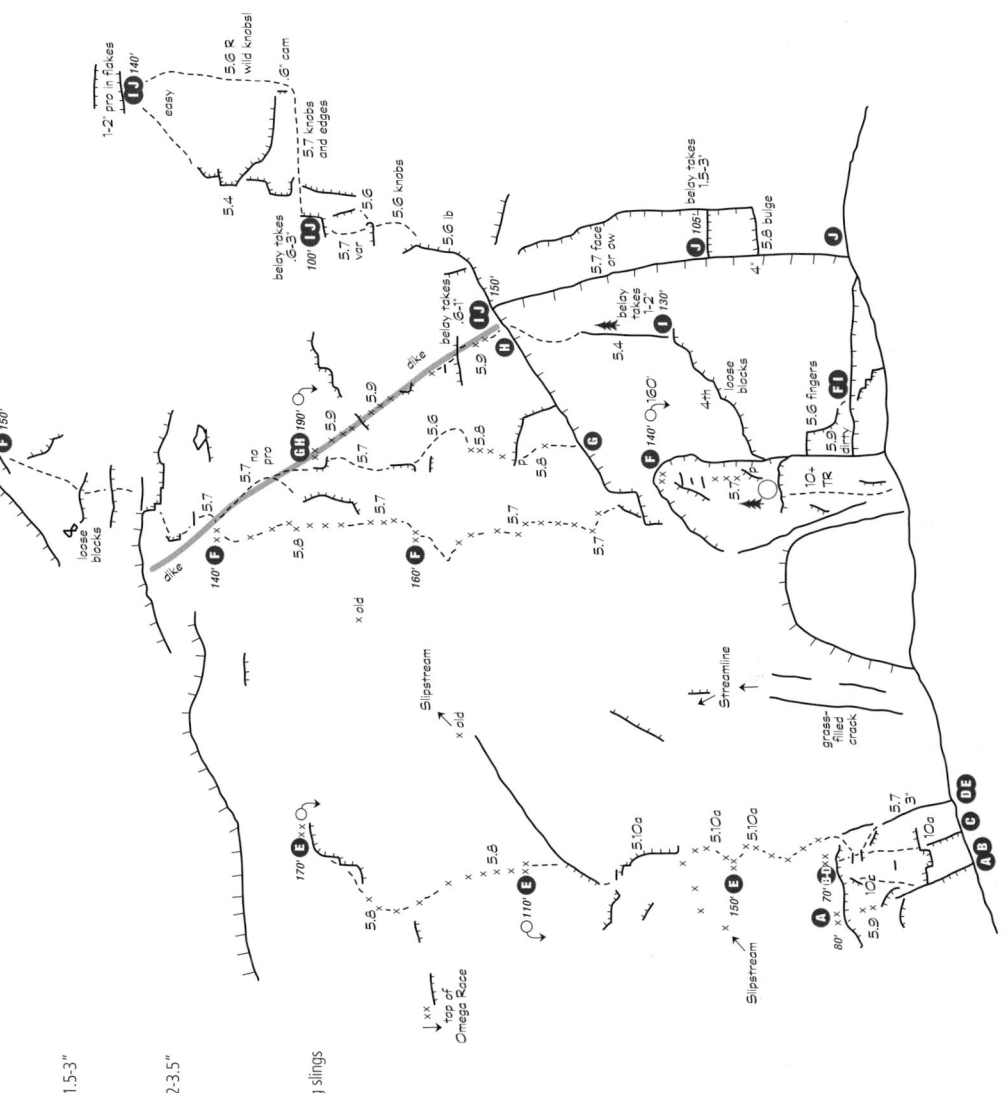

A. Beer 5.9★★★ nuts: 1 set cams: 2 ea. 0.6-1.25" 1 ea. 1.5-3"

B. Beernuts 5.10c★★ toprope

C. Donuts 5.10a★★★ toprope

D. D'oh 5.7★★★ nuts: 1 set; cams: 1 ea 1.25-1.5" , 2 ea 2-3.5"

E. Excellent, Smithers 5.10a★★★★ nuts: 1 set; cams: 1 ea .3-3.5"; 9 quickdraws

F. Shagadelic 5.8★★★★ nuts: 1 set; cams; 1 ea .3-2", opt. extra .6-.75", 10 quickdraws

G. Fook Mi 5.8 R★★ nuts: 1 ea med; cams: 1 ea 1"; long slings

H. Goldmember 5.9★★★★ nuts: 1 set; cams: 1 ea .6-1.5" , 9 quickdraws

I. Piss Easier 5.6 R★ nuts: 1 set; cams: 2 ea .6-1.5", 1 ea 2-3"; many long slings

J. Piss Easy 5.8 R★★★ nuts: 1 set; cams: 1 ea .4-5", 2 ea .6-4"; opt. extra1 ea 3-5"; many slings

A. Beer   5.9★★★

FA: Greg Barnes, Bryan Law, June 2007.

Fun left-leaning cracks to flakes and a short crimpy face past two bolts. It's easy to traverse from the anchor of Beer to the anchor for the first section of Excellent, Smithers. The first half of this route was an old toprope that continued across the face to the right at 5.10.

B. Beernuts   5.10c★★

From the anchor for D'oh!, toprope the first half of Beer then up the face.

C. Donuts   5.10a★★★

Excellent toprope up a small knobby dihedral and through a cool roof. This climb is straight under the anchor of D'oh.

D. D'oh!   5.7★★★

FA: unknown, 1950s or 1960s.

D'oh! appears to be an inviting, clean, wide hand crack on a slab, yet it has surprisingly sharp knobs inside the crack (where the name comes from). Take care to avoid slicing up your hands – a perfect climb for Hand Jammies or heavy tape gloves. From the anchor, toprope Beernuts and/or Donuts.

E. Excellent, Smithers   5.10a★★★★

FA: Greg Barnes and Karin Wuhrmann, July 2002.

This is one of the few face climbs of its grade in Tuolumne with good protection. Crossing through the slab testpiece Slipstream (5.11c) on its third pitch, and neighbored by such climbs as the unfinished slab route Vapor Lock (5.11c), no one would expect this line to go at such a moderate rating. The first ascent team did not even intend to do this route, just to put a good anchor on the obvious fun crack at the start (D'oh!), which previously had only a single hangerless 1/4" bolt as the anchor.

Carry two 60m ropes to rappel. Thunderstorms have a nasty habit of sneaking up on Medlicott from behind. In a downpour this route becomes a waterfall.

F. Shagadelic   5.8★★★★

FA: Greg Barnes and Barry Hutten, June 2001.

With fun knob climbing up a gray waterstreak, Shagadelic is the longer and better-protected version of Golfer's Route. It is perfectly positioned in the middle of Medlicott Dome, with the spectacular buttress of the Wailing Wall and The Yawn to one side, and a view all the way to Half Dome on the other. While very well protected by Tuolumne standards, it is not a sport climb. Be careful, especially at the start of the fourth pitch where a tricky horizontal .3-.4" cam placement is the only protection for the first 40 feet.

This could have been another runout Tuolumne face climb, but the first ascent team wanted the average 5.8 leader to enjoy the route.

The route is wet in early season. It is common to have wet sand and pebbles on the first pitch after a thunderstorm. The route is a waterfall in a downpour.

G. Fook Mi   5.8 R★★

FA: Greg Barnes and Karin Wuhrmann, June 2002.

Fun and strange face climbing and mantels lead to some huge runouts (don't break a knob.). The anchor (shared with Goldmember) is in a cool hole along a dike. You can toprope Fook Mi after leading Goldmember (two 60m ropes required). The pitch is a rope-stretcher with a 60m rope (195 feet). A fun second pitch (5.7 X) up the dike crosses through Slipstream to join Shagadelic at its third anchor, but has no protection at all, so most will rappel (two 60m ropes required).

H. Goldmember   5.9★★★★

FA: Jake Whittaker, free solo, 2001. Possibly soloed earlier.

Goldmember is a great and well-protected climb on slab and edges so slick that they are reminiscent of climber-polished limestone or the Glacier Point Apron. Unbeknownst to the first roped ascent team, this route had previously been free-soloed. The roped team offered to remove their bolts, but the soloist declined the offer.

I. Piss Easier   5.6 R★

FA: unknown.

The easiest way to the top of Medlicott, Piss Easier starts on Shagadelic, then follows a very easy but loose ramp and crack system to the top of the second pitch of Piss Easy thereby avoiding the best, but also the hardest, climbing on the latter route.

J. Piss Easy   5.8 R★★★

FA: Tom Higgins and Bob Kamps, June 1968.

Great climbing up a huge white book, Piss Easy (aka West Face of Medlicott) used to be rated 5.7 as most climbers were far more proficient at wide cracks and liebacking. Now rated 5.8, Piss Easy is good, awkward climbing with unusually good protection for its wider cracks. It is an excellent introduction to offwidth climbing. The third pitch follows an easy flake to a fairly short, unprotected 5.6 face. Above, easy climbing up dirty corners leads to the top.

After the second pitch you can access the previous three routes using the huge 4th class ramp (often has loose pebbles and sand).

The upper pitches are usually wet in early season – if there is a snow patch on top, there is probably water running down the slabs. A snow bank is common at the base in early season. A fat resident marmot awaits those foolhardy enough to leave anything (edible or not) at the base.

Cedar Wright on High Heels with Medlicott Dome in the background. Photo by Corey Rich.

Medlicott Dome, Right

Approach time: 30–45 minutes

Sun exposure: mid-morning to sunset

Height of routes: 100-700'

This is the widest and perhaps most beautiful dome in Tuolumne and is home to some of the hardest and scariest face climbs in California. The infamous testpiece Bachar-Yerian ascends the first large black streak on the golden right side of the dome. Yet among the 5.11 X and 5.13 climbs are some overlooked classics of the 1960s and 1970s, plus some fun easier sport climbs. The base of Medlicott Dome is 500 feet higher than the parking lot, and many people underestimate the hike at altitude.

Approach

(See page 118 for directions to the parking area.) From the parking lot, follow the obvious trail through a muddy bog – stay on the trail, don't damage the delicate meadow by trying to shortcut. Immediately after the meadow the trail contours right, then intersects a hiking trail after another 100 yards. Head uphill on the most traveled trail here (not right!), and follow the trail carefully as it heads up and far to the right.

Resist the temptation to cut straight up to the dome. After about 0.25 mile, the trail gets into rocks and passes some drop-offs, then cuts back up left to the base of the Bachar-Yerian area. The trail continues right and eventually takes you to the Cathedral Lakes (this trail is the Cathedral Lakes fishing trail). Note carefully where you come out of the trees – you will need to find the trail when descending. For The Coming area, hike left along a climbers' trail at the base of the wall. For the Bachar-Yerian area, the 5.6 approach starts below the left side of the huge ledge 80 feet above. For the Ciebolla area, hike right for about 200 yards.

Descent

Rappel the routes. If topping out on The Coming, hike right and around back to the bottom. Retrace the approach.

A. The Coming   5.9 R★★★★

FA: Tom Higgins and Bob Kamps, 6/68.

The Coming is steep and sustained up a big right-facing corner. It's a great climb for the well-rounded climber with a bit of everything from chimney to steep hands to tricky liebacking to knobby face. This is a stellar 1960s route that was established by the master Tuolumne free climbers of the era.

The first two pitches are fairly well protected at the harder sections. The first pitch is somewhat loose and dirty, but the intimidating chimney is easy due to hidden cracks in the back. An excellent alternate start to the right is 5.10a, and recommended over the original start.

The third pitch huge runout on 5.6 knobs gives the climb an R rating. This section can be avoided with a better-protected, yet still runout, 5.8 face.

If rappelling, be aware that two 60m ropes are mandatory unless you have a 20-foot section of webbing to leave around a large block on a ledge left of the second pitch anchor. Also, the rappel anchor on top of the third pitch is two fixed medium nuts, which may or may not be there, so be prepared to leave nuts if you intend to rappel.

B. Come and Get It   5.10b R★★★★

FA: Scott Burk, August 1990.

Beautiful climbing up a knobby arête and face. The tricky crux comes right before you can clip a bolt, where a nasty fall will launch you around the arête into the corner. It is easily toproped by rappelling from the fixed nuts on top of The Coming's third pitch.

C. Approach Pitch   5.6★

A short, easy climb used to access all the climbs above.

D. Peace (Pitch 1)   5.10b R-★★★

FA: Pitch 1: John Bachar; Pitch 2: Ron Kauk.

The first pitch has fun knob climbing that is a bit runout. Check out the insane second pitch, currently one of the hardest face climbs (5.13c) in Tuolumne.

E. Pretty in Pink Point (P 1)   5.10a★★★★

FA: Steve Schneider, July 1990.

One of the best moderate knob sport climbs in Tuolumne. The tricky roof start is the crux, and the climbing higher up is just downright fun. The second pitch is 5.12c.

F. Unknown   5.10d★★★

Good sport climb with a distinct crux at the top. A 5.9 move before the first bolt has ankle-breaking potential, so get a good spot.

G. 15 Minutes of Fame   5.11a★★★★

FA: Errett Allen, Ken Yager, Karen Young

Excellent thin face climbing.

H. Big Time   5.11b★★★★

Another top-quality face climb.

I. Shady Rest   5.10c R-★★

Slick face to thin slab.

J. Hill Crest Drive   5.10a R-★★

Circuitous slab – short leaders may have trouble clipping bolts.

K. Lechlinski Flake   5.11a R-★★★★

FA: Mike Lechlinski and John Bachar, 7/81.

This Tuolumne classic climbs a spectacular thin flake on the right side of the Bachar-Yerian wall. Lechlinski Flake is not to be missed, yet it is rarely done. The anchor had terrible 1/4" bolts, but they were replaced by the ASCA in 2002.

The first pitch has two options; a fun 5.7 flake system, or a serious, but excellent, wandering 5.10b R pitch. You can lower off the second pitch anchor with a single 60m rope, but two ropes are required to rappel off the first pitch. At the belay ledge, try to spot a black bolt high on the black knobby face to the right – this is the first bolt on the classic (and massively runout) Bachar testpiece, You Asked For It (5.10c X).

The crux second pitch has thin and often hollow pro, and the leader must often fire up a distance before getting a placement. It's a somewhat serious, off-balanced, and burly lead. The 5.11c R/X Bachar and Kauk route Swinger continues above.

L. Ciebolla   5.10b★★★★★

FA: Vern Clevenger, Bob Harrington, and Alan Bartlett, 6/77.

The slick and polished first pitch often scares people off. But the second pitch, an excellent sustained face with knobs and edges, is one of the best face pitches in Tuolumne.

You can do two rappels to the ground from the original anchor with a single 70m rope using the anchor for Alien, which was replaced in 2002 by the ASCA.

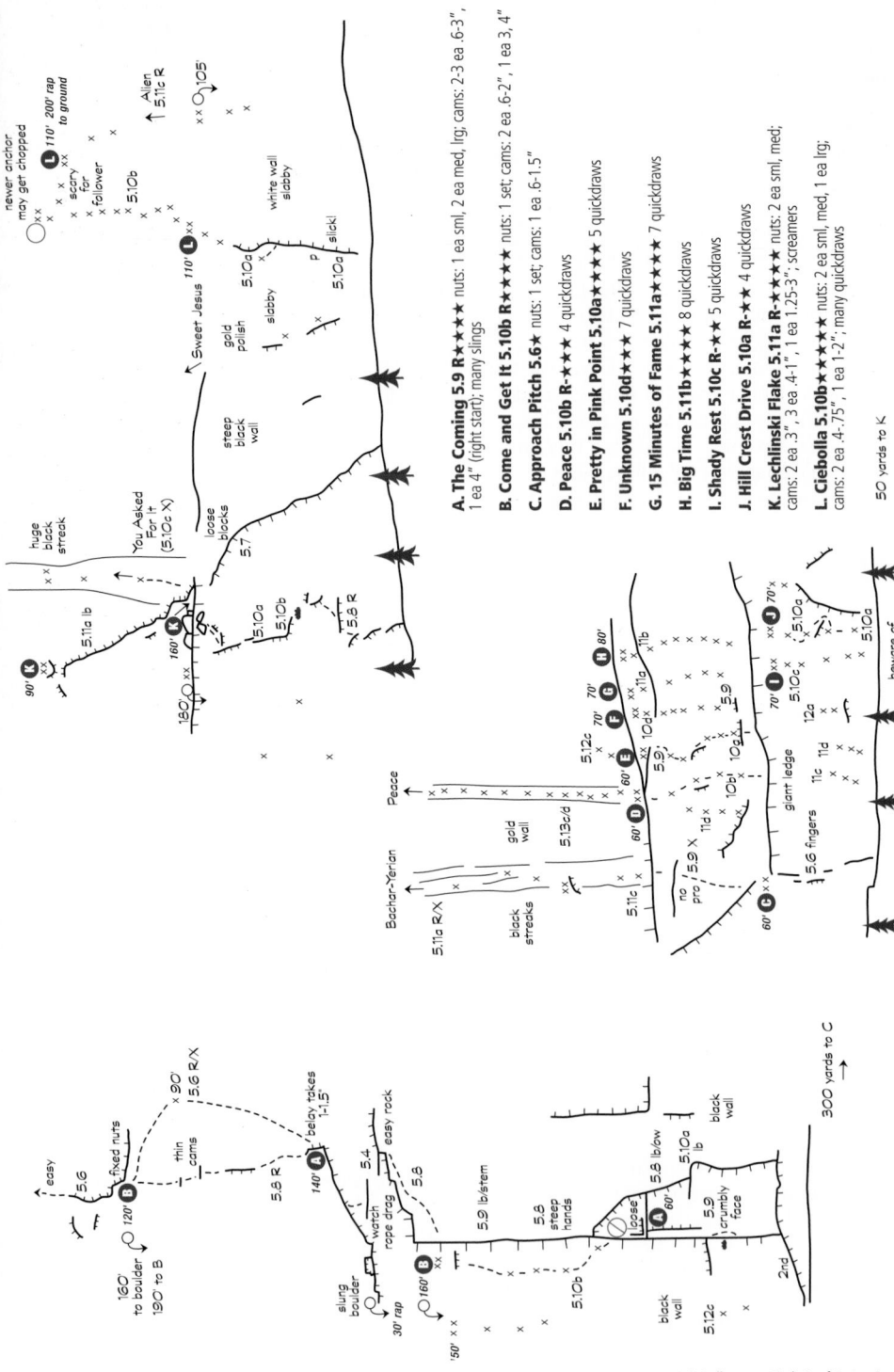

A. The Coming 5.9 R ★★★★ nuts: 1 ea sml, 2 ea med, lrg; cams: 2-3 ea .6-3", 1 ea 4" (right start); many slings

B. Come and Get It 5.10b R ★★★★ nuts: 1 set; cams: 2 ea .6-2", 1 ea 3, 4"

C. Approach Pitch 5.6 ★ nuts: 1 set; cams: 1 ea .6-1.5"

D. Peace 5.10b R ★★★ 4 quickdraws

E. Pretty in Pink Point 5.10a ★★★★ 5 quickdraws

F. Unknown 5.10d ★★★ 7 quickdraws

G. 15 Minutes of Fame 5.11a ★★★★ 7 quickdraws

H. Big Time 5.11b ★★★★ 8 quickdraws

I. Shady Rest 5.10c R ★★★ 5 quickdraws

J. Hill Crest Drive 5.10a R ★★ 4 quickdraws

K. Lechlinski Flake 5.11a R ★★★★ nuts: 2 ea sml, med; cams: 2 ea .3", 3 ea .4-1", 1 ea 1.25-3"; screamers

L. Ciebolla 5.10b ★★★★ nuts: 2 ea sml, med, 1 ea lrg; cams: 2 ea .4-.75", 1 ea 1-2"; many quickdraws

50 yards to K →

Joi Gallant on Pitch 2 of Pretty in Pink Point (5.12c). (Corey Rich)

M. Bachar/Yerian   5.11c X★★★★★

FA: John Bachar, Dave Yerian, August 1981.

The most famous psychological testpiece in the U.S., the Bachar/Yerian takes the huge black streak up the golden wall of the right side of Medlicott. While rated X for the first half of the first pitch, the reputation comes more from lots of steep, sustained, hard climbing with R/X runouts. Many climbers have whipped big off the psychological crux second pitch (often because they got lost in the knobs and ended up too far to the side from a bolt to clip), and the slab climbing on the third pitch is no giveaway. It was originally rated 5.10d and, amazingly, also criticized for the "questionable ethics" of drilling from hooks instead of stance (which would be impossible on the vertical and gently overhung wall). The story of the second ascent by Steve Schneider is harrowing, since he broke a big knob, barn-doored out, saved it and swung back in, clung desperately for a while, then did the exact same thing again on another knob.

N. Peace   5.13c★★★★★

FA: Ron Kauk, Chris Falkenstein, 1995.

One of the hardest climbs in Tuolumne, Peace takes the narrow black streak right of the Bachar/Yerian up a very long pitch of golden knobs. The first pitch and the first few bolts on the second pitch were placed by John Bachar, who called his incomplete project Die Hard.

O. You Asked For It   5.10c X★★★★★

FA: John Bachar, Ron Peers, July 1981.

The largest black streak on Medlicott Dome is the heinously runout Bachar testpiece You Asked For It. With precisely four bolts and one cam placement in three pitches of sustained face climbing and slab, You Asked For It is even more runout than another black streak that Bachar established a month later – the Bachar/Yerian. The rating of the crux first pitch is old-school, with moves that on a modern sport climb would be called 5.11 – yet even when old-school ratings were standard, Bachar originally sandbagged locals, calling it 5.10a. The right start variation is Free For All, established three years later by Bachar and Mike Lechlinski. Despite the easier rating, You Asked For It sees far less traffic than the Bachar/Yerian, probably because the hard climbing is more dangerous, slabs are not in fashion, and the climb is "only 5.10." You Asked For It has a ledge to hit for the crux first pitch, and sustained slab climbing with gigantic fall potential on lower-angled rock, while 50 to 90-foot falls off of the Bachar/Yerian result in huge air time but not that many serious injuries.

M. Bachar/Yerian 5.11c X★★★★★
4 quickdraws
cams: 1 ea. 0.6-3"
thin sling/cord for knob tie-offs on first pitch

N. Peace 5.13c★★★★★
many quickdraws (15+?)

O. You Asked For It 5.10c X★★★★★
2 quickdraws
cams: 1 ea. 0.6-3"

easy

Ⓜ

5.9 dirty

black
streak

Ⓜ 100'
3"

5.10d
slab

Ⓜ xx   Ⓝ xx 130'

5.11a   Peace
                     5.13c

Shipoopi

Ⓜ
0.75"
knob tie-off
5.11c   Ⓝ
              old

5.9 no
pro

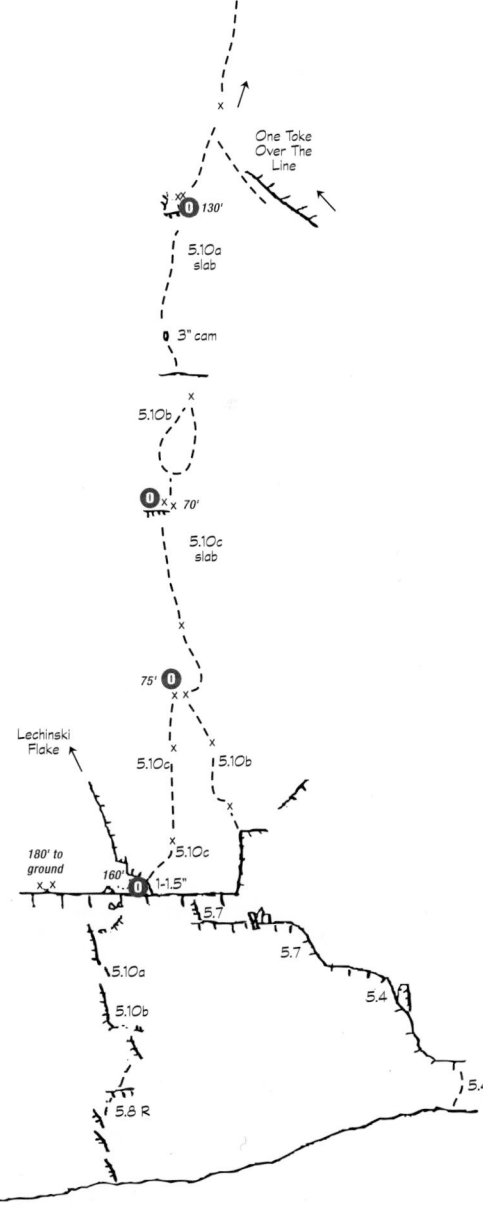

One Toke
Over The
Line

Ⓞ 130'

5.10a
slab

3" cam

5.10b

Ⓞ xx x 70'

5.10c
slab

75' Ⓞ

Lechinski
Flake

5.10c   5.10b

180' to
ground   5.10c
160' Ⓞ 1-1.5"

5.7

5.7

5.10a   5.7

5.10b   5.4

5.8 R   5.4

Sticks and Stones Cliff

The short, steep Sticks and Stones cliff is easily missed since it's below the middle of the huge face of Medlicott Dome. Burly, steep crack climbs are the name of the game at this cliff. It's possible to top out on this cliff as an approach to the main wall of Medlicott.

Approach

Take the Cathedral Lakes fishing trail, the same trail as for the right side of Medlicott Dome. The trail starts climbing steeply shortly after crossing the park service trail. About 200 yards up, the trail starts traversing right. At this point, head up and left to the 200-foot tall Sticks and Stones cliff. Don't go too far right - the cliff is basically straight above the four-way intersection of the fishing trail and the NPS trail.

Descent

You can either descend the 4th class slabs to the right (often wet in early season), or hike down either the Medlicott Center or Right trails. You can also climb The Coming or other routes on Medlicott. If you leave packs at the base, either take the 4th class slabs or, if too wet, hike right, go down the fishing trail, then back up to the base.

A. Sticks and Stones 5.10c★★★

FA: Jim Pettigrew, Will Tyree, Phil Bircheff 1972

Sticks and Stones is an awkward, burly, powerful, steep climb up a wavy hand/finger crack in a flare – and that's only the crux first pitch. Old-school 5.10a, it's a great reminder that it's not only old 5.9+ routes and offwidths that can be sandbags. The one big detractor from this great route is a short, nasty, slimy, wet section through a thorn bush (thorns in Tuolumne?!?) on the first pitch. This section has a micro-spring that is wet even in the driest years. The second pitch is an ominous offwidth to chimney, but it's way easier than it looks and pretty mellow, especially for wide cracks rated 5.9 in Yosemite. The final pitch is stellar 5.8 up intermittent cracks and knobs in a shallow corner.

   The wet section through the thorn bush detracts greatly from the star rating of the climb. A 3.5" and a 4" cam can be used in

the wet area.

The wide crack of the second pitch is not that bad, and has a huge knob to hang out on before tackling the wide crack crux.

The last pitch has intermittent, but solid, small pro protecting fun knob, flake, and dihedral climbing.

B. Chili Air   5.10a★

FA: Greg Barnes, Julie Haas, July 2007.

Crack climbing with substantial munge, a couple wide sections, and a steep sport-climbing like crux. The wide sections are hand jams in the back of awkward flares, and they are good practice for some of the wide sections on Sticks and Stones. Despite the burly short flares, be ready to switch out of crack climbing mode for the top section.

Sticks and Stones

A. Sticks & Stones 5.10c★★★
nuts: 1 set small-medium, double large
cams: 1 ea 0.5-0.75", 1 ea 4"
  2 ea 1-3.5"
  optional extra 3"

B. Chili Air 5.10a★
nuts: 1 set
cams: 1 ea. 0.6-1.5", 4"
2 ea. 2-3"

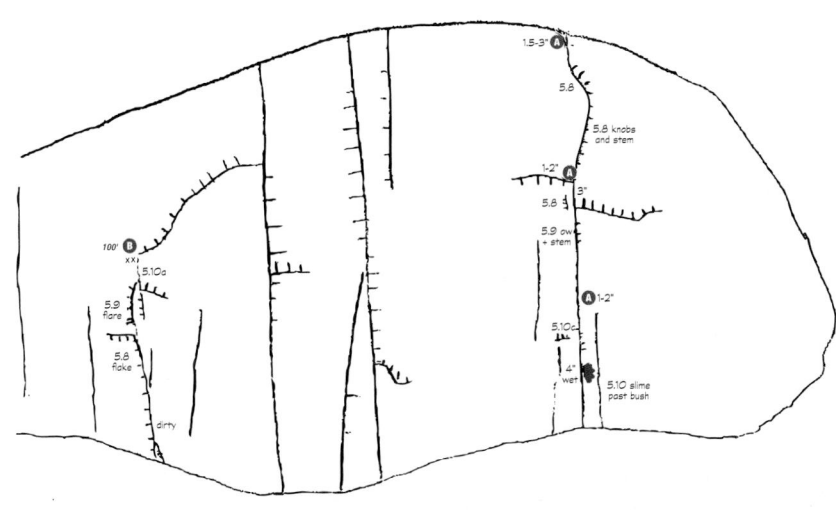

Dozier Dome

The left side of Dozier Dome, known for the classic Holdless Horror, has seen a huge amount of activity in the last few years. Dozier Dome is now home to the highest concentration of quality easier routes in all of Tuolumne, with stellar knobby faces, slabs, dikes, and cracks. A few massively runout old routes (one of which is a 500-foot 5.9 free solo!) were established many years ago, and likely never even had second ascents.

Long-time local guide Grant Hiskes had his eye on the wall for 15 years, and recently continued an old abandoned project of former local Errett Allen (an author of the 1988 Sierra Eastside climbing guide) to create the fun route Errett Out. Since then, Grant, John Shewchuk, Bill Serniuk, George Ridgley, Bryan Law, Dave Lane, and others have developed tons of high-quality routes, most with good protection (by Tuolumne standards).

Note that while these routes are well-protected for the grade in Tuolumne, they are nearly all somewhat runout in various places, as indicated on the topos. Some bolts can be hard to spot in the knobby faces. Many of these newer routes also rely heavily on knobs, and as on all knob routes in Tuolumne (particularly the new routes), knobs can and do break. Use small, sharply jutting, and/or fractured knobs with care.

These modern routes nearly all require 60m ropes to lead, and two 60m ropes to rappel. You can hike off some routes, but not all routes top out, so two 60m ropes are required for many routes.

Dozier Dome, especially this portion of the Dome, is often a waterfall of snow runoff in early season.

Approach

There are two parking areas for Dozier Dome. The first is along the road shoulder on the east side of the road about 100 yards west of the large paved Low Profile Dome pullout. Follow cairns downstream for 50 yards, then into the forest to an open slab with small boulders. You cross a major hiking trail when you reach the slab. The second is 150 yards further at the Knobs bouldering area, which is large dirt pullouts on both sides of the road at the near end of a flat straightaway. Hike east into the forest

for a few yards to pick up a major hiking trail. Follow this left (north) for 200 yards to the same open slab with small boulders.

From here, travel due east along the slab with small boulders, then follow a good trail to the right about 20 yards before the slab ends in the forest. This trail contours around swampy areas and through dense forest, and cuts the old approach time in half while avoiding the swamp. It crosses a slab, then comes up below and right of Blitzo's Balcony. Hike right to get to most of the routes. Please make sure to stay on the trail.

Descent

If you top out and don't rappel, hike around to the right (toward Tenaya Lake), then back to the base. The walk-off has several spots with running water in early season.

History

We originally suggested Lebrado Dome as an appropriate name that reflected Tuolumne Meadows history. However, the alliteration of Dozier Dome was too attractive to the Tuolumne climbing group in the early 1970s and this name made it into Tom Gerughty's binder and thence the Reid-Falkenstein guide. A few times I tried to describe the location of Lebrado Dome, only to get the "Oh, you mean Dozier Dome" response.

Now nearly 40 years later, I like the name! It's not as grand as Salathé Wall, Reed Pinnacle, or Pratt's Crack, but they were more important to the development of Yosemite climbing than I. When people learn there is a dome in Tuolumne named after me, they treat me more respectfully, as least for a day or so. This is good.

I spent most of the summers of 1970-72 working on my PhD thesis – on channel morphology in gravel bed streams, using the Dana Fork for the measurements. With a variety of partners (Eric Beck, Steve Thompson, TM Herbert, David Green, and my cousin Lance Dozier), I did many of the Dome's routes that are in the Reid-Falkenstein guide, though nothing harder than about 5.8. I thought we had put these into Gerughty's binder, but there was just a single copy of the binder, so some route descriptions were lost (e.g., Marmot's Revenge on the cliffs above the southeast side of Tenaya Lake).

When TM Herbert, Steve Thompson and I did Holdless Horror, from the approach walk the crack appeared to be smooth – climbable but maybe difficult – then we discovered there were holds inside the crack! TM said he always wanted to name a climb Holdless Horror and please could this be the one?

– Jeff Dozier, December 2007

A. Cheeseburgers & Beer 5.8★★★

FA: Bryan Law, George Ridgley, John Shewchuk, August 2005.

Fun climbing with a distinct thin crux right after the second bolt. Make sure to protect the follower from pendulums with a cam placement above the last bolt.
Rack: cams: 1-2 each 1.25-2", 7 quickdraws

B. Scandalous Summer 5.7★★

FA: John Shewchuk, Grant Hiskes, Billy "Blitzo" Serniuk, 9/04.

Slabby climbing with the crux right after the last bolt.
Rack: cams: 1 ea. 0.75-1.5"

C. White Lie 5.8 R★★★

FA: John Shewchuk, Grant Hiskes, Bill Serniuk, August 2004.

Slab with great incut edges leads to a knobby headwall and face. Walk out right on the ledge for 50 feet. There is no pro for a "ground" anchor, and there is a cruxy move before the first bolt. While there is one optional pro placement mid-pitch, gear is definitely needed for the anchor.
Rack: cams: 1 ea. 1-1.25, 2", 2 ea 1.5", 6 quickdraws

The big ledge with trees is Blitzo's Balcony, with four routes starting from the ledge.

D. Tourette's 5.10b★★★★

FA: John Shewchuk, George Ridgley, August 2007.

Excellent, sustained, and tightly-bolted route in a spectacular location. Climb one of the first tier routes to approach the ledge. A single 70m allows lowering to the ledge, but it requires two 60m ropes to rappel the approach pitch.
Rack: cams: 1.25-2" for ground anchor
13 quickdraws

E. Wrest Day 5.9★★★

FA: Lucho Rivera et al, August 2007.

Burly, old-school hourglass squeeze chimney and bombay flare/fist crack. Traverse left to anchor of Tourette's.
Rack: cams: 1 ea. 0.6-2", 2 ea. 3-4", optional 5"

F. Dumpster Evangelist 5.10a★★★★

FA: Bryan Law, George Ridgley, October 2008.

2 60M ROPES NEEDED FOR MOST ROUTES

Another top quality climb up the blunt arête right of Wrest Day. After a few pro placements up a short crack, a reachy crux past the first bolt leads to fun knob, overlap, and dike climbing.
Rack: cams: 1 ea 1-2", 10 quickdraws

G. City Girl 5.10c★★★

FA: George Ridgley et al., October 2008.

A deceptively difficult slab to shallow corner with technical slab and knobs at the top, the only reason City Girl doesn't get more stars is a section of very easy climbing in the middle of the pitch. Amusingly, the hardest route off of Blitzo's Balcony was intended to be the easiest!
Rack: 11 quickdraws, including some long draws, optional 1-1.5" pro for ground anchor

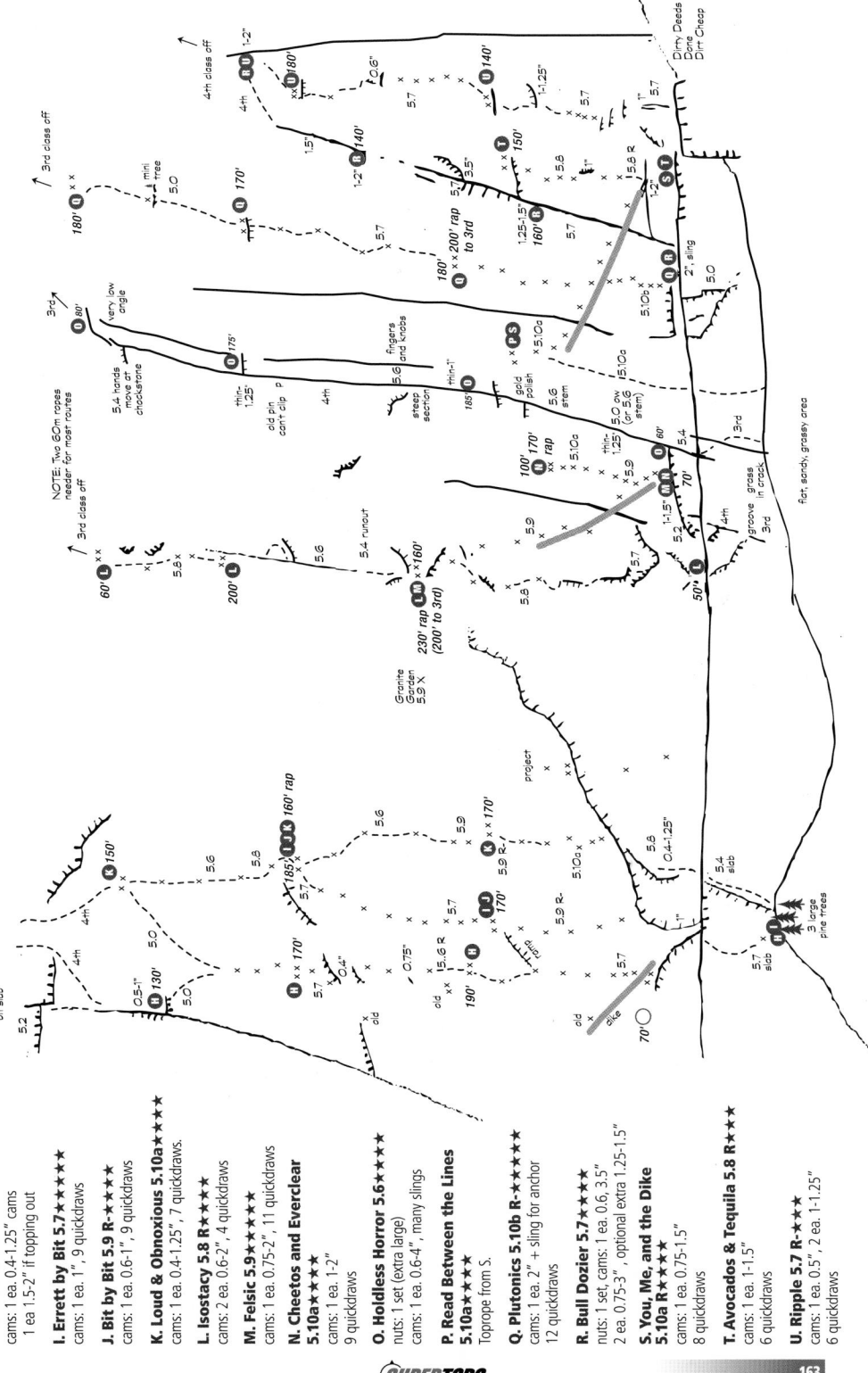

H. Errett Out 5.7 R-★★★★
cams: 1 ea. 0.4-1.25" cams
1 ea 1.5-2" if topping out

I. Errett by Bit 5.7 ★★★★★
cams: 1 ea. 1", 9 quickdraws

J. Bit by Bit 5.9 R-★★★★
cams: 1 ea. 0.6-1", 9 quickdraws

K. Loud & Obnoxious 5.10a ★★★
cams: 1 ea. 0.4-1.25", 7 quickdraws.

L. Isostacy 5.8 R ★★★★
cams: 2 ea. 0.6-2", 4 quickdraws

M. Felsic 5.9 ★★★★★
cams: 1 ea. 0.75-2", 11 quickdraws

**N. Cheetos and Everclear
5.10a** ★★★★
cams: 1 ea. 1-2"
9 quickdraws

O. Holdless Horror 5.6 ★★★★
nuts: 1 set (extra large)
cams: 1 ea. 0.6-4", many slings

**P. Read Between the Lines
5.10a** ★★★★
Toprope from S.

Q. Plutonics 5.10b R-★★★★★
cams: 1 ea. 2" + sling for anchor
12 quickdraws

R. Bull Dozier 5.7 ★★★
nuts: 1 set, cams: 1 ea. 0.6, 3.5",
2 ea. 0.75-3", optional extra 1.25-1.5"

**S. You, Me, and the Dike
5.10a R** ★★★★★
cams: 1 ea. 0.75-1.5"

T. Avocados & Tequila 5.8 R ★★★
cams: 1 ea. 1-1.5"
6 quickdraws

U. Ripple 5.7 R-★★★
cams: 1 ea. 0.5", 2 ea. 1-1.25"
6 quickdraws

To the right of White Lie on the broad face over to Errett Out are several multi-pitch routes with no bolts at all. Extremely runout, these routes are The Silence of the Cams, Unknown Route, Circus Maximus, Easy Walk, Repo Man, and Vacillation. In the vicinity of Errett Out and Bit by Bit, Jeff Dozier and Eric Beck climbed a route in 1971 called Vacillation. No bolts were used on their very runout route, which is probably closest to the modern route Errett Out and the 80s route Repo Man.

H. Errett Out   5.7 R-★★★★

FA: Grant Hiskes, John Shewchuk, Bill Serniuk, Errett Allen, September 2003.

Slab, knobs, knobs, and more knobs on three long pitches. You can rap from the top of Pitch 2 with two 60m ropes. Start up the slab past a bolt 15 feet up, then move 40 feet to the left on the ledge to a optional two-bolt belay. This belay is recommended for anyone leading near the grade of the route. Continue straight up to a hard-to-spot anchor after the 6th bolt – the belay anchor to the right is for Bit by Bit. The second pitch starts with runout knobs to a bolt 40 feet up, but you can diagonal left and clip the hidden anchor of Repo Man if you use long slings and are ready for some rope drag.

Pro 0.4-1.25" cams (first 2 pitches), a couple extra pieces in the 1-2" range for topping out.

Long-time local guide Grant Hiskes saw a bolt with a retreat biner on this route many years ago, and suspected that eastside local Errett Allen might have started the route just before leaving the area. After over a decade, Grant headed up on the route, and sure enough, the retreat biner was stamped "Errett".

I. Errett by Bit   5.7★★★★★

This is a link up of Pitch 1 of Errett Out and Pitch 2 of Bit by Bit, and it is perhaps the best face climb of its grade in Tuolumne. Skip the last bolt on Pitch 1 of Errett Out and traverse right to the anchor on Bit by Bit (easy ramp). Continuing on Bit by Bit is a final fun pitch with a few moves of 5.8.

J. Bit by Bit   5.9 R-★★★★

FA: John Shewchuk, Grant Hiskes, Bill Serniuk, George Ridgley, July 2004.

Shares the start with Errett Out, but goes straight up from the first bolt. The first pitch has sustained climbing on small knobs, and is a tad runout. The second pitch is a stellar, long knob pitch. Pay attention while looking for bolts, since it's easy to miss a few (particularly the last one). The third pitch goes past a short bulge to easy climbing. A final 4th class pitch is needed if you want to walk off instead of rappel.

K. Loud and Obnoxious   5.10a★★★★

FA: John Shewchuk, Grant Hiskes, Bill Serniuk, 2005.

The first pitch is a long, fun pitch with tightly-bolted 5.10a knob climbing and lots of sustained 5.9. Second pitch has a well-bolted 5.9 section on golden rock followed by some runouts on easy terrain. An old route called Knob Job climbed through the same section of the wall as this route, but had only one ¼" protection bolt, a single ¼" anchor bolt, and no other pro has been found – perhaps even including no-pro "belays" on sloping stances.

L. Isostacy   5.8★★★★

FA: Bryan Law, George Ridgley, Linda Jarit, October 2007.

Fun varied climbing with a sweet 195-foot 5.6 crack second pitch. After a short 3rd class approach, the first pitch climbs straight up past thin crack, overlaps, knobs, and edges. The anchor on Pitch 2 is 230 feet from the ground, so if you don't want to walk off, either rap with two 60m ropes and downclimb the 3rd class to the ground, or rap over right and set a base anchor, climb Cheetos & Everclear, and then rap to the ground. To the left of Isostacy is Granite Garden (5.9 X), a 500-foot free solo.

Stir Crazy   5.8 R

FA: Jeff Dozier, Eric Beck, 1971.

This is the next crack left of Holdless Horror. The start is the same as Isostacy. The crack disappears into runout face halfway up the dome.

M. Felsic   5.9★★★★

FA: Bryan Law, Greg Barnes, Linda Jarit, August 2007.

A stellar pitch following a cool natural feature, with lots of variety and sustained climbing in the 5.8/9 range. Climb the narrowing dike past the Stir Crazy crack and then up the face. Shares the anchor with Isostacy and is a good alternative first pitch. You can't rappel to the ground unless you have two 70m ropes, but you can rappel to the slab and downclimb easy (3rd class) grooves.

N. Cheetos and Everclear   5.10a★★★★

FA: Bryan Law, George Ridgley, Greg Barnes, August 2007.

Start up Felsic (the dike left of the second pitch of Holdless Horror), then after four bolts go straight up the thin, sustained face.

O. Holdless Horror   5.6★★★★

FA: TM Herbert, Steve Thompson, Jeff Dozier, 1971.

A splitter crack system up a low-angle knobby face, Holdless Horror is anything but what its name implies. Bomber protection, relatively easy climbing, and straight-forward routefinding make this a perfect introductory multi-pitch climb. However, some low-angle offwidth/ chimneying and a few steep sections remind you that nothing in Yosemite or Tuolumne is ever really that easy.

Side Dish 5.8 R

FA: Jeff Dozier, Steve Thompson, David Green, Lance Dozier,71.

This is the next crack to the right of Holdless Horror, with the crux being unprotected face gaining the crack.

P. Read Between the Lines   5.10a★★★★

Long, quality toprope from S.

Q. Plutonics   5.10b R-★★★★★

FA: Bryan Law et al, August 2007.

After a short approach to the start ledge, Plutonics heads up a technical slab to endless slab and knob climbing. A bit runout in spots. Long first pitch. The second pitch is easier but runout, and the final pitch is very easy. The final rappel is 210 feet to the ground or 200 feet to the ledge just above ground.

R. Bull Dozier   5.7★★★★

FA: Jeff Dozier et al, 1971.

Excellent crack route with lots of finger to hand cracks, cool pockets, and only one short awkward section. This route is probably even better than Holdless Horror, but it is a lot shorter.

S. You, Me, and the Dike   5.10a R★★★★

FA Dave and Jen Lane, 2007.

The right-hand of the two big left-leaning dikes, You, Me, and the Dike is a classic dike route on perfect rock. Runout for leader and follower, it crosses both Bull Dozier and Side Dish. The original crux can be avoided by keeping feet on the dike instead of hands.

T. Avocados & Tequila   5.8 R★★★

FA: Bryan Law, George Ridgley, Grant Hiskes, August 2007.

Good route with some runouts, particularly the one getting to the first bolt. Start off the ledge left of the Ripple boulder, at the start of the left-leaning dike.

U. Ripple   5.7 R-★★★

FA: George Ridgley, Bryan Law, Sabine Schirm, August 2005.

Fun climbing with a stellar crux section on the second pitch. Sections of easy climbing mixed with fairly well-protected (but not tightly bolted) knob and small shelf (or ripple.) climbing, plus runout easy slab. A huge boulder with a killer flat-topped hang-out marks the start of the route. You need two 60m ropes to rap, or you can walk off after a pitch of 4th class up and right.

Dirty Deeds Done Dirt Cheap (aka Crack of Disgust)   5.9

FA: Jeff Dozier, David Green, Lance Dozier, 1971.

This is the crack right of Ripple, and there's a reason "dirt" appears twice in the name. The newer name wasn't the original, as AC/ DC fans could figure out since the song came out five years after the first ascent, but Jeff Dozier likes the new one. Not recommended unless the belayer brings an umbrella for the dirt raining down from the leader!

Bryan Law on the first ascent of Turbine at the Wind Tunnel. Photo by Eric Odenthal

Climbers on Cheetos and Everclear. Photo by Bryan Law

Pywiack Dome

There's no better spot in Tuolumne to watch climbing than in front of Pywiack Dome. The road travels right next to and about 80 feet above the base of the dome, putting climbers directly in the view of motorists and often causing RVs and SUVs to stop in the middle of the road and watch the "crazy mountain climbers" do their craft. The climbing on Pywiack Dome is good, but not spectacular by Tuolumne standards. The main appeal is the all-day sun, short approach, and beautiful view of Tenaya Lake.

Approach

This approach takes between two and three minutes. On Highway 120, drive sevens miles west of the Tuolumne Store and park in the dirt pullout in front of Pywiack Dome. The approach is obvious.

Aqua Knobby
Park at the large dirt pullout on the side of the road, overlooking Pywiack Dome. Hike down across the creek, then up left along the edge of the dome to below the left edge of the huge roof. Hike up 3rd class knobby slabs and belay at small ledges.

Descent

There are two descent options for Dike Route and Zee Tree: 1) From the summit, walk to the northeast corner of the dome and look for rappel slings. After a steep 40-foot rappel, walk north down 4th class slabs and contour around back to the base of the route. 2) From the middle of Pitch 4 of Dike Route, rappel the route with two ropes or one 70m rope. This is the most popular descent option, but avoids the final pitch of the route.

Aqua Knobby
Rappel 40 feet off the back side of the dome, immediately back from the top of Aqua Knobby. Hike down 3rd class gullies about 100 feet away from the dome, then into the talus field, or for an easier descent, hike along the ridge past a short cliff, then down the talus. Once at the base, reverse the approach.

Aqua Knobby 5.9 R-★★★★

Time to climb route: **2–3 hours**

Approach time: **5 minutes**

Descent time: **15 minutes**

Sun exposure: **glancing midsummer, late afternoon**

Height of route: **400'**

Aqua Knobby follows a line of sweet knobs and flakes up a gray water streak on the north side of Pywiack Dome. Despite being right next to the road, stories about the runout 5.6 slab first pitch and the horrendous old bolt protecting a crux 5.8 runout have kept most away. The ASCA replaced the bolt in 2001, and the first pitch is easier than rumored. While most of the climbing on Aqua Knobby is easy and low-angle, the steep crux pitch is one of the finest in Tuolumne.

FA: Lloyd Price and Joe Fitchen, 7/72.

Strategy

You can evaluate crowds on the route without leaving the car. Aqua Knobby can be wet – and stay wet – for some time in early season. It's pretty obvious from the road if the route is still wet.

The first pitch is an intimidating 5.6 runout slab. Luckily, a line of hard-to-spot knobs heads straight up to the left side of the angled roof, making the slab not particularly difficult. The crux second pitch follows knobs and flakes, and requires many thin nuts and thin cams. Be aware that if you use the optional second pitch belay, the leader could take a nasty fall onto the belayer. The final pitch has only ten feet of climbing harder than 5.6, and that section is well protected by medium nuts.

The right start to the first pitch is dry in early season when the normal start is wet. It is harder but well-protected. Beware of water higher on the route when this is the case – if the 4th pitch crack is wet, it's still possible to climb it at a slightly harder grade, but make sure that the runout on pitch 3 is dry!

Aqua Knobby only gets glaring (in your face) sun in midday in mid-season. Thus, it is cold and a good choice for warmer days. Since it is so close to the road, many do Aqua Knobby in late afternoon after climbing other routes, such as Dike Route or Zee Tree.

Retreat

Retreat requires leaving gear. With a longer rope, or two ropes, you'll leave less gear. As the name suggests, this route is a watercourse and will become a waterfall in minutes during a thunderstorm.

D. Needle & Spoon   5.10a R-★★★★

FA: Dennis Oakeshott, Bruce Morris, Peter Mayfield, 1975.

NOTE: Topo on page 171
Needle & Spoon is a beautiful slab route on glacially polished golden granite. While rated only a step harder, Needle & Spoon is far more sustained than the Dike Route, especially on the second pitch (first slab pitch). The bolting is much tighter than the Dike Route, and was considered to be a "sport" route for the era. Not by any means a sport route by today's standards, multiple long falls have been taken on the first pitch, at least one of which resulted in a YOSAR call-out because the leader wasn't wearing a helmet and sustained a bloody head injury and concussion (http://www.friendsofyosar. org/rescues/2001/8-12-01_Pywiack.html).

The first pitch is up a slab with an intermittent thin crack, and a few pieces of pro are nice unless soloing 5.6 is fine with you. The second pitch (first slab pitch) is a very sustained slab with polish and shallow dishes. There's a bulge near the start of the pitch that is easiest to pass far to the right, where there is an old bolt. If you clip the bolt, be prepared for rope drag higher on the pitch - it's good to use at least a shoulder-length sling. The third pitch has a short crux that is well protected, and it is much less sustained than the previous pitch. High on the pitch there are a couple of long runouts on easy terrain, but compared to lower on the route, they will seem casual.

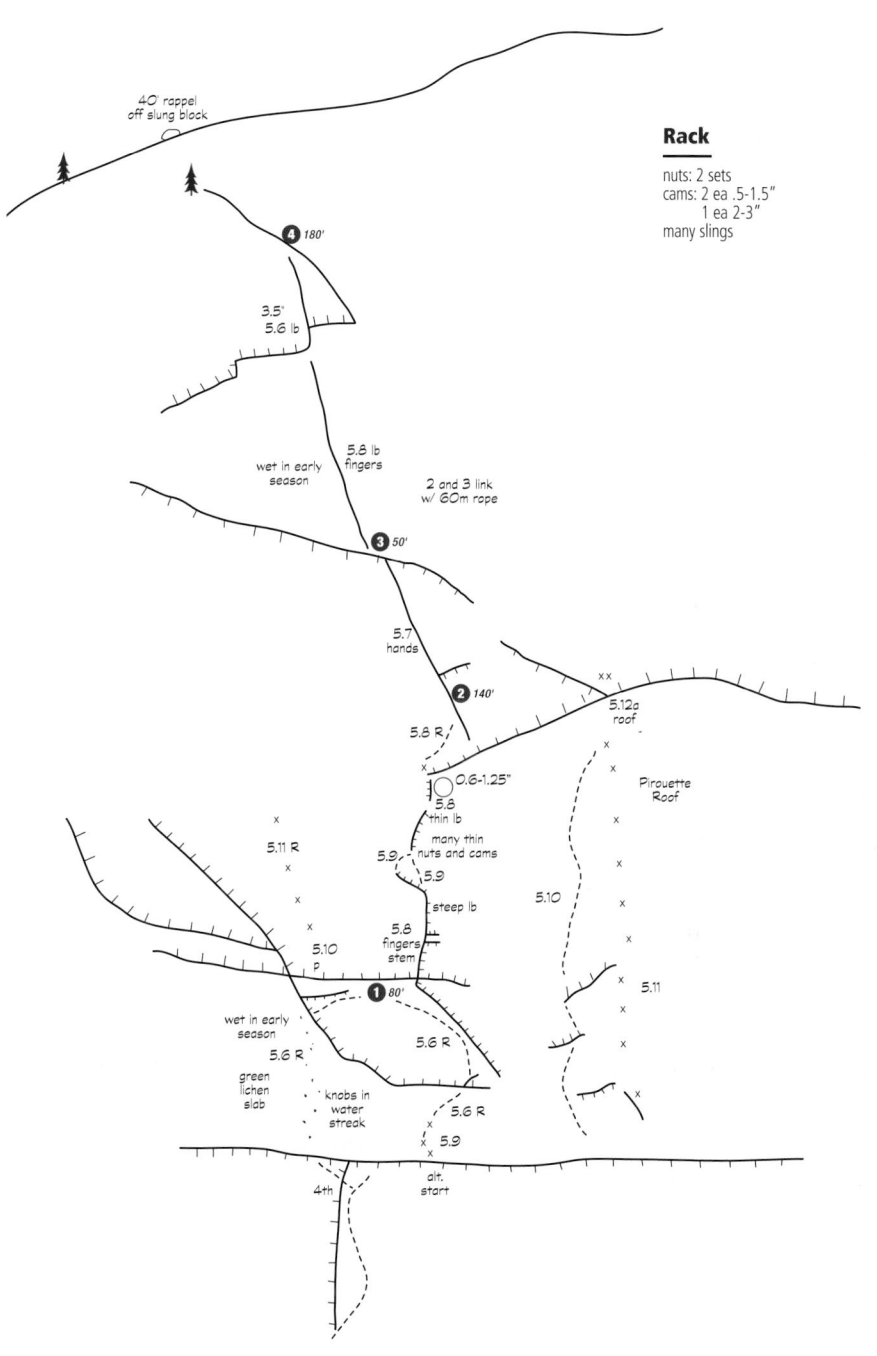

Rack

nuts: 2 sets
cams: 2 ea .5-1.5"
1 ea 2-3"
many slings

Dike Route 5.9 R★★★★

Time to climb route:	**2–3 hours**
Approach time:	**2–3 minutes**
Descent time:	**20–30 minutes**
Sun exposure:	**afternoon to sunset**
Height of route:	**700'**

The Bachar/Yerian is to 5.11 climbing what the Dike Route is to 5.9 climbing – classic and tremendously runout. Up until the crux, the route follows an amazing white dike that diagonals up the granite wall. At the crux, the climbing moves up small knobs, edges, and smears.

FA: Tom Gerughty, Roger Evje, and Dave Meeks, 8/66.

History

This thrilling route was the brainchild of an obsessive climber named Tom Gerughty. Strong as the proverbial ox, the stout Gerughty was best known as a crack climber, and it was a miracle that he could also perform ballet on low-angle rock. He talked quietly and hesitantly and this demeanor made it certain that practical jokes would come flying his way. He took these in stride, grinning his slow grin as the outcome dawned on him. Around 1966 Gerughty began climbing in Tuolumne more than in the Valley, and a tiny curving rib – or dike – on Pywiack Dome's northwest flank caught his eye. This dike, sometimes ultra prominent, sometimes vague, offered an obvious route. But how to protect it? The dike itself had no cracks and drilling stances looked grim, especially in the places where the dike disappeared. It would be a route for a calm and brave person.

Gerughty was certainly a brave lad, but calm he was not as he approached the crux, high on the route, with Roger Evje and Dave Meeks. He had been at this spot twice before on earlier attempts. Fear had overcome greed both times, for the crux was thin and runout. And because

of a higher bulge, there was no way to see what lay ahead. Maybe a stance to get in a bolt? Maybe even thinner? This was long before the days of previewing, so the word "unknown" was full of meaning.

On that second day, at the crux bulge, Gerughty whimpered and moaned as he got farther and farther above his last bolt. Soon he was making 5.9 moves 50 feet out. Downclimbing seemed out of the question. Finally, trembling, he reached a tiny ledge and got in a poor bolt. Above was easier climbing and Gerughty's sense of relief must have been immense.

Tom Higgins later wrote that "Tom [earned] the respect of numerous climbers who imagine leading the last pitch with two less bolts, since added with Tom's permission."

– Steve Roper

Strategy

Dike Route is all about balance, smearing and, most importantly, keeping your head cool when faced with a big fall. Be extremely confident on 5.9 slab climbing before attempting this route. During warm conditions start the climb early when the face is in the shade.

Most of the runout climbing on the first three pitches is in the 5.5-5.7 range. Then, the fourth pitch captures your full attention with 5.8 friction high above that last bolt (some climbers never find this bolt and risk a 150-foot fall).

Retreat

You need two ropes or one 70m rope to retreat from this route. All anchors are set up to rappel from except for belay number 5 which takes natural gear.

A. Zee Tree 5.7★★★★

FA: Dan Zimmerlin, early 1990s.

This is one of the few easy well-bolted slab routes in Tuolumne and a great introduction to face climbing. Bring gear for the upper pitches, and two ropes if rappelling.

Dike Route 5.9 R★★★★
cams: 1-2 ea 2.5-4.5" (for Pitch 6 only), 3 quickdraws

A. Zee Tree 5.7★★★
nuts: 1 set, cams: 1 ea .6-4.5", 10 quickdraws

B. Unknown 5.4 R/X★★
1 or 2 quickdraws, 2 ropes

C. Unknown 5.6 R★★
1 quickdraw, 1 ea. cam 1"

D. Needle & Spoon 5.10a R-★★★★
cams: 1 ea. 0.6-1.5" 7 draws, include extra long draw if clipping
the bolt out right on the second pitch.

B. Unknown   5.4 R/X★★

This unknown old route climbs small steps
and knobs up to a couple bolts in dishes in
the middle of nowhere. The lower, right-
hand bolt was recently replaced. The left-
hand upper bolt is still old. From the bolts,
easier terrain leads to a three-bolt anchor.
Not a good route for inexperienced leaders
since there is very little pro and it would be
easy to miss both the bolt(s) and the anchor!

C. Unknown   5.6 R★★

Leading up from the right edge of the tan
"cave" to the right of Zee Tree, this old
route has a crux right off the belay, and
easier climbing after the pro bolt. Wander
left past the left edge of a flake, then left
again to a bolted anchor. Various wandering
routes continue upwards – and experienced
climbers often just walk down the low 5th
class slabs in this area after finishing the
Dike Route.

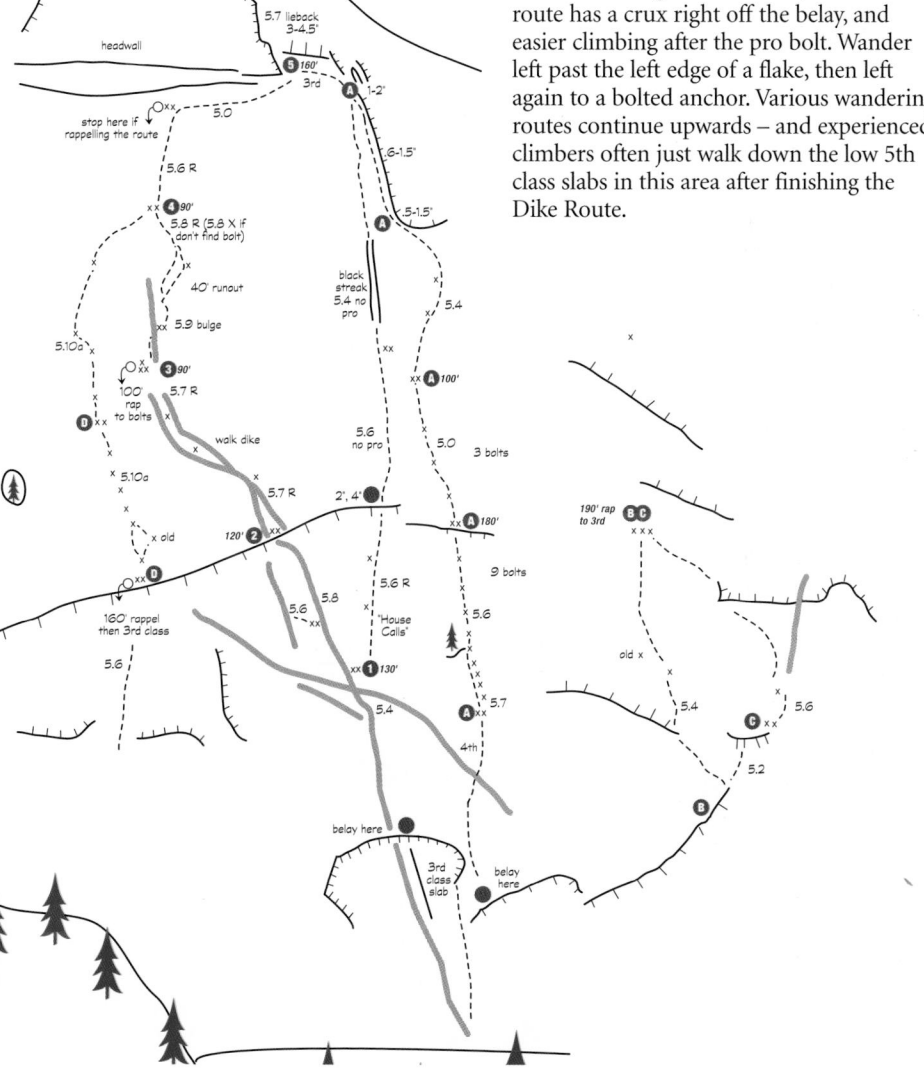

Tenaya Peak

Tenaya Peak is unusual rock for Tuolumne – predominantly slick, cleanly fractured with no knobs – similar to the rock found right next to the car at the base of Stately Pleasure Dome. From the top, an amazing view is had of Half Dome to almost every spot in Tuolumne, with Mt. Conness in the distance, and Matthes Crest to the east.

Approach

Park at the large parking lot with bathrooms, about 300 yards northeast of Tenaya Lake. Hike straight across the woods and meadows, aiming for the toe of the buttress. Work up surprisingly good deer trails to the left, then scramble and bushwack a bit to reach the toe of the rock. If you get on the main lower ledge, a short polished scramble leads up a waterchute, or simply work back left and go up and around. In general, the scrambling is easier than it looks. Look for trails and paths around difficulties.

Descent

Hike west down the ridge from the summit, generally staying to the left side of the actual ridgetop. After about 0.5 miles, start looking for an open bouldery area about 200 yards below some large rock formations on the ridgetop. Work around to the right and join the main ledge system. It helps to have carefully eyed the ledge system from the car ahead of time. There are some hard climbs on steep cliffs above the ledge once you start down. Follow the ledge all the way back (but be very careful, it's easy to get on dirty steep slabs). Once back at the start of the ledge, descend back down where you came up (or thrash down almost anywhere).

An easier, but longer, alternative is to keep hiking down the ridge until you reach a major hiking trail, then follow this back to the right. When the trail splits, the left branch leads to the road at the Sunrise trailhead at the west end of the lake, and the right contours along the lake back to the beach. This latter trail is very beautiful, with perfect views of the lake and Stately Pleasure Dome on the far side.

Northwest Buttress

descent

Northwest Buttress 5.5★★★★

Time to climb route: **5–7 hours**

Approach time: **30 minutes**

Descent time: **1–1.5 hours**

Sun exposure: **afternoon to sunset**

Height of route: **1500'**

This route looks loose and blocky, but in reality it climbs clean and amazing white granite. Unlike the knobby, flaky granite of Cathedral Peak and Matthes Crest, the granite here is slick and cleanly fractured. The crux moves are 5.5 friction and almost every pitch is 5.0-5.4 – not 3rd or 4th class blocks like many other long, easier routes.

FA: Wayne Merry and John Ward, 7/61.

Strategy

Snow can be a problem on this route. Often a snow patch sits in the middle of the route until late June or July, and large slab avalanches have been seen in May. The snow condition is obvious from the road; if there's any snow on the buttress, wait until later in the season. The snow patch normally sits at the crux of the route, and to bypass it to the right will involve harder climbing on unknown terrain.

The route is popular but even if others are on it there are dozens of ways to pass slower parties during the first half of the route. Do not underestimate the length – the route appears foreshortened while you are on it and that tree that looks like it's one pitch up may well be four rope lengths ahead!

Getting to the start of the route is straightforward until the last few hundred feet, where wet conditions, trees, loose rocks, and small cliffs must be negotiated. Unusually good trails, apparently from deer, are found in the lower brush.

There are a few options to finish the route: an easy traverse off left, a steep 5.8 hand crack or a loose, blocky finish up and right. If you feel comfortable dealing with loose rock, the right finish is the most direct and easiest route to the top, but the traverse off left is the standard finish. The 5.7 finish is fun, but somewhat grainy and mossy so it is not recommended unless you're comfortable at the grade.

Retreat

Since the route is longer than it looks and ascends a high point, watch out for storms. It's possible to retreat off left at many points in the first half of the route, but rappelling involves leaving a lot of gear. There are many old fixed pitons in the upper half of the route and a few trees, but again gear is likely needed for rappel stations. Two ropes are not mandatory for retreat, but allow more rappelling options.

Rack

nuts: 1 set
cams: 2 ea .6-2"
     1 ea 3-4"

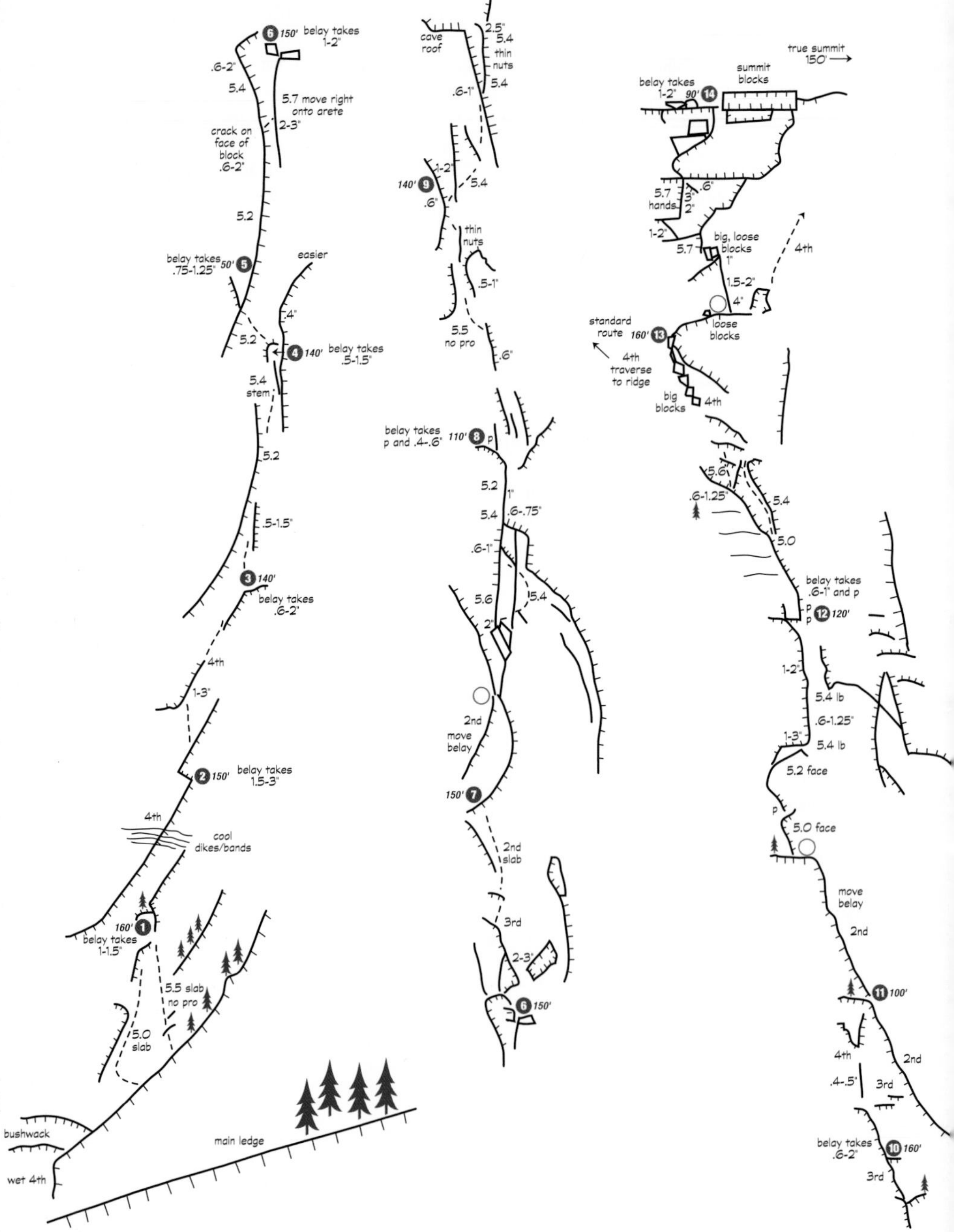

6 150' belay takes 1-2'

.6-2"
5.4

5.7 move right onto arete 2-3'

crack on face of block .6-2"

5.2

belay takes .75-1.25' 50' 5

easier

.4'

5.2

4 140' belay takes .5-1.5'

5.4 stem

5.2

.5-1.5'

3 140' belay takes .6-2'

4th

1-3'

2 150' belay takes 1.5-3'

4th

cool dikes/bands

1 160' belay takes 1-1.5'

5.5 slab no pro

5.0 slab

bushwack

wet 4th

main ledge

cave roof

2.5'
5.4 thin nuts

5.4

.6-1"

1-2'

140' 9
.6'

5.4

thin nuts

.5-1"

5.5 no pro

.6'

belay takes p and .4-.6' 110' 8 P

5.2 1"

5.4 .6-.75'

.6-1"

5.6

5.4

2'

2nd move belay

150' 7

2nd slab

3rd

2-3'

6 150'

true summit 150' →

summit blocks

belay takes 1-2' 90' 14

5.7 hands .6'
3'
2'
1-2'
5.7 1"

1.5-2'
4'

standard route 160' 13
4th traverse to ridge

big, loose blocks

4th

loose blocks

big blocks 4th

5.6
.6-1.25' 5.4

5.0

belay takes .6-1" and p

p 12 120'
p

1-2'

5.4 lb
.6-1.25'
1-3'
5.4 lb

5.2 face

p

5.0 face

move belay

2nd

11 100'

4th
2nd
.4-.5' 3rd

belay takes .6-2'

10 160'

3rd

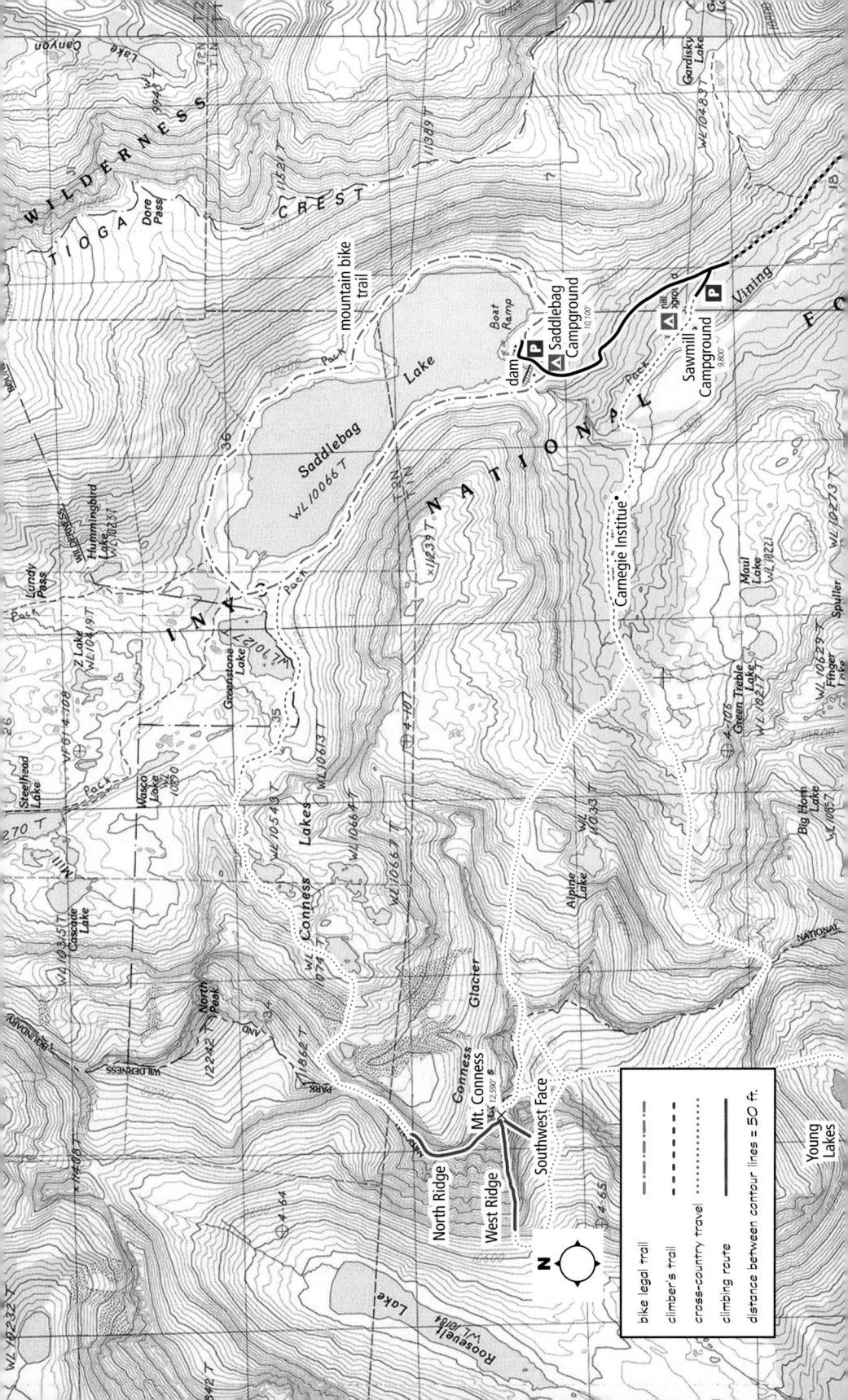

Mt. Conness, North Ridge

The North Ridge provides the perfect alpine experience without too many logistics. The approach passes streams, lakes, and a glacier and the climb ascends an aesthetic, exposed ridge. You cover a variety of terrain from low-angle scrambling to steep downclimbing to exposed traversing – all on solid white granite.

Approach - see map on page 175

The approach takes 2-3 hours, is about 4 miles long, and gains 1,700 feet in elevation. Of that, 1.7 miles are on hikers' trail and about 2.3 miles are on climbers' trail and cross-country. This is a relatively moderate and straightforward approach by High Sierra standards.

From Tioga Pass, drive east 2.2 miles on Highway 120 and turn onto the Saddlebag Lake Road just east of the Tioga Pass Resort. Follow this sometimes paved and sometimes dirt road 2.5 miles and park at the dam. (Remove all food and scented items or bears will trash your car.)

Hike north on the trail on the west shore of Saddleback Lake (or pay for a ferry crossing in the summer). After 1.3 miles, when the trail forks at a distinct boulder, go left and walk to the west end of Greenstone Lake where the trail fades. Cross the inlet of the lake and walk west, passing a sign that says "No camping or wood fires in Hall National Area." Follow a faint trail across a meadow until it gets more defined, starts trending right, and goes up a hill that parallels the creek. After a few hundred yards you reach a meadow and a waterfall. Scramble right of the waterfall on slabs and then trend left, above the waterfall, to Conness Lakes.

Stay on the right (north) shores of Conness Lakes and at the last lake head up and skirt the right side of the talus. At the top of the talus, meet a wide 300-foot-tall cliff band right (northwest) of a moraine in front of the Conness Glacier (see photo). Climb up sand and scree on the left-most manageable-looking gully (some 4th class) that is just right of where the cliff band becomes steep and 5th class. It's hard to see what gully to take – if the gully looks too steep then move right to another gully.

At the top of the gully, traverse left above the cliff band staying just above the bushes. Continue traversing until you gain the ridge just above a col and the start of the North Ridge. Walk on the ridge for a few hundred yards as the ridge transitions from 2nd to 3rd class. When the ridge steepens to 4th class, rope up and start climbing.

Descent

The West Ridge and the North Ridge share the same descent, which is also the approach for the West Ridge. From the summit, go down the 2nd class southeast ridge trail to the large sandy plateau. Walk to the northeast corner of the plateau (don't lose elevation when traversing the plateau even if other trails go down).

4th class

Drop down the East Ridge and head a little right (south) to a flat section. Continue east and find a way down a cliffy section and then aim for the bottom of the valley. Eventually you'll reach a faint trail that gradually gets more pronounced until it turns to a major trail. Pass the Carnegie Institute and continue east past the Sawmill Campground to the road. Walk up the road about 0.5 mile to Saddlebag Lake and your car.

Approach GPS Coordinates

Parking area at Saddlebag Lake dam:
    37.96475, -119.27278
Split in trail at distinct boulder:
    37.97846, -119.29278
Inlet of Gemstone Lake:
    37.977933, -119.29273
Just before waterfall below Conness Lakes:
    37.98016, -119.29795
150 yards above last Conness Lake:
    37.97538, -119.31355
Col at the start of the North Ridge:
    37.97451, -119.31905
Summit of Mt. Conness:
    37.96690, -119.32130

A view of the crux downclimb from below.

North Ridge 5.6★★★★

Time to climb route: 3–8 hours

Approach time: 2–3 hours

Descent time: 2–3 hours

Sun exposure: partial sun to shade

Height of route: 800'

This great introduction to alpine rock climbing ascends long stretches of 3rd and 4th class occasionally interrupted with an exposed 5.6 move. Even the 3rd class sections are interesting and fun. You choose the exposure and climbing difficulty by either staying directly on the ridge (harder) or moving to either side of the ridge (easier). Following the climbing route is straightforward but the approach and descent are more devious and require skill using a USGS map. Located at a relatively low elevation, this climb is usually warm enough to climb up until the first snow of the year (usually in November). Compared with Cathedral Peak, the North Ridge has less technical climbing but much more hiking, routefinding, and elevation gain.

FA: Galen Rowell and Barry Hagen, 1969.

Strategy

It's best to climb the route car-to-car in a day. Because the descent doesn't pass by where you would camp at Conness Lakes, bivying on the approach means hiking back at least four miles round-trip to recover your gear after the climb.

Most climbers need a full day for the climb and should start at dawn. The first half of the climb receives sun in the morning and the second half gets sun in the afternoon. The climbing can be quite cold in the shade so bring gloves and warm clothes. The time to climb the route will vary from three to eight hours depending on how many sections you rope up for. If you plan to rope up for much of the climb, get a pre-dawn start. The route is relatively popular but there are many ways to pass other climbers. For a rack, bring a lightweight lead line and a small selection of nuts and cams. Many climbers free solo the route except for the 5.6 downclimb, which is rappelled with one 120-foot-long rope.

Route description

From the col at the beginning of the North Ridge, walk a few hundred yards until the ridge steepens. Rope up when necessary. Climb about 300-400 feet (two roped pitches) of 3rd then 4th class until the ridge flattens. Walk for a few hundred feet to just below First Tower, which has a distinct visor. Traverse under First Tower staying on the east side of the ridge on exposed 3rd class. Downclimb into a notch then climb up a few hundred feet of 3rd and occasionally 4th class to the top of the Second Tower. Stop here for a snack, take in the view, and prepare for the crux downclimb.

The crux starts just below Second Tower by either rappelling 30 feet from slings or downclimbing 5.5 to a second set of slings. From here, either rappel 60 feet or downclimb a big 5.6 corner. After the downclimb/rappel, ascend 500 feet of sustained 4th class with the occasional 5th class move. For the best and most exhilarating climbing, stay near but not on the ridge. When the ridge flattens out, walk a few hundred feet to the summit.

For super fast and motivated climbers, consider climbing the West Ridge before or after the North Ridge.

Retreat

Carry one 50m or 60m rope to retreat. From before Second Tower, reverse the route, which will either require downclimbing or rappelling and leaving gear (there are few fixed anchors). From after Second Tower, the easiest option is to finish climbing the route. If you are caught near the summit and must bivy or take cover, there are some stonewall bivy spots southwest of the summit.

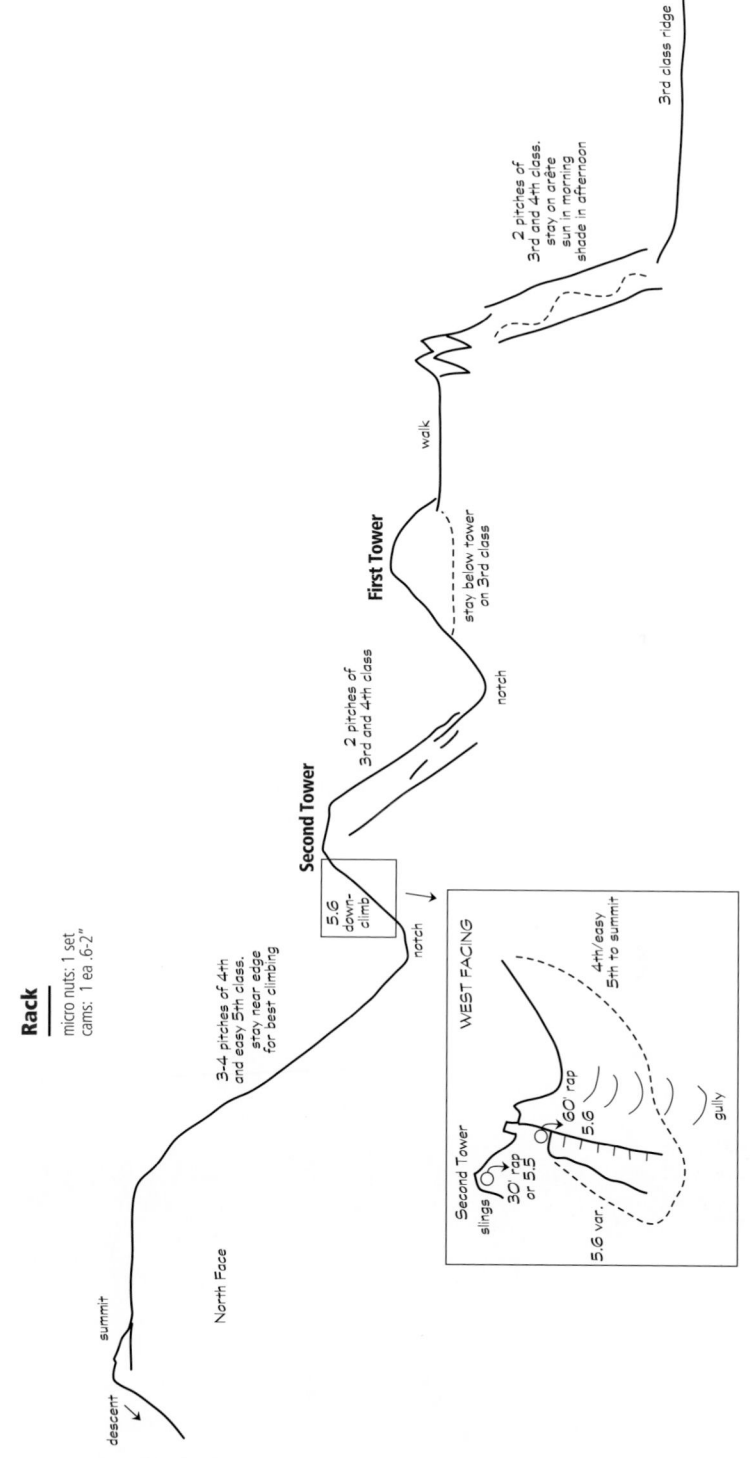

Rack

micro nuts: 1 set
cams: 1 ea .6-2"

3-4 pitches of 4th
and easy 5th class.
stay near edge
for best climbing

descent

summit

North Face

Second Tower

5.6
down-
climb

notch

2 pitches of
3rd and 4th class

First Tower

stay below tower
on 3rd class

notch

walk

2 pitches of
3rd and 4th class.
stay on arête
sun in morning
shade in afternoon

3rd class ridge

WEST FACING

Second Tower
slings

30' rap
or 5.5

60' rap

5.6

5.6 var.

4th/easy
5th to summit

gully

Mt. Conness, West Ridge and Southwest Face

Unlike most Sierra peaks that have gentle western slopes leading to eastern drop-offs, Mt. Conness has an attention-grabbing 1,200-foot southwest face. The wall is so impressive it's easy to overlook the gentle sweep of the West Ridge on the left. This once obscure feature has been rediscovered in the last ten years as maybe the best 5.6 ridge in the Sierra.

Approach

The approach takes three to six hours, is about 4.5 miles long, and gains 2,500 feet in elevation then loses about 800 feet at the end. Of that, one mile is on hikers' trail and about 3.5 miles is on climbers' trail and cross-country. This is a strenuous and confusing approach. Do it with someone who has done it before and give yourself plenty of time.

Take the Saddlebag Lake road off of Highway 120, 2.2 miles outside the East Entrance to the Park, just below the Tioga Pass Resort, and about 0.5 miles above Ellery Lake. Follow the sometimes paved and sometimes dirt road for 1.6 miles and park in the Sawmill Campground parking area on the left. If you reach Saddlebag

Lake, you have gone too far.

Follow the dirt road to the campground for a couple hundred yards to a trail junction; stay left on the road (right trail leads to Saddlebag Lake). Continue through the campground and along a stream (cross where possible – depends on water level) and continue following the road left up a hill past the Carnegie Institute (just a dilapidated wooden shed). The road turns to trail and then dies out after another five to ten minutes.

After the trail first dies out, it appears and disappears multiple times. The GPS coordinate for where to leave the trail is 37.96053, -119.28935. However, you can leave the trail at almost any point when it starts to fade.

This is where the approach gets confusing, so orient yourself to your surroundings with a compass and the USGS map. Travel cross-country to the northwest, aiming for a subtle gully system that leads to a notch/low point in the cliffy section. At the top of this, the terrain flattens a little and you get your last water source. Continue west staying near and finally on the East Ridge on the right. A final section of sandy scrambling puts you on the expansive sandy plateau that leads to the summit of Mt. Conness. Don't go to the summit; instead, move down and west aiming for

North Ridge

Southwest Face

West Ridge

approach

approach

Carnegie Institute

Chris McNamara

an indistinct gully. There are many gullies to choose from, most of which cliff out (danger!). Only go down the one from which you can see the entire southwest face of the cliff.

Head straight down the gully for several hundred yards, following sandy, loose, and steep 2nd class trails. When you encounter a steep section, stay to the left – the obvious right path dead-ends in a loose 4th class slab with a treacherous 5th class section at the bottom. Once past the steep section, head right, aiming for the low-angle slabs.

For the West Ridge: continue down staying about 300 feet away from the southwest face. The West Ridge starts just left of the obvious toe of the buttress. There are two arêtes separated by a gully. The route starts on the left arete.

For the Southwest Face: aim for the left side of the steep part of the face. The route starts about 80 feet left of a plaque in memory of Don Goodrich, who was killed on the face. The route starts in grassy cracks (usually wet)to the right of a series of tiered roofs and right-facing corners.

Alternate approach: get a Wilderness Permit in Tuolumne, park at Lembert Dome and backpack into the Young Lakes or a bit beyond (consult the permit rangers). Camp here. Climb the next day with the lightest, smallest pack possible. Enjoy the far more leisurely pace required to do the route and for fun pick the best looking line on the upper pitches, avoiding the easier 4th class in favor of endless easy 5th class. This approach is best for those less experienced at mountain travel, since the normal approach assumes familiarity with 3rd class boulder hopping and a fair degree of overall speed in order to succeed in a day. However, the Young Lakes approach is too long for a one-day car-to-car climb.

Descent

The West Ridge and the North Ridge share the same descent, which is also the approach for the West Ridge. From the summit, go down the 2nd class southeast ridge trail to the large sandy plateau. Walk to the northeast corner of the plateau. Don't lose elevation when traversing the plateau even if other trails go down. From here, reverse the approach.

West Ridge 5.6★★★★★

Time to climb route: **3–6 hours**

Approach time: **3–5 hours**

Descent time: **2–3 hours**

Sun exposure: **noon to sunset**

Height of route: **1500'**

The West Ridge of Mt. Conness is perhaps the best moderate alpine climb in Tuolumne. With the competition including Cathedral Peak and Matthes Crest, this says a lot. TM Herbert described it as "great fun, like two Cathedral Peaks stacked on top of each other." Peter Croft called it the best route he had done in the Sierra backcountry (albeit before embarking on some of his recent mega-traverse link-ups). Those familiar with the numerous options climbers encounter on Cathedral and Matthes will be overwhelmed with Mt. Conness – there are hundreds of possible starting points, and nearly every pitch has dozens of possible variations.

The West Ridge is an indistinct line with many options, and several veteran climbers have said that the most classic option starts a hundred yards down and right of the topo route on the ridge edge/arête to the right. Many options are available and all are fun, so don't limit your options, especially if other parties are ahead. The ridge is clean, but the farther you stray from the true ridge, the more loose rock you will find.

FA: Dick Long et al, 1957.

Strategy

Like many alpine climbs, the West Ridge of Conness must be climbed swiftly to be done in one day. Slower climbers, or those simply out to enjoy a beautiful backpack in the Sierra, should consider backpacking into the Young Lakes from Tuolumne. Due consideration for the availability of Wilderness Permits should be taken – don't expect to get one without planning in advance.

The weather on Mt. Conness can be more severe than surrounding areas due to the height and the sheer southwest face. Winds can be tremendous and lightning danger is extreme. Do not attempt this climb if thunderstorms are expected or if any clouds are seen.

Much of the approach is loose and sandy 2nd/3rd class. In early season snow and boggy conditions should be expected and footwear should reflect this. Even in late season a pair of light gaiters will help keep sand out of your boots.

Retreat

Retreat is not recommended due to the high probability of rope snags and pulling rocks on your head. If retreat is required, try to avoid the gully or anything that could snag the rope. Perhaps traverse a ways for each rappel to be sure that falling rock will not hit you. Gear must be left to retreat.

Do not get on this climb if there is any possibility of a storm.

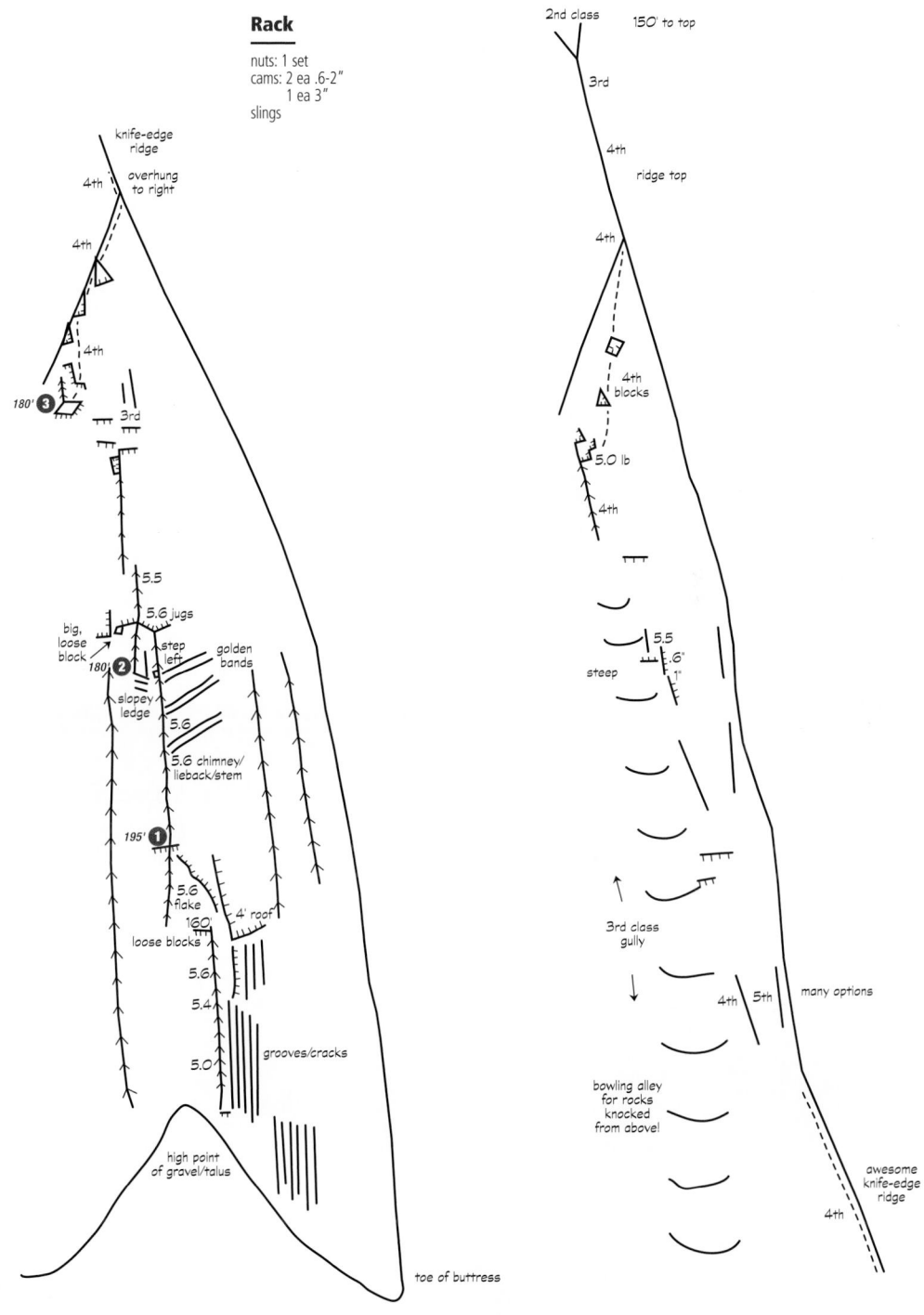

Rack

nuts: 1 set
cams: 2 ea .6-2"
      1 ea 3"
slings

knife-edge ridge
4th
overhung to right
4th
4th
180' ❸
3rd
5.5
5.6 jugs
big, loose block
step left
golden bands
180' ❷
slopey ledge
5.6
5.6 chimney/lieback/stem
195' ❶
5.6 flake
160'
4' roof
loose blocks
5.6
5.4
5.0
grooves/cracks
high point of gravel/talus
toe of buttress

2nd class
150' to top
3rd
4th
ridge top
4th
4th blocks
5.0 lb
4th
5.5
.6"
1"
steep
3rd class gully
4th   5th
many options
bowling alley for rocks knocked from above!
awesome knife-edge ridge
4th

Nabeel Atique on the upper part of the West Ridge.

Climbers on the lower part of the West Ridge.

Southwest Face 5.10c★★★★

Time to climb route: **6-9 hours**

Approach time: **3-5 hours**

Descent time: **2-3 hours**

Sun exposure: **all day**

Height of route: **1,200'**

The sheer 1,200-foot white Southwest Face is the most prominent and alluring face in the Tuolumne area. If you climb 5.10 and you see it enough times, (and you will, since it is visible from Half Dome, Cathedral Peak and anywhere in between), you will eventually need to climb it. Standing at the base, the route looks impressive and intimidating with a big roof and steep corner looming midway up. Stout, wild, and exposed climbing is mixed in with lower angle moves. You must be in good offwidth shape for the sustained crux 5.10 wide pitch. The offwidth makes this climb just a touch harder than the Incredible Hulk's Red Dihedral. This route will help you get in shape for Keeler Needle. This route has one of the more incredible views of any Sierra peak: You look across Tuolumne Meadows, Grand Canyon of Tuolumne, Half Dome, Fairview Dome, and Cathedral Peak.

FA: Warren Harding, Glen Denny, Herb Swedlund, 9/59.
FFA: Galen Rowell, Chris Vandiver, 7/76.

History

When Warren Harding and his crew completed The Nose of El Capitan in November of 1958, Yosemite climbers started asking, "What's next?" One obvious answer was to take the methods of El Cap success to other walls, including the Sierra high country. Wally Reed was one of Harding's stronger El Cap partners, and during the long months of Park Service enforced interims on Nose work in 1958, Reed was the first to look carefully for the possibilities for new walls around Tuolumne Meadows. He and Chuck Pratt came back from the first ascent of Fairview Dome in August of 1958, and their news of superb rock probably added to the impetus to check out the big face that a variety of wandering climbers had seen north of Tuolumne, the southwest face of Mt. Conness.

Early the next season, Don Goodrich organized a team to try this face. Just a few weeks before he had pioneered a classic new route to the top of a slab lying against the Glacier Point Apron. On Conness, just 150 feet up, Goodrich pulled on a block that came off; he fell with it and was killed.

Goodrich was well-liked, and the tragedy traumatized the Yosemite climbers. Soon though, they built a determination that an ascent of the wall in his name would be a fitting memorial. By September, Warren Harding collected a pair of relative newcomers: Herb Swedlund, a wiry man who would pioneer some great new routes in the Tetons in subsequent years; and Glen Denny, a tall, redheaded employee at Yosemite Lodge who had started climbing with Harding a year before on Washington Column.

Conness's face suggested that Goodrich's route choice had been a good one, but there was a short, loose section where he simply had met some very bad luck. His blood still discolored the rock, and as Swedlund led past the dark stain his head spun and his stomach turned. He finished the pitch but announced that his energy for leading had withered. He would haul as Harding and Denny led, and, in classic Harding style they took their time and enjoyed the struggles of nailing pins and jamming cracks and hauling gear. After a night on a ledge they worked up a chimney that led to a wide crack. Harding, an innovator at improvising wide pitons, hadn't packed much big iron to this backcountry wall, and so they drilled protection bolts to the right of the worst offwidth section. This took up enough time that they spent a second night on the wall, enjoying the wine that Harding always brought along. After a (probably hanging) bivouac higher up, they finished the route.

A few years later, Galen Rowell found some of his profound inspiration while climbing with Harding, and by the mid-1970s Rowell was aiming for technical routes in the Himalaya. He decided that Sierra winter ascents would be good preparation, and in February of 1976 he came to this face on Conness, with Dennis Hennek and Mike Graber. In full winter regalia it took them an afternoon to fix a couple of pitches, then a full day of aid and booted freeclimbing to reach an alcove where they hung in hammocks, waiting a cold night a couple of pitches below the top.

Four months later, Rowell hiked back in with Chris Vandiver, who figured he could make the first free ascent of the route. Starting the crux second pitch, Vandiver tried to climb directly upward. He couldn't work in any reliable protection, so he shifted to a tenuous rightward traverse. After struggling to get in a series of hexes and pitons in a flared horizontal crack, he committed to some desperate and scary moves, clipping his haul line into one piece so that Rowell could give him a two-rope belay. He panted and pulled an overhang, and found one foothold to pause on before working back toward the original route. A couple of more moves of 5.11 got him to easier terrain.They rappelled to the ground, leaving two ropes to ease their way to the first free ascent the next day.

– Andy Selters

Strategy

Many climbers do this route car-to-car in a day. However, to ensure success, you might consider camping somewhere on the approach or at Young Lakes. Despite the high elevation, temperatures can be scorching because the route faces south and is wind-sheltered. Bring plenty of water and wear versatile clothing so you can adjust your layers as the temperatures change. This is a great climb to do in late season when other climbs are too cold. A 60m rope allows you to link many pitches but is not mandatory.

The first pitch is the worst on the climb and can feel like 5.9 if dry and 5.10c if wet (it's usually wet). The second pitch starts with tricky routefinding: don't be suckered by the beautiful right-leaning crack. The second part of the second pitch is the technical crux of the route, but the business is the offwidth crux on the fourth pitch. This pitch has a few 5.10 moves between long stretches of 5.8 and 5.9 offwidth and chimney. A 7" cam might protect the crux (Big Bros certainly will). Otherwise you rely on a handful of ancient bolts for protection.

The next pitch has the exposure crux of the route where you must make a somewhat devious 5.10 face move right. You can link this pitch with the next in order to bypass a cramped belay, but beware of bad rope drag. The next few pitches are pretty straightforward with many belay options.

Retreat

It's possible to retreat with one 60m rope, but you will have more options and leave less gear with two ropes. There are some retreat stations just right of the route for the first few pitches. After that you must leave gear in order to retreat.

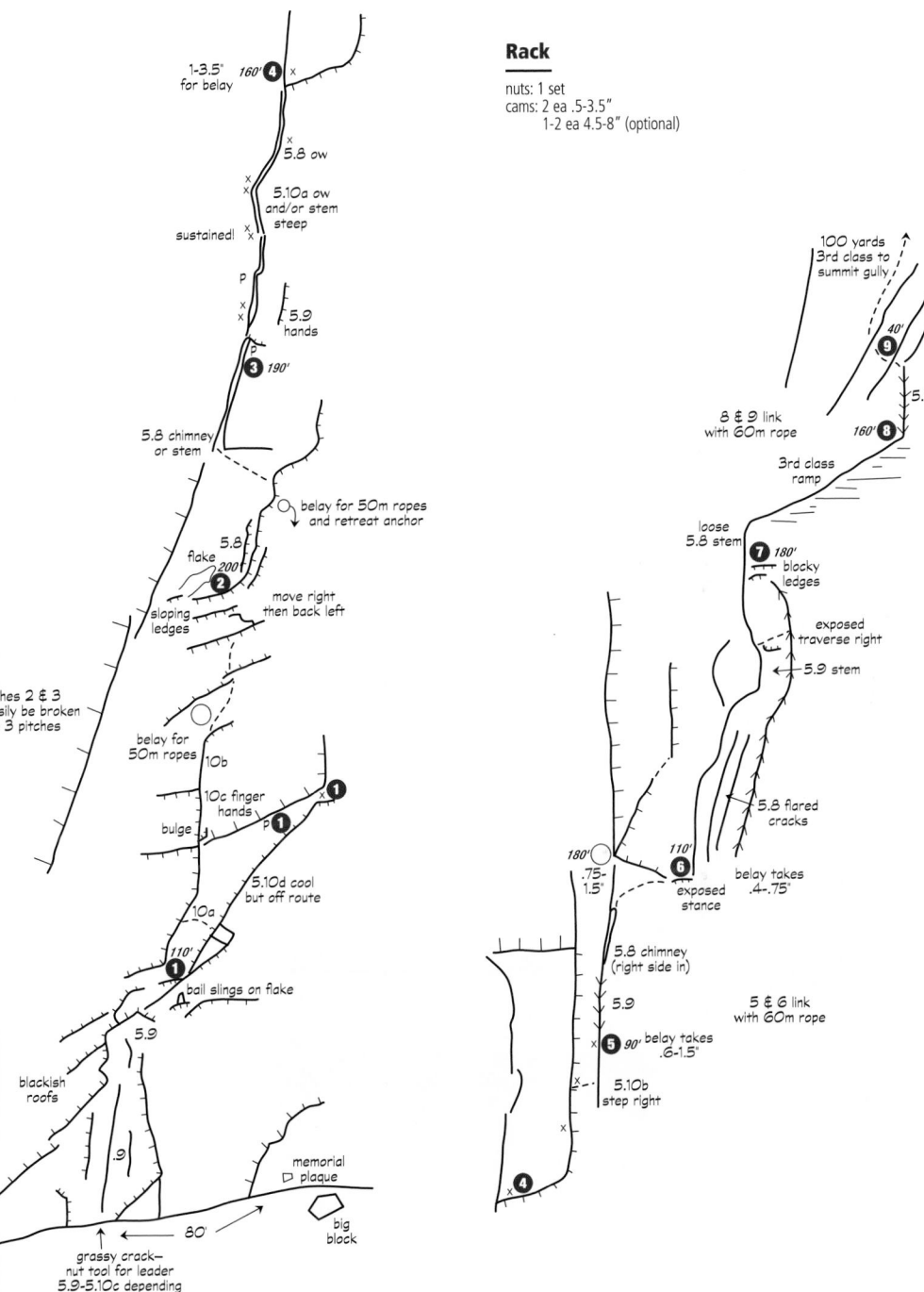

Rack

nuts: 1 set
cams: 2 ea .5-3.5"
      1-2 ea 4.5-8" (optional)

1-3.5' 160' ❹ x
for belay

5.8 ow

5.10a ow
and/or stem
steep

sustained!

5.9
hands

❸ 190'

5.8 chimney
or stem

belay for 50m ropes
and retreat anchor

5.8
flake
❷ 200'

sloping
ledges

move right
then back left

tches 2 & 3
asily be broken
o 3 pitches

belay for
50m ropes

10b

10c finger
hands

bulge

❶
P ❶
x ❶

5.10d cool
but off route

10a

110'
❶

bail slings on flake

5.9

blackish
roofs

.9

memorial
▱ plaque

80'

big
block

grassy crack—
nut tool for leader
5.9-5.10c depending
on how wet

100 yards
3rd class to
summit gully

40'
❾

5.9

8 & 9 link
with 60m rope

160' ❽

3rd class
ramp

loose
5.8 stem

❼ 180'

blocky
ledges

exposed
traverse right

5.9 stem

5.8 flared
cracks

180'
.75-
1.5'

110'

❻

belay takes
.4-.75'

exposed
stance

5.8 chimney
(right side in)

5.9

5 & 6 link
with 60m rope

❺ 90' belay takes
.6-1.5'

5.10b
step right

❹

Third Pillar of Dana

From Mono Lake, the Third Pillar of the Dana Plateau looks like a huge shark's tooth – the most prominent point on an escarpment of large cliffs. From the west, the Third Pillar is invisible until you are on top of it at the dramatic edge of an expansive plateau. The first sight when you get to the edge is of a steep, blocky, yet sheer pillar, and the skeptic expects any route that ascends such a steep final pitch to be 5.12. But only a few hours later, a stellar photograph of your partner will be had from the same point, on top of the pillar, victorious after some of the best (and most accessible) alpine climbing in the Sierra.

Approach

Park at the Tioga Lake Overlook (0.8 miles east of the Tioga Pass Entrance Station along Highway 120). Behind the bathrooms, find a wide fisherman's trail that leads down to the west end of Tioga Lake. Remain on the trail another 200 yards as it turns and parallels the south shore of Tioga Lake. When Glacier Creek meets Tioga Lake, leave the trail and walk cross-country following the east edge of the creek for a few hundred yards until a climbers' trail appears. This trail parallels the creek for about a mile to Glacier Canyon – a long shallow valley that rests between Mount Dana on the west and the Dana Plateau on the east. At this point the well-defined climbers' trail ends (from this point on there is a combination of climbers' trails and cross-country travel). Continue on the trail for another 200 feet and gradually diagonal east up a rocky slope on a faint climbers' trail that may be hard to see. After 200 yards, a second meadow is reached. Walk along the east end of the meadow for another few hundred yards until it is possible to head southeast up a large gully filled with orange talus (a distinct climbers' trail appears after a few minutes on the north edge of the gully). After a few hundred yards a climbers' trail will traverse right and then disappear into a shallow, grassy valley in the middle of the Dana Plateau. Walk east up the shallow valley until you eventually reach a large field of one- to four-foot boulders. Walk east through the boulders all the way to the edge of the Dana Plateau. The striking prow of the Third Pillar of Dana will be visible 100 yards before you reach the dramatic edge of the plateau, and the top of the descent buttress is immediately to the west of the Third Pillar. Descend the buttress via low-angle 3rd class terrain; generally stay to the left, or 4th class drops must be negotiated.

Cross the snow field to prominent ledges near the bottom of the snow chute, about 150 feet above the bottom of the rock on the Third Pillar.

Descent

Reverse the approach.

Regular Route 5.10b★★★★★

Time to climb route: **3–5 hours**

Approach time: **2–3 hours**

Descent time: **1–1.5 hours**

Sun exposure: **sunrise to noon**

Height of route: **600'**

This route has four pitches of three-star climbing leading to maybe the most dramatic and highest quality single pitch in the High Sierra. The setting is much different than the Meadows: the climb is perched 5,000 vertical feet above Mono Lake with expansive high-desert scenery and 13,000-foot mountains in the distance. Every 5.10 Tuolumne climber should do this route.

FA: Phil Bircheff and Bill Bonebreak, 8/76.

Strategy

While the approach is relatively mild, the elevation coupled with the chance of afternoon thunderstorms dictate a dawn start. The Third Pillar is very popular and it is common to have more than one party on the route.

In early season (or all season in heavy snow years) there's a short snow slope just before the start of the climb. If you're careful and the snow is soft, you can usually kick steps in the snow with approach shoes. However, if the slope seems too steep or icy, continue downclimbing the 3rd class and cross once the snow gully is at a lower angle. An ice axe could be used but is rarely necessary, unless the temperature is so low that climbing would not be enjoyable.

There is plenty of tricky routefinding and at least two variations to each pitch.

While the route generally offers excellent protection, there is one short scary face section. Right off a ledge mid-fourth pitch, a thin piton on the right protects tricky moves left into a small lieback flake. Although the moves are not too difficult once you commit, they look spooky and drive many climbers to attempt a bypass either to the left or the right. Both bypasses are dangerously runout and harder than they appear. Place protection on the ledge in case a fall pulls the piton and place RPs immediately below the piton.

After the flake in the midst of the 4th pitch, a cruxy face has become easier recently since a flake fell out. Thin pro (RPs) helps protect the moves to a big jug, then higher climb left to a small corner with a cruxy, but well-protected, move. Many climbers attempt to bypass this face either to the left or the right, but both are harder and poorly protected. Place good pro on the ledge just in case the thin pro pops.

Retreat

There are few fixed anchors so bring extra slings to leave on rock horns and chockstones (you may also have to leave nuts and cams). Only one rope is necessary for rappelling (if you made longer raps with two ropes they would likely get snagged).

The Dana Plateau is exposed to lightning danger, so check weather forecasts beforehand and retreat at the first sign of thunderstorm activity. Should you get caught in a serious thunderstorm on top, descend the 3rd class buttress to the bottom of the climb or lower and wait for the storm to dissipate, then re-ascend and hike out.

More at SuperTopo.com

Before climbing this route, check the latest snow conditions in the approach gully at: www.supertopo.com/rockclimbing/ route.html?r=tuthregu

Rack

nuts: 1 ea micro
2 ea sml-med
1 ea lrg
cams: 1 ea .4, 3"
2 ea .5-2.5"
many slings

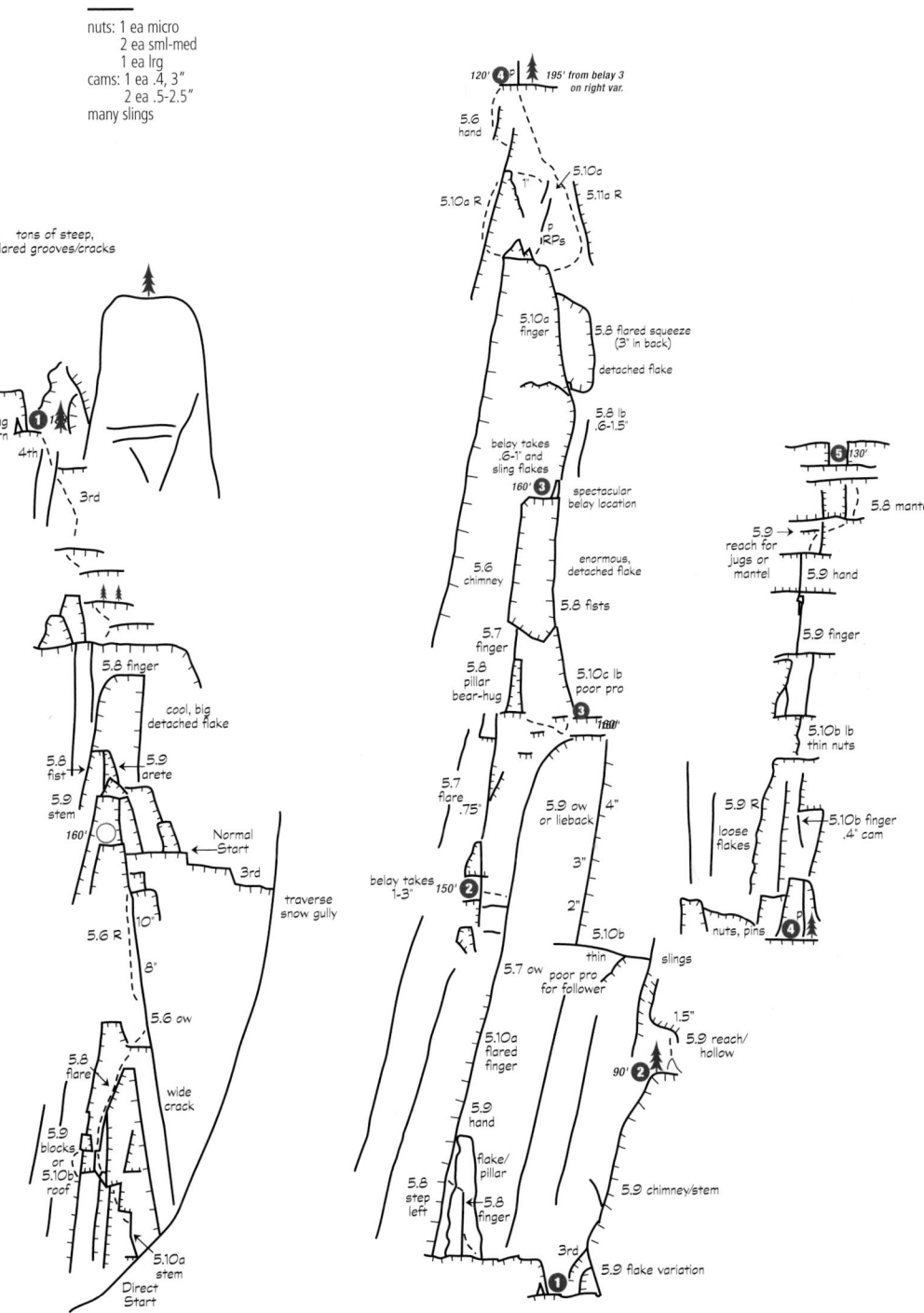

Ellery Lake

Approach time: 5–10 minutes

Sun exposure: midday to afternoon

Height of routes: 30–70'

The Ellery Lake crag is outside of the Park below the Ellery Lake dam spillway. Bolted toprope anchors abound in this area and there are a few short leads as well. The most popular toprope, Gold Mine, is the only one without a bolted anchor. Many bolted routes and anchors are found on surrounding rocks, and it's fun to do some exploration and toproping.

For toproping, you will need 1 ea 1.5-3" cams for Gold Mine, and just slings and biners for the rest.

Leading is rare; for Gold Mine bring nuts: 1 set; cams: 1 ea .6-1.25", 2 ea 1.5-3"

Approach

Ellery Lake (9,500 feet) is the last lake before Highway 120 dives down Lee Vining Canyon. Park at the dam at the east end of the lake (a popular area for fishing). Walk across the dam then go east on an old flat jeep road at the top of an aqueduct (leaks in this old pipe are the main source of the ice for Lee Vining ice climbing). After a few hundred yards, the small angular crag of Gold Mine is immediately on the right. After another 50 yards, the road passes by the top of the second (and larger) cliff.

A. Dihedral   5.10a★★

Slab to fun fingercrack dihedral.

B. Groove   5.10d★

Somewhat grungy steep dihedral.

C. Roof   5.10b★

Various options available.

D. Gold Mine   5.9★★

Good hand jamming and steep edges. Fun lead as well.

E. Arête   5.10d★★

A four-bolt sport climb. Be careful setting toprope. Bolts are at the edge and some might want a belay to set a toprope.

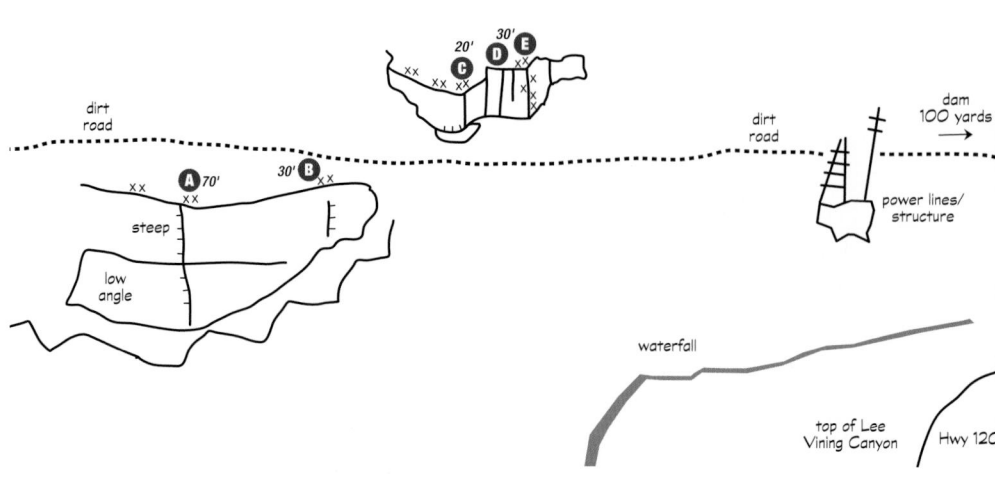

Chris McNamara on the 11,500-foot Third Pillar with Mono Lake in the distance. (Greg Barnes)

A. Speed of Life   5.11b★★★★★

FA: Don Reid, Chris Falkenstein, 1981.

Speed of Life is an awesome two-pitch crack located above Ellery Lake on the east side of Tioga Pass. The route has beautiful, clean rock, sharp flakes and splitter cracks, with two long, burly pitches at high altitude that will tax your lungs as well as your muscles. It is guarded by a deceptively long and loose approach up scree fields, and a large snow bank during most of the summer. The first ascent of this classic crack was an impressive on-sight by Don Reid in 1981.

The first pitch takes steep cracks to a short, powerful crux with good, but very thin, gear. After the crux, an easy but wide flake/offwidth leads to a traverse right around a corner. If you don't bring a large cam, this traverse is protected only by a tiny cam in a horizontal.

The crux second pitch starts with a traverse to a wildly exposed technical section to gain the base of the enduro wide hand crack. The crux of the route hits near the top when you're gassed from the long steep crack at altitude.

The messy, sketchy fixed anchors (one of which had one old bolt, an old piton, two knot jams and three nuts, and involved a large loose block) were upgraded to good bolts in 2006 at the request of both members of the first ascent team. Be careful on the rope pull off the first pitch, as stuck ropes are common on a flake/notch.

Approach

Park at the dam, cross the dam, and start the slog. The base of Speed of Life is about 10,700 feet and the 1200-foot vertical approach is longer and looser than it looks from the car. A snow bank is common at the base of the route and you may need to chop steps in snow if it's cold, so boots are recommended in early season. The route gets glancing sun in mid-summer but is mostly shady most of the time.

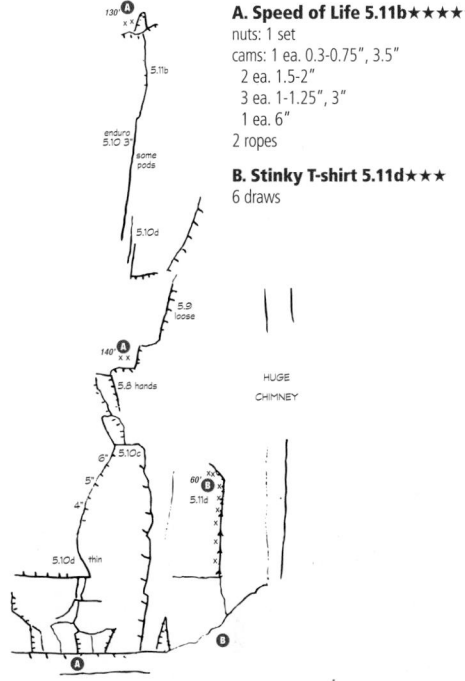

A. Speed of Life 5.11b★★★★★
nuts: 1 set
cams: 1 ea. 0.3-0.75", 3.5"
    2 ea. 1.5-2"
    3 ea. 1-1.25", 3"
    1 ea. 6"
2 ropes

B. Stinky T-shirt 5.11d★★★
6 draws

B. Stinky T-shirt   5.11d★★★

FA: Vic Lawson, Paul Rasmussen, August 2008.

The clean, technical arête about 80' right of Speed of Life.

About the Authors

Keith Barnes photo

Greg Barnes - Lead Author

Greg has been climbing since 1994, and he can tell you every move on every route he's done, draw a topo from memory, give you his opinion on the rating of any pitch, repeat anything written in any guidebook, and tell you about the weather that day. He is Director of the American Safe Climbing Association. From 1998 to 2008, Greg replaced 408 bolts in Tuolumne by hand drilling, which takes 20-30 minutes of work per bolt. From Great Pumpkin to the Dike Route to OZ to Blues Riff, Greg has worked hard to make climbing safer for all of us. Please support him and the other volunteers of the ASCA by visiting www.safeclimbing.org and donating. When not road tripping to Bishop, Yosemite, Tuolumne, Joshua Tree, and Red Rocks, Greg lives in the Bay Area. Greg has also authored SuperTopo books for Red Rocks and Yosemite Valley.

Lita Collins photo

Chris McNamara - Contributing Author

Climbing Magazine once computed that three percent of Chris McNamara's life on earth has been spent on the face of El Capitan – an accomplishment that has left friends and family pondering Chris' sanity. He's climbed El Capitan over 50 times and holds nine big wall speed climbing records. In 1998 Chris did the first Girdle Traverse of El Capitan, an epic 75-pitch route that begs the question, "Why?" Outside Magazine has called Chris one of "the world's finest aid climbers." He's the winner of the 1999 Bates Award from the American Alpine Club and founder of the American Safe Climbing Association, a nonprofit group that has replaced over 7,000 dangerous anchor bolts. He also serves on the board of directors of the Access Fund.

Joe McKeown photo

Steve Roper - History Author

Roper was never much of a fan of topos until now. "Routes were vague back in the old days," he says, "and by using vague words we guidebook writers could ensure that climbers would get just as lost as we did." Later, when topos first appeared, he saw their usefulness but was disgusted by their crude appearance. And a wordless description meant that the history of the route was also lost, perhaps forever. In Roper's many books about climbing and backpacking, he stresses history, feeling it's an integral part of the overall experience. "Think of doing the Nose without knowing the name Warren Harding!" The skeptic Roper is now at peace with SuperTopos, feeling that a few hundred well-chosen words placed next to a beautifully drawn topo is the best of all worlds.

Staying Alive

by John Dill, NPS Search and Rescue

Most climbers do a good job coping with the hazards of their sport, yet more than a hundred climbing accidents occur in the Park every year. What factors contribute to them? What, if anything, can climbers do to avoid them? And just how dangerous is climbing, anyway? With these questions in mind, the National Park Service (NPS) examined most of the serious accidents that occurred in the park from 1970 through 1990. The conclusions provide interesting reading for those who wish to stay alive.

Fifty-one climbers died from traumatic injuries in that period. A dozen more, critically hurt, would have died without rapid transport and medical treatment. In addition, there were many serious but survivable injuries, from fractured skulls to broken legs (at least 50 fractures per year), and a much larger number of cuts, bruises, and sprains.

Not surprisingly, most injuries occurred during leader falls and involved feet, ankles, or lower legs; for many, these are the accepted risks of climbing. However, leader falls accounted for only 25 percent of the fatal and near-fatal traumatic injuries; roughly 10 percent were from rockfall, 25 percent from being deliberately unroped, and 40 percent from simple mistakes with gear. Many cases are not clear cut; several factors may share the credit, and it is sometimes hard to quantify the weird adventures climbers have.

Not to be overlooked in the body count are environmental injuries. Inadequately equipped for the weather, four climbers died of hypothermia and perhaps 45 more would have died of the cold or the heat if not rescued.

Fifteen to 25 parties require an NPS rescue each year. Sixty more climbers stagger into Yosemite's medical clinic on their own, and an unknown number escape statistical immortality by seeking treatment outside the park (or at the Mountain Room Bar).

Most Yosemite victims are experienced climbers: 60 percent have been climbing for three years or more, lead at least 5.10, are in good condition, and climb frequently. Short climbs and big walls, easy routes and desperate ones – they all get their share of the accidents.

The NPS keeps no statistics on how many climbers use the park, but 25,000 to 50,000 climber-days annually is a fair estimate. With this in mind, a few serious injuries and 2.5 deaths per year may seem a pretty low rate. It's much too high, however, if your climbing career is cut short by a broken hip, or worse. It's also too high when you consider that at least 80 percent of the fatalities, and many of the injuries, were easily preventable. In case after case, ignorance, a casual attitude, and/or some form of distraction proved to be contributing factors to the accidents.

As the saying goes, "good judgment comes from bad experience." Condensed in the following pages are 21 years of bad experience – the situations Yosemite climbers faced, the mistakes they made, and some recommendations for avoiding bad experiences of your own. This information comes in many cases from the victims' own analysis or from those of their peers.

Environmental Dangers

On October 11, 1983, a climber on El Cap collapsed from heat exhaustion. On October 11, 1984, a party on Washington Column was immobilized by hypothermia. You can expect this range of weather year-round.

Heat
No Yosemite climber has died from the heat, but a half-dozen parties have come close. Too exhausted to move, they survived only because death by drying-up is a relatively slow process, allowing rescuers to reach them. Temperatures on the sunny walls often exceed 100° F, but even in cool weather, climbing all day requires a lot of

water. The generally accepted minimum, two quarts per person per day, is just that, a minimum. It may not replace what you use, so don't let the desire for a light pack be an overriding concern, and take extra for unanticipated delays.

If you find yourself rationing water, remember that dehydration will seriously sap your strength, slowing you even further. It's not uncommon to go from mere thirst to a complete standstill in a single day. Continuing up may be the right choice but several climbers have said, "I should have gone down while I could."

Storms
We still hear climbers say, "It never rains in Yosemite." In fact, there are serious storms year-round. Four climbers have died of hypothermia and almost 50 have been rescued, most of whom would not have survived otherwise. Several were very experienced, with winter alpine routes, Yosemite walls, and stormy bivouacs to their credit – experts, by most measures. In many cases they took sub-standard gear, added another mistake or two, and couldn't deal with the water.

Mountain thunderstorms are common in spring, summer, and fall. They may appear suddenly out of a clear blue sky and rapidly shift position, their approach concealed by the route you are on. A few minutes warning may be all that you get. Thunderstorms may last only a couple of hours, but they are very intense, with huge amounts of near-freezing water often mixed with hail, strong winds, and lightning. The runoff can be a foot deep and fast enough to cause rockfall. A common result is a panicky retreat, a jammed rope, and cries for help.

No climber has died thus far in such a storm because rescuers were able to respond. No climbers have died from lightning either, but there have been several near misses, and hikers on Half Dome and elsewhere have been killed. Get out of the way of a thunderstorm as fast as you can, and avoid summits and projections.

The big Pacific storm systems have proven more dangerous. They sweep through the Sierra at any time of year, most frequently from September through May. They are unpredictable, often appearing back-to-back after several weeks of gorgeous, mind-numbing weather. It may rain on Half Dome in January and snow there in July. These storms are dangerous because they are usually warm enough to be wet, even in winter, yet always cold enough to kill an unprotected climber.

With no soil to absorb it, rain on the walls quickly collects into streams and waterfalls, pouring off overhangs and down the corner you're trying to climb up. Wind blows the water in all directions, including straight up.

Once cold and wet, you are in trouble and your options run out. Even with good gear, water runs down your sleeve every time you reach up. As your body temperature drops, you begin making dumb mistakes, such as clipping in wrong or dropping your rack. Once you become seriously hypothermic, you will just hang there, no longer caring. It happens quickly. In two separate incidents, climbers on the last pitch of The Nose left what protection they had to make a run for the top. They all died on that pitch.

Staying put may be no better. If you need help, no one may see you or hear you, and reaching you may take days. Don't forget your cell phone! Survivors say they had no idea how helpless they'd be until it happened to them. To find out for yourself, stand in the spray of a garden hose on a cold windy night. How long will you last?

How to Prepare for Bad Weather

• Check the forecast just before you start up but don't rely on it. For several parties it provided no warning whatsoever.

• Evaluate ahead of time the problems of retreat from any point on the route.

• If it's starting to rain, think twice about climbing "just one more pitch" – once wet you won't dry out.

All such hints and tricks aside, the bottom

line is your ability to sit out the storm. Your first priority is to keep the wind and outside water away. Second is to be insulated enough to stay warm, even though you are wet from your own condensation.

- Stick with high quality gear in good condition, and don't leave key items behind to travel lighter. Don't go up with a poorly equipped partner; it will be your neck as well.

- For insulation, never rely on cotton or down (even if it's covered with one of the waterproof/breathable fabrics). Even nylon absorbs water. Wool, polypropylene, and polyester insulators stay relatively warm when wet, and the synthetics dry fastest. Take along warm pants, long underwear, sweater, jacket, balaclava/hat, gloves, sleeping bag, insulating pad, extra socks or booties, and plenty of food and water – dehydration hastens hypothermia.

WARNING: Several climbers have blamed the waterproof/breathable fabrics for their close calls. They claim that no version of it can take the punishment of a storm on the walls. Whether true or not, you must be the judge; test all of your gear ahead of time under miserable conditions, but where your exit is an easy one.

Unplanned Bivouacs

Getting caught by darkness is common, especially on the longer one-day climbs and descent routes, e.g., Royal Arches and Cathedral Rocks. It happens easily – a late start, a slow partner, getting off-route, a jammed or dropped rope, or a sprained ankle. Usually it's nothing to get upset about, but if you are unprepared, even a cold wind or a mild storm becomes serious. One death and several close calls occurred this way. To avoid becoming a statistic:

- Consider the following gear for each person's day pack: long underwear, gloves, balaclava, rain jacket, and pants (which double as wind protection).

In warmer weather, all can be of the lightweight variety. If that's too heavy for you, at least take one of those disposable plastic rain-quilts or tube tents that occupy virtually no space. Take more warm clothes in colder weather. A head lamp with spare bulb and new batteries is very important for finding safe anchors, signaling for help, or avoiding that bivy altogether. Matches and heat-tabs will light wet wood. Food and water increase your safety after a night of shivering.

- Keep your survival gear with you whenever practical, not with your partner – climbers get separated from their gear, and each other, in imaginative ways, sometimes with serious consequences.

- Standing in slings on poor anchors is not the way to spend a night. If a bivy is inevitable, don't climb until the last moment – find a safe, sheltered, and/or comfortable spot while you've got enough light.

Descents

Consult the guidebook and your friends, but be wary of advice that the way down is obvious; look the route over ahead of time. If you carry a topo of the way up, consider one for the way down, or a photograph. Your ultimate protection is routefinding ability, and that takes experience. Some trouble spots: North Dome Gully, the Kat Walk, Michael's Ledge.

Many rappel epics are born when an easy descent, often a walk-off, is missed. Search for it thoroughly before you commit to a big drop – it may be well worth the effort.

Conversely, footprints and rappel anchors often lead nowhere – they were someone else's mistake. Be willing and able to retrace your steps and remember that the crux may not be at the top.

Any time you can't see anchors all the way to the ground, take the gear to set your own. This includes established descents.

Consider taking a second (7-9mm) rope, even for one-rope descents and walk-offs.

You'll save time, depend on fewer anchors, leave less gear, and more easily reverse the climbing route in an emergency. This is one advantage of leading on double ropes. But don't forget that thinner ropes are more vulnerable to sharp edges.

Friction from wet or twisted ropes, slings, ledges, cracks, and flakes may jam your rope. Plan ahead when you rig the anchor and be willing to leave gear behind to avoid friction. You can retrieve the gear later.

Rappelling through trees? Consider short rappels from tree to tree. It's slow but avoids irretrievable snarls.

Is your rope jammed? You can go back up and rerig if you still have both ends, so keep them until you're sure it will pull or you have to let go. If you do have to climb that rope, be careful that it isn't jammed by a sharp edge. Don't forget to untie the knots in the ends before you pull.

Loose Rock

There's plenty of it in Yosemite. Ten percent of all injuries are associated with rockfall, including six deaths and one permanent disability to date. In several other deaths, loose rock was implicated but not confirmed, e.g. possible broken handholds and failed placements. Spontaneous rockfall is not the problem – all the fatal and serious accidents were triggered by the victim, the rope, or by climbers above.

Rocks lying on ledges and in steep gullies are obviously dangerous. Not so obvious is that old reliable mantel block, five times your weight, wedged in place, and worn smooth by previous climbers. Yet with distressing regularity, "bombproof" blocks, flakes, and even ledges collapse under body weight, spit out cams, or fracture from the pressure of a piton. The forces placed on anchors and protection, even from rappelling, may be far higher than you generate in a test. Handholds may pass your scrutiny, then fail in mid-move. The rock you pull off can break your leg after falling only a couple of feet. Finally, watch out for rotten rock, responsible for at least two of these fatalities. It's common on the last couple of pitches of climbs that go to the rim of the Valley (e.g. Yosemite Point Buttress and Washington Column).

The East Buttress of Middle Cathedral Rock is a well-known bowling alley and the site of many rockfall injuries. The Northwest Face of Half Dome is another, with the added excitement of tourist "firing squads" on the summit. But the most dangerous, surprisingly, may be El Cap; on rock so steep, loose blocks balance precariously and big flakes wait for an unlucky hand to trigger the final fracture.

Some rockfall accidents may not be preventable, but being alert and following a few guidelines will cut the injury rate:

- Wear a helmet. (See "Helmets")

- Throw in an occasional piece on long, easy runouts as insurance against the unpredictability of the medium.

- Avoid rotten rock as protection, even if you can back it up. When it fails it endangers everyone below you.

- Ropes launch almost as many missiles as climbers do. Watch where you run your lead rope. Use directionals to keep it away from loose and sharp stuff, and check it frequently. Keep in mind that your bag or pack, when hauled, may dislodge everything in its path. When you pull your rappel ropes, stand to one side, look up, and watch out for delayed rockfall.

- You have no control over a party above you, and by being below you accept the risk. If you are catching up, don't crowd them – ask for permission to pass. You can probably get by them safely, but remember that climbers have been killed or hurt by rocks dislodged by parties above, including those they allowed to pass. The party you want to pass may have gotten an early start to avoid that risk, and they have no obligation to let you by. When you are above someone else, including your partner, put yourself in their shoes. Slow down and watch your feet and the rope.

Climbing Unroped

Everybody does it to some extent. There's no reason to stop, but good reason to be cautious: 14 climbers were killed and two critically injured while deliberately unroped. At least eight climbed 5.10 or better. Most, if not all, of those accidents were avoidable. You may find yourself unroped in several situations – on 3rd class terrain, spontaneously on 5th class, and while deliberately free-soloing a route.

Third class terrain may be easy, but add a bit of sand, loose or wet rock, darkness, plus a moment of distraction, and the rating becomes meaningless. Four climbers have died this way, typically on approach and descent routes such as North Dome Gully, all in spots that did not demand a rope.

Sometimes you lose the way on the approach, or unrope at what you thought was the top of the climb, only to find a few feet of "easy" 5th class blocking your way. Your rope is tucked away in your pack, and you're in a hurry. Before you go on, remember that you didn't plan to free-solo an unknown quantity today. Four died this way, falling from 5th class terrain that they were climbing on the spur of the moment.

Seven of the 14 killed were rappelling or otherwise tied in. They unroped while still on 5th class rock, for various reasons of convenience, without clipping into a nearby anchor. Three slipped off their stances, a ledge collapsed under another, one decided to downclimb the last few feet, and two tried to climb their rappel ropes hand-over-hand to attend to some problem. Like the previous group, they all went unroped onto 5th class terrain on the spur of the moment. In addition, they all had a belay immediately available. Did its nearness give them a false sense of security?

Only one true free-soloer has been killed, although another one, critically hurt, survived only by the speed of his rescue. Is the free-soloer more alert to the task, having planned it in advance, than those who unroped on the spur of the moment? Were the unlucky 14 still relaxed in their minds, not quite attuned to their new situation? We can only speculate.

Keep these cases and the hidden hazards in mind as you travel through any steep terrain. Be aware of what is underfoot, and in hand, at each moment. Be patient enough to retrace your steps to find the easy way.

Leading

Nine climbers died and six were critically injured in leader-fall accidents involving inadequate protection. Most fell simply because the moves were hard, and several were victims of broken holds. They were all injured because they hit something before their protection stopped them. Either they did not place enough protection (one-third of the cases) or it failed under the force of the fall (the remaining two-thirds). In every case, their injuries were serious because they fell headfirst or on their sides – the head, neck, or trunk took a lethal blow. Half fell 50 feet or less, the climber falling the shortest distance (25 feet) died, and the longest (270 feet!) survived.

Were these catastrophes avoidable? It's sometimes hard to tell, but the answer is often yes. Here are a few lessons frequently learned the hard way:

• Climbers frequently describe the belaying habits they see on Yosemite routes as "frightening." Before you start up, how frightening is your belay? Can the anchor withstand pulls in all directions? Is there more than one piece, with the load shared? Is the tie-in snug and in line with the fall force? Is your belayer experienced with that belay gadget and in position to operate it effectively when you fall? (You'd be surprised.) Will you clip through a bombproof directional as you start up, even on an easy pitch?

• Don't cheat on your ground fall calculations. (A good belayer will keep you honest.) With rope stretch and slack in the system, you may fall twice as far below your last protection as you are above it – if it holds.

• Nuts want to fall out. One that self-cleans below you may turn a comfortable lead

SUPERTOPO

into a ground-fall situation. Or, during a fall, the top piece may hold just long enough for the rope to yank the lower nuts out sideways, and then also fail. For more reliable placements, set those nuts with a tug and sling them generously. A tug on a marginal nut however, is worthless as a test. Be especially cautious about placements you can't see. Back them up.

• Camming devices "fail" regularly, but it's seldom the fault of the device. It's more likely due to haste, coupled with undeserved faith in technology. As with nuts, a blind placement – often in a lieback crack – may feel solid but be worthless.

• Fixed pitons loosen from freeze-thaw cycles and repeated use. They may not have been installed well to begin with. A hammer is the only reliable way to test and reset them, but you don't see many hammers on free routes these days. You don't see them on rappel routes, either, but you may find yourself hanging from anchors that belong in a museum. If you don't test pitons properly, do not depend on them – routinely back them up.

• There is no reliable way to test bolts but plenty of reasons to want to. For example, the common 3/8 split-shaft type was not designed or intended for life support, let alone for rock climbing. Their quality varies; several have broken under body weight, and others like them await you. Reliability also depends on the quality of the rock and the skill of the bolter. Add years of weathering and mistreatment by climbers and the result is many bolts that are easily pulled out by fingers or a sharp yank with a sling. Several bolt hangers have cracked as well, with one fatal accident so far.

• Never test a bolt with a hammer. Instead, examine the surrounding rock, the bolt, and the hanger for cracks, and hope they are large enough to see. Is the bolt tight and fully seated in the hole? Is the nut snug?

• Back up all untested fixed protection. Leave gear, even cams, before rappelling off of antique pieces. Is your life worth a cam?

Okay. So you know this stuff. You're a little shaky on the lead right now and you've had some trouble getting your pro to stick, but the book said this was 5.10a. It's only 20 feet more and one of those pieces is bound to hold. Think for a minute. Are you willing to free-solo this pitch? Keep your answer in mind as you climb, because poorly placed protection amounts to just that – you may not be deliberately unroped, but you might as well be.

About Falling
There's an art to falling safely – like a cat. Bouldering helps build the alertness required. Controlling your fall may be out of the question on those 200-foot screamers, but it will reduce the risk of injury from routine falls. Whenever possible, land on your feet – even if you break your leg, absorbing the shock this way may save your life. Liebacks and underclings hold special risks in this regard – you are already leaning back, and if you lose your grip the friction of your feet on the rock may rotate you into a headfirst – and backward – dive.

Pendulum falls are particularly dangerous. If you swing into a corner from 20 feet to one side of your protection, you will hit with the same bone-breaking speed as when striking a ledge in a 20-foot vertical fall. The crucial difference is, you are "landing" on your side, exposing vital organs to the impact. Two climbers died this way and others suffered serious injuries. Even small projections are dangerous: a 20-foot swing on Glacier Point Apron fractured a skull, and another smashed a pelvis. In a pendulum there is no difference between a leader and a follower fall; don't forget to protect your second from this fate as you lead a hard traverse.

Learning to Lead
Four of the 15 killed or critically injured in leader falls were good climbers on

well-defined routes, but the majority were intermediates, often off-route. There may be a couple of lessons in that.

- Don't get cocky because you just led your first 5.8 or your protection held on your first fall. Experienced climbers have died from errors "only a beginner would make," so you have plenty of time left in your career to screw up.

- Climbing and protecting are separate skills but both keep you alive. Don't challenge yourself in both at the same time – you may not have the skill and presence of mind to get out of a tight spot. If you're out to push your limits, pick a route that's well defined and easy to protect, place extra pieces for practice, and be willing and equipped to back off.

- Routefinding is another survival skill. A mistake here can quickly put you over your head in climbing, protecting, or both. Learn to look ahead and recognize what you want to avoid. Climb it mentally before you climb it physically.

- Some "easy" terrain in the valley is actually pretty dangerous. Low angle gullies are often full of loose blocks cemented together with moss. Opportunities for protection may be scarce and routefinding subtle. These are not usually cataloged routes. Three or four climbers have been killed, or nearly so, on such terrain while looking for easy routes to climb.

The Belay Chain

Whether you are climbing, rappelling, or just sitting on a ledge, the belay chain is what connects you to the rock. There are many links, and mistakes with almost every one have killed 22 climbers, 40 percent of all Yosemite climbing fatalities. In every case the cause was human error. In every case the death was completely preventable, not by the subtle skills of placing protection on the lead, but by some simple precaution to keep the belay chain intact. Experienced

climbers outnumbered the inexperienced in this category two to one. Mistakes with the belay chain can occur at any time. Make one and you'll fall to the end of the rope . . . or farther. Minor injuries are rare. Here are some key points to remember:

- Before you commit yourself to a system, always apply a few pounds of tension in the directions in which it will be loaded, analyzing it like an engineer – what if this happens . . . or that? Check every link, from the buckle of your harness to the rock around your anchor. You would be amazed at the inadequate systems often used by experienced climbers, even though it takes only a few seconds to run a proper check. Both lives depend on that system, so go through it with your partner. Nine climbers have died in multi-victim accidents.

- Check the system periodically while you're using it. Forces may change direction (two died when their anchors failed for this reason), ropes and slings can wear through (serious injuries and one death) and gear can come undone (two died when a wiggling bolt hanger unscrewed its nut – they were relying on a single bolt).

- Are you about to rappel? Stay clipped to the anchor for a few seconds. Check both the anchor and your brake system, as above. If one anchor point fails, will you remain attached to others? Are the knots in your rappel slings secure? Did you check every inch of those fixed slings for damage? Skipping these precautions cost eight lives plus serious injuries, from poorly tied slings, partially dismantled anchors (a simple misunderstanding), relying on single carabiners, and other reasons. The next accident may be caused by something new, but it will have been preventable by double-checking.

- Two climbers died by rappelling off the ends of their ropes, even though both had tied knots in the ends as a safety measure. In one case the knots pulled

SUPERTOPO
TUOLUMNE FREE CLIMBS: SUPERTOPOS

through the brake. In the second, the victim forgot to double-check the ropes after a knot had been untied to deal with a problem. Knots are still a recommended safety procedure, but do not take anything for granted. Tie both strands into one knot or knot each separately – there are pros and cons to each method.

• When rappelling in unpredictable circumstances – darkness, wind, poor communications, unknown anchors below – consider a Prusik Hitch or a mechanical ascender as a safety. If improperly handled, neither one may stop you if you fall – they are primarily for quickly but deliberately stopping yourself to deal with other emergencies. Both of those who rappelled off their ropes would have survived with safeties.

• Self-belayers should also tie in short – one died when his Prusik belay melted during a fall (a Prusik cord too large for the rope). At least two were treated to close calls when other types of self-belay systems jammed open.

• Clip into a new belay point before unclipping from the old one. During those few, vulnerable seconds, pitons have pulled, hero loops have broken, rocks have struck, and feet have slipped.

• Three climbers were killed and one critically injured by "failures" of single-carabiner tie-ins and rappel anchors. Be careful of relying on a single non-locking carabiner for any link in the chain. The rope or sling may flip over the gate and unclip itself, especially if it is slack, or shock loaded. Even if you watch it carefully and/or it is "safely" under tension, you may become distracted. One climber died when his Figure Eight descender unclipped while he was busy passing a knot on rappel. (He should have tied in short.) For those critical points, use either two non-locking carabiners with gates opposed and reversed, or a locking carabiner. Don't forget to lock it! For many applications the two-carabiner method is safer and faster to operate.

• Ropes have been cut in three fatal accidents. They did not break, but were stressed over sharp edges, a condition never intended by the manufacturer. Two of these accidents were avoidable: one climber should have tied in short to prevent a 100 foot fall that cut the rope; the other should have protected a fixed rope from a well-defined sharp edge. Ascending a rope produces a weighted, see-sawing action that can destroy it, even over a rounded, moderately rough, edge.

• As with ropes, most gear failure falls into the misuse category. Failure from a design or manufacturing flaw is rare. It was the initiating factor in one fatal accident – three climbers died when a bolt hanger broke at a two-bolt rappel anchor. The tragic outcome would have been avoided, however, had the climbers noticed they were not properly backed up to the second bolt.

These cases illustrate one of the rules most commonly overlooked: BACK YOURSELF UP. No matter what initially pulled, broke, slipped, jammed, or cut, the incident became an accident because the climber did not carefully ask himself, "What if . . .?" By leaving yourself open, you are betting against a variety of unpredictable events. You don't lose very often, but when you do, you may lose very big.

Beginners

From your first day on the rock, you have the right to inspect, and ask questions about, any system to which you're committing your life. It's a good way to learn, and a good way to stay alive. If your partner or instructor is offended, find someone else to climb with. Never change the system or the plan, however, without your partner's knowledge.

Helmets

While we can never know for certain, helmets might have made a difference in roughly 25 percent of the fatal and critical trauma cases. They would have significantly increased – but not guaranteed – the survival chances for five of those fatalities. Furthermore, helmets would have offered excellent protection against less serious fractures, concussions, and lacerations. There are no compelling reasons not to wear a helmet on any Yosemite climb and many reasons why you should.

States of Mind

This is the key to safety. It's impossible to know how many climbers were killed by haste or overconfidence, but many survivors will tell you that they somehow lost their good judgment long enough to get hurt. It's a complex subject and sometimes a touchy one. Nevertheless, at least three states of mind frequently contribute to accidents: ignorance, casualness, and distraction.

Ignorance

There is always more to learn, and even the most conscientious climber can get into trouble if unaware of the danger ("I thought it never rained . . . ") Here are some ways to fight ignorance:

Look in the mirror. Are you the stubborn type? Do you resist suggestions? Could you be a bit overconfident? (Ask your friends.) Several partners have said of a dead friend, "I wanted to give him advice, but he always got mad when I did that. I didn't realize he was about to die."

Read. The climbing magazines are full of good recommendations. Case histories in the American Alpine Club's *Accidents in North American Mountaineering*, a yearly compilation of accident reports, will show you how subtle factors may combine to catch you unaware. Such accounts are the next best (or worst?) thing to being there.

Practice. Reading may make you aware but not competent. In fact, you can be dangerously misled by what you read, including this report – important details are often left out, the advice may be incorrect, and in the long run you must think and act for yourself. Several climbers, for example, waited to learn how to prusik until it was dark, raining, overhanging and they were actually in trouble. They had read about it, but they had to be rescued despite having the gear to improvise their own solutions. Book-learning alone gave them a complacency that could have proved fatal.

Casualness

"I just didn't take it seriously," is a common lament. It's often correct, but it's more a symptom than a cause – there may be deeper reasons for underestimating your risk. Ignorance is one, and here are some more:

Habit reinforcement. The more often you get away with risky business the more entrenched your lazy habits become. Have you unconsciously dropped items from your safety checklists since you were a chickenhearted (or hare-brained) beginner? Your attitudes and habits can be reinforced by the experiences (and states of mind) of others. The sense of awe and commitment of the 1960s is gone from the big wall trade routes, and young aspirants with no Grade VIs, or even Vs, to their credit speak casually about them. Even for experts, most accidents on El Cap occur on the easier pitches, where their guard is down.

Memory Decay. "I'm not going up again without raingear – I thought I would die!" A week later this climber had forgotten how scared he had been in that thunderstorm. Raingear was now too heavy and besides, he was sure he'd be able to rap off the next time. Many of us tend to forget the bad parts. We have to be hit again.

Civilization. With fixed anchors marking the way up and ghetto blasters echoing behind, it may be hard to realize that the potential for trouble is as high in Yosemite as anywhere. Some say the possibility of fast rescue added to their casualness. Maybe, but who wants a broken leg, or worse, in the first place?

Distraction

It is caused by whatever takes your mind off your work – anxiety, sore feet, skinny-dippers below – the list is endless. Being in a hurry is one of the most common causes. Here are two ways it has happened:

• Experienced climbers were often hurt after making "beginner errors" (their words) to get somewhere quickly. There was no emergency or panic, but their minds were elsewhere – on a cold beer, a good bivy – or just sick of being on that route for a week. (It's often called "summit fever.") Their mistakes were usually shortcuts in protecting easy pitches, on both walls and shorter climbs. As one put it, "We were climbing as though we were on top."

• Darkness had caught two day-climbers for the first time. Unprepared, upset, and off route, they rushed to get down, arguing with each other about what to do. After several errors, which they knew how to avoid, one died rappelling off the end of his rope.

Rescue

Despite the best of attitudes, an accident can happen to anyone. Self-rescue is often the fastest and safest way out, but whether it's the wise course of action depends on the injury and how well prepared you are. Combining with a nearby party will often give you the margin of safety you need, but do not risk aggravating an injury or getting yourself into a more serious predicament – ask for help if you need it. (Sometimes a bit of advice, delivered by loudspeaker, is all that's required.) In making your decision, keep an eye on weather and darkness – call for help early.

If you don't have formal first aid training (which is strongly recommended), at least know how to keep an unconscious patient's airway open, how to protect a possible broken neck or back, and how to deal with external bleeding and serious blood loss. These procedures are lifesaving, do not require fancy gear, and are easy to learn.

Head injury victims, even when unconscious, may try to untie themselves. If you have to leave one alone, make escape impossible.

Risk and Responsibility

The NPS has no regulations specifying how you must climb. There is a regulation, however, requiring that all park users act responsibly. This applies to climbers, in that the consequences of your actions put rescue and other climbers at risk. One rescuer has been killed in the park so far. Thus, if your own negligence got you into trouble, you may be charged with "creating a hazardous condition" for others. As an example, a climber was fined because he became stranded by a hailstorm while attempting to free-solo the Steck-Salathé on Sentinel Rock. Storms had been predicted and his rescue should not have been necessary.

Even avoidable accidents are understandable, thus legal charges are not frequently filed. Of all park users, however, climbers should be particularly aware – they know that their sport is dangerous, that safety lies in education and training, and that there is an information network available. So take what you'll need with you on the climb, or have competent friends ready to back you up.

Climbing will always be risky. It should be clear, however, that a reduced accident rate is possible without seriously restricting the sport. You have a right to choose your own climbing style and level of risk, but you owe it to yourself and everyone else to make that choice with your eyes wide open.

Accident/Hazard Reporting

If you know of dangerous route conditions such as loose rock, consider posting the information on the bulletin board at Camp 4 or at www.supertopo.com. If you know of bad anchors, email the ASCA at greg@safeclimbing.org. Your information will help other climbers.

Nearby Mountain Biking

Bikes are allowed only where cars are allowed in Tuolumne, and the only spot that they are useful inside the Park is for navigating the immense, pothole-filled campground. However, since many visiting climbers have their mountain bikes with them, here is a guide to the limited mountain biking near Tioga Pass. Mammoth Mountain Bike Park is the only destination biking area nearby, but at less than 1.5 hours away, it's pretty close! Current (2009) Mammoth bike park passes are $39/day for lift-served, and $10/day for pedal power access. www.mammothmountain.com

Tioga Pass area

There's limited biking, but what's here is pretty fun for experienced bikers. The trails aren't all that long, but they make for a fun break from climbing. Do not underestimate the effects of the altitude – it's high! Technical and rocky is the name of the game. Please use excessive courtesy when encountering fishermen, hikers, equestrians, and other trail users – mountain biking in these areas is currently allowed, but it could easily be closed.

Bennetville Mine Road – about 2.5 miles round trip

This old mine road is fairly flat and very scenic, but it requires some riding on rocks including riding along a rocky streambed/old road. The altitude is just shy of 10,000' and the road is often too snowy in early season. It also tends to have insane mosquitos in mid-season. Park at the big paved turnout above Tioga Lake (the first pullout on the eastside of Tioga Pass). Ride 50yds down the road, and cross (carefully!) to a pullout at the start of an old road (the road is blocked with large rocks). It's also possible to park at the pullout. Bike along

the old road about 100 yds to another set of blocking rocks, and take the uphill (left) branch. Follow this road past a couple of very photogenic (and very mosquitogenic!) small ponds, then up a short hill to an open ridgetop. This section of the trail is pretty easy. Next, drop down a short steep hill and start battling up the old roadbed along a stream. Wet, technical rock crawling leads to an open bowl. Follow the road to a big flat mine entrance platform, with old machinery and a gated mine entrance (with stream coming out of the mine). The trail continues for a short distance into meadows, but the trail is narrow and side-hilled, and while legal, probably not worth riding considering how short it is. Reverse the road on the way back!

Saddlebag Lake Trail – about 4 miles

This trail/road is best done counter-clockwise, saving the loose rocky stuff for when you're warmed up (and allowing you to just turn around and reverse the trail if it gets too tough). Please avoid this trail on popular weekends mid-summer (when you'll have trouble finding parking anyway!). The elevation is a bit over 10,000'. Park in the main parking lot, then follow the main trail to the right along the lake. The trail/road crosses some rocky water troughs but is generally pretty easy. At the opposite end of the lake, you'll intersect a maze of trails. Go straight at the first intersection along the old road (the left trail just goes to the lake), then left at the next intersection, staying left to parallel the lake shore. You'll have to walk across a log bridge. DO NOT GO RIGHT anywhere in here – you're nearly at the Wilderness boundary, and all bikes are prohibited in Wilderness. Any transgression, even an accidental one just a few yards past the boundary, will jeopardize access to the lake trail.

Once past the bridge, join the trail paralleling the lake. This trail is very rocky, and even the best trail riders will probably not make every section. Watch out for your derailleur on the rocks! Follow the elbow-battering loose rock trail past the small dam and back to the road.

Mono Lake area

Log Cabin Mine Road

This is a big, no holds barred hill climb at altitude, gaining 2400' to the mine at 9600'. You reverse the way you climb so you can bail at any point. About ¾ of a mile up Hwy 120 from the Mobil station in Lee Vining, park at the USFS administration center or at the water spigot pullout (50 yds down the road). The USFS center has bathrooms as well. Fill up with plenty of water, then cross the highway and head up the signed Log Cabin Mine Road. After a few yards a utility road takes off right – ignore this and head left and up. There is some private property once you gain the big bench, so just stay on the main road and keep grunting your way up. Few will be able to ride the whole thing, as it's not only high – it's also both steep and loose. There's a cool plateau with old mine buildings and a sweet view – if you make it to the top!

Horse Meadow

Upper and Lower Horse Meadow are on the giant glacial moraine on the south side of Lee Vining Canyon, with great views of the Third Pillar of Dana and Mono Lake. The Mobil Station is at the very toe of the moraine. The Forest Service actually has a marked mountain bike route, but the descent section is not a good bike route. The ride outlined here shares the same uphill as the USFS route, but explores branches with good surfaces and great scenery and avoids the poor descent. A substantial, but relatively moderate, climb up a dirt road leads to the beautiful lower meadow. The angle eases through the meadow, and there's a side road near a small rock tower that is fun to explore. On the way up to the upper meadow, a very steep section is typically hike-a-biked, but those who are in great shape (and acclimated) can climb it. The upper meadow winds around, with various side roads that are fun to explore. The marked bike route takes a sharp left, and after a short climb you reach a cool ridge. This is the beginning of the descent for the marked USFS bike route. Instead of descending

The author at Upper Horse Meadow. Karin Wuhrmann photo.

the USFS bike route, explore up and down the ridge (if you go all the way to the east there's a steep hill climb to a superb viewpoint), then return down to the Horse meadows and descend as you climbed.

The marked mountain bike route descends roads that are poor biking. The descent is better for motorcycles than bikes, with loose small rocks on dirt roads, soft sand, and motorcycle grooves in the sand. If you want to do the marked route, be aware that more than half of the intersections are missing signs.

In early season, swarms of micro-size gnats can plague the bike ride, especially down low near the highway. During the fall hunting season, it's best to avoid this heavily used area.

Other options

There are many open jeep roads around Mono Lake, but they are nearly all very soft volcanic pumice. Unfortunately this holds true for nearly everything else in the immediate area. If you bother coming this far, just go to Mammoth! If you are heading north and want to stop for some biking, you can explore jeep trails and side roads near the turn off for Bodie, and further north, in the Sweetwater mountains.

Climbs by Name

NOTE: routes with a * are new to the second edition of this book.

15 Minutes of Fame 5.11a 153

A

Acapulco Gold (pitch 1) 5.10c R 134 *
Ace in the Hole 5.10a R/X 66
Age of Darkness 5.11a 30 *
Aileron 5.9+ 55 *
Alimony Crack 5.8 76
American Wet Dream 5.10b 50
Anatolio (pitch 1) 5.11b 134 *
Anduril 5.10b R- 114 *
Apex Predator 5.11b 52
Aqua Knobby 5.9 168
Arete 5.10d 192
Auto Bond 5.11b 32 *
Avacados & Tequila 5.8 R 165 *

B

Bachar/Yerian 5.11c X 156 *
Ballroom Dancing 5.10b R 84 *
Battle of the Bulge 5.8 R 98 *
Beer 5.9 150 *
Beernuts 5.10c 150
Beginner's Route 5.4 R- 93 *
Big Time 5.11b 153
Billiard Room 5.10a X 87 *
Biscuit and Gravy 5.8 54
Bit by Bit 5.9 R- 164 *
Black Diamond 5.9 R 54
Black Leather 5.8 R 28 *
Black Nepalese 5.7 136 *
Black Widow (pitch 1) 5.7 61
Black Widow (pitch 2) 5.9 R 61 *
Blown Away 5.9 71
Blues Riff 5.11b 58
Bombs Over Tokyo 5.10c 70
Bull Dike 5.7 R- 28 *
Bull Dozier 5.7 165 *
Bust It Out 5.10a 65 *
By Hook or By Crook 5.11b 44

C

Carpet Crawler 5.10a R/X 128
Cathedral Peak, Southeast Buttress 5.6 102
Cheeseburgers & Beer 5.8 162 *
Cheesecake 5.5 R- 79 *
Cheetos & Everclear 5.10a 165 *
Chicken Little 5.9 R 146 *
Chili Air 5.10a 159 *
Chinese Handcuffs 5.10d 44
Chop the Hogs 5.7 116 *
Ciebolla 5.10b 153
City Girl 5.10c 162 *
Come and Get It 5.10b R- 153
Comfortably Numb 5.10c 84 *
Cooke Book 5.10a 69
Cottage Cheese 5.10b 81 *
Crescent Arch 5.10b 73
Cross Reference 5.11a R 37 *
Cry Baby 5.8 R- 92 *
Crying Time Again 5.10a R 92
Crystal Meth 5.8 R- 136 *
Cucamonga Honey 5.10b R 96 *
Cyclone 5.10b 44 *

D

DAFFy Duck 5.5 R 79 *
Darth Vader's Revenge 5.10a 61
Dastardly Rascal 5.8 116 *
Deadheads Delight 5.9 R 66
Deimos 5.9 58
Dihedral 5.10a 192
Dike Route 5.9 R 170
Disintegration 5.10d 84 *
Dixie Peach 5.9 R 39 *
Do or Fly 5.11c 98
D'oh! 5.7 150
Donuts 5.10a TR 150
Dope Show 5.8 136 *
Double Feature 5.11d 30 *
Dumpster Evangelist 5.10a 162 *

E

Eddie Muenster 5.7 79 *
Eichorn's Pinnacle, North Face 5.4 108
Eichorn's Pinnacle, West Pillar 5.9 108
Eichorn's Pinnacle, West Pillar Direct 5.10b 108
Enemy Within 5.10b 31 *
Errett by Bit 5.7 164 *
Errett Out 5.7 R- 164 *
Euro Trash 5.10c 136 *
Excellent, Smithers 5.10a 150

F

Fairview Dome, Regular Route 5.9 119
Falkenstein Face 5.10d TR 63
Family Affair 5.9 R- 61 *
Faux Pas 5.9 R 48 *
Felsic 5.9 165 *
Fingertips 5.10a R 76
Five Ten, You Wuss 5.10c 127 *
Flash of the Blade 5.10a R- 116 *
Flintstone 5.10b R- 83 *
Fluoridation 5.11a 32 *
Fook Mi 5.8 R 150
Footnote 5.10c R 37 *
Frogger 5.7 33 *
Fuel Rod 5.10d 55 *

G

Galen's Crack 5.10c 63
Geekin' Hard 5.10d 80 *
George's Toprope 5.9+ 142 *
Getting in the Groove 5.11d 33 *
Gold Mine 5.9 192
Goldmember 5.9 150
Golfer's Route 5.7 R 61
Gortlough RA 5.9 33 *
Gram Traverse 5.10d 131
Grease Monkey 5.9 R- 30 *
Great Circle 5.10a R- 76
Great Pumpkin 5.8 R 124
Great White Book 5.6 R 38
Green Eggs and Ham 5.9 R 66
Grenade Launcher 5.12c 99
Groove 5.10d 192
Guide Cracks 5.5-8 76

H

Happy Hour 5.10b R 50 *
Head Rush 5.10a R 97 *
Heat Sensitive 5.12b 44
Hermaphrodite Flake 5.8 37
Hill Crest Drive 5.10a R- 153
Hobbit Book 5.7 R 141
Hogwash 5.10c R- 76
Holdless Horror 5.6 165
Hoodwink 5.10a R 43
Horseshoes and Handgrenades 5.12a 99
Hot Crossed Buns 5.6 54
How Does it Feel? 5.11a R 50 *

I

Ice 5.12d 134 *
Isostacy 5.8 164 *
It is Finished 5.11a R- 76
Ivory Tower Center 5.10a 31 *
Ivory Tower Left 5.8 31 *

J

Jailbreak 5.9 R- 128 *
Joe Mamba 5.10a R- 52
John Henry 5.10a R- 92 *
John Lee Hooker 5.11b 58 *
Just Say No (pitch 1) 5.11a R 134 *

K

Kick Back Crack 5.10a R 87 *
Kill Pickle 5.10c R 87 *
Knobnoxious 5.10d 85 *
Knobulator 5.10c 85 *
Knobvious 5.11a R 85 *

L

Lampoon 5.9+ R/X 128 *
Lechlinski Flake 5.11a 153
Left Water Crack 5.7 R 96 *
Lembert Dome, Direct NW Face 5.10b 92
Liberation 5.10c R 76
Life in the Cretaceous 5.10a 83 *
Linda's Sandbag 5.8 83 *
Liposuction 5.11a 84 *
Little Sheba 5.10a 128
Lock of Ages 5.10c 30 *
Loco Yokel 5.10d 146 *
Lord Caffeine 5.10d 30 *
Lord of the Overhigh (pitch 1) 5.8 136 *
Loud & Obnoxious 5.10a 164 *
Lucky Streaks 5.10c 122

M

Mandric 5.10c R 32 *
Mandric Direct 5.11b 32 *
March of Dimes 5.10a R- 66
Matthes Crest Traverse 5.7 111
Mega Bleam 5.10a 93 *
Memo From Lloyd 5.11b 61
Mere Image 5.7 R- 54
Metalhead 5.10c 116 *

M (cont)

Middle Earth 5.10b R 140 *
Mmmm...Crackahol 5.9 142 *
Mordor 5.10c 139 *
Mosquito 5.7 R 39 *
Mt. Conness, North Ridge 5.6 178
Mt. Conness, Southwest Face 5.10c 185
Mt. Conness, West Ridge 5.6 182

N

Narsil 5.10d 115 *
Needle & Spoon 5.10a R- 168 *
New Tricks for Old Dogs 5.10b R 66
No Rock Nazis 5.11c 44
Northwest Books 5.6 93
Northwest Buttress 5.5 173

O

Obviously Not 5.7 R 55 *
Old Folks Boogie 5.10d R 84 *
On the Lamb 5.9 127
One-Eyed Jack 5.10d X 86 *
Orange Man 5.10c 61
Orange Plasma 5.11a 84 *
OZ 5.10d 131

P

Pac Man 5.8 33 *
Pasture-ized 5.8 R- 79 *
Peace (first pitch) 5.10b R- 153
Peace (pitch 2) 5.13c 156 *
Pencilitis 5.11a R 80 *
Pencil-Necked Geek 5.11a R- 81 *
Penguin Café 5.11a 33 *
Perspiration 5.11c 76
Phobos 5.9 58
Pippin 5.8 R 48 *
Piss Easier 5.6 R 151
Piss Easy 5.8 R 151
Plutonics 5.10b R- 165 *
Polski Wyrob 5.11b R- 87 *
Pothole Dome, TR #1-3 5.0-6 89
Pothole Dome, TR #4-6 5.0-6 90
Potluck 5.11 89
Pretty in Pink Point (first pitch) 5.10a 153
Puppy Crack 5.7 98
Push It 5.11a 135 *
Pussy Paws 5.10c X 146 *

R

R2-D2 5.8 R- 60 *
Read Between the Lines 5.10a 165 *
Right Water Crack 5.8 R 96 *
Ripple 5.7 R- 165 *
Rise and Fall of the Albatross 5.13a/b 69 *
Roof 5.10b 192
Roof Rat 5.7 135 *
Rover Take Over 5.10d R- 85 *
Scandalous Summer 5.7 162 *
Scorpion 5.11b 147 *
Seconds to Darkness 5.8 142
Shady Rest 5.10c R- 153
Shagadelic 5.8 150
Shit Hooks 5.10b 61
Silicone Corner 5.7 R- 65 *
Slasher 5.9 116 *
Sleeper 5.9 R 128
South Country 5.10c 146 *
South Crack 5.8 R 42
Speed of Life 5.11b 193 *
Stemulant 5.10a 135 *
Sticks & Stones 5.10c 158 *
Stinky T-shirt 5.11d 193 *
Stomper 5.10a 139 *
String Cheese 5.6 78 *
Sudden Impact 5.13a 87 *
Sunshine (pitch 1) 5.9 R/X 135 *
Super Chicken 5.9 146
Sweet'n Low 5.7 87 *

T

Table of Contents 5.10d R- 37 *
Tectonomagmatic 5.10b 127 *
The Boltway 5.10b 37
The Coming 5.9 R 152
The Shadow Nose 5.9 R 34 *
The Stanley Edge 5.10c 31 *
The Sting 5.10b R 44
The Thrill is Gone 5.10d 31 *
Third Pillar of Dana, Regular Route 5.10b 190
Third World 5.11b 44 *
Tideline 5.11a 31 *
Tips Ahoy 5.11a R 76
Tooled 5.11b 128 *
Touch of Grey 5.9 R 66
Tourette's 5.10b 162 *
Trendy Bendy 5.10a 55 *
Trick Shot 5.9 87 *
Truck'N Drive 5.9 R 96 *
Turbine 5.10a 79 *
Twisted Sister 5.6 28 *

U

Udder Chaos 5.8 R- 78 *
Undisputed Truth 5.10a R 47 *
Unknown (East Cottage Dome) 5.10d 85 *
Unknown (Medlicott Dome) 5.10d 153
Unknown (Pywiack Dome) 5.4 R/X 171 *
Unknown (Pywiack Dome) 5.6 R 171 *
Unnamed (Daff Dome) 5.7 R 76

V

Vice Gripped 5.10c R 50 *

W

Wailing Wall (pitch 1) 5.11d 147 *
Werner's Wiggle 5.8 R 97 *
West Country 5.7 36
West Crack 5.9 72
West of the Witch 5.8 R- 70 *
White Flake 5.7 R 34 *
White Lie 5.8 R 162 *
Wild in the Streaks 5.7 54
Witch of the West 5.9 R- 70
Wrest Day 5.9 162 *

X

X-wing 5.9 33 *

Y

You Asked For It 5.10c X 156 *
You, Me, and the Dike 5.10a R 165 *

Z

Zee Tree 5.7 170

Climbs by Rating

5.0-5.4

Pothole Dome, TR #1-3 5.0-6 89
Pothole Dome, TR #4-6 5.0-6 90
Eichorn's Pinnacle, North Face 5.4 108
Beginner's Route 5.4 R- 93
Unknown (Pywiack Dome) 5.4 R/X 171

5.5

Northwest Buttress 5.5 173
DAFFy Duck 5.5 R 79
Cheesecake 5.5 R- 79
Guide Cracks 5.5-8 76

5.6

Cathedral Peak, Southeast Buttress 5.6 102
Holdless Horror 5.6 165
Hot Crossed Buns 5.6 54
Mt. Conness, North Ridge 5.6 178
Mt. Conness, West Ridge 5.6 182
Northwest Books 5.6 93
String Cheese 5.6 78
Twisted Sister 5.6 28
Great White Book 5.6 R 38
Piss Easier 5.6 R 151
Unknown (Pywiack Dome) 5.6 R 171

5.7

Black Nepalese 5.7 136
Black Widow (pitch 1) 5.7 61
Bull Dozier 5.7 165
Chop the Hogs 5.7 116
D'oh! 5.7 150
Eddie Muenster 5.7 79
Errett by Bit 5.7 164
Frogger 5.7 33
Matthes Crest Traverse 5.7 111
Puppy Crack 5.7 98
Roof Rat 5.7 135
Scandalous Summer 5.7 162
Sweet'n Low 5.7 87
West Country 5.7 36
Wild in the Streaks 5.7 54

5.7 (cont)

Zee Tree 5.7 170
Bull Dike 5.7 R- 28
Errett Out 5.7 R- 164
Mere Image 5.7 R- 54
Ripple 5.7 R- 165
Silicone Corner 5.7 R- 65
Golfer's Route 5.7 R 61
Hobbit Book 5.7 R 141
Left Water Crack 5.7 R 96
Mosquito 5.7 R 39
Obviously Not 5.7 R 55
Unnamed (Daff Dome) 5.7 R 76
White Flake 5.7 R 34

5.8

Alimony Crack 5.8 76
Biscuit and Gravy 5.8 54
Cheeseburgers & Beer 5.8 162
Dastardly Rascal 5.8 116
Dope Show 5.8 136
Hermaphrodite Flake 5.8 37
Isostacy 5.8 164
Ivory Tower Left 5.8 31
Linda's Sandbag 5.8 83
Lord of the Overhigh (pitch 1) 5.8 136
Pac Man 5.8 33
Seconds to Darkness 5.8 142
Shagadelic 5.8 150
Cry Baby 5.8 R- 92
Crystal Meth 5.8 R- 136
Pasture-ized 5.8 R- 79
R2-D2 5.8 R- 60
Udder Chaos 5.8 R- 78
West of the Witch 5.8 R- 70
Avacados & Tequila 5.8 R 165
Battle of the Bulge 5.8 R 98
Black Leather 5.8 R 28
Fook Mi 5.8 R 150
Great Pumpkin 5.8 R 124
Pippin 5.8 R 48
Piss Easy 5.8 R 151
Right Water Crack 5.8 R 96
South Crack 5.8 R 42
Werner's Wiggle 5.8 R 97
White Lie 5.8 R 162

5.9

Aqua Knobby 5.9 168
Beer 5.9 150
Blown Away 5.9 71
Deimos 5.9 58
Eichorn's Pinnacle, West Pillar 5.9 108
Fairview Dome, Regular Route 5.9 119
Felsic 5.9 165
Gold Mine 5.9 192
Goldmember 5.9 150
Gortlough RA 5.9 33
Mmmm...Crackahol 5.9 142
On the Lamb 5.9 127
Phobos 5.9 58
Slasher 5.9 116
Super Chicken 5.9 146
Trick Shot 5.9 87
West Crack 5.9 72
Witch of the West 5.9 R- 70
Wrest Day 5.9 162
X-wing 5.9 33
Family Affair 5.9 R- 61
Grease Monkey 5.9 R- 30
Jailbreak 5.9 R- 128
Bit by Bit 5.9 R- 164
Black Diamond 5.9 R 54
Black Widow (pitch 2) 5.9 R 61
Chicken Little 5.9 R 146
Deadheads Delight 5.9 R 66
Dike Route 5.9 R 170
Dixie Peach 5.9 R 39
Faux Pas 5.9 R 48
Green Eggs and Ham 5.9 R 66
Sleeper 5.9 R 128
The Coming 5.9 R 152
The Shadow Nose 5.9 R 34
Touch of Grey 5.9 R 66
Truck'N Drive 5.9 R 96
Sunshine (pitch 1) 5.9 R/X 135
Aileron 5.9+ 55
George's Toprope 5.9+ 142
Lampoon 5.9+ R/X 128

5.10a

Donuts 5.10a TR 150
Bust It Out 5.10a 65
Cheetos & Everclear 5.10a 165
Chili Air 5.10a 159
Cooke Book 5.10a 69
Darth Vader's Revenge 5.10a 61
Dihedral 5.10a 192
Dumpster Evangelist 5.10a 162
Excellent, Smithers 5.10a 150
Ivory Tower Center 5.10a 31
Life in the Cretaceous 5.10a 83
Little Sheba 5.10a 128
Loud & Obnoxious 5.10a 164
Mega Bleam 5.10a 93
Pretty in Pink Point (first pitch) 5.10a 153
Read Between the Lines 5.10a 165
Stemulant 5.10a 135
Stomper 5.10a 139
Trendy Bendy 5.10a 55
Turbine 5.10a 79
Flash of the Blade 5.10a R- 116
Great Circle 5.10a R- 76
Joe Mamba 5.10a R- 52
John Henry 5.10a R- 92
March of Dimes 5.10a R- 66
Crying Time Again 5.10a R 92
Fingertips 5.10a R 76
Head Rush 5.10a R 97
Hill Crest Drive 5.10a R 153
Hoodwink 5.10a R 43
Kick Back Crack 5.10a R 87
Needle & Spoon 5.10a R- 168
Undisputed Truth 5.10a R 47
You, Me, and the Dike 5.10a R 165
Ace in the Hole 5.10a R/X 66
Carpet Crawler 5.10a R/X 128
Billiard Room 5.10a X 87

5.10b

American Wet Dream 5.10b 50
Ciebolla 5.10b 153
Cottage Cheese 5.10b 81
Crescent Arch 5.10b 73
Cyclone 5.10b 44
Eichorn's Pinnacle, West Pillar Direct 5.10b 108
Enemy Within 5.10b 31
Lembert Dome, Direct Northwest Face 5.10b 92

Roof 5.10b 192
Shit Hooks 5.10b 61
Tectonomagmatic 5.10b 127
The Boltway 5.10b 37
Third Pillar of Dana, Regular Route 5.10b 190
Tourette's 5.10b 162
Anduril 5.10b R- 114
Come and Get It 5.10b R- 153
Flintstone 5.10b R- 83
Peace (first pitch) 5.10b R- 153
Plutonics 5.10b R- 165
Ballroom Dancing 5.10b R 84
Cucamonga Honey 5.10b R 96
Happy Hour 5.10b R 50
Middle Earth 5.10b R 140
New Tricks for Old Dogs 5.10b R 66
The Sting 5.10b R 44

5.10c

Beernuts 5.10c 150
Bombs Over Tokyo 5.10c 70
City Girl 5.10c 162
Comfortably Numb 5.10c 84
Euro Trash 5.10c 136
Five Ten, You Wuss 5.10c 127
Galen's Crack 5.10c 63
Knobulator 5.10c 85
Lock of Ages 5.10c 30
Lucky Streaks 5.10c 122
Metalhead 5.10c 116
Mordor 5.10c 139
Mt. Conness, Southwest Face 5.10c 185
Orange Man 5.10c 61
South Country 5.10c 146
Sticks & Stones 5.10c 158
The Stanley Edge 5.10c 31
Hogwash 5.10c R- 76
Shady Rest 5.10c R- 153
Acapulco Gold (pitch 1) 5.10c R 134
Footnote 5.10c R 37
Kill Pickle 5.10c R 87
Liberation 5.10c R 76
Mandric 5.10c R 32
Vice Gripped 5.10c R 50
Pussy Paws 5.10c X 146
You Asked For It 5.10c X 156

5.10d

Falkenstein Face 5.10d TR 63
Arete 5.10d 192
Chinese Handcuffs 5.10d 44
Disintegration 5.10d 84
Fuel Rod 5.10d 55
Geekin' Hard 5.10d 80
Gram Traverse 5.10d 131
Groove 5.10d 192
Knobnoxious 5.10d 85
Loco Yokel 5.10d 146
Lord Caffeine 5.10d 30
Narsil 5.10d 115
OZ 5.10d 131
The Thrill is Gone 5.10d 31
Unknown (East Cottage Dome) 5.10d 85
Unknown (Medlicott Dome) 5.10d 153
Rover Take Over 5.10d R- 85
Table of Contents 5.10d R- 37
Old Folks Boogie 5.10d R 84
One-Eyed Jack 5.10d X 86

5.11a

15 Minutes of Fame 5.11a 153
Age of Darkness 5.11a 30
Fluoridation 5.11a 32
Lechlinski Flake 5.11a 153
Liposuction 5.11a 84
Orange Plasma 5.11a 84
Penguin Café 5.11a 33
Push It 5.11a 135
Tideline 5.11a 31
It is Finished 5.11a R- 76
Pencil-Necked Geek 5.11a R- 81
Cross Reference 5.11a R 37
How Does it Feel? 5.11a R 50
Just Say No (pitch 1) 5.11a R 134
Knobvious 5.11a R 85
Pencilitis 5.11a R 80
Tips Ahoy 5.11a R 76

5.11b

Anatolio (pitch 1) 5.11b 134
Apex Predator 5.11b 52
Auto Bond 5.11b 32
Big Time 5.11b 153
Blues Riff 5.11b 58
By Hook or By Crook 5.11b 44
John Lee Hooker 5.11b 58
Mandric Direct 5.11b 32
Memo From Lloyd 5.11b 61
Scorpion 5.11b 147
Speed of Life 5.11b 193
Third World 5.11b 44
Tooled 5.11b 128
Polski Wyrob 5.11b R- 87

5.11c/d

Potluck 5.11 89
Do or Fly 5.11c 98
No Rock Nazis 5.11c 44
Perspiration 5.11c 76
Bachar/Yerian 5.11c X 156
Double Feature 5.11d 30
Getting in the Groove 5.11d 33
Stinky T-shirt 5.11d 193
Wailing Wall (pitch 1) 5.11d 147

5.12

Horseshoes and Handgrenades 5.12a 99
Heat Sensitive 5.12b 44
Grenade Launcher 5.12c 99
Ice 5.12d 134

5.13

Sudden Impact 5.13a 87
Rise and Fall of the Albatross 5.13a/b 69
Peace (pitch 2) 5.13c 156

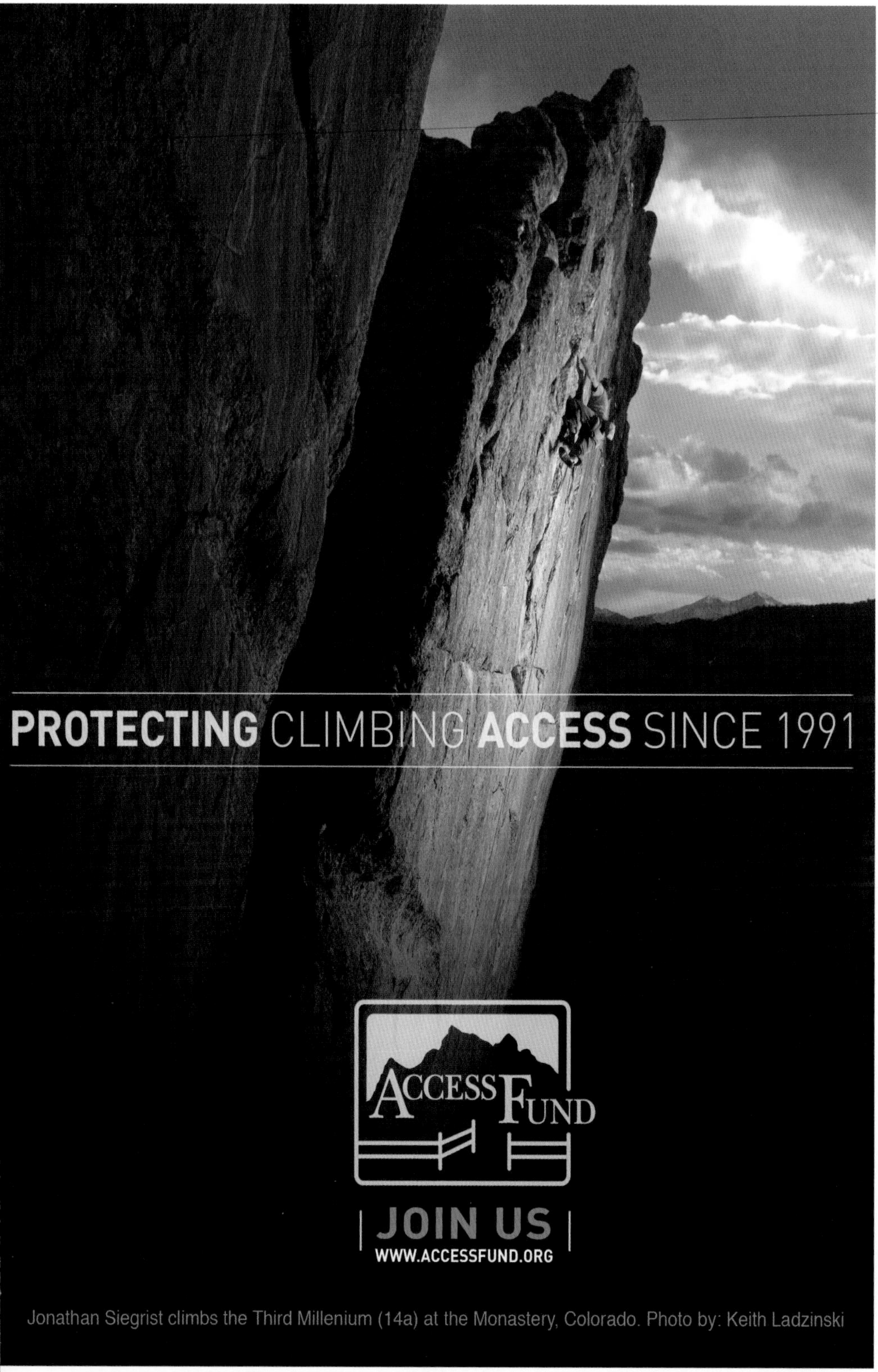

MORE FROM SUPERTOPO

TUOLUMNE BOULDERING

$16.95 Available at www.supertopo.com

Tuolumne Bouldering showcases 20 of best bouldering spots. It has more than 275 of the best boulder problems in one of the most pristine alpine rock playgrounds on Earth. Tuolumne has a little something for everyone— golden diorite knob pinches, splitter crack jams, gnarly old school mantels and a little bit of every other style of bouldering challenge. Located above 8000 feet, Tuolumne Meadows is covered in snow every winter and the only road in is closed. But when summer is on the horizon and the snow is melting, the road will open just in time for you to escape the heat and crowds of popular lower elevation areas such as Bishop and Yosemite Valley.

HIGH SIERRA CLIMBING

$24.95 Available at www.supertopo.com

This guidebook includes 26 of the best High Sierra alpine climbs, ranging in difficulty from 3rd class to 5.11c. Most of these climbs are well-protected, 10 to 15 pitches long, and ascend some of the best alpine granite anywhere. Whether you plan to scramble up the 3rd class East Ridge of Mt. Russell, climb the 5.7 East Face of Mt. Whitney, or ascend the epic 18-pitch Sun Ribbon Arête, our guidebook ensures you spend minimum time getting off-route and maximum time enjoying the climbing.

YOSEMITE VALLEY FREE CLIMBS

$29.95 Available at www.supertopo.com

This guidebook includes over 230 of the best routes in Yosemite Valley, from 16-pitch trad climbs to one-pitch sport routes. While many hard Yosemite test-pieces are included, this book focuses on topropes, crags, and multi-pitch climbs in the 5.4-5.9 range. We also include formerly obscure climbs to provide more options for avoiding crowds. As in all SuperTopo books, the authors personally climbed and documented each route with meticulous care to create the most detailed and accurate topos ever published.